D1233325

Henry James
AND THE JACOBITES

Henry James

AND THE JACOBITES

Maxwell Geismar

1963
Houghton Mifflin Company Boston
The Riverside Press Cambridge

First printing

To Van Wyck Brooks,
Grand Historian of Native Letters

Henry James *was* the Age.   *New Critic, circa 1960*

There are some things which for the credit of America should be left unsaid, perhaps; but these very things happen sometimes to be the things which, for the real benefit of Americans, ought to have prominent notice.

Mark Twain, *The Innocents Abroad*

Everyone, in the last analysis, experiences only *one* conflict in life, which only disguises itself differently all the time and shows up somewhere else — mine is, to make life and work agree in a purest sense; where the infinite commensurable work of the artist is concerned, the two directions are opposed. Many have helped themselves by taking life lightly, surreptitiously snatching from it, so to speak, what they did nevertheless need, or transforming its values into intoxications the murky exhalation of which they then swiftly flung over into art; others had no way out save the turning away from life, asceticism, and *this* means is of course cleaner and truer by far than that other greedy cheating of life for the benefit of art. But for me this does not come into consideration either. Since in the last analysis my productivity springs from the most direct admiration of life, from the daily inexhaustible marvelling at it (how else could I come to produce?), so I would see a lie in that too, in rejecting at any time the streaming of it towards me; every such renunciation, however much one's art may potentially gain from it, must finally come to expression in that art as *hardness*, and have its revenge: for who would be entirely open and acquiescent in such a sensitive domain, if he have a mistrustful, constraining and timid attitude toward life!

RILKE, *Letters*

In the course of evolutionary development, the profound tragedy in the human heritage (and the base of culture) was the loss of the Plenary-Pagan state — which became the trauma of "original sin" in the dialectical manner of human thought, and from whence came the Edenite memory and dream. And it appears to become increasingly clear that this was also, inevitably, the moment of an evolutionary self-destruction. For how can modern man understand the "meaning of life," when the meaning of life is contained in the natural pleasure of living — an area which is steadily decreasing with each "advance" of modern civilization.

JACK JONES, *To the End of Thought*

Raised the elk at noon those golden and triumphant antlers.

Folk Romance

The stately homes of England!
How beautiful they stand,
Amidst their tall ancestral trees,
O'er all the pleasant land!

FELICIA DOROTHEA HEMANS

Acknowledgments

THE author's thanks are due to the following magazines which have printed selections from this book prior to publication: *The American Scholar, The Anthologist* (Rutgers University), *The Atlantic Monthly, Nineteenth-Century Fiction, Panorama* (Chicago Daily News), *Ramparts,* and *Studi Americani.*

The following publishers have generously granted permission to quote illustrative passages in the present volume: Oxford University Press for passages from *The Notebooks of Henry James,* edited by F. O. Matthiessen and Kenneth B. Murdock, copyright 1947 by Oxford University Press, New York, Inc.; William Sloan Associates and Methuen & Co., Ltd., for passages from *Henry James: His Life and Writings,* by F. W. Dupee, copyright 1951, 1956 by William Sloan Associates, Inc.

The author also wishes to thank the following publishers for the use of shorter illustrative quotations in the present book: Charles Scribner's Sons for passages from the New York Edition of Henry James; Oxford University Press for passages from *Henry James: The Major Phase,* by F. O. Matthiessen; Random House for passages from *The Short Stories of Henry James,* edited by Clifton Fadiman; Grove Press for passages from *The Sacred Fount;* Criterion Books for passages from *Henry James: Autobiography,* edited by F. W. Dupee; Viking Press for passages from *The Portable Henry James,* edited by Morton Dauwen Zabel.

Contents

The Early Years

1. Illusions, Enchantments and Magics

YES, I KNOW there is no "real" Henry James. Every notable artist is subject to diverse interpretations; the more the better. Each age has its own view of every artist. James himself was neglected, even ridiculed, towards the end of his career. He was the idol of a little coterie of esthetes; though he drew back from the refined British decadence of the *Yellow Book* set.

In the 1920's he had a small but definite position of prominence. He was read by Scott Fitzgerald, for example, among the other writers of the period; his first editions were collected by the sophisticated. In the thirties again, age of social concern and radical belief, of thwarted hopes and twisted careers, of disenchantment, yes; but of vitality and excitement too — poor James was put back in his familiar corner of obliquity.

It was only in the mid-forties, in the decades following the Second (perhaps last) World War, that James was "discovered," and rediscovered, and discovered again, until he took on, with each passing year of our own period, a greater and greater importance. Isn't he now the source of a whole literary, academic and critical foundation: an industry? Like his own scoundrelly philosopher of "The Coxon Fund" — strange irony! — James has become an institution. He is considered today not only a major figure in world literature but, along with Melville perhaps, as the greatest American artist; or sometimes as *the* American writer of modern times.

Thus the self-acknowledged pariah and literary outcast of his own period is the present figurehead of a dominant, and power-ful, and fearsome literary establishment. Now I don't wish to deny Henry James the kind of belated justice and recognition which has come to him, and which in part he surely deserves. But he de-serves it for different reasons, I believe, than those which are gen-erally advanced for his art. The present extent, the intensity, the proportions of his recognition are not only formidable but ful-some; are exaggerated, absurd, and unreasonable. It appears that justice, like anything else, can be overdone.

Why this vogue, this Jamesian tidal sweep? That is one of the questions this book tries to answer. But here, as elsewhere in my other work, the central purpose is the study of Henry James's own temperament, character and literary achievement — that marvelous prodigy indeed, blooming like some esoteric orchid (though James was always consumed by fear and anxiety) in the otherwise vulgar garden, or jungle, of life and literature. And that body of fictional work which is surely unlike, and for good reasons, anything else which has ever been written.

But the Henry James of this study is very different from the figure which has been established in the artistic consciousness of the United States in the mid-twentieth century. We might call him the "other Henry James." If I must summarize briefly, for the sake of clarity, the conclusions which are reached in the following dis-cussion of James's big body of work, let me say first that this writer was not a major writer at all — that he is a major *entertainer* (some-thing quite different) of a rare and exotic sort, a cross, if you like, between the master magician which James used to describe himself, and the kind of literary monster which he really was.

He was not a major writer not only because of the narrow — if immensely elevated — range of his work; but because his chosen area of art was completely artificial and fanciful; neither British nor American at base, but only compounded of adolescent, or preado-lescent, visions of what such a world *should* be like. Wasn't it com-posed at least half of a gloried British "aristocracy," just beneath whom a few proletarian butlers perhaps, like the famous "Brook-smith" so often commended by the Jamesian critics; or the "revolu-tionary" little bookbinder Hyacinth Robinson of *The Princess Casamassima*; or the murky journalist Densher of *The Wings of the Dove*; beneath whom a few, as I say, of the Jamesian "working-class" protagonists simply yearned to ape this spurious nobility? Now this was also a world of rentiers and inheritors, for the condi-tion of human freedom, according to James, was primarily to have inherited a fortune. Even his less successful heroes and heroines have a *little* fortune. And when they don't, they must be adopted by the British or American nobility which does have a fortune, as with Isabel Archer of *The Portrait of a Lady*. Or else, as with Kate Croy of *The Wings of the Dove*, they must set out to gain a fortune illegitimately, evilly, corruptly — and hence (to James) sexually.

In this leisure-class literary cosmos, the idea of *making* a fortune — and that is not to say, earning a living — was unthinkable, ex-cept for those vulgar American financiers of James's work, or those quaint, childlike, sweet millionaires (from Newman of *The Ameri-can* to Adam Verver of *The Golden Bowl*) who have come to Eu-rope to be "educated." Very much like Edith Wharton, James thought the function of the artist was to teach the rich how to use their money better. Wasn't he in fact the perfect novelist of our primitive finance-capitalism in its first flowering of titans and rob-ber barons; the complete Veblenian "artist" (though Veblen neg-lected to use him) of conspicuous display and ostentatious con-sumption in the arts?

The Jamesian style, in its later phases, was a key to this: a style, as it were, for the sake of style; a style which was intended to de-ceive or mislead the reader quite as often as to inform him; a style whose abundance grew richer, more verbose and orotund, as its ma-terial grew thinner. For even within the restricted confines of this upper- and leisure-class literary orbit which James had laid out for himself — and as early, quite literally, as his pubescent years when his reading of the English Victorian novelists, his yearning for "romance," and his encounter with the great European art galleries all coalesced into the dream of Europe, the nightmare of America — even within *this* thin and artificial and fanciful literary orbit, the Jamesian range of emotions, of human feelings and relations, was narrowed down even more by temperamental considerations.

His view of womankind was essentially that of a childlike purity, sweetness, goodness, along with wealth of course. His vision of sex was essentially voyeuristic. A whole series of infantile Jamesian "observers" — some of them, as in *What Maisie Knew*, actually being children — stand outside of a mysterious realm of adult "intimacy," which always turns out, however, to be coarse and vulgar, if not actually sinful. And when the later James did actually break through a lifelong sexual inhibition, as in *The Sacred Fount*, what even stranger "theories" of sexual behavior and sexual motivation emerged: fabulous, incredible and fantastical indeed. In this esoteric Jamesian universe — a literary world that was comprised of one-half of the upper one per cent of the human race at best; and one-quarter of *their* emotions — the worst crime, next to being poor, was to be sexual. In the later Jamesian women, such as Kate Croy, or Charlotte Stant of *The Golden Bowl*, poverty not only accompanies sexuality, but appears to cause it. Now of course I don't mean real poverty but, as it were, relative poverty — not being as rich as your rich friends, or as noble as your noble friends.

Do I exaggerate? Yes, a little, probably; it is hard not to, once we have caught the real key to this Jamesian vision of life, which then becomes comic in essence. And not comic by the Jamesian intention; but because he absolutely and completely believed that this was the only true vision of life, and he founded an autocratic and despotic empire of art around it. James has been praised over and over again (by the James cult, I mean) for having removed the "auctorial presence" of the nineteenth century novelists from the novel form. But the "points of view," or the "centers of illumination," which he substituted were all completely *James's* point of view. Behind them he lurked, he plotted and planned and schemed, more despotic and dictatorial than any old-fashioned novelist lecturing his readers about the sins and frailties of human character. And the later Jamesian characters, as we shall see, become inhuman. Or at least, in their limited area of experience, with their limited range of emotions, they are human only in the sense that power and scheming are human. Without the capacity for love, fearful even of friendship as another "trap" of the human spirit, living on fabricated human relations, controlled only by the yearnings and demands of an immaculate egotism which eschewed all the ordinary solaces, rewards and supports of human experience, these Jamesian literary figures are also puppets of the Jamesian *plots* — most typically a combination of sentimental romance and of cunning melodrama.

The famous "dramatic method" which James brought over to the novel form, from his unhappy, his traumatic, experiences on the English stage, also removed all possibilities of freedom in the novel itself. Thus the typical Jamesian chronicle was one of *manipulation*, rather than of human revelation — of characters preying upon each other, of James preying upon them all, for the sake of those grand dramatic "effects," those theatrical entrances and exits, those tricky stage climaxes. No character in the later James fiction, the so-called "major phase," can lead either a normal or a full life because James was in absolute control of their behavior, their thought, their being; and James had no other life except this fabricated and manipulated world of his fiction. That is why, in this sense, the Jamesian esthetic is valid in concentrating on the work of art rather than on the artist himself; for the work of art, in the Jamesian case, *is* the artist. And that is why, in the present study, I am concerned with James's fiction rather than with his life or his time. For, just as he had no life outside of his art, he knew nothing at all about the life of his time; or the barest minimum that a writer can know — and he cared less.

Strange and incredible, exotic indeed, that is the simple truth about Henry James. His earliest description of the American scene was a formidable list of lapses and omissions, most of which had nothing to do with the American scene. That was the nightmare of James's youth, as we shall see; which was set against his earliest dreams of European "art," "culture," and "life" itself, in a temperament which was comprised of such polar opposites, where illusion was pitted against illusion, and reality, maturity or the experience of living had little place to enter. Yes, it is the artist's vision of life which counts most, which makes his work notable and durable; but the crucial question here is the amount of life contained in that vision — of the connections it makes with the recognized, shared experience of the human race. What shall we say, then, of a "major artist" who is *all* vision — or illusion, or enchantment, or magic — and has no recognizable life?

Well, very little life then; the barest minimum again, which serves to make all the Jamesian fictions almost seem convincing while you read them, and before you think about them. Isn't he the perfect symbol of all our own deepest youthful yearnings for the way "things should be," even though we know they never are that way; and in Henry James's case, never even could be, and never were? Along with Herman Wouk, say, or J. D. Salinger, wasn't James also the perfect figurehead, since he easily surpassed the contemporary writers in talent and achievement, for the American fifties: an age itself of social and cultural make-believe whose own yearnings for illusion and magic — for a false, blind enchantment at the cost of all reality — met and matched James's native capacity for entertainment? Was *that* the reason why the James cult of native critics instinctively and unanimously selected this master for their study and worship, their marvelous works of explication and exegesis, soaring ever higher into the empyrean void of absolute and immaculate art?

At least James couldn't have suited them better. He was nonpolitical; that is to say, he was a "royalist" in the politics which he disdained. He thought of America as the lost colony (England's, of course), while the American Revolution became the "King's

War." Even more than the late nineteenth century British nobility, James preferred the early nineteenth century English scene simply because the older nobility appeared to be more noble — and even to that he preferred the great and glorious French Empire of the *ancien régime.* James was non-historical, since his notion of "history" was that of legend, romance and the picturesque. The French Revolution of *The Ambassadors* is a matter of blood and terror; and of those delicate, cultivated, ancient French noblewomen who gallantly await their turn at the guillotine. (There is much more on this subject in our study of his other works, in particular *The Princess Casamassima* and *The American Scene,* which was in fact one of the weirdest social documentaries ever to be written.) And James, though again he has been hailed as the "father of the modern novel," was absolutely non-Freudian and non-psychological; in place of which he used something I can only call "psychomorality." (That is: a noble moral ending to a very dubious human situation.)

How else could he have been, also, so obviously, so patently, sometimes so ludicrously ignorant about his own motivation, his own behavior, his own literary achievement — all of which he revealed in the utmost detail, and in the sublime conviction of his own essential "rightness"? The Jamesian "stream of consciousness" is simply that; the unconscious would have been as vulgar to him as Zola's novels of peasants and workers. Now again the interest of studying James lies partly in what he does to, how he interprets, how he again — and always — "uses" the unconscious material that is inherent in the act of writing itself. But certainly this cluster of limitations in James, of "lacks" almost as large as those which he saw in his earliest picture of American life, would be enough to draw to this writer all those contemporary critics who had turned away from the radicalism of the thirties; or who had been against it in the first place; or who, in the next generation of the forties and fifties no longer wished to concern themselves with anything remotely bearing on the social question. In the epoch of the cold war, of McCarthyism, Birchism, Walkerism, of governmental purges and investigations, of both a forced conformity of thought and a natural, self-induced one, Henry James was the perfect symbol of safety, propriety and gentlemanly behavior.

Or even more: of a "pure art" that, claiming to be advanced, modern, sophisticated, was actually reversionary or reactionary. The U.S.A. of the forties and fifties, just like the England which faced the real (non-Jamesian) French Revolution in Herman Melville's *Billy Budd*, was afraid to look beyond itself; for within all was comfort, complacency and safety — and beyond, but not beyond *enough*, were anarchy, chaos and world revolution. Just as in the case of Melville's Captain Vere, the esthetic authoritarianism, if not absolutism, which James had created, and which the James cult elaborated into the Book of Good Taste, held in it the seeds of fear and panic; and of that Jamesian anxiety which is the single dominant emotion in his fiction. The wonder of it is that this Jacobite cult could have gone so far on so little: piling flattery upon praise, rationalization upon rationalization — even falsehood upon falsehood.

Thus *The Portrait of a Lady*, another Jamesian romance of renunciation, sensitive and touching as it is, but embroidered upon a highly improbable melodrama, is compared with *Moby Dick* itself. (And what a mate for Ahab would Isabel Archer be!) Thus *The Turn of the Screw*, a tricky and fabricated ghost story by James's own admission — and based upon the "evil" of sexuality forced upon "pure" childhood — is solemnly discussed as a Freudian masterpiece. Thus *The Princess Casamassima*, one of James's poorest and most tedious novels, is revalued as a brilliant study of the "Anarchist Movement" in the 1880's: about which, judging from the novel itself, James knew only what was contained in the scare-headlines of the daily newspapers. Thus *The Bostonians*, into which James poured all his scorn for the New England intellectual scene which he hardly cared to understand, is a "devastating" picture of the Abolitionist-Transcendental movements. Thus even the Jamesian plays, which were hissed off the British stage, and which he wrote as sheer melodramas and pot-boilers, have now been collected for the edification, one supposes, of our budding academic playwrights. Thus even those famous "transposed chapters" in *The Ambassadors* — which is incidentally one of the silliest and most uninformed novels about American business and French art alike — have finally been put in their proper order in the new New York Edition, though for fifty years nobody noticed that they were out of place.

And so on. Were these contemporary Jacobite critics honest and self-deluded — the victims of the historical period which they wished to ignore? Or were they disillusioned and cynical, using James's work as a marvelously elaborate "screen" for their own lack of any real conviction or belief in life and in art alike — or any real involvement? (This writer, James, who was himself so full of screens, of blinds and dodges, of reflectors and reverberators of a reality that was always described second or third hand.) Or were they simply clever and conformist — mass-minded, and other-directed, herd-minded, that is, and opportunistic, sensing in this new literary trend the fastest, best way to a university chair, a book-reviewing podium, the columns of the informed literary quarterlies (all more or less alike), or, in short, a safe, fashionable and comfortable area of intellectual activity?

They are, at any rate, entrenched in the sensitive, the powerful, areas of our academic, scholarly and journalistic life today. (And they will greet this "unauthorized study" of Henry James with something less than enthusiasm.) But the peak of their authority and influence — if not of their malice, another trait they have inherited from their master — is already waning, for the simple reason that they have pushed the Jamesian canon as far as it can go. Nothing more can be said about this artist in praise and false praise; now it remains only to tell the truth. The most recent work of the Jacobite cult — it can hardly be called criticism — is Oscar Cargill's *The Novels of Henry James* (1961). It is, among other things, a gathering-in of the universal modern encomia for all of James's books — good, bad and indifferent — in which the author of the compendium quarrels with the other Jacobites who have dared to criticize, well, to differ with, even the poorest or weakest literary productions by James. Well, so be it, and the Imperial James still rules over the American Academy today — but this has always been a sanctuary, or a resting place, to be euphemistic, for art, rather than a creative or germinal area. Henry James is also the perfect academic novelist; but among our younger fiction writers today, many have realized, quite intuitively, or naturally, that this particular Emperor is naked.

I am afraid that, during the course of the present study, while noting the commentary of the Jamesian cult wherever it seemed useful, I have not treated their most typical or representative critics with sufficient respect. For I believe that their worst fault, intellectually speaking, is that they have not understood the real nature of the artist whom they have elevated into such dubious prominence. They are ignorant about Henry James, since they accept the premises that James himself gave to them on esthetic, historical, social, psychological and human grounds. And the Jamesian premises, like his "rules," "principles," and "laws" of art — or like the whole structure of the Jamesian "esthetics" — were almost always a rationalization of his own weaknesses and failures. His "triumph," in his own mind surely, and now, as it appears, in the mind of a whole bewitched generation of Jamesian explicators, analysts, and apologists, was simply that he converted every loss, every failure, every defeat, every debacle in his own career, into an imaginary victory. He is a supreme example of the Rationalizing Ego (in non- or pre-Freudian terminology) which must repress the least hint of danger, either in itself or in the world around it, by a series of ever ascending, ever more elaborate "explanations" which remove it farther and farther from any kind of troublesome reality. Henry James is indeed a whole course in the non-Freudian psychology of "survival," and of triumphant ascendancy, at the cost of all truth.

The great writers start first of all from self-knowledge, while James reveled in self-ignorance — which he then proclaimed and codified as "universal law." But how can a writer who is not "great," or "major," or even "important" in any important sense; or perhaps even *relevant* in the long workings of time for the majority of the human race — since James's vision of life was *so* singular, his experience so limited, his sensibilities so restrained: how can such a writer, finally, still remain so interesting? I have no intention here of destroying, or even debunking Henry James himself — that would be too easy, in a sense, and too cheap. When the present Jacobite cult has vanished from our literary scene (and no loss) James himself will remain as a remarkable phenomenon. Remarkable just because he is a phenomenon never before glimpsed on literary land or sea; and probably never to appear again. Henry James is indeed the most singular curiosity in the whole wide reach of literary history.

2. The Seventies: The Nostalgic Poison

"THE STORY OF A YEAR," published by Henry James, Jr., in the *Atlantic Monthly* in 1865, is usually considered to be this author's first story. (Though Leon Edel has discovered a still earlier one, "A Tragedy of Error," in 1864.) According to F. O. Matthiessen, "The Story of a Year" is notable for its portrait of a vacillating heroine and the "power of evil" to haunt a New England village like an unlaid ghost. Well, this tale was in fact a romantic melodrama of passion and the martial spirit — both of which the young Henry knew very little about.

It was nearly a decade later that he published the first collection of early stories which he thought worth preserving, and this was the decade of intense emotional conflict about his future life, his art, his home: about Europe and America. There was the problem of the Puritan heritage in New England culture, so he felt, of "this subdued, largely joyless existence" which marked American life. There was the passage in his *Notebook.* "In a story, some one says — 'Oh yes, the United States — a country without a sovereign, without a court, without a nobility, without an army, without a church or a clergy, without a diplomatic service, without a picturesque peasantry, without palaces or castles or country seats or ruins, without a literature, without novels, without an Oxford or Cambridge, without cathedrals or ivied churches, without latticed cottages or village alehouses, without political society, without sport, without fox-hunting or country gentlemen, without an Epsom or an Ascot, an Eton or a Rugby . . . !' "

This famous passage became the basis for James's later indictment of Hawthorne, though, as Professor Matthiessen observed, he
dropped out "a picturesque peasantry" and added "no museums, no
pictures." But there was enough here to indicate the prevailing
bent of the young artist's temperament, his determination to do
without these "withouts." (To William Dean Howells' rejoinder
that in the absence of "these dreary and worn-out paraphernalia"
of European society, the American writer had simply the whole
of human life left, James argued that "you beg [to my sense] the
question.") There were deeper and more personal problems involved in the international conflict of the young artist, as we shall
see, but meanwhile there is no doubt that A *Passionate Pilgrim and
Other Tales* (1875) was a pleasant collection of early fiction.

Two of these stories are still interesting, and a third has its psychic illuminations. The later James himself, in his Preface to the
New York Edition, volume XIII, had some pertinent comments
on the personal background of his early fiction. "I had in the
spring of 1869, and again in that of 1870, spent several weeks in
England, renewing and extending, with infinite zest, an acquaint-
ance with the country that had previously been but an uneffaced
little chapter of boyish, or — putting it again far enough back for
the dimmest dawn of sensibility — of infantine experience; and
had, perceptively and aesthetically speaking, taken the adventure
of my twenty-sixth year 'hard,' as 'A Passionate Pilgrim' quite sufficiently attests."

The story was really a romantic fairy tale of a young man's infatuation with English heraldic lore; but it is of much documentary
interest about the early Jamesian crisis as to Europe and/or America. The narrator-observer is present at a conversation where the
dingy and ailing Mr. Searle stakes his dubious claim to an old
English estate. This American claimant, or pretender, is an equivocal character whose cause is taken up with total enthusiasm by
the young Jamesian spokesman. (The declining American spirit is
revived only by the diseased fantasy of inheriting an English title,
and property.) Indeed it is the narrator even more than the shrink-

ing "hero" Searle who is obsessed by the legendary claim to Hampton Court. "Just the scene around me was the England of one's early reveries. Over against us, amid the ripeness of its gardens, the dark red residence, with its formal facings and its vacant windows, seemed to make the past definite and massive; the little village, nestling between park and palace, around a patch of turfy common, with its taverns of figurative names, its ivy-towered church, its mossy roofs, looked like the property of a feudal lord."

It was in this dark composite light, the narrator says, that he had read the British classics. "It was this mild moist air that had blown from the pages of the poets; while I seemed to feel the buried generations in the dense and elastic sod." "A Passionate Pilgrim" is filled with details of legendary British life that could only have come from the pages of English novels, and could only have been retained by a young, infatuated, romantic temperament. There is the young girl who comes cantering down the shallow glade of the avenue on a fine black horse: "one of those little budding gentlewomen, perfectly mounted and equipped, who form to alien eyes one of the prettiest incidents of English scenery" — the budding gentlewoman who drops her riding crop, the mounted servant, dashing after her, who touches his hat to the visiting Americans. They meet also a rural vagrant, "an immemorial vagrant — the disowned in his own rich way, of all the English ages," who embodies, one supposes, the picturesque peasantry of James's earlier fantasies. A reduced hostler, with his greasy bonnet and grimy red scarf, he is very different apparently from the American workmen or the American tramps who, in the post-Civil War decades, were to mark the epoch of a rising and unfettered finance capitalism. "His face was pale haggard and degraded beyond description — as base as a counterfeit coin, yet as modelled somehow as a tragic mask. He too, like everything else, had a history."

This "history," to the early Jamesian fantasy, was no doubt different from the real story of the industrial revolution which in the early seventies was ravaging the pleasant English countryside;

in fact the true history of contemporary Great Britain would never appear in Henry James's work. But meanwhile "A Passionate Pilgrim," set as the story was amid peacocks, great paintings, horses and dogs, centered around an evil feudal baron who was also a "consummate conservative, breathing the fumes of hereditary privilege and security" (and how the young Henry James yearned for those hereditary fumes!), ended on a note of pure melodrama — just as the artist-hero in "The Madonna of the Future" turned out to be another odd, but revealing, expatriate.

It was this American, or ex-American painter in Italy who again expressed the central Jamesian lament about the vulgar, raw, barren culture of his native scene. "We're the disinherited of Art! We're condemned to be superficial! We're excluded from the magic circle! The soil of American perception is a poor little barren artificial deposit!" Was this enough, and was it clear enough in this exclamatory mood? There was more: "Yes, we're wedded to imperfection! An American, to excel, has just ten times as much to learn as a European! We lack the deeper sense! We have neither taste nor tact nor force! How *should* we have them? Our crude and garish climate, our silent past, our deafening present, the constant pressure about us of unlovely conditions, are as void of all that nourishes and prompts the artist as my sad heart is void of bitterness in saying so."

But was this "sad heart" quite void of all bitterness? The story's hero, "brooding in charmed inaction, for ever preparing for a work for ever deferred," also embodied a deep personal fantasy of the young James who viewed himself as perhaps equally condemned to a perfectionism, a sterility, an impotence in art. The later James of the Prefaces had a further word, too, about the conflicted young American writer of the seventies faced by all the rich opportunities and dangerous perils of European culture. "A part of that adventure had been the never-to-be-forgotten thrill of a first sight of Italy . . . so that a return to America at the beginning of the following year was to drag with it, as a lengthening chain, the torment of losses and regrets . . . The nostalgic poison had been distilled for him, the future presented to him but as a single intense question: was he to spend it in brooding exile, or might he somehow come into his 'own'? — as I liked betimes to put it for a romantic analogy with the state of dispossessed princes and wandering heirs."

Exiled royalty, and dispossessed orphan princes in truth; and however cleverly the argument of Europe and America was to be dramatized in the early Jamesian fiction, there was only one possible solution. The terms of the problem were in themselves curiously reversed. America was torment — not promises — for the repatriated victim; while Europe was the true homeland for the brooding "exile," the wandering, illegitimate "heir" who had been dispossessed of his own —

I had from as far back as I could remember carried in my side, buried and unextracted, the head of one of those well-directed shafts from the European quiver to which, of old, tender American flesh was more helplessly and bleedingly exposed, I think, than to-day: the nostalgic cup had been applied to my lips even before I was conscious of it — I had been hurried off to London and to Paris immediately after my birth, and then and there, I was ever afterwards to feel, that poison had entered my veins. This was so much the case that when again, in my thirteenth year, re-exposure was decreed, was made effective and prolonged, my inward sense of it was, in the oddest way, not of my finding myself in the vague and the uncharted, but much rather restored to air already breathed and to a harmony already disclosed.

Look Homeward, Angel, indeed; and was this inflammatory arrowhead of "culture" lodged in the tender American flesh; this "nostalgic cup" feeding the poisoned veins, this unutterable yearning for the prebreathed air and already disclosed promise of *Europe:* was this really in the infantine as well as the elderly Henry James? Was it an inherent proclivity, almost a biological sensitivity — so "immediately after my birth," or perhaps even before it — to a "harmony" commonly considered Edenite, which was now merely European?

In the same volume of tales, "Madame de Mauves" described a sympathetic heroine; though the story was again based on a fanciful, a fabricated conflict between American and European culture; and in the familiar, weak-willed Jamesian hero, the analysis of his passion for Euphemia — the name of this romantic heroine was amusing, and revealing — took the place of any action, even the heart's action. Longmore — these early Jamesian names again — even wonders if his emotion for Euphemia really does constitute a "passion," and thus sets the pattern for a central but unresolved theme in James's work: the theme of Eros.

But if James had spent a decade perfecting the shorter forms of his work, he also, at the age of thirty-three, published his first novel in the same year of 1875.* *Roderick Hudson* has become a kind of standard item in American fiction, though it is perhaps the least interesting longer work of the Jamesian apprenticeship. It is an early and imperfect example of the more or less romantic "art novel," a genre which James developed along with Edith Wharton and Willa Cather, and which came to an uneasy climax in the 1920's. Roderick, like Henry, yearns to become "the typical, original, aboriginal American artist" — just as though no Transcendentalist movement and no flowering of New England had ever touched the meager, dry, provincial country-town life of New England which James described here. In fact, this sculptor-hero has all the marks of a rebellious *southern* aristocrat (a notion James developed in *The Bostonians*) amid the puritanical northern climate. On one level perhaps the satire on Northampton's (Massachusetts) "Main Street," and on "the custom of the country" — a phrase that Mrs. Wharton used for her later novel — led into the similar, but sharper, provincial satire of Sinclair Lewis. And Rowland Mallet was a novelty in the national letters too: this rich, idle American "gentleman," dedicated to esthetic purposes, whose whole purpose in life is served by bringing Roderick to Rome. (There is

* *Transatlantic Sketches* (1875) was a collection of travel articles by James written in the early seventies and first published in such magazines as *The Nation, The Atlantic Monthly* and *Galaxy*.

an element of plain fairy tale in the parable of untutored native genius being "rescued" by a wise, generous, selfless godfather-benefactor.) The close, rather touching, wholly innocent masculine friendship of Roderick and Rowland is at the center of the novel. But the "double hero" of *Roderick Hudson* is closer to the splintered halves of a single personality which is debating, often at length, the nature of art and the artistic life.

The "artist-doer" and the yearning for "pagan life" are embodied in Roderick; there are hints of Hawthorne's romances in the sensuous appeal and temptations of the Eternal City which lead him astray. Yet Roderick is not altogether convincing as the artist, and often ends up as an adolescent egoist; while Rowland, the man of "moral passion," is sensitive, thoughtful and weak, if not improbable. It is mainly with the advent of Christina Light that Roderick's doom is sealed; and that the pleasant but slow-moving and almost entirely superficial novel to this point — the novel in the later Jamesian critical jargon of "the contributive value of accessory facts" — gains in interest. Willful, discontented, witty, an early flapper type of the seventies, the unacknowledged daughter of her American mother's romance with an obscure Italian "cavaliere," Christina is the spoiled princess of the international set who flaunts her charm, her wiles, her power, her restlessness and her emptiness.

Being prepared for the marriage mart, she is still half in love with Roderick; while Rowland reflects uneasily that this "complex, wilful, passionate creature" might easily draw the innocent sculptor down into "some strange underworld of unworthy sacrifice" — and that is to say, of passion or love. Now what is interesting in the early Henry James is a certain kind of *conceptual* boldness (for his period, at least), and then the swift return of emotional restraints and inhibitions which are not merely Victorian either. In the early James this was a boldness of the mind rather than of the flesh. There is that noted scene in the Colosseum when Christina declares: "I suppose we have not climbed up here under the

skies to play propriety." But to "play propriety" is just what
Roderick Hudson does, while it pretends to play bohemian.
Christina, for all her tormenting of the moody super-artist, turns
out, alas, to be merely a superior version of the "nice girl" in the
fiction of the period; and the lack of any real relation between the
two lovers is the reason why Roderick's disintegration appears so
extreme as well as useless.

The end of the novel foundered again upon the abstract discussion of moral or "passional" conflicts; the familiar vein of melodrama takes over the plot — and in the later Preface to this book
James, admitting this failure, changed the whole focus of the story
from Roderick's story to his friend Roland's. "My subject, all bliss-
fully," was not Roderick's adventure, so James stated, but "his
patron's view and experience of him." Was this criticism of the
novel, or a superior form of auctorial rationalization? At any rate
the elder James believed that the younger James had already turned
away from the direct action of life to the reflection and mirroring of
that action in the human consciousness: in "the very drama of
that consciousness" which Rowland Mallet recorded in the story.

Moreover, Rowland's own shy passion for Mary Garland — the
Northampton girl whom Roderick has "betrayed" in Italy, or even
worse, has forgotten about — is never even suggested to her. Yet
Roderick Hudson was still an interesting first novel for its texture
and sensibility, and for the evocation of its Italian landscape
through its sculptor-hero's eyes. "In Rome his first care was for
the Vatican; he went there again and again. But the old imperial
and papal city altogether delighted him; only there he really found
what he had been looking for from the first, the sufficient negation of his native scene." — And whatever this hero's bias was. The
minor personages of the novel, such as Gloriani, the cynical artist;
Sam Singleton, the Dickensian little painter; Miss Blanchard of the
artistic fraternity in Rome, and Mme. Grandoni, the aristocratic
intimate of Christina Light; all these were well-drawn types.
The picture of Roman life, with the rich blending of culture,

"race" and wealth which the early James instinctively associated with the life of art, was dazzling enough, perhaps, to overcome even those readers who objected to the writer's own negation of his native scene. And it almost appeared that James's next novel, *The American*, in 1877, was designed expressly to project the best aspects of a smiling American financial society, if not its meager provincial esthetics.

In the Jamesian world of inherited wealth, even poor artists ride horseback on the Campagna, or spend their mornings strolling through famous art galleries, while Italian princes, with eight hundred years of "history" displayed in their faces, still manage to have their fortunes intact. But Christopher Newman is the New World's self-made rich man at his best. This long, lean, shrewd and genial hero (probably based, as Constance Rourke has suggested, on the humorous folklore of the period) was the first of the "good millionaires" in American fiction; his successor, Silas Lapham, would appear seven years later, and Dodsworth took another half a century. And on him James lavished all his praise. "The ideal completeness . . . the mould of race . . . the superlative American . . . the general easy magnificence of his manhood . . . a muscular Christian quite without doctrine . . . a liberal looseness, a grenadier on parade . . . He had never tasted tobacco." Nor does Christopher Newman, whose name could hardly be more symbolic, care a fig for European "race" or culture. He is happy to buy all the paintings of the little French copyist, Mlle. Noémie, whom he meets at the Louvre with her pathetic and tedious father, M. Nioche.

The opening of *The American* is all warmth, good-humor, entertainment. This was the parable of the true American "innocence," of the earliest American promise, of the Edenite idyll before the (financial) Fall, of the lyrical childhood of the western race. No wonder that Newman's first talk was with his old friend Tristram at the Palais Royal where under the lime trees "buxom, white-capped nurses, seated along the benches, were offering to their infant charges the amplest facilities for nutrition." The imagery is of happy, abundant, generous infancy — of "a kind of primordial, pastoral simplicity" — though, to be sure, of highly artificial foster-motherhood. Newman's history, so James said, was "with intensity a tale of the Western world," and it showed, in that bright alien air, "very much as fine desiccated, articulated 'specimens,' bleached, monstrous, probably unique, show in the high light of museums of natural history" — though again the simile had a curious dissonance. Which was life; which was the bleached and desiccated specimen in this new chronicle of Europe and America; and where was the museum?

There was a certain ambiguousness in the record of Newman's financial career. "It dealt with elements, incidents, enterprises, which it will be needless to introduce to the reader in detail; the deeps and the shallows, the ebb and flow, of great financial tides." After the Civil War, San Francisco was the scene of Newman's "most victorious engagements," where he had added dollars to dollars and gouged out his fortune.* But indifferent to "culture," or the amenities of old society, he is "fond, in all circumstances, of the society of women," and it is through the expatriate Tristrams that he meets Mme. de Cintré.

The Tristrams are one of those domestic couples whom the later James would develop into full-fledged reverberators and reflectors of the main action. The Bellegardes of the Faubourg Saint-Germain, whose daughter Mme. de Cintré is, are the primary French aristocracy of the novel. "With these people the family's everything; you must act not for your own pleasure but for the advantage of your race and name," says Mrs. Tristram. Surrounded and guarded by family ritual in the gray depths of her inhospitable-looking house, the strange, pretty, suffering, silent heroine of the novel is indeed another fairy princess in the "enchanted

* Newman has been successful in copper, but very mixed in other mining adventures, and has had to take a back seat in oil, so James adds. But this "great Western barbarian," this noble American Titan, is rather like one of J. J. Rousseau's purehearted primitives.

castle" of hereditary privilege, protected by the moats of class and caste — or of the social amenities; ringed round, as though by fire and water, with all the proprieties of "noble" custom. This is the castle which Newman must assail to gain the hand of Mme. de Cintré; this is the trap which has been laid for him at the rosy dawn of the novel.

But the Bellegardes are in reality perfect examples of the petty, ingrown prejudices of the French *haute-bourgeoisie*. One is struck by the deference which James accords to a group whose rigid, narrow, suspicious and materialistic values had already been dissected by a line of native French writers from Stendhal and Balzac on. "The Bellegardes don't recognize the Bonapartes," says Count Valentin, who is instructing Newman in the subtleties of race. And "old races have strange secrets." The young Urbain de Bellegarde is "an incarnation of the maintained attitude" which Newman had never yet been confronted by. Mme. de Cintré herself gave him "the sense of an elaborate educating, of her having passed through mysterious ceremonies and processes of culture in her youth, of her having been fashioned and made flexible to certain deep social needs." Again, however, the two lovers in this royal romance are so separated by a wall of virtue and propriety — as well as by the barriers of different cultures and different "races" — that there is no real relation between them; while Madame herself becomes little more than a charming symbol of whatever deep social needs she is supposed to represent. She is subordinated to her family and to her society. She is a mysterious suffering romantic woman; but her real character is unknown. The narrative slows down towards the middle of the novel, and is little more than a domestic chronicle of high society and exalted personages on a foreign shore.

It is Mme. Urbain, the rebellious daughter-in-law, who comes closer to the truth. "But why should I bother about my ancestors? I'm sure they never bothered about me." In his own way, the later James of the Prefaces acknowledged these defects in *The American*. "The great house of Bellegarde, in a word, would, I now feel, given the circumstances, given the *whole* of the ground, have comported itself in a manner as different as possible from the manner to which my narrative commits it . . . They would positively have jumped then, the Bellegardes, at my rich and easy American, and not have 'minded' in the least any drawback." But the early James was infatuated with the romance of "great people" like the Belle- gardes to whom he might impute "with a fine free hand, the arro- gance and cruelty, the tortuous behaviour, in given conditions, of which great people have been historically so often capable." As to Mme. de Cintré, James conceded that with this lady altogether "I recognize, a light plank, too light a plank, is laid for the reader over a dark 'psychological' abyss. The delicate clue to her conduct is never definitely placed in his hand." But what the later James of the Prefaces did *not* concede, or at least acknowledge, was that Christopher Newman himself was just as romanticized and ideal- ized a portrait of the new American millionaire — the western titan — as the Bellegardes were of ancient French nobility.

Thus both poles of *The American* were essentially false; or at least imaginary and artificial; the product of a youthful literary imagination rather than of experience and reality. To keep the tale going, James fell back on sheer melodrama in the episode of Valentin's duel with the vulgar Strasbourg brewery scion over the "rising" little courtesan, Noémie. The sequel of the letter which Newman receives containing the "dark secret" of the Bellegardes, and which he burns, is even worse. Yet what is notable in the novel again, with all its false premises and heavy stage props, is the narrative skill through which James created the illusion of verisimilitude, if not of truth. *The American* was another "topo- graphical novel" of French scenery, French society and French cul- ture, well suited to an American audience which now had, in the gilded age, the leisure, the money and the desire for such literature, and such "life." The lack of the economic base in the early James, or of any real interest in the social-economic nature of his prosper- ous, materialistic post-Civil War American society, would hardly

disturb this audience either, which was trying to put the best
façade forward, so to speak, for its purely acquisitive instincts. If
this "defense" of the New World in the novel was just as inadequate as the glorifying of the Old World, the narrative's warmth
and wit, its sophistication and its scene alike, all managed to
obscure the awkward plot, and the author's inadequate view of his
material.

The new "race" of oil kings and copper barons in the mid-
seventies would hardly have recognized the "world of the inheritors" in which Christopher Newman really moved: the world of
second or third generation wealth with no other object, and no
other obligation, than the single purpose of acquiring culture. (So
too an attractive heroine like Mme. de Cintré was sacrificed to the
false conflict of these two "social groups.") "We really can't réc-
oncile ourselves to a commercial person," says the grand Mme. de
Bellegarde. "We tried to believe in an evil hour it was possible, and
that effort was our great misfortune. We determined to persevere
to the end and to give you every advantage . . . We let the thing
certainly go very far — we introduced you to our friends. To tell
the truth it was that, I think, that broke me down." "It was your
commercial quality in the abstract," says Mrs. Tristram in turn,
"and the mere historic facts of your wash-tubs and other lucrative
wares that they couldn't swallow." And these peculiar Jamesian
statements reflected not merely the opinions of his lofty European
personages but the depth of his own aversion to the barely hidden
commercial origins of the James family itself. It was the prejudice
not indeed of European nobility during the seventies, anxious to
shore up its declining estate with new fortunes, but of the new
American "leisure-class" itself, which had so much money and so
little history.

In the revised version of *The American*, too, which James prepared for the New York edition, there are evidences of the "em-
bellished declarative" which he developed in his late period. Newman, we are told, "almost panted" or "rejoicingly declared," while

Mme. de Bellegarde "inordinately fluted" and other characters
"candidly smiled," or they simply quaver. How is it then that
during the poorish end of this false fairy tale James maintains
his drama and keeps it so interesting when it is so barely probable?
It is the intensity — rather than the validity — of the literary
"illusions" in James's work which keeps you interested in these
early novels, and even in such a minor tale as *The Europeans* in
1878.*

James was fond of twisting all situations. (This early he showed
signs of being a "metaphysical" novelist.) The new book was designed as a sort of companion piece in reverse to *The American*
in which the aristocratic European woman seeks a husband (and a
fortune) in mid-nineteenth century New England. The theme was
again that of old-world sophistication and American "innocence"
so complete as to be insipid, or farcical. The first view of the States
is hardly consoling to the Baroness Eugenia. "This dreadful country," she exclaims, while to her brother Felix it is "this comical
country, this delightful country." Their distant cousins, the Went-
worths, in their old-fashioned country house near Boston, are natural, primitive, patriarchal American types. The daughter, Gertrude
Wentworth, is a kind of aboriginal sleeping princess whose "dull
eyes" — which James stressed — are to be awakened by the
European prince to a vision of true gaiety, love and pleasure.
"Duty" is the single American standard before the advent of the
cultivated Europeans. This was a virtuoso little fable in which any
pretense of reality was suspended; could James have *believed* this?
Yes, the little novel was "thin," as William James complained at

---

* *Watch and Ward* (1878; but serialized in the *Atlantic Monthly* in 1871) was
technically James's first novel. An overt romance of sibling rivalry on the part of two
"cousins" who struggle to gain the love of a young girl who has previously been
"adopted" by the weakish, ailing, neurotic "hero-cousin" of the narrative, this novel
brought into early focus the uneasy family, parental and sexual tensions which under-
lie all of James's life and work — though later he concealed them more carefully;
and still later they poured out again in another phase . . . *French Poets and Novelists*, also in 1878, was a collection of early essays on Musset, Gautier, Baudelaire,
Balzac, among others.

the time, rather tactfully; since it was also artificial, and insipid. Yet in our own period such a critic as Philip Rahv could still declare obliviously, it might appear, that "in that exquisite little narrative, the irony directed at the angular conditions of New England life is scarcely distinguishable from the charm and serenity of the presentation."

Well, to the present writer this irony is quite distinguishable as one of James's most deeply rooted preconceptions or prejudices; while "the charm and serenity" of *The Europeans* hardly conceal the "exquisite" novel's essential absurdity. James was on firmer ground, and a less self-revealing one, when his American figures went to Europe; and the young heroine of *Daisy Miller: A Study*, in 1879, was perhaps the most famous of all the early Jamesian maidens. But even here there was the same deliberate flatness and smallness of character in the portrait of Daisy herself. This pretty girl from Schenectady, the heiress of the new "western" fortunes in James's eyes, was also the first of a new type. A product of pure poetry, as the later writer claimed, a child of nature and freedom, despite the "grossness" of the American readers who had originally protested her behavior, Daisy became the prototype for all James's "self-made American girls" who came forth to conquer Europe (or "life") without benefit of family, tradition, or culture.

Wasn't this a kind of Horatio Alger story about the children of the new millionaires — the lowest social level to which the Jamesian imagination could really penetrate?

Hence Daisy's little brother Randolph with his "hard harsh little voice" and altogether spoiled behavior; this improbable little man who represents *the* American boy of the period. Hence Daisy's mother, idle, ignorant, ailing, with her "mild fatalism," her querulous voice, her dyspepsia. And hence the missing father of the story, somewhere back in the western wilderness, enormously rich, and yet presumably preoccupied solely with the making of the money which supports this traveling family group. What James had very early caught was the fluidity of family life among the new-rich classes in American life where the children — ignorant, spoiled, idle as they might be — could dominate their "less culti-vated" parents. But what James also established here, despite the grace and humor of his own treatment, was a kind of stereotype of the provincial American family that would persist in our letters from Edith Wharton to F. Scott Fitzgerald.*

But Daisy, another pre-flapper of the seventies, with her charm, with her audacity, along with her "impatient confiding step" and her desire to make "a little fuss," is still attractive. But was she or wasn't she a "nice girl"? That was the problem which stirred up the readers of her time, and which concerned the respectable hero of the tale, Winterbourne, whose name suggested the contrast be-tween him and the wild flower of the western earth. And here again the craft of the tale exemplified how much the young Henry James could do with so little content. For Daisy's indiscretions appear very mild today, and Winterbourne's doubts about her are those of a priggish young man who uses his moral scruples to shield his temperamental weakness. Their love affair is both tenuous and adolescent; and yet it is Winterbourne's own conflict, his repressed love for Daisy, the attraction beneath his disapprobation, which carry the story along.

And there is the risk she embodies to his social status. Is it her dubious carrying-on with the disreputable Italian fortune hunters of the story that Winterbourne objects to; or the fact that she has been exiled from the American colony in Rome; or that his aunt

---

* This family pattern, or lack of it, became more obvious among the later immi-grant groups in American society, whose children often repudiated their parental origins, and values, and culture, so completely as to become a particularly rootless and superficial middle class in the twentieth century United States. But while James caught this family (and social) configuration very early, and it became in fact a recurrent and standard item in his descriptions of American life, we shall notice also how he *shared* this embarrassment or shame about his own background, both in respect to the Irish and the commercial elements. He was indeed very closely linked, emotionally, with all these "self-made" American heiresses who are forced to reject, to disown, the families which nevertheless and so "mysteriously" supply them with the money for their cultural ambitions.

has declared her "cheap" and vulgar? When he takes that fatal
evening walk beneath the Arch of Constantine, past the vaguely
lighted monuments of the Forum, and sees Daisy and Giovanelli
sitting together in the dusky circle of the Colosseum — at eleven
o'clock! — his horror is compounded with a final relief. "It was
as if a sudden clearance had taken place in the ambiguity of the
poor girl's appearances and the whole riddle of her contradictions
had grown easy to read. She was a young lady about the *shades* of
whose perversity a foolish puzzled gentleman need no longer trouble his head or his heart. That once questionable quantity *had* no
shades — it was a mere black little blot." But those are the accents
of anger and jealousy, of a lover's heart as well as a gentleman's
code; and Daisy plays up to his indignation. "Why it was Mr.
Winterbourne! He saw me, and he cuts me dead." What a clever
little reprobate she was, the Jamesian hero thinks, and how smartly
she feigned. "How promptly she sought to play off on him, a sur-
prised and injured innocence!" — and yet walking her back to her
carriage, "he tried to deny himself the small fine anguish of looking at her, but his eyes themselves refused to spare him."

It is "the fortunate Italian," too, who takes the seat beside her in
the carriage. Rather like the typical Victorian sexual encounter,
Daisy's one trip to the Colosseum by moonlight does lead to the
perniciosa, the Roman fever of which she dies, and it is Giovanelli
who pronounces the final verdict. "She was the most beautiful
young lady I ever saw, and the most amiable . . . Also — naturally! — the most innocent." Daisy simply "did what she liked."
Both she and the disreputable Latin lover of the story come out
rather well, or are simply human, compared with the proper
Anglo-Saxons of the narrative, and *Daisy Miller* is still a touching,
if a somewhat dated, minor tale. For here, unlike *The Europeans*,
the weight was very evenly divided between the accents of desire in
the hero — repressed as he is, and limited as was the object of his
desire — and the dictates of social convention. If Daisy is both
too perverse and too ungrammatical; if Winterbourne is too in-

hibited and careful, or as "stiff" as Daisy says; if they are a typical pair of "lovers" in this early tale of James's — who talk out their passion rather than live it — it is still their tension and their feeling which keep the story alive. But on another level, the social "code" is too silly here; the rebellious heroine is too empty. "It was the most charming innocent prattle he had ever heard," so Winterbourne thinks about Daisy, and perhaps the early James was a master of that milieu.*

The British edition of *Daisy Miller* carried two other stories on Europe and America, "An International Episode" and "Four Meetings." The first of these was the tale of two young English visitors and two American women of Newport society, which again revealed the weakness in the early Jamesian concepts both of American business and British nobility. Bessie Alden finally turns down Lord Lambeth, in another variation on the international theme, but it hardly matters, because the story stressed the "grim truth . . . that in America there is no leisure class." "Unfortunately we haven't got a 'Peerage' like the people in Thackeray," Bessie remarks. And in London she feels, intensely, "the many-voiced appeal of the capital of the race from which she had sprung." The British lord is himself more impressive in his own surroundings. "He would be an unconscious part of the antiquity, the impressiveness, the picturesqueness of England: of all of which things poor Bessie Alden was terribly at the mercy." Or was it the poor young Henry James? "Ah, you're fond of castles?" says Her Grace, the Duchess of Bayswater. "It has been the dream of my life to live in one," says Bessie, who in her rejection of these old-world temptations shows her democratic mettle.

---

* On the subject of the "nice girl" in American fiction — a theme which dominated our literature during the period when the lords of finance were at a peak of immorality — it is interesting to compare William Dean Howells' *The Lady of the Aroostook* (1879), in which a young American girl makes a trip to Europe, unescorted, on a boat that is naturally run by men; and also Edith Wharton's later short story, "Roman Fever," where the young heroine, also having a romantic encounter at night in the Colosseum, contracts not a fatal illness, but a child.

"Four Meetings" was an even slighter story which illustrated again the deep enchantment, the fatal allure, which the "dream of Europe" held for the early, the literary, the adolescent and possessed Henry James.* "You've the great American disease, and you've got it bad," says the "European" to the New England schoolteacher: "the appetite, morbid and monstrous, for colour and form, for the picturesque and the romantic at any price —

I don't know whether we come into the world with it — with the germs implanted and antecedent to experience; rather perhaps we catch it early, almost before developed consciousness — we feel, as we look about, that we're going (to save our souls, or at least our senses) to be thrown back on it hard. We're like travellers in the desert — deprived of water and subject to the terrible mirage, the torment of illusion, of the thirst-fever . . . So we with our thirst — except that with us it's more wonderful: we have before us the beautiful old things we've never seen at all, and when we do at last see them — if we're lucky! — we simply recognize them. What experience does is merely to confirm and consecrate our confident dream.

The spinsterish heroine in "Four Meetings" listens to this peroration on the dream of Europe with "rounded eyes," we are told, and so perhaps does the modern reader. For wasn't it the most illuminating and revealing, the most eloquent and odd description of the "American disease" which Henry James, alone among our major writing talents, had become subject to, if not "antecedent to experience," at least surely very early in infancy or childhood?

Now this appetite, morbid and monstrous, for the picturesque and the romantic at any price; this terrible mirage and torment of illusion; this sense of returning to and recognizing "the beautiful old things" of Europe as the confirmation of a dream — and then

* So how can this story possibly be one of James's "most felicitous versions of the international theme," as Morton D. Zabel states in his *Portable Henry James* — "and a flawless example of his art in the pathos of privation." The pathos of the privation of *Europe*, that is — and such peaks of critical eloquence, based on such shaky foundations of fact, were typical of the Jacobite cultists of the 1950's.

the returning "home," to Europe, naturally, of the exiled, stricken and deprived child-orphan! Well, the famous little book on Hawthorne, in the same year of 1879, spelled out some further details about the early James who was consumed by this curious vision.

Was this volume, written for the English Men of Letters series, "perfect of its sort and its sort is rare," as F. W. Dupee roundly claimed? "A kind of hail and farewell to Hawthorne and his New England age, it is both tender and urbane," this critic adds — although the book is also ignorant, improvised, unjust, patronizing above all to the American literary scene and deliberately ingratiating, at once fawning and snobbish, where its British audience was concerned. James did indeed pay tribute to the older American writer who was "on his limited scale a master of expression." But then Hawthorne borrowed an added relief "from the absence of competitors in his own line, and from the general flatness of the literary field that surrounds him." Very early in the book James announced his own conviction and belief. "The moral is that the flower of art blooms only where the soil is deep, that it takes a great deal of history to produce a little literature, that it needs a complex social machinery to set a writer in motion." And what James meant by soil, history and a complex social machinery was equally clear. "Poor Hawthorne was indeed thousands of miles away from Oxford and Cambridge." *

Here came the famous passage (which I have already quoted from the *Notebooks*) on the "items of high civilization" that were missing in American life from Hawthorne's day to James's: the artistic lacks of "a simple, democratic, thinly-composed society." And what James appeared most to lament in American history was the passing away of King George's representatives "in his only loyal but finally alienated colony." If James either patronized or ignored the

* This refrain has echoed down some quarters of American thought from the time of James to those New Critics of the 1950's who apparently associated an artist's creative talent with his university (and preferably British) training. Nothing could be falser, even in England itself, as the English writers have told us.

whole group of writers who surrounded Hawthorne in the first flowering of the national letters — Emerson, Thoreau, Melville, Whitman — he was hardly more favorably impressed by the Transcendental movement itself. In the domestic annals of New England, said he, this was only the "ingenious attempt of a few speculative persons to improve the outlook of mankind." It was a "harmless effusion of Radicalism," a "little epoch of fermentation," or at best "the free, frank and stainless companionship of young men and maidens in the mixture of manual labour and intellectual flights." From the first exchange of musket shots between the King's troops and the American insurgents to the advent of the foreign immigration — and particularly the "salt Hibernian spray" — upon "the rural strongholds of the New England race," there was nothing in American culture to nourish its native talent. Nothing, that is, except the American's famous capacity to laugh at himself. "It would be cruel, in this terrible denudation, to deny him the consolation of his natural gift, that 'American humour' of which, of late years, we have heard so much."

How did poor Hawthorne manage to write as well as he did? That is the question which haunts the modern reader of James's *Hawthorne*. But there were still other revealing elements in this study. There was a consistent attempt to devalue or deny just those characteristics which gave density, depth and humanity to the earlier novelist's work. There was in Hawthorne's writings, said Henry James, "something cold, and light, and thin, something belonging to the imagination alone — which indicated a man but little disposed to multiply his relations, his points of contact, with society." Had the French critics of the period already described him as a "Romancier Pessimiste"? James found no sign of a "dusky and malarious genius" in Hawthorne. He was in fact "rarely even what I should call tragical." Surely *The Scarlet Letter* was the "most consistently gloomy of English novels," James said again, yet nothing was more curious and interesting "than this almost exclusively *imported* character of the sense of sin in Hawthorne's mind." The italicizing of "imported" was apparently important to James, and he went on to compare "the passionless quality of Hawthorne's novel, its element of cold and ingenious fantasy" with a now almost forgotten novel, *Adam Blair*, by John Gibson Lockhart. Lockhart was "a dense, substantial Briton," while Hawthorne was a "thin New Englander with a miasmatic conscience."

This was surely one of the most curious passages in a very curious book. Here the early James was not only ignorant but insufferable. Was it his own jealousy and insecurity that made him deny the depth of Hawthorne, the deep and tangled strain of sexual sin, the brooding compassion? Or was it James's own psychic bloc about this central area of human behavior which had precisely distinguished the earlier "romancer"? If, as he sensed, Hawthorne was his single great American competitor (Melville was unknown to him; the early Whitman he scorned), did he have to hew the ground around his distinguished confrere quite so level, and then adroitly dispose of his confrere also? The question at stake was the psychological realism of Hawthorne's emotions versus the psychological illusion of the Jamesian "manners." And if James had to survive — ridden as he was by the deep obsession of "Europe" — then Hawthorne had to go. America could *not* have its genius that flourished so unconventionally, so inconveniently and so richly.

And Hawthorne never understood the English! With all its merits, *Our Old Home* was the work "of an outsider, of a stranger, of a man who remains to the end a mere spectator (something less even than an observer), and always lacks the final initiation into the manners and nature of a people of whom it may most be said, among all the people of the earth, that to know them is to make discoveries." James was acknowledging his own qualifications on the basis of Hawthorne's limitations (though the prophetic note of self-illumination remained). And while the Italian Note-Books of the older writer were pleasant reading, Hawthorne's Puritanism also kept him from any real contact with the country and its people. For so acute a critic, James was perhaps deliberately obtuse in his discussion of *The Marble Faun*, too (which he persisted in calling by its English title of *Transformation*). Puritan or not, Hawthorne's Italian "romance" reached deeper levels of sensuous and pagan feeling than even the best later work of James's. But perhaps the real difference in timbre between these two American writers came in the discussion of the Civil War. To Hawthorne, whose somber humor lay beneath the sophisticated wit of James, John Brown's crime was a "preposterous miscalculation of possibilities" for which he should have been hanged. To James, John Brown was "the dauntless and deluded old man" who proposed to solve a complex political problem "by stirring up a servile insurrection."

Yes; these were two very different epochs of the American republic which clashed so oddly beneath the "tender and urbane" surface (Dupee) of James's *Hawthorne*. And this was not so much a hail and farewell to the New England age which James knew so little about, as it was a prophetic and illuminating and self-revealing book by James *about* James — rather than about his ostensible subject. But now James was on the edge of one of his most interesting early works, the *Washington Square* of 1880.* Was this the single work of James's, as F. O. Matthiessen suggests, which is always admired by those people who don't really like James? Well, one can admire very different works (and periods) in this writer, and also try to discriminate between good and bad works by the same prodigious author.

Was the story also the product of "the single tension" (Matthiessen) caused between Catherine Sloper and her father? James did

---

* *Confidence* (1879; a year when James was pouring out material) was another romance melodrama in the vein of *Watch and Ward*, centering on the triangle of two "friends" in love with the same ambiguous heroine; a situation from which James evoked endless complications but not much literary merit. A *Bundle of Letters* (1880), was a rather pleasant sketch of a group of Americans, British and Europeans all discussing each other's manners through their correspondence — but not a sufficiently important work to deserve Clifton Fadiman's encomium in his *Short Stories of Henry James*.

complain to Howells that in doing a tale purely American, the writing made him feel acutely "the want of paraphernalia." Yet even from his childhood memories, the temple of Republican simplicity in Old New York, the ideal of "quiet and genteel retirement" in Washington Square society, are effective in the background of the story.* And from Catherine's first appearance, in her red satin gown trimmed with gold fringe; and from the Doctor's "fatherly" remark to her — "You are sumptuous, opulent, expensive . . . You look as if you had eighty thousand a year" — the story's tension is set up. Or rather the tangled skein of avarice and incest becomes apparent as the emotional fabric of *Washington Square.* Catherine is another sleeping-princess heroine, surrounded by a wall of cash rather than fire. The noble stranger is the indolent, charming, calculating Morris Townsend. Doctor Sloper is the stern, "protective" father-god figure of property, duty and righteousness whose motives and behavior are finally revealed to be as ambiguous as his name.

Yet James's ironic treatment of this odd cluster of literary elements, and particularly the tender treatment of Catherine Sloper herself, were good; while all the subordinate characters in the domestic drama cast their various lights on the central action. Catherine, with her innocence, happiness and softness in her first love affair, but her deep sense of filial loyalty, duty and respect for the father whom she knows to scorn her, is very different from the spoiled American maiden-princesses of the later age of the great fortunes. She is closer to Jennie Gerhardt than to Daisy Miller. "Love demands certain things as a right; but Catherine had no sense of her rights; she had only a consciousness of immense and

---

* The story was suggested to James by Mrs. Kemble's anecdote of her brother's engagement to "a dull, plain, common-place" British girl, whose father threatened to cut off her money if the marriage went through. In James's *Notebook* entry, it was Mrs. Kemble herself (the elderly actress-and-writer friend of the young American) who warned the girl not to marry her weak and pleasure-loving brother . . . But in transplanting this story to the American scene of his youth, James also gave it another dimension of parent-child relations.

unexpected favours." When Morris prepares her, with his kisses on her lips and cheeks, for her encounter with the Doctor over her engagement, and forewarns her that her father will accuse her suitor of being mercenary — "I am very glad we shall be rich," Catherine says simply. She has the flat feminine realism about money; but her doubts lie in other quarters. "Morris . . . are you very sure you love me?"

She is caught between father and lover, neither of whom has any real concern for her happiness — for her. The Doctor slowly emerges as a monster-egoist, almost monomaniacal in the destruction of his daughter's only chance for love. But Morris Townsend doesn't so much break against the father's iron will as he wilts at the prospect of losing the larger fortune which Catherine is to inherit from her father. On the surface, *Washington Square* is hardly a modern story of passion. It is closer to the old-fashioned Balzacian tale of "the passions" — of pride, greed, avarice, or cunning. In a sense the good Doctor is right; and Morris is not after a comfortable marriage on Catherine's own income, but only after her fortune. It is Catherine's humanity which redeems the solid cash basis of the narrative; her renunciation of life, and her lifelong suffering.

But can you live so deeply on the tragic memories of a single love affair, never consummated and mercenary in essence, and rather inadequately described? This was to become the Jamesian hypothesis of the "heightened sensibility" which was set off against all the low vulgar experience of existence. In *Washington Square* this concept was both projected and maintained — and the fictional "illusion" was given true life — from another source. Does the power of the story, then, depend on the Freudian depths which a later generation has seen there, and which the stage play, *The Heiress*, suggested rather dramatically? Was the Jamesian stress on solid (inherited) cash simply a covering mechanism for the love-hatred-jealousy emotional pattern of a classic father-daughter relation? There is much to support the thesis in the story, and this writer was to become still more involved — to dwell among — even more complex incestuous and oedipal family relationships. One might say his instinct drew him here, and his "reason" drew him back, which accounts for another celebrated Jamesian virtue of "ambiguity."

But meanwhile it is clear that the story was written during the period of James's own stuggle to emancipate himself from his own family; to create his own mold of self and individuality, via Europe rather than America — and that *this* self-struggle was projected into the dramatic structure of *Washington Square*. Catherine Sloper is almost too submissive and pious. She is not restrained so much by her father's power and threats as by her own sense of filial devotion. (Another heroine, another heiress, might simply have gone off with her young man and her own money.) "She had an immense respect for her father, and she felt that to displease him would be a misdemeanour analogous to an act of profanity in a great temple; but her purpose had slowly ripened, and she believed that her prayers had purified it of its violence." Catherine had indeed "the sentiment of duty developed in a very high degree." She is the backward and "dull" member of a bright family, as the Doctor reminds her. That James also felt himself in very much the same family position is clear, just as this heroine's "resolution" of silent suffering and emotional repression, of self-sacrifice and abnegation, forecast the typical Jamesian resolution to all the tangled affairs of life.*

The inner theme of *Washington Square* was thus that of the exploited and backward child who gains dignity and individuality in what has been described as "almost a system of inverted family relationships." Yes, where the father quite hopelessly loves the beautiful "lost" mother at the expense of the ugly-duckling daugh-

---

* On the deeper psychological levels, which are revealing in the case of James, the "castrated son" identified himself with the deprived daughter. But what is curious here is the early James fantasy of the beautiful "dead" mother in *Washington Square*, and the tyrannical father-image which is different from anything in James's own family relations.

ter (or say, son). And this situation, and this intensity of feeling derived quite directly, not perhaps from the *facts* of James's own childhood and youth, but certainly, as we shall see, from his most profound and permanent fancy of those facts. Centered on these deeply personal and "experienced" (if only in the Jamesian fantasy) emotions, the tale was a good one; and it was the prelude to what is still the most notable work of James's first period, *The Portrait of a Lady*, in 1881.

Rather like *The American*, the opening of the new novel was that of leisurely, old-fashioned social comedy; the tone was warm, genial, entertaining. Again there were the overtones of great wealth, high culture, and "old world" sensitivity in the exchange of pleasantries between Lord Warburton and the Touchetts, and when the charming young American girl first encounters the vista of the lawn, the great trees, the silvery Thames, the old house, the British dogs. In one sense the *Portrait of a Lady* was an engaging domestic drama of the international scene; on this level it summarized and capped all of the early James's romantic visions of "the dream of Europe." We first see the eccentric Mrs. Touchett, who has brought Isabel Archer to England, when she is completely dressed for dinner and embracing her son with her gloved hands.

If the mother image in *Washington Square* was that of a beautiful and dead woman, the psychological cause of her daughter's ruin, the Mrs. Touchett of the *Portrait* is also separated, by her choice of an Italian residence, from her British-American family. Isabel herself, with her innocence and cleverness, her "irregular education," her strong will and high temper; her determination to learn about life and not to be bored, is a superior evocation of the series of young American girls who are the products of wealth and the victims of Europe. Is she a limited medium of literary consciousness, a rather thin and cool and "intellectual" figure as a heroine and a woman? But this whole line of early Jamesian heroines, these young American girls who were in reality rich, spoiled, untutored products of the new American fortunes, were romanticized and idealized by a writer whose own charm of craft carried along these rather dubious vehicles. Similarly Lord Warburton is a curious type of nobleman of the newest pattern, "a reformer, a radical, a contemner of ancient ways." He has a hundred thousand (pounds) a year, and owns fifty thousand acres. He has half a dozen houses to live in, a seat in Parliament, elegant taste in literature, art, science and in charming young ladies. But "the victim of a critical age," he is James's concept of a royal revolutionist.

"I should delight in seeing a revolution," says Isabel Archer herself. But in such a case, she adds, "I think I should be a high, proud loyalist. One sympathizes more with them, and they've a chance to behave so exquisitely. I mean so picturesquely." Yes, the England of the 1870's was in the throes of a social crisis produced by the injustices of the industrial revolution. But again the early James notion of "history," very much like his heroine's, was concerned not so much with principles as with the pictorial. "If I were he," says Isabel to the nobleman's two sisters, the Misses Molyneux, "I should wish to fight to the death: I mean for the heritage of the past . . . I should hold it tight." Yet Warburton was acceptable to James as an upper-class radical, at least, or as the symbol of one rather than the fact. The only valid social criticism, or social commentary, in *The Portrait of a Lady* is in the portrait of Henrietta Stackpole, the brassy American lady journalist who snoops around the British aristocracy for the benefit of the democratic "free press." She is an amusing caricature at times; she does indeed "smell of the Future — it almost knocks one down!" as James said. But Howells, before James, and Edith Wharton after him were equally sharp on the yellow journalism of the period.

The sensitive and sick Ralph Touchett is the familiar Jamesian observer in the novel. The spiritual guardian of Isabel, and then her material benefactor, he is really the other half, the conscious half of Isabel, or of a central protagonist in the *Portrait* which is feminine in essence. (Ralph's family name is a cross between "touching," which he is, and one who hardly dares to touch; while the large share of the family fortune which he gives to Isabel as a token of his affection is in the best vein of Jamesian romance about the world of the inheritors.) James had actually divided up his own sensibilities between these two central figures, as in *Roderick Hudson*; while the arrival of Caspar Goodwood in the novel points up the emotional deficiency in Lord Warburton himself. "She liked him too much to marry him, that was the truth," Isabel reflects about the British lord, but he was indeed a *personage*. "She had never yet known a personage; there had been no personages . . . in her life; there were probably none at all in her native land."

Thus *The Portrait of a Lady* was a compendium of early James prejudices, and Caspar himself is a rude, aggressive symbol of "New World vitality." But there are other elements here — his mere arrival "made the air sultry" around Isabel, and she is terrified of him, as she admits. "There was a disagreeably strong push, a kind of hardness of presence, in his way of rising before her . . . Caspar Goodwood expressed for her an energy — and she had already felt it as a power — that was of his very nature." He is the only symbol of biological or sexual energy in the novel; this post-Civil War American industrialist is a kind of early D. H. Lawrence character. "But it was as if something large and confused, something dark and ugly, would have to call upon him: he was not after all in harmony with mere smug peace and greed and gain . . ." And Isabel, drawn to him physically, has to get rid of him. "Yes, you don't at all delight me, you don't fit in, not in any way, just now." "One would think you were going to commit some atrocity!" says Caspar in return, directly before the entrance of Mme. Merle. And he is right. This is an effective climax in the early part of the *Portrait*; even though one notices that James has divided off the qualities of love, for Isabel, between two equally impossible suitors.

Mme. Merle is the old-world magician, as her name indicates, whom Isabel has been asking to initiate her into the "mystery of life," and who leads her into her fatal entrapment. Here again

James used a "false," or at least a highly melodramatic plot to carry forward the action in the last half of the novel; and yet, on such an improbable base, the last half is perhaps the best part of the novel. What is remarkable is the virtuosity of James's craft which could carry forward such a thin, pure heroine — empty of all real knowledge or real experience — and such a limited view of life, based on such peculiar propositions, even to this point. It is Mme. Merle who sets Gilbert Osmond after Isabel's fortune for the sake of little Pansy, the child of a previous affair between these two former lovers. (These two lovers, who know each other so well, have no love left, apparently; no affection, no memories, except a cold understanding of material gain.) Yes, melodrama, plus an Italian travelogue, constitute the real medium of the second half of *The Portrait of a Lady*, which is also in a sense a completely different, or a second novel.

Osmond himself, with his old curtains and crucifixes; with his bibelots, his pictures, his medallions and tapestries, and his dependence on "beauty" as the secret of existence, is the portrait of a pure esthete; a "collector." "He had consulted his taste in everything — his taste alone, perhaps, as a sick man consciously incurable consults at last only his lawyer," James wrote, and he was projecting another facet of his own temperament. "I had no prospects, I was poor . . . I had no talents even; I was simply the most fastidious young gentleman living," Osmond tells Isabel. Yet he and Mme. Merle liven up this cold-blooded and unbelievable plot to entrap the American heiress; these two, and the "Fayaway" young Pansy, and the Countess Gemini herself. This highly compromised character, as James said, by no means a blank sheet, but one that had been written over "in a variety of hands," and who exhibited "the mere floating fragments of a wrecked renown," is another message of warning to poor blind Isabel.

What Isabel is seeking from Osmond is the life of experience; what she gets from their marriage is the cold life of cultivation. This mistress of rejection arrives only at an apex of renunciation.

And now James piled twist on twist of narrative complication to
sustain the climax of *The Portrait of a Lady*. Ralph is slowly dying,
just living long enough, as he says, for his "curiosity" to glean the
conclusion of Isabel's tragic marriage — an odd motive for survival. Lord Warburton, now the "famous radical" of the London
Times at least, re-enters Isabel's life as a potential suitor for
Pansy's hand, this foster-daughter of the foster-mother whom he
still loves. How fond James is of these deliberately contrived and
ambiguous human relations! Notice the ingenious "domestic" and
love relationships that prevail at large in the novel. Pansy's true
mother, Mme. Merle, marries off her former lover for the sake of
her daughter. Isabel's own child dies shortly after her marriage,
while she devotes herself to Osmond's (and Mme. Merle's) child,
whom the father scorns. Warburton returns as the father-lover of
Pansy, while he still desires the lost wife-mother figure of Isabel.
The touching relation of Isabel and Ralph becomes that of
brother and sister, but of an "adopted" brother who also confers
on Isabel the fortune which is meant to bring her happiness and
leads to her ruin.

Was this a curious kind of oedipal fantasy, or mere fictional ingenuity, or something else still? That is the question to be determined. It is a central issue in James's craft, in his real view of
life: a causative agent as well as a literary curiosity, compounded
of incest and ambiguity. Meanwhile Isabel, symbol of Puritan conscience, is determined to atone for her own errors of judgment. "It
was impossible to pretend that she had not acted with her eyes
open; if ever a girl was a free agent she had been. A girl in love was
doubtless not a free agent; but the sole source of her mistake had
been within herself. There had been no plot, no snare; she had
looked and considered and chosen. When a woman had made
such a mistake, there was only one way to repair it — just immensely (oh, with the highest grandeur!) to accept it . . ." But
this "grandeur" of the Jamesian heroine, and this lofty, touching
moral suffering and resignation, were also highly suspect — were
theatrical, and based on an altogether false foundation. In fact,

there *was* a plot and a snare (James's own plot and snare); and it was Isabel's pride and her vanity, and perhaps her fear of life, which prevailed over her common sense, and her capacity for experience.

The later portrait of Isabel Archer contained some of James's most effective and famous descriptions of the life of restriction, depression, failure. "It was the house of darkness, the house of dumbness, the house of suffocation." These were the emotions that James knew best; and which paralleled some of his personal passages of anxiety and renunciation in the *Notebooks*. But there also was a final paradox in his famous early heroine and his own view of life. When Isabel Archer realizes the depths of her own degradation — and the absolutely contrived situation which has led her there — why shouldn't she pick up and go? Or rather, pick up her fortune and go? It is bad enough to be trapped by life; but it is totally inexcusable — isn't it? — to remain trapped by altogether contrived circumstances in life. Isabel's relation with Pansy is never convincing, while the child herself is a dubious symbol of the European jeune fille. Isabel's power over Mme. Merle, in the end, is sufficient to send that sorceress into exile in America; the worst of all possible Jamesian fates. Just as the plot of the *Portrait* is never quite credible, except as entertainment, the resolution of the novel is strained to fit the Jamesian moral rather than the realities of the European existence he was describing. The human truth of the story is constrained, or contorted on the Procrustean frame of both the author's initial concept and his limited sense of experience — or of the lack of alternatives in human choice.*

The *Portrait* was in this sense a Victorian "novel of complica-

---

* But compare Robert W. Stallman (*The Houses That James Built*, 1961), one of the most recent and fervent converts to the New Criticism, who declares that — "Second to *Moby Dick*, *The Portrait of a Lady* strikes me as the richest perfection in American literature." Well, I've already suggested that Isabel Archer would make a strange mate for the demonic, rebellious Ahab; and what poles, what worlds apart these two novels are in fact. How can recent American criticism lose all sense of values, of distinctions, of judgment in this infatuated, absurd fashion?

tions" raised to a new height of moral or intellectual analysis. It used an early and quite orderly "stream of consciousness"; but never the true currents of the unconscious; which yet, in a curious way, James somehow suggested. He could be far more free sexually, about the disreputable Italian Countess Gemini — "with her trunks, her dresses, her chatter, her falsehoods, her frivolity, the strange, the unholy legend of the number of her lovers." Nevertheless, all of his *heroine's* relations, perhaps her marriage itself, must remain pure, lofty, exalted, and, in the end, self-sacrificial, renunciatory, chaste. There is another interesting scene where Caspar Goodwood is almost overcome by his passion for Isabel —

Now that he was alone with her all the passion he had never stifled surged into his senses; it hummed in his eyes and made things swim round him. The bright, empty room grew dim and blurred, and through the heaving veil he felt her hover before him with gleaming eyes and parted lips.

But if Caspar's seizure is almost feminine in essence, Isabel, frightened of what she reads in his face, preserves her forced smile and her composure. " 'I suppose you wish to bid me good-bye?' she said."

There is still the embrace he forces upon her, which confirms all her distaste for him. "His kiss was like white lightning, a flash that spread, and spread again, and stayed; and it was extraordinarily as if, while she took it, she felt each thing in his hard manhood that had least pleased her, each aggressive fact of his face, his figure, his presence, justified of its intense identity and made one with this act of possession. So had she heard of those wrecked and under water following a train of images before they sank. But when darkness returned she was free." Free indeed: to continue her solitary existence of suffering, the pursuit of her own heightened sensibility at the expense of all common human pleasure, companionship, fulfillment in human relations. In this sense the ending of the novel was never ambiguous. The first major heroine of James's was a woman who teased, flirted with and then fled from all of her possible lovers; while she took the one man who would never awaken her, and who had to destroy her.

This was the meaning of *The Portrait of a Lady* in any kind of depth interpretation, and perhaps it is still the reason why, despite the inadequacy of the story's origins and conclusions — and of its professed and "conscious" moral — the novel still attracts, even while it may puzzle us. Was the early James even dimly aware of the true nature of this heroine whom he described with such charm and grace and then with such magniloquence of moral grandeur? But this was a writer, as we shall see, whose unconscious emotions continued to project a series of figures, situations, and relations which are often directly opposed to, in flat contradiction to, the conscious purposes of his craft. This great "analyst" of modern American fiction, and of modern criticism, was aware of everything except his own inner springs of creative action.

The skill of craft, apparent even as early as this novel, was designed to compensate for, even to conceal, the inadequate fictional concepts of James's — to bridge the gap between his dubious propositions and his foreshortened conclusions. On the conscious level *The Portrait of a Lady* must be viewed only as a kind of superior romance melodrama which is entertaining to read, and completely inadequate as serious literary commentary on the life of James's period, or certainly our own. That the novel has another hidden source of interest is due simply to the unacknowledged conflict between the intuitions of the artist, including his own sexual fears, inhibitions and aversions which are projected through his revealing heroine, and the "literary intention" which he consciously rendered to his readers and, yes, to himself.

3. The Eighties: Nightmare and Fairy Tale

ISABEL ARCHER was not merely the young American girl of the 1870's casting her arrow into the blue, and meeting that "ghost" of European experience which, as James said, alone entailed true life, suffering and tragedy. She was also the descendant, symbolically, of the frigid huntress, Diana or Artemis, who, linked with the moon, was the guardian of perpetual celibacy.

If this first major novel, like other works of James's, is more memorable while you read it than it is afterwards — if the illusion which the artist created is more immediate than durable — you may also note that this romance deals almost exclusively with the feminine interests of courtship and marriage. The fortune which Isabel "inherits" from Ralph Touchett's family; the travelogue of European culture against which the novel's action is set: these are part of the leisure-class Jamesian world of the inheritors which hardly allows for even the semblance of masculine action or enterprise. The American Caspar Goodwood is dismissed as being too crude and too sexual.

James could be called the great novelist of a feminine age in letters, as F. W. Dupee says — and Dupee's *Henry James* is perhaps the most sensible of all the "James-ite" books. At least this critic is aware of certain deficiencies in the Master's work; though he too casts a passing glance at such matters, rather than giving them full consideration. The real trouble with all the Jacobites is that they are wholly committed to their cause. Thus they are no longer critics so much as apologists — or esthetic theologists — who must rationalize every issue in favor of their royal subject, their literary emperor, if not their god.

Perhaps Henry James might better be described as the greatest feminine novelist of *any* age; the artist who brought the domestic realm of a Jane Austen, say, to the edge (if no further) of world literature. Now the later James himself, the James of the Prefaces, acknowledged that "the mere young thing" was a frail vessel for the purposes of major fiction. But what better field "for a due in-genuity," he added, than this problem itself: to make the most of a limited subject, a limited heroine, a limited consciousness — to gain "the maximum of intensity from a minimum of human ex-perience." And didn't this formulation of the specific Jamesian "problem" also give the whole thing away? For what one really demands from literature is a maximum of intensity from a *maxi-mum* of human experience. In addition to this, however, the later theorist (James) pointed out that the earlier novelist (James) had stressed the interior drama of Isabel's consciousness to the point that her reverie, just beyond the middle of the book, is the high moment of the novel. "It is a representation simply of her motion-lessly *seeing*, and an attempt withal to make the mere still lucid-ity of her act as 'interesting' as the surprise of a caravan or the identification of a pirate." James's use of imagery was revealing, as though it came from the romance literature of his own childhood, even while he changed the stress from outside to inside melo-drama, from extreme action to intensities of being. "But it all goes on without her being approached by another person and without her leaving her chair. It is obviously the best thing in the book, but it is only a supreme illustration of the general plan."

What was it also that in her supreme moment this heroine did *not* see? — that James himself felt and scented, half projected and then left dangling in the abyss of his typical ambiguity at the close of the novel: the vision of Isabel's *un*conscious motives? Mean-while he had rewritten *Daisy Miller* into a three-act comedy for the stage (published in 1882) and collected three new stories for the volume called *The Siege of London*, in 1883. "The Pension Beaurepas" was an entertaining satire of western American wealth. The title story was an "Anglicized" — that is, purified, refined, genteel — version of a Dumas play, *Le Demi-Monde*, which was both deliberately and also unconsciously amusing. In these tales of our crude new fortunes, the rise of sensational journalism, the growing incidence of easy divorce in late nineteenth century society, James was, to be sure, anticipating certain themes of the new literary realism, extending from the Howells of his own generation to Frank Norris and Ellen Glasgow and Theodore Dreiser.

But with what a different point of view! For James still described the American West as a colony, rather, of the eastern coast; just as he saw the United States itself as the lost colony of England. The vulgar, brassy heroine of "The Siege of London" — this "shining smiling rustling chattering daughter of the Territories" — is worse than immoral perhaps. She is ignorant, pushing and presumptuous. What chance has she really got with an English nobility who were so wrapped up in a community of ideas, of traditions that "they understood each other's accent, even each other's deviations." The noblemen with "their clean complexions, their well-hung chins, their cold pleasant eyes"; the noblewomen, very handsome, "half-strangled in strings of pearls," who appear to look at nothing, and support silence with such grace, and sometimes talk a little "in fresh rich voices." Against this glowing vision of British society, what American heroine could make *any* headway? And Mrs. Headway herself, the Nancy Beck of the far West, is "fearfully common," a "flaming barbarian" at best. "What I see," says Littlemore's Anglo-American sister, who has made good — "What I see is a fine old race — one of the oldest and most honourable in England, people with every tradition of good conduct and high principle — and a dreadful disreputable vulgar little woman, who hasn't an idea of what such things are, trying to force her way into it."

And that was just what Henry James saw, too. For the third

story in *The Siege of London*, "The Point of View" — a continuation of his earlier "Bundle of Letters" — carried James's most
bitter indictment of American culture, society and art to this point.
The period of real doubt and conflict, up to *The Portrait of a Lady*,
was over. Now the die had been cast — and the Jamesian literary dice were loaded. There were "very few gentlemen, pure and
simple," in the American scene of the early eighties. There were
no "brilliant types of personalities," and no "personages." The
prevailing mediocrity of democratic society which Tocqueville
had feared had arrived with a vengeance. "The most important
people seem to lack dignity . . . The men have no style; the
women, who are fidgety and talk too much, have it only in their
tournures." This was from "Miss Sturdy's" account of her travels;
and James recited another of his familiar complaints about American life. The servants were *rude* — there was really no servant class!
There were also no yeomen in New England, according to the
Right Hon. Edward Antrobus, M.P. There were no gentry; while
the political life of the nation was almost wholly confined "to the
lower middle class," or "the upper section of the lower class."

These sentiments were very close to James's own confidential passages to himself in the *Notebooks* and Journals of these years; and
there was more —

*I think of your warm rich Paris; I think of the Boulevard Saint-Michel
on the mild spring evenings; I see the little corner by the window (of
the Café de la Jeunesse) where I used to sit: the doors are open, the
soft deep breath of the great city comes in. The sense is of a supreme
splendor and an incomparable arrangement, yet there's a kind of tone,
of body, in the radiance; the mighty murmur of the ripest civilisation
in the world comes in; the dear old peuple de Paris . . . There's no
form here, dear Harvard; I had no idea how little form there is. I don't
know what I shall do; I feel so undraped, so uncurtained, so uncush-
ioned; I feel as if I were sitting in the centre of a mighty "reflector."
A terrible crude glare is over everything; the earth looks peeled and
excoriated; the raw heavens seem to bleed with the quick hard light.*

This was another version of the pure white American air and light which the royal travelers of *The Europeans* felt to be the single asset of the New England landscape. The terrible crude glare, the peeled and excoriated earth, the raw and bleeding heavens; those were close to the imagery of a nightmare; and the Boston hotel where this Jamesian spokesman of "The Point of View" was staying is hardly more soothing. There is the arrogant desk clerk, "where you write your name in a horrible book where every one may come and stare at it and finger it." There is the "savage Irishman" who is the bellboy who receives the key from the clerk.

"Take him away," he seems to say to the Irishman; but it's all done in silence; there's no answer to your own wild wail — "What's to be done with me, please?" "Wait and you'll see," the awful silence seems to say. There's a great crowd round you, but there's also a great stillness; every now and then you hear some one expectorate. There are a thousand people in this huge and hideous structure; they feed together in a big white-walled room. It's lighted by a thousand gas-jets and heated by cast-iron screens which vomit forth torrents of scorching air. The temperature's terrible; the atmosphere's more so; the furious light and heat seem to intensify the dreadful definiteness. When things are so ugly they shouldn't be so definite, and they're terribly ugly here. There's no mystery in the corners, there's no light and shade in the types. The people are haggard and joyless; they look as if they had no passions, no tastes, no senses. They sit feeding in silence under the dry hard light; occasionally I hear the high firm note of a child.

Even the black servants whom the earlier James had considered objects of esthetic merit, if not of moral fervor, become the accessories of these domestic horrors. "They've no manners; they address but don't answer you; they plant themselves at your elbow . . . and watch you as if your proceedings were strange. They deluge you with iced water; it's the only thing they'll bring you; if you look round to summon them they've gone for more." He was dying of iced water, of hot air, of flaring gas, said this hypersensitive Jamesian spokesman, and his bedroom was no refuge from the prevailing horrors and tortures of the New World:

I sit in my room thinking of these things — this room of mine which is a chamber of pain. The walls are white and bare, they shine in the rays of a horrible chandelier of imitation bronze which depends from the middle of the ceiling . . . I rise and put out the gas — when my room becomes even lighter than before. Then a crude illumination from the hall, from the neighbouring room, pours through the glass openings that surmount the two doors of my apartment. It covers my bed, where I toss and groan; it beats in through my closed lids; it's accompanied by the most vulgar, though the most human sounds. I spring up to call for some help, some remedy; but there's no bell and I feel desolate and weak. There's only a strange orifice in the wall, through which the traveller in distress may transmit his appeal. I fill it with incoherent sounds, and sounds more incoherent yet come back to me. I gather at last their meaning; they appear to constitute an awful enquiry. A hollow impersonal voice wishes to know what I want, and the very question paralyses me. I want everything — yet I want nothing this hard impersonality can give! I want my little corner of Paris; I want the rich, the deep, the dark Old World; I want to be out of this horrible place. Yet I can't confide all this to that mechanical tube; it would be of no use; a barbarous laugh would come up from the office.

Thus the dream of Europe in James's mind was balanced by — or did it indeed derive from — the nightmare of America. If this writer also stressed the complexity of his art in "The Point of View," the capacity to see every angle in an idea, or every possible twist and reverberation of his theme, there was no doubt that both the theme and the tone of the story were close to a Kafka-esque vision of frustration and horror. This aversion to his native scene was morbid at its core; concealed as it so often was by irony or wit or a deliberate ambiguousness. It was, in these passages and others like them, almost a physical, a sensory, an *organic* aversion — on the part of this solitary sufferer in the contrived inferno of a Boston hotel — to his native climate and his native residence.

There was an element of prophetic horror here, too, that antici-

pated the air-conditioned nightmare of Henry Miller's America of
the 1950's. But would "the rich, the deep, the dark Old World"
provide the true refuge — womblike and sexual — that this harried
protagonist in "The Point of View" was searching for? And what
were the real, and the earliest, sources of this oddly balanced equation of dream and nightmare, or more precisely, of nightmare and
dream, in the mind of the young Henry James? Meanwhile, however, there was a curious and exorbitant revulsion to his native
scene; an intense psychic wound that, not often revealed so clearly
under the rational and polished surface of this civilized and urbane artist, was nevertheless almost always described in identical
terms.

Beneath the literary "masks" of this story, or the "angles of vision" on which James prided himself, the writer's own point of
view was only too apparent. To the voice of the young esthete,
Louis Leverett, yearning for his little corner of Paris, was added
that of M. Gustave Lejaune of the French Academy, commenting
that the country was "a colossal mediocrity," and the public conscience an "abyss." The United States was the last word in democracy — and the word was platitude. This intense and absolute rejection of every phase of American life; this deeply physical
as well as emotional and intellectual repudiation, was the true
"point of view" in the story; and in James's next two nouvelles, the
two poles of the international theme were elaborated again.*

The story called "Lady Barberina," in *Tales of Three Cities*
(1884), opened in Hyde Park at the height of the season. The
fantasy of the cultivated and gracious life in the Jamesian mind —
the "great exhibition of English wealth and health, beauty, luxury
and leisure" — was again obvious in this minor entertainment.

---

* *Portraits of Places* (1883) was a collection of European travel sketches. A *Little
Tour in France* (1884) was about a little tour in France . . . For these publication
dates I am indebted to A *Bibliography of Henry James*, compiled by Leon Edel and
Dan H. Laurence, which is perhaps the most useful work of the Jamesian scholarship
after *The Notebooks of Henry James*, edited by F. O. Matthiessen and Kenneth B.
Murdock.

The American expatriates of the story have found it much more possible to economize at Dresden or Florence than at Buffalo or Min-
neapolis. The saving was greater and the strain was less; indeed
"they had found their native land quite ruinous." (Thus James
gave an economic base, a financial as well as moral validity to his
vision of English culture.) This couple is, so to speak, an example
of the poorer American rich class; while the hero, Jackson Lemon,
with his seven or eight millions, mounted on his shiny big horse,
also parades before the densely packed mass of spectators.

For "royalty was approaching — royalty was passing — royalty
had passed." The scene was striking and pictorial to James's eyes,
a great composition, with "the contrasted tones of a thousand polished surfaces." Faces were the great effect everywhere, said
James — "above all the fair faces of women on tall horses" with
their well-secured helmets, their neat compact heads, their straight
necks, their firm tailor-made armor, their frequent hardy bloom. Or
take the British horsemen with hats of "undulating brim, good
profiles, high collars, white flowers on their chests, long legs and
long feet." Or even the British ladies who are *unmounted* but
"quite ready to spring into the saddle," with their diffused look of
happy expansion, all limited and controlled, "which came from clear
quiet eyes and well-cut lips . . . on which syllables were liquid
and sentences brief." "They're often very good-looking," says Mr.
Freer. "They're on the whole the finest whites," while before this
handsome throng rides the most perfect nobleman of all, "a
thoroughly splendid apparition," despite the fact that his usual
orchid is missing: Lord Canterville, with his two handsome
daughters — "an eminent trio" followed by their groom.

The early James had the vision of Europe "educating" America.
The mixture of the "best" of the two "races" would provide a kind
of cultural elite. "Lady Barbarina" (James modified the spelling in
the New York Edition) was also a propagandistic fairy tale. Jackson Lemon has about five hundred horses in his riding stable, we
are told. "If I had known you were coming here I'd have given

you a mount," he tells his old pal, Dr. Feeder from Cincinnati, yet Lady Barb says to her fiancé in some dismay: "Are *all* your friends doctors?" and she wishes him to abandon his profession altogether. Indeed the marriage of a British noblewoman and an American doctor was a subject for satire that Thackeray would have yearned for, so James said. But was it specifically *American* doctors that the British nobility scorned, in the Jamesian notion of British nobility? (For later on, in *The Wings of the Dove*, the great British specialist in tuberculosis is treated with the utmost reverence.) Jackson Lemon accepts his inferior social status with equanimity, however, for the Cantervilles are not only noble but well off. "He himself had a great deal of money, and money was good even when it was new; but old money was somehow *more* to the shilling and the pound." Thus the Jamesian economics; and Lady Barb is moreover, in her flexible virginal form, a wonderful compendium of those elements in English womanhood which most appeal to the story's hero. "He saw her as she might be in the future, the beautiful mother of beautiful children in whom the appearance of 'race' should be conspicuous."

This odd concept of "race," incidentally, was closer to snobbery than to biology. It was a mixture of physical appearance, genealogy, and wealth, rather than a mixture of blood, in which the American stock was definitely inferior to, if not utterly different from, the pure Anglo-Saxon British. "I've never supposed I should marry a foreigner!" exclaims Lady Barb at the party at Portland Place which contained "an assembly of five hundred persons and a band of music concealed in a bower of azaleas." These scenes in "Lady Barbarina" outdo even a Scott Fitzgerald's gaudy visions of wealth and gaiety; and it was probably from James and Edith Wharton that the later writer fashioned his own web of glittering illusion.

But was the Jamesian worship of this British nobility any different in essence from Dreiser's early note of awe at the "costly salons" of Chicago or New York; or Thomas Wolfe's lyrical praise of the Hudson Valley "aristocracy," near the "Enfabled Rock"; or Jack London's Martin Eden, speechless and fumbling before the spectacle of California "culture"? Here the different strains, or even "schools," of our native letters struck a common chord of provincial aspiration. Here they were all most American — though what was important was the *manner* in which they resolved their earliest or infantine vision of the "great life." From this pitch of wealth, breeding and luxury, however, and this rosy vision of British nobility, "Lady Barbarina" descended to a rather heavy parody of the American society which the elegant (and rather mute) English heroine simply couldn't bear. And with these peculiar sentiments James himself was on the edge of his first famous "nouvelle" (or novelette), "The Author of Beltraffio," in 1885.*

This was the first solid short story in the new vein of art-and-artist tales which James would develop from *Roderick Hudson* to such later tales as "The Figure in the Carpet," "The Lesson of the Master," and "The Middle Years." The setting was the late nineteenth century English literary world, pre-Raphaelite but not quite Yellow Book, "fleshly," "sensuous," but still quite respectable, which was marked by such esthetes as Walter Pater, Robert Louis Stevenson, Oscar Wilde, and Swinburne. This was the pagan revolt, as it were, of the British gentlemen of letters; and it was rather subdued when compared with the French or Continental movements of the same type. Mark Ambient, the story's hero, was almost a fusion of all these typical English figures. (He was actually, as James's *Notebooks* indicated, based on John Addington Symonds — about whose extreme "and somewhat hysterical aestheticism" James had some private doubts.) But was this Jamesian figure, as Philip Rahv enthusiastically declared, "the very best portrait in fiction of the English gentleman-aesthete of the late Victorian age"? Well, maybe; and maybe not.

---

* This was the title story of a collection in which also appeared the tale called "Pandora," about another young American heiress who had to leave her impossible family behind her, and make her own way socially — in this leisure-class version of the Horatio Alger success story.

Ambient is, at any rate, a rather decent, sensible and serious
writer who is completely at the mercy of his wife's narrow, puritanical, or even fanatical, moral code. Yet would such a mother
really forbid her child — their child — to read the father's books;
would she be *so* terrified that the father's moral, or literary,
taint would contaminate the young child's innocence? Who was it
but James himself who projected a series of such angelic infant-
victims of adult coarseness and cruelty — those young orphan
princes, small, wounded heroes, noble to the core, and always "corrupted" by life's vulgarity? In "The Author of Beltraffio," little
Dolcino has the face of an angel — "the eyes, the hair, the more
than mortal bloom, the smile of innocence." There is something
touching and alarming in his beauty, we are told, which is composed of elements "too fine and pure for the breath of this world,"
and he again is described as "an orphan, or a changeling," or as
"stamped with some social stigma." He is indeed "too charming to
live," though his parents have not yet perceived it.

But the reader has — and that is the primary flaw of the nouvelle. This doomed child is already inalterably fixed as the puppet
of the parental conflict; and the lyrical tone of "innocence
betrayed" is exaggerated to the point of melodrama, or a horror tale
of the mind. As is the case so often with the Jamesian infants, this
little Dolcino — and what a name; even for the pre-Raphaelite
background of the narrative — is the victim not merely of parental
evil, but of the story's plot: of the *author*'s own literary designs
upon his angelic beauty, his purity of soul. He is not so much a
credible child as the dupe of the wicked world. "Mark Ambient's
child is the little brother of Pansy in *The Portrait of a Lady*," we
are solemnly advised by the inestimable Philip Rahv — "and of
Maisie in *What Maisie Knew*, and of Morgan Moreen in 'The
Pupil,' and of course of those two strange children in 'The Turn of
the Screw' who are really beyond everything." But this whole line
of exotic, wounded, or betrayed Jamesian child prodigies is "beyond
everything" in a sense that our admiring and complacent Jacobite

critic hardly intended. (To give the secret away, I may as well say here that all these curious literary infants are the projections of James's own fantasies about his own childhood.)

Mark Ambient himself, this rich, cultivated, elegant literary figure, who is defending above all the freedom of the artist against the stupidity and prejudice of the typical Anglo-American reader (as personified in the evil wife), and whose "paganism" is expounded against the background of "dusky, delicate bindings of valuable books," was also in part a projection — a dramatization — of the younger James's own literary aspirations. On the matter of Ambient's passion for form, James said, the attempt at perfection of surface was a quest to his mind like "the real search for the holy grail"— and here we are approaching the later Jamesian religion of art. The portrait of Ambient's wife, this cold, high-bred British beauty who has "a mortal dread of things as they are" is well done, however; and the story was in essence an eloquent sermon, if again rather pedagogical and propagandistic at base, on the inadequate taste, the narrow moral standards, of both the British and the American reading public.

But even such a woman as Beatrice Ambient, with her air of incorruptible conformity, her "tapering monosyllabic correctness": would such a woman and such a mother deliberately sacrifice her child, sick with diphtheria, merely to justify her aversion to her husband's literary views — to "protect" this angelic infant (through his death) from the father's "poisonous influence"? "The Author of Beltraffio," for all its merits as symbol and parable, was another tour de force, made more convincing by its own "perfection of surface" while you read it than when you think about it. The real psychological element in the story was missing. The "evil" was unmotivated and improbable, except as dictated by James's own convictions about art, and his own "moral"— to which again the human content of the nouvelle was sacrificed. If this drama was "a piece of wonderful invention from beginning to end," according to Mr. Rahv — why, that is just the point! It *was* invention; and "invention," to justify the Jamesian thesis of the story, which wandered too far from the reality principle either in art or life.

The volume called *The Author of Beltraffio* contained several other minor tales. "Georgina's Reasons," a melodrama of western American army life, was based on an anecdote told to James at dinner by Mrs. Kemble, who had heard it from Edward Sartoris, who had in turn heard it from his daughter-in-law, Mrs. Algernon Sartoris, who was a daughter of Ulysses S. Grant. Thus the eminent, if highly convoluted, sources of those air-borne and dinner-born "seeds" and "germs" of the Jamesian tales, which then flourished in his fancy; but not always with effective literary results. "The Path of Duty" was a romance of an English lord who is in love with one woman and has offered his hand to another. "The question, as a matter of ethics," James wrote in the *Notebooks*, "seems to me to have but one answer; if he had offered marriage to Miss Rosslyn . . . by that offer he should abide."

Yet if he were "a Frenchman or a naturalist," James added, he could have imagined other endings for the story; including that of the hero marrying the young woman but taking his true love, the English lady, as his mistress . . . What was interesting in this little debate was the Jamesian stress on duty and "ethics" at the expense of both psychology and social reality, which he here consigned only to the French and to the naturalists. Wasn't he then, in his personal preference, sharply qualifying that freedom of art which he had affirmed in the story of "Beltraffio" — and marking off his own position at the halfway house of modern literature? There were even more ambiguous and contradictory elements in his next novel, *The Bostonians*, in 1886.*

At the height of his early popularity, James received $4000 (a

---

* *Stories Revived* (1885) was a three-volume collection of James's early tales, revised, rewritten, and published again, from "The Romance of Certain Old Clothes" and "Master Eustace" in the 1870's. Though none of these stories had previously appeared in England, most of them, with the exception of "Beltraffio," and perhaps "Pandora" for its entertainment value, were among the lighter and poorer works of James.

considerable price in those days) for the rights to this story from
the Boston publisher J. R. Osgood. (When Osgood failed in 1885,
Macmillan published the book.) And there was a critical furore
over the novel in the press as well as among friends and family.
The longest and most ambitious work of James's on a specifically
American theme was considered a failure by him. As a satiric study
of Boston in the seventies — the decline of the Transcendentalist
and Abolitionist spirit in the post-Civil War epoch — it was
rejected by the official opinion of the time, and James himself never
included it among his collected works. The "Miss Birdseye" of the
narrative was recognized as Elizabeth Peabody, the sister-in-law of
Hawthorne and Horace Mann; and James's satire was sharp. "The
whole moral history of Boston was reflected in her displaced spec-
tacles." In the study of the suffragette movement — "the situation
of women, the decline of the sentiment of sex"— there was the central description of a "morbid" feminine relation that hardly helped
matters.

"The relation of the two girls should be a study of one of those
friendships between women which are so common in New England," James wrote in his *Notebooks*. But he had got the idea from
Daudet's *Evangéliste* of a "curious" psychological study — just
how curious he did not himself, from his own comments, quite realize.* Poised against a background of "witches and wizards, mediums and spirit-rappers, and roaring radicals" — of female Jacobins
and nihilists — the novel's hero was a post-Civil War Southern conservative, a traditionalist who is almost a royalist, a virile masculine
soul who is haughty, noble and exotic. "His discourse was pervaded
by something sultry and vast, something almost African in its rich,
basking tone, something that suggested the teeming expanse of the
cotton-field." Much of the action is seen through Basil Ransom's

---

* The theme and tone of *The Bostonians* may have derived in part from Hawthorne's study of the "new thought" of the period in *The Blithedale Romance*, and
perhaps also from Oliver Wendell Holmes's early treatise on feminine neurosis in
Elsie Venner — though it was typical of James to mention only a European source
for his "completely American" novel.

eyes. He is close to being the Jamesian spokesman here, and his verdict on Boston society is hardly flattering.

There is the early scene in the novel in which all the varieties and oddities of the social reform movements were lumped together by James, it seemed, in one ugly and distasteful mélange to which Ransom is introduced by Miss Chancellor. Miss Birdseye herself "belonged to the Short-Skirts League, as a matter of course; for she belonged to any and every league that had been founded for almost any purpose whatever —

This did not prevent her being a confused, entangled, inconsequent, discursive old woman, whose charity began at home and ended nowhere, whose credulity kept pace with it, and who knew less about her fellow-creatures, if possible, after fifty years of humanitary zeal, than on the day she had gone into the field to testify against the iniquity of most arrangements.

To the Jamesian spokesman-observer, she was "a revelation of a class." And a multitude of "socialistic" figures, or of cranks, eccentrics, fanatics were grouped behind her:

She looked as if she had spent her life on platforms, in audiences, in conventions, in phalansteries, in séances: in her faded face there was a kind of reflection of ugly lecture lamps; with its habit of an upward angle, it seemed turned toward a public speaker, with an effort of respiration in the thick air in which social reforms are usually discussed. She talked continually, in a voice of which the spring seemed broken, like that of an over-worked bell-wire; and when Miss Chancellor explained that she had brought Mr. Ransom because he was so anxious to meet Mrs. Farrinder, she gave the young man a delicate, dirty, democratic little hand . . .

Was Miss Birdseye, indeed, the symbol of the decaying, confused, and ineffectual Boston "conscience" — or of the American and democratic one? Mrs. Farrinder, the apostle of feminine emancipation, is, by contrast, a copious, handsome woman whose origi-

nal angularity "had been corrected by the air of success." There
was a lithographic smoothness about her, James said, "and a mixture of the American matron and the public character." To an
audience composed mainly of "mediums, communists, vegetar-
ians," she lectured on temperance and the rights of women. "The
ends she laboured for were to give the ballot to every woman in the
country and to take the flowing bowl from every man." And to
complete this odd and motley group, in an apartment which looked
like an enormous streetcar, and smelled of india-rubber overshoes,
with its workman's audience dressed in "the garb of toil" or in
"weary-looking overcoats," there was Doctor Tarrant, the mesmeric
healer, and his daughter Verena who is "of old Abolitionist stock."

Now there is no doubt that this is entertaining and sharp satire.
James's pen fairly flew here, showering epigrams upon one or another of these "humanitary hacks." But what was evident to the
Boston audience of the time, and what is obvious today, is the note
of malice behind the satire. This was the clever, smart, "sophisticated" young James who lumped together all movements of social
reform, abolitionism, socialism, mesmerism, vegetarianism, into
one large stew of quackery. Even the Civil War, by implication,
was another kind of colossal fraud in these bright, sparkling pages;
while the economic injustices and abuses — the moral crimes — of
the post-Civil War barons and titans of finance were ignored. By
the mid-eighties William Dean Howells was also increasingly discontented with the declining moral fervor of the New England
spirit; he plunged into the Christian or Utopian socialism of New
York life instead. But James's real position in this satire was conservative, traditional or reactionary; uninformed, abstract and
aloof.

It is interesting to compare the Jamesian descriptions of social
reform and reformers with the very similar scenes in Howells's *A
Hazard of New Fortunes* (1890) which describe the immigrants
and aliens, the anarchists, socialists and Utopian communists of
the New York intellectual scene. But Howells overcame his origi-

nal prejudices about these "aliens" for the sake of his own deep social convictions, while James retreated to — or rather, had never emerged from — a more or less "royalist" (or often quite medieval) bastion of esthetic disdain. *The Bostonians* marked his real break with Boston. Beneath the satire, farce and parody, the animating spirit of the novel was James's own, never quite publicly acknowledged — perhaps never conscious — anger at Boston itself, which, even when he was overtly denying it in his most personal passages during these early years, was transparently clear. Or was it hatred, even; and there was also an element of guilt and shame about his own Civil War behavior in this scornful repudiation of New England's Abolitionist and Transcendental fervor.

In the auctorial figure of the aristocratic, conservative, disapproving Southern hero of the novel, offshoot that he is "of the old slave-holding oligarchy," we are also told by Mr. Rahv that James had created "with remarkable prescience" the type of intellectual who has come to the fore in the English-speaking world of the last few decades. "Thus James anticipated . . . one of the major tendencies in twentieth-century thinking." Now it is true that it was a group of mainly Southern "traditionalists" and conservatives (most of them spiritual fugitives, as in the case of Allen Tate, John Crowe Ransom or Robert Penn Warren, from the legendary South which they extolled) who had a large hand in the ascendancy of Henry James's work during the 1940's and '50's. But if James's Basil Ransom is really their forerunner and figurehead, what are we to think of this "major tendency" of our period?

No, it is only in the central triangle of Basil, Verena and Olive Chancellor that *The Bostonians* has any real validity. But was James really aware that with Olive and Verena he was creating an almost classic study of lesbian love? "With equal prescience," adds Mr. Rahv (and could James be endowed with any *more* "prescience" in any more areas of literature than by this infatuated Jacobite, speaking in these accents of unadulterated eulogy?), "he had grasped the emotional economy of the lesbian woman."

And: "His intuitive grasp of the psychic process of repression and displacement is astonishing indeed." Now, really, this isn't quite so astonishing, precisely because James *himself* was a supreme and unique example of the psychic process of repression and displacement, as you'll see — and in *his* case it was altogether unconscious. If he represented this process so well in *The Bostonians,* it was because he was simply projecting the depths of his own temperament. The emotions he attributed to Olive Chancellor are the emotions which are at the core of *all* the Jamesian love relations. They are close to being James's central notion of love.

We shall notice further the deep Jamesian inhibition, already evident in his work to this point, on sexual matters; and his remarkable and childlike "innocence" about this area of human behavior — along with the deeply unconscious depths of *his* frustration and anxiety; and more. "How tragical was her nature," he wrote about his Olive Chancellor, "how anxious, suspicious, exposed to subtle influences." As was his own; as was that of a whole series of Jamesian lovers to come! The physical symptoms of Olive's love are acutely described in the novel — and that is to say, her "palpitations of dread" that she will lose her love. We are reminded at points of Isabel Archer's sexual panic, and her flight before the blunt presence of Caspar Goodwood's masculine power: of those true under-depths of human passion which James (until his very late and very curious sexual breakthrough) would increasingly ignore or sublimate ("psychic displacement" indeed!) in his rarefied "drama of consciousness" or in the often laborious intricacies of his "moral analysis."

Yet Olive's tragical nature is never fully realized in *The Bostonians.* James had too little sympathy for her. And the study of lesbian pathology (which would have horrified this author if he had been aware of it) was sublimated to the romance-melodrama ending where the noble Ransom defied the Boston "mob" of free-thinkers; and carried off Verena as the natural (and henceforth inaudible) mate for his old-fashioned, conservative Southern virility.

The novel as a whole was less effective than its good sections. The novelist's own bias was too clear; his ignorance and prejudice about New England's great tradition of moral reform was unmistakable. James himself could hardly understand why *The Bostonians* never, "even to my much-disciplined patience, received any sort of justice." But to seek justice from an audience to which his chronicle had accorded so little justice was perhaps another example of a sublime vanity, or of a notable optimism, and the fate of *The Bostonians* (which, with all its faults, was still a lively chronicle) was a prelude to a worse debacle for Henry James of this period — the failure of the huge, intricate, heavy novel which followed it.

The Princess Casamassima, in 1886, was the chronicle of an illegitimate English bookbinder who gets caught up in a mysterious (even to the reader) web of "socialists and anarchists," who are of the same category to the disdainful Jamesian spirit as the New England "radicals" of the previous novel. The little hero, Hyacinth Robinson, whose name presumably implies the innocent flower, or bird, of the social dung heap, gets a brief glimpse of the *true* life of leisure, wealth and culture which is symbolized to him by the Princess Casamassima, a Jamesian sequel to the Christina Light of *Roderick Hudson*. And finally the tender, weak-willed, sensitive little hero is torn apart by his conflicting loyalties (to the radicalism of his youth; the conservatism of his maturity) and commits suicide rather than carry out an equally mysterious act of "terrorism" and murder allotted to him by the stern anarchist discipline.

Now I summarize this plot in outline but accurately; because this Jamesian novel too had its revival in the American literary scene of the mid-fifties owing mainly to its "discovery" by Lionel Trilling. Because of this tedious, solemn, pretentious, implausible and dull chronicle of a revolutionary movement which its author confessedly knew little about, and cared less, Henry James was acclaimed as a brilliant social historian who had caught, in an Orwellian sense, the whole drift of the modern age. Implausible, incredible on the face of it, if you simply read the novel — and yet the Jacobite cult eagerly grasped this lead or this bait thrown to them by such an eminent practitioner of the contemporary critical spirit. Thus *The Princess Casamassima* was "the most considerable product of the social historian in James," said F. W. Dupee echoing the Trilling thesis — and perhaps this was unconsciously a completely true statement: since James was no social historian at all. The same critic also compared the novel's view of London life with the Balzacian studies of Paris, completely ignoring the obvious Dickensian base of the book; since Dickens had gone out of favor in the epoch which elevated Henry James above all the crude, fanciful, careless and loose Victorian social realists. And one notes that even this little lower class hero of James's, this dubious, illegitimate, anarchistic little radical hero, even he, like every true Jamesian hero, has inherited his modest legacy (though obviously smaller than most) from his unknown but noble father.

It was this legacy indeed, as Dupee adds, which "symbolized his passing-over morally into the leisure class." It was this experience with the leisure class which makes poor Hyacinth conclude "that civilization and art necessarily rest on privilege, and that his anarchist friends are motivated by a destructive envy in wanting to overturn society." To be sure, Dupee adds, he cannot make out as good a case for the novel as Lionel Trilling has; but, with this premise so explicitly stated, can you make out any case at all for *The Princess Casamassima* as a study of social revolution? And what are we to think of Edmund Wilson's perhaps even more astounding statement that Hyacinth "died of the class struggle"? One of James's weakest heroes, little Hyacinth more likely died of frustration and jealousy — or of pure inertia. He died *in fact* to prove James's own leisure-class, morally prejudiced, and quite ignorant concept of what he believed to be the class struggle.

One must add, however, that James himself was far more cautious, if not apologetic, in his own earlier estimate of the novel. The Preface to *The Princess Casamassima,* also hailed as an extraordinary document by the Jamesian critics, is a highly ambiguous one. The novel derived from the writer's first year in London, we are told, when he had few social contacts, and when, like the later Tom Wolfe in New York, he prowled the streets of the unknown city. *The Princess* was "the ripe round fruit of perambulation," in the later James vocabulary, when he had seen all around him the unsolved mysteries of London, the "dense categories of dark arcana"; and when he frankly admitted (*vide* his later critics!) his own state of exclusion and ignorance — himself without "experience of the meaner conditions, the lower manners and types, the general sordid struggle, the weight of the burden of labour, the ignorance, the misery and the vice." Here spoke the creative spirit aware of its own limitations; and yet James's resolution of this problem was curiously tangential. But after all, the affair of the writer or the painter, he added, in one of those sudden grand generalizations — or rationalizations — that in a later age was proclaimed as an immutable esthetic principle: "But the affair of the painter is not the immediate, it is the reflected field of life, the realm not of application, but of *appreciation*."

Thus in effect James did not have to *know* anything about the lower class origins and life of Hyacinth Robinson; he only had to imagine and to invent. His hero like himself would be an outsider, a "small obscure but ardent observer" of the London world, his disinherited but swelling spirit cramped by poverty and obscurity. And then, said James about this hero, who was so obviously an imaginative reconstruction of his own state of mind in an alien setting: "His being jealous of all the ease of life of which he tastes so little, and bitten, under this exasperation, with an aggressive, vindictive, destructive social faith, his turning to 'treasons, stratagems and spoils' might be as vivid a picture as one chose."

The lurid colors of James's "picture" are interesting, of course; and he referred to "the more than 'shady' under-world of militant socialism," which was, in his own mind, equated with anarchism or communism or worse. His sensitive, wronged hero — "dabbling deeply in revolutionary politics of a hole-and-corner sort" — was to find a social, as well as socialistic connection. He would find a door somehow open to him into "the appeased and civilised state, into that warmer glow of things he is precisely to help to undermine." This was the function of the Princess Casamassima herself; her intervention would be a prime factor "in the life of the dingy little London bookbinder whose sensibility, whose flow of opinions on 'public questions' in especial, should have been poisoned at the source." Here James indeed, like any good upper-class capitalist, in the primary age of American finance capitalism, was speaking with the voice of his race and his class. Perhaps he was only less harsh on *British* radicalism because it was, at least, not American. And here the fairy-tale romance of English life, to James, took on a momentarily fearsome and ominous quality. The fairy tale was being threatened. "My scheme called for the suggested nearness (to all our apparently ordered life) of some sinister anarchic under-world, heaving in its pain, its power and its hate." The obverse of the fairy tale was an anxiety-ridden melodrama. Thus James wanted to present not a social picture of sharp particulars "but of loose appearances, vague motions and sounds and symptoms, just perceptible presences and general looming possibilities."

Loose appearances, vague motions, sounds, symptoms; barely perceptible "presences" and general looming "possibilities": was *that* the way to write a great, "prescient" historical novel of James's own time — or was it an accurate description of all the bugaboos of social chaos, anarchy and revolution which haunted the polite, the terrified, the inhibited and haunted ex- or post-radical U.S. intellectuals of the 1950's? The true and acrid history of the *actual* British social conflict in those decades was being written out before James's eyes in the pages of the daily newspapers — a history of labor conflict and a battle for elementary human rights which we know from so many sources (and just lately again from Helen Lynd's *England in the Eighteen-Eighties*), to have been so completely different from this prevailing Jamesian fantasy of an abhorrent, wicked, nightmarish (and completely vague) anarchist conspiracy.

What was interesting too was the manner with which James still combined the elements of his British fairy tale with the horrid vision of a social nightmare. Little Hyacinth, as the product of an unknown British nobleman and a French courtesan who has murdered the royal (but erring) father, has nevertheless the "air of race" about him even as a child. But what was the true aim and ambition of Henry James's famous "revolutionary" hero? It was "the hope of being carried to some brighter, happier vision — the vision of societies where, in splendid rooms, with smiles and soft voices, distinguished men, with women who were both proud and gentle, talked of art, literature and history." But this elevated vision of society — an odd one for a radical or revolutionary — was also, quite obviously, Henry James's own earliest fantasy of the "great life," just as this infantine noble hero was the projection of a central Jamesian emotional complex.*

Equally obviously this theme and this hero of *The Princess Casamassima* had no possible bearing on the radical social movements of the time with which James was ostensibly dealing. Even more, the novel's social milieu had nothing to do with the real world of English working-class people, reformers, Fabians and social idealists of the late nineteenth century. It was at best another little circle of lower middle class gentility — and this was as far down the social spectrum as Henry James could ever penetrate.

If the *Princess Casamassima* is a key book in any sense, it is only in respect to Henry James's own most abiding prejudices, social ignorance, and infantine obsessions. Hyacinth Robinson, quite like

---

* The orphan theme is recurrent in the Jamesian fiction, as we already know; at the close of the present study we will see its real significance. But perhaps *The Princess Casamassima* shows most clearly (to this point) the fantasy world of a "declassed" or socially ostracized Mother, who has, in addition, destroyed the Royal Father — who has, in his turn, refused to acknowledge his true son. This was a lurid form of the Oedipus complex, which had the merit of eliminating *both* parental figures under the guise of killing the father — or indeed then, it was *not* an Oedipal complex at base.

James himself, also confesses to a passion for the theater, which was full of "sweet deception" for him. But this sweet deception, which is at the base of the Jamesian craft of fiction — is *that* the meaning of the major fiction whose outstanding practitioner this uneasy romancer is supposed to be? Again, the Mme. Grandoni of this novel comes close to expressing James's auctorial view of his revolutionary theme. "I take no interest whatever in the people; I don't understand them and I know nothing about them. An honourable nature, of any class, I always respect; but I won't pretend to a passion for the ignorant masses, because I have it not." Now this statement wasn't of course even democratic or American in essence — not to mention the dread specter of bloody socialism; and as to any belief in the ignorant masses, James, too, had it not.

But what did he, or his Italian Madam, mean about an "honourable nature" — if not honorable by virtue of class, breeding and wealth? In the *Princess*, the Jamesian notion of history again stressed the romance of the past, rather than historical facts. Yet in the novel's noble but dispossessed hero, the Jamesian genetics was almost a matter of social aspiration rather than chromosomes. And wasn't the fairy princess of the romance also illegitimate and "self-made" in much the same sense as the budding young proletarian prince? The Christina Light of *Roderick Hudson* was a restless, discontented, witty young Euro-American girl, also of dubious social background, hovering on the edge of "good society." In the present novel, married to the Prince Casamassima for the sake of his fortune, bored to death by her royal spouse, and taking revenge upon him for his "mysterious crime" — and what a convenient one! — she throws herself into all kinds of social causes with more fervor than discrimination.

She rushes to the "séances of the Revolution" which are described in much the same manner as those of the spiritualists in *The Bostonians* — and was there any real difference to James? She contacts the "subversive little circles in Bloomsbury." She is a rather good portrait of a discontented, bored, neurotic and empty

society woman struggling to amuse herself; but in the process of her
improbable behavior she also loses all the charm and gaiety of her
earlier portrait. To Hyacinth it appears that her rejection by the
Casamassima family "had evidently planted in her soul a lasting
resentment and contempt." And: "The forces of reaction and revenge might carry her far, make her modern and democratic and
heretical *à outrance* — lead her to swear by Darwin and Spencer
and all the scientific iconoclasts as well as by the revolutionary
spirit." What an odd "revolutionary spirit" this was again, which
embraced Spencer the great social reactionary, as well as Darwin,
the pure scientist; but all manifestations of the "modern spirit"
were apparently equally distasteful to the younger Henry James.
And "resentment," "contempt," "revenge," not to mention envy, or
jealousy or the desire to destroy one's "betters": those were to
James, or to his now-almost-noble little spokesman Hyacinth, the
only true motives for social change or social reform. Any form of
social idealism, including that of personal devotion to a social
cause, or personal sacrifice for its sake — although these traits too
marked the history of the socialist and anarchist movements in the
Europe of his time — was inconceivable to Henry James, except, of
course, among his imaginary or "noble" upper class "radicals."

And "modern," "democratic," "heretical" — these were the
milder synonyms for socialism and anarchism. Was it in fact
against the "revolutionary," or against the *democratic* spirit that
the true burden of *The Princess Casamassima*'s message was directed; since to James they were equally odious, they were akin.
(Just as, in the American forties and fifties, the concept of socialism
itself, in any of its various forms, became suspect, became treasonable among certain reactionary spokesmen of the intellectual scene,
since socialism led to communism — and democracy, by implication, to socialism!) James was indeed "prescient" in this sense; but
what a sorry sense it was.* And meanwhile in the novel itself, it

* And here Mr. Lionel Trilling's social bias becomes clear; just as another former
radical of the 1930's, John Dos Passos, equated the New Deal with socialism and
communism: as all being equally abhorrent to the Radical Right of the American
fifties.

was Hyacinth's trip to France, via his little legacy, which completed his moral renunciation of the group of bookbinders, watchmakers, chefs, cosmeticians, butchers — in short, *tradespeople* — who in the Jamesian view of history comprised the bulk of the anarchistic conspirators.

And so the Jamesian refutation of "democracy, revolution, socialism" — as *The Princess Casamassima* finally stated its true theme — became also a defense of position and fortune, of social class and caste, and of that "immemorial inequality" which little Hyacinth finally is "educated" to accept — and to cherish. For James himself, touching upon the real mass of human misery and discontent in the late nineteenth century European and English social scene — even so vaguely, so ominously, so fastidiously as he did; for it was *dirty*, it was poor, it was dangerous! — had no other solution for the problem except his familiar recourse to the ancient British (or French) nobility, visionary as that was also in his mind. And he made no real distinction, he had no real interst in, the different methods of social reform which here, as in *The Bostonians*, were all equally distasteful to him, were all lumped together indiscriminately in a witch's brew of discontent.

A series of later American writers visiting England, including Jack London, Willa Cather, Theodore Dreiser, were quick to notice the elements of social misery and degradation which were the by-products of the industrial revolution in the nineteenth century; and with which the best English minds of the period were seriously concerned. But to James himself — living in the midst of this scene, and withdrawing into an almost baroque social conservatism, a feudal royalism beyond that of the British ruling class itself — the only answer was to recoil from this poverty and misery in horror and distaste. Moreover, just as the social-economic areas of *The Princess Casamassima* were so largely imaginary, fanciful, contrived and "gotten up," the novel is curiously lacking in human relationships also, in any kind of love relation beyond the "ideal" or the platonic — or in the biopsychological bases of the literary craft itself. Perhaps the dense verbiage of the style, the two volumes of extended and often rather heavy prose, was an implicit acknowledgment on James's part — a covering up, a verbal screen — of the novel's lack of content.*

But what is finally illuminating about the *Princess* is that the prevailing American literary taste of the 1950's should have selected just this novel as not only one of the best works of James (when it is one of the poorest), but also as a key "revolutionary" (or counter-revolutionary) document. How in the world could Lionel Trilling solemnly state that James's social texture was "grainy and knotted with practicality and detail"; that his social observation was "startlingly *prescient*" — and there is that favorite Jacobite term again! Furthermore, said Mr. Trilling, *The Princess Casamassima* belonged to the great line of nineteenth century European novels from *The Red and the Black* and *Père Goriot* to *War and Peace* and *The Idiot*. This is utter nonsense — a virtual abdication of critical responsibility. Perhaps no literary judgment of the 1930's — an epoch belabored by the same critic for its subordination of literary to political values — was so sweepingly wrong as this Trillingesque verdict rendered in the name of pure morality; and flying in the face of common sense. For Mr. Trilling also praised the "fairy-tale" quality of the *Princess* in the name of magic and primitive myth; he lauds the novel's "notable insights into the temper of radicalism." He insists that James gave "a very accurate account of anarchism" — though he admits that anarchism had very little impact on the English social scene which James was dealing with. Nevertheless — "Quite apart from its moral and aesthetic authority, *The Princess Casamassima* is a brilliantly precise representation of social actuality."

* Millie Henning's "betrayal" of Hyacinth with Captain Sholto — also harped upon by the Jamesian cult — is no real betrayal, since "Hy" has already rejected her open physical advances, just as he rejects or is indifferent to every other woman in the novel . . . But in this "proletarian" romance, James was showing the vulgar treason of the flesh, too. And note the language: "That was rather a nice little girl in there," says Sholto. "Did you twig her good bust? It's a pity they always have such beastly hands." Hands, of course, soiled and deformed by labor — and does Mr. Trilling also commend this as art?

But then, of whose social actuality? Of the alienated American author, prowling the streets of that unknown London which he had accepted as his true "ancestral home" in his dreamlike fantasy life, and conjuring up his dark visions of a fanatic and extremist revolutionary group which he abhorred (but seized upon for its melodramatic literary value), while all about him lay the true conditions of British social misery and the real course of its future social reforms, ignored, unnoticed, and never touched upon in his "great novel" of social revolution?

Such mundane matters as the abolition of child labor or the twelve-hour working day; or the battle for the right to vote, for women's rights, for the rights of minority and disenfranchised religious groups; or the Luddite revolt against the machine; or the agrarian revolts and the crucial demand for parliamentary reform; or of the Manchester massacre, and the Reform bills of 1832, 1867, 1884 — these were among the events *not* mentioned in *The Princess Casamassima*, which in all probability James had based on his romance-readings about the *French* revolution.

No, Mr. Trilling's "brilliantly precise representation of social actuality" corresponded not in the least to the *Princess*; but it did represent the mood of the disenchanted American political thought of the 1950's, now parading under the banner of an abstract moral "humanism" which, as in this esoteric essay, had reached such a point of lofty detachment that it could no longer distinguish between fact and fancy. Trilling's essay was a tour de force of academic scholarship which attempted to prove that every obvious weakness in *The Princess Casamassima* was a hidden virtue. But its whole web of learned fantasy (Jamesian in essence) only showed to what extremes of folly the purified "liberal imagination" of Mr. Trilling's invention could reach when it was divorced from that "vulgar progressivism" (Mr. Trilling's phrase) which at least should know a good book from a bad book.

This was the kind of "liberal imagination" which could discern in the mediocre and quite Dickensian Paul Muniment of the

Princess — a budding Commissar. Or which again, as in the similar case of the disillusioned John Dos Passos, chose to find the demons and houris of social revolution beneath every American cupboard and bedstead (and political desk), while the plain broad facts of an inevitable social revolution throughout the rest of the world — responding to general and urgent human needs — were beneath the notice of its elevated and distrait stare.

Yes, the prevailing and reversionary time-spirit of the American fifties was the real reason for the "re-discovery" of *The Princess Casamassima* — but the wonder of it was that these critics could establish such a gross delusion even momentarily in the academic communities of the Anglo-American world, at least. (Perhaps even the Russian scholars, the Africans, the Asians, would be forced to take notice eventually of such a massive burden of "received opinion." But not yet; and meanwhile Henry James was the sole glory, or perhaps the hidden weapon of western democracy's high culture.) The critics of James's own time were more accurate in describing the novel as improbable, implausible and, above all, tedious. It was; and it is. It had been written in haste, and carelessly, after the failure of *The Bostonians*. It was the second of James's "big" novels to become a debacle; and the next three years of his career were devoted to essays, stories, and one nouvelle.

Partial Portraits (1888) was a collection of literary essays which ranged from studies of George Eliot and Anthony Trollope to those on Turgenev and Daudet. "The Reverberator," in the same year, was a rather weak and overwritten (and overextended) satire on another "social" theme about which James did care deeply. He had been interested in the "queer incident" of a young woman visiting Italy and then writing for an American newspaper "that inconceivable letter about the Venetian society whose hospitality she had just been enjoying." He had been outraged at Julian Hawthorne's newspaper story of an interview with James Russell Lowell about English affairs, which James described in his *Notebooks* as a monstrous, "beastly and blackguardly betrayal" of confidence.

"One sketches one's age but imperfectly," he wrote, "if one doesn't touch on that particular matter: the invasion, the impudence and shamelessness, of the newspaper and the interviewer, the devouring *publicity* of life, the extinction of all sense between public and private. It is the highest expression of the note of 'familiarity,' the sinking of *manners*, in so many ways, which the democratization of the world brings with it."

Other American writers of the period were concerned with the rise of the yellow press in their native scene, and with the increasing sensationalism of the newspapers. They saw this issue with a wider social reference, but with a less intense personal feeling than James, who had been maligned or made fun of in some of the British "society journals." * By the eighties and nineties, wasn't the real question here not a matter of personal privacy, annoying as that might be, or the violation of personal confidence in the general democratic "sinking of manners" — alarming as that might be — wasn't the basic question that of the *place of a free press* in a democratic society which was being increasingly subordinated to the pressures of finance-capitalism; as Howells, for example, perceived in the Haymarket Case; and as James never perceived at all? However, "The Reverberator" turned out to be an innocuous light comedy tale based on the familiar international theme. The Dossons were the typical American family in Paris. The Proberts were the "Europeanized Americans" who were completely merged, thanks to their wealth and sensitivity, *"dans le monde du Faubourg"* — *et* — I mean and — *"dans les vieilles idées."*

The American father of the tale was another of the "innocent millionaires" of James's fancy who had nothing to do in Europe except to take care of his daughters. (The apotheosis of this rather implausible social type was to be reached in the infinitely richer

---

* Or perhaps it was possible that certain other aspects of Henry James's life had already been hinted at in the gossip and scandal sheets of British society. We shall see these strains of the Jamesian temperament emerge much more clearly in the later work of this writer; though Mr. Leon Edel chooses not to mention them in the three volumes of his "definitive" biography published to date.

"infant father" of *The Golden Bowl*.) Gaston Probert was the European-American who fell in love with Francie Dosson. And here the line was even more rigidly drawn between the two cultures, or the "two races." The European castle was even more impossible of access; the moat of American vulgarity and ignorance — to recast the image — was broader and deeper and muddier. Even Probert's painter friend, Charles Waterlow (the romance-fiction names of high British gentility are revealing) complains about "the rigidity of the conception of the family among people who had adopted and had even . . . improved upon the 'Latin' ideal." The "appendages" of Francie Dosson (that is to say, her father and sister) are the delicate point; for social commerce with such *malheureux* is difficult. "Marry whomever you like," says Gaston's Latinized sister, Mme. de Brécourt, "only let her be the best of her kind. Let her be at least a gentlewoman. Trust me, I've studied life." And: "You know what our feelings are," she tells her brother even more ardently, "our convictions, our susceptibilities. We may be wrong, we may be hollow, we may be pretentious, we mayn't be able to say on what it all rests; but there we are, and the fact's insurmountable. It's simply impossible for us to live with vulgar people."

It *was* somewhat difficult to say on what all this rested; this last stand in romance fiction of an "adopted" French society which was even more devout in snobbery than the original models in James's work — for didn't the "adoption theme" itself logically destroy the whole argument of the story? This was again the world of the Jamesian inheritors — this time the inheritors of the ancient French culture — and if a Mme. de Brécourt could become so completely "assimilated" within so short a time, why couldn't a Francie Dosson? This was the realm of the Jamesian social parvenus who upheld a contrived "social code" so fiercely just because they were so insecurely and so inadequately established. Gaston Probert teaches Mr. Dosson to "live" through buying him a beautiful pair of horses. The sweet, kind, ignorant old millionaire's main interest has been in "the great markets, the sewers and the Bank of

France." But is a knowledge of horseflesh really so superior to this? The Proberts are "tremendous Catholics," as we learn; they have all the subtle resignation "of old races who have known a long historical discipline" (despite their recent adoption of the Latin culture). The "poor Dossons," whom James can pity and even handle with a certain affection *after* he has defined their true social status, are simply out of their element. Mr. Probert senior has his money still in the United States, however. "He resembled other discriminating persons for whom the only good taste in America was the taste of invested and paying capital." His name indeed is a curious mixture of "probity" and "property," which belong quite naturally together in the Jamesian concept of the international novel.

Yet Francie Dosson notices that "in proportion as the Proberts became majestic they became articulately French," particularly on questions of art. "They go back a thousand years," she tells the young American journalist Flack; forgetting that James has already told us that some of them go back only thirty years. And it is Flack's article about them which lets loose a flood of rubbish and impudence "on decent quiet people who only want to be left alone." "They were the last people in France to do it to. The sense of desecration, of pollution, you see . . ." says the despairing Gaston to the beautiful, charming but socially untutored Francie. But were they really? Don't they belong to that narrow little upper-class stratum of French bourgeois society — respectable, comfortable, prejudiced, and inflexible — which James had already described in similarly romantic terms in *The American;* and wasn't "The Reverberator" itself a more popular projection — an exaggeration — of this same idealized French "aristocracy"? And just as we noticed with *The American,* a group of native French realists — from Stendhal and Balzac to Flaubert and Zola — had already described the French ruling-class society in somewhat less glamorous, less enchanted terms than those offered to us by the international fantasy of Henry James. Even the more sophisticated and acute American novelist, Edith Wharton, could see the parallels (in her best work) between this group of *haute-bourgeois* "nobility" and her own "old New York" Dutch society.

Moreover, this Jamesian "horror" and high moral dudgeon at the cheap publicity given to the Proberts — this sense of "desecration, of pollution" — was a curiously suspect emotion on the part of a writer who craved above all (and was never given) fame, renown, a place in the world of affairs and who would turn to — of all places, and shortly after this — the *stage* itself. The element of voyeurism is strong in James's work, as we shall see directly, in stories where the life of art becomes mainly a matter of snooping and prying; and where the artist himself is compared to a "publishing scoundrel," or a scurrilous "newspaper man kicked out." Wasn't indeed the typical figure and the typical form of James's art as a whole that of the "observer-hero" relating secondhand experience — that is to say, watching, listening to, *spying on* life, rather than experiencing it? This dominant trait in James himself also helps to explain his curiously phobic, more than genuine moral indignation at what he believed to be the modern invasion of social or personal "privacy." At least "The Reverberator" was one of the poorest of the international tales; its only charm, again, being that of light entertainment based on an implausible plot. It was written as a serial for *Macmillan's Magazine*; to some degree it was a kind of potboiler designed to restore James's literary position with his popular audience.

Yet from this low point of his popular writing, James went on to create one of his interesting early nouvelles. "The Aspern Papers" in 1888 was the title story of a volume which contained two other tales.* It was the second of James's "famous" nouvelles — or

---

* One of these, "Louisa Pallant," was a rather nice story in James's old-fashioned and sentimental vein, of a mother who discovers that her daughter has grown up to be hard, grasping, and "evil." The mother, however, blaming herself, destroys the daughter's chances for a "good marriage" through the typical use of the Jamesian "psycho-morality" which is completely noble at the cost of any deeper implications. The real interest of the story lies in the unexpressed mother-daughter rivalry or competition, which, typically again, James sketched out — and ignored.

novellas, or long short stories; or "little novels," which they really weren't — coming after and superior to "The Author of Beltraffio." The story itself was based on a curious anecdote (related to James, as we are told, by Eugene Lee-Hamilton, who was the half brother of Vernon Lee; but what difference?) about a certain Captain Silsbee, a Boston art critic and Shelley-worshiper, who had learned that a former mistress of Byron, Claire Clairemont — do you follow this? — was still living in Florence with her niece; and who, the Boston art critic, I mean, established residence with the two ladies in hopes of recovering the private papers of Shelley still in their possession. James made the "great poet" of "The Aspern Papers" American in origin, and also rather Byronic in essense, in the attempt, as he said, to suggest "the lost age of romance." He was intrigued — and now I mean James — by the notion of "the Shelley fanatic" — his watchings and waitings — and "the way he *couvers* [sic] the treasure."

This narrator-spy, seeking the lost Aspern papers, is brilliantly described in the narrative. He is a reputable American scholar who acquits himself of any "grossness" in his plan to recover the priceless documents. He is wholly convinced that "no man could have walked straighter in the given circumstances," although he admits that his dealings with the ancient Miss Bordereau will involve the diplomatic arts. "Hypocrisy, duplicity are my only chance." He is the first in the line of the "obsessed" Jamesian protagonists whose appeal lies in the fact that not only do their actions belie their words, but that their words belie their words.

The ancient, empty palace; the curiously dim and fleeting appointments of the three protagonists (usually two, and usually at night); the "impenetrable regions" where the manuscript treasure is concealed in the bedroom of the "divine Juliana" of Jeffrey Aspern's ancient romance who is now "tremendously old," a "hideous relic," a grinning skull that mocks at love — all this contributes to the dream-and-nightmare effect of the story. The scholar-thief-narrator wanders around this castle with his heart beating "as I had

known it to do in dentists' parlors" in his childhood. He is consumed
by a terrible anxiety, an implacable purpose. "She would die next
week, she would die tomorrow — then I could pounce on her possessions and ransack her drawers." Meanwhile this curious hero
who "can't live without flowers" works in his garden, sends his
floral tributes to the "high tremulous spinster" who is Juliana's
niece and present guardian; and pays out his own treasure of gold
pieces for his "rent." During the hot summer season when the
American socialites close up their Venetian houses, and the Misses
Bordereau celebrate in their darkened rooms "the mystic rites of en-
nui," he waits and watches, plans and schemes, and forms his uneasy
alliance, almost to the point of courtship, with Miss Tina herself.

Tina is one of those modest small souls of English fiction, who
begins to bloom under the narrator's dupery and wiles. But Juliana
turns out to be "a sarcastic profane cynical old woman," as the narrator says, a cunning, vicious, evil old lady who knows exactly what
he wants, and outwits him at every turn. She offers him a picture of
Jeffrey Aspern at a fantastic price. Knowing love, art and the world
far better than he ever can, though she also speaks "out of the white
ashes of her vanity," she makes him feel like a fool, like a child, like
the impotent "collector" that in actuality he is. She is an evil old
witch-mother, even though he has contrived to get into her mysterious, darkened bedroom (when she has had a fit of "oppression")
to study the furniture and the "queer superannuated coffer of
painted wood" which holds (he thinks) the priceless letters about
her vanished love affair, from her dead lover. On the bed itself Juliana lies in a faint, her face covered by a dingy muslin mask. (The
veiled "secret" of sexuality, to the infantine Jamesian fancy.) And
in this scene of "dire confusion," the Jamesian narrator recognizes
an "appetite" in himself which is "well-nigh indecent in the presence of our dying companion." He admits the "grossness" of his
anxieties which are not about the dying woman but about the
"treasure" which he seeks from her.

Here the innermost core of the Jamesian sexuality was being

revealed in an early form — though we'll see more complex examples of it. There is another odd climax in "The Aspern Papers" when this narrator, at night again, persuading himself that the opened door to this evil, mysterious or shameful bedroom of Juliana's is a sign from Tina to enter, yields to the depth of his compulsion — only to discover Juliana herself, in her nightdress, and with her "mask" at last removed from her face, her "extraordinary eyes" glaring at him, and revealing him as a thief. "Ah, you publishing scoundrel!" she cries, before her death; and before Tina offers the papers, the portraits of Aspern, everything he wants, on the condition that he becomes a "relative" of the family, that he should marry her. "That was the price — that was the price!" the narrator cries in panic. "And did she think I wanted it, poor deluded extravagant lady? . . . Did she think I had made love to her even to get the papers? I hadn't, I hadn't . . ." But he has, rather; and retreating from this agonizing form of bribery which the gentle Tina has placed before his outstretched hands, he still has a moment of weakness when he almost persuades himself that she is not a ridiculous old woman, but that with her look of absolution and forgiveness for his own sins, she is beautiful, angelic, young. "It seemed to me I *could* pay the price."

As in the best psychological mystery tales of James, the whole structure of his yearning and desire collapses upon this possessed, deluded and "cunning" narrator-hero. But is "The Aspern Papers" just the parable of a "damned publishing scoundrel," as R. P. Blackmur says? (Mr. Blackmur also insists on calling Miss Tina "Miss Tita.") Or is it "a great reverberating story on the themes of art, time and passion," as F. W. Dupee has stated in reverberating tones? Perhaps it includes both these interpretations, and maybe more, in a particularly Jamesian fashion. For if the story is only another variation of James's outspoken antipathy to the "modern publicity" that followed the vulgar democratization of manners in his period, then what shall we make of the specifically Jamesian hero who is admittedly a voyeur and a "spiritual thief" —

who spends his whole life in the story in merely peeping and spying upon the "secrets" of this ancient, witchlike mistress-mother symbol? And if the story's themes are really those of "art, time and passion," then we must state it is an art which is embalmed in the "priceless" letters of a dead poet — it is more likely the lesser "art" which is the collector's mania. It is the time of a romantic past which is here made dark, mysterious and nightmarish; and of a passion whose remaining symbol is a sick, ugly, avaricious old woman.

Yet Juliana does in her own way outwit the scheming "voyeur-collector" of the tale, perhaps simply because she has known the reality of life, love and art; and she carries her "secret" to the grave with her. If Mr. Dupee's interpretation of "The Aspern Papers" has more depth than Mr. Blackmur's, it is mainly because he identifies the lodger-scholar with the "artist-type." This odd hero "has all of the artist's presumption and ruthless curiosity," Dupee adds. He has the artist's "right" to make public that which is intrinsically private, in "publishing" those secrets "which because of fear, pride, delicacy or shame all 'decent' people are resolved to keep to themselves." Now this is very close indeed not to the general concept of "the artist" — but to the specifically *Jamesian* mode of art. James was indeed identified with the central "observer" (or snooper) of "The Aspern Papers," even while he was here ironically detached from him. He had in fact *objectified* his own deepest drives and obsessions; this story (the first in such a series) derived from his hidden depths, perhaps even from his dream-and-nightmare visions. That "ruthless curiosity," that bland (lofty) moral presumption of the artist's "right" to discover the "secrets" of other human beings, and particularly their sexual secrets here described in barely veiled terms, and symbolized in Juliana's "mask"; that obvious voyeurism around which the story is built, and then all that frustrated teasing and being teased about the "object" of the narrator's quest: this whole emotional complex was typical of Henry James, both in his private communings in his *Notebooks,* and in a series of similarly compulsive and obsessive stories to come.

This was at the core of "The Aspern Papers"; though all the various moral or intellectual (or "esthetic") interpretations miss the real point. The whole psychological, or primary human basis of the story is, of course, a barely concealed infantile-sexual "curiosity" and guilt. It's interesting too that James concealed, obscured, darkened the great romantic love affair of his narrative — the act itself! — by making it deliberately remote and vague . . . back yonder in "the age of love." Jeffrey Aspern was a "devil," says Tina, and that is all we ever learn directly about this romance. The rest is the bundle of "secret" documents hidden in the room (or in the bed?) of his former mistress who is now herself a mysterious, evil, diseased symbol of ancient sexuality — if not the "grinning skull" of the Jamesian anti-sexuality. What a marvelous "womb" of opaque sexuality is the darkened chamber with its invaluable "treasures," where lies also the dying mistress of the great poet! What a moment of revelation when she finally drops her mask to reveal those remarkable "eyes." Even her sexuality thus becomes visual, voyeuristic; though what is being suggested here, by implication, is of course her naked face, or the naked mistress, or even (to the infantile observer of this transposed grandmother figure) the naked mother. But then, how involved this secondary, or tertiary sexuality also is with age, ugliness, horror, sickness and death. And how this infantile sexual fantasy has been rationalized and sublimated, and transposed in turn into the obsessive drives of "curiosity" on the part of the narrator-hero, and of his overpowering — if scholarly — acquisitiveness.

Yes, but wasn't there also an equal guilt and anxiety on the part of the publishing scoundrel who is trying to ferret out these ancient "secrets"— or a moral presumptuousness, in short, which is laden with an uneasy moral disapprobation. He is "horribly ashamed" when Juliana, in her bedclothes, lifts the "everlasting curtain" which obscures her face — as he should be. And his avarice, his deception, his schemes, wiles and lures as bait for his projected "theft"— those twists and turns of "reason" and logic to justify his projected crime — those "grins" and "groans" which are the verbal and physiognomic accompaniment of his "success" or failure, in this description of the Jamesian pathology! At the end of "The Aspern Papers" the narrator-hero of the story becomes its chief victim. His importunate, trembling yearning for the "evidence" of this ancient sexuality does indeed constitute "an appetite well-nigh indecent," as he knows; though Henry James himself also appears to be as unconscious as his protagonist about the true sources and the real nature of this "passion." And even the most antique love affairs leave their residue of tenderness and truth in the human heart (and does the narrator, frustrated snooper that he is, perceive this dimly too in his own torment?) even though the wily and grotesque Juliana is also being "punished," perhaps, for having been the "loose woman" of the romantic past. Now probably all artists have an element of this peeping, prying, infantile core of sexuality within the depths of their psychic unconscious, or sometimes even consciousness. But most writers, at least the good ones, have lived out this strain on a more adult level of emotion and physical love — while few have fallen back upon it, as Henry James did here, as he will do again, as the dominant, almost the only and single mode of behavior; and as the true emotional center of their art.

Curiosity, greed, abstract manipulation and neurotic desire are at the center of "The Aspern Papers," with its midnight scenes of morbid sexuality, its background of gold and flowers. And this was the real climax of James's fiction in the 1880's, although he published one more volume of short stories. *A London Life* (1889) contained "The Liar," an entertaining kind of variation on the snooping observer in "The Aspern Papers," while the title story of the volume dealt with the smart, fast, dissipated and "modern" area of English aristocracy.

Certain unpleasant or more realistic facts about this society were becoming apparent to James — if only after two decades or more of his infatuation with the romance of this British nobility, and almost ten years after he had settled his life and career in London.

The story's drama was centered around Lady Selina's children whom her American sister Laura protects while the errant mother is off with a certain Lady Ringrose in Paris. And from Selina's husband Lionel, Laura learns that Lady Ringrose has had at least "fifty" love affairs — the number does seem exorbitant — while Selina herself has had other lovers and is planning to run off with one of them.

Modern times, indeed! But the flaw in the nouvelle — granting this Jamesian notion of sexual laxity in the British smart set — was that the heroine Laura herself was surely "a little sister bristling with righteousness." She repulses her American suitor, Wendover, because she has discovered "the dishonour of her race" — in her sister, that is. Thus the fairy-tale tags still lingered on in this later international romance; even though it marked the ending of a literary dream, in fact; and a dream which was beginning to turn into the familiar obverse of the Jamesian nightmare. For notice the artist's own indignation, as well as his heroine's — the obvious exaggerations about the sexual "perversity" of the new British upper classes which is also the mark of James's outraged, his wounded, his put-upon innocence. In the story, it is the aged Lady Davenant who still represents the true moral values of the older British nobility; just as henceforth all of James's *true* English aristocrats will tend to be elderly relics of the past. It is also the shallow, frivolous *American* girl — rather than an English lady — who is the prime symbol of the "modern" corruption. In this sense, James appeared to really blame the decline of English morals upon the American influence. For Selina, who is a shallow, pretending cat, and "incorrigibly light," is described as "New York scrap."

James was reluctant to give up his early, embedded vision of European and British nobility. It would take another decade to develop this process of disenchantment, which James also would never quite consciously face — and for which he found every reason, every excuse, except the fact that it had been there right before his eyes from the start . . . Now we've seen that his view of American "innocence" (a cultural generalization to which his Selina is a sudden, gross exception) was equally blind, equally contrived. As in "The Reverberator," the whole "international theme" was the product of the abundant Jamesian fancy without relation to the available and equally abundant facts. It was a literary proposition without validity as to both the American and European poles; sustained only by the remarkable capacity of James to create such an illusion of "life" without any trace of reality. Thus the real international marriages of the period — where the American "heiresses," that is, the daughters, the widows, or the divorced wives of the new class of American financiers, simply *bought up* the titles of the impoverished European nobility — who in their turn were glad to snatch at these God-given (or Mammon-given) saviors of their dwindling royal estate: thus, as I say, the real international marriages of the period were very different things, in reality, from the Jamesian romances.

Was the innocent, pure, "good" millionaire-father of "The Reverberator" — who existed only to ensure a proper European marriage for his daughters — really a creation of "James's warmest humor," as Matthiessen and Murdock stated in *The Notebooks of Henry James* — or was he a creation of James's own innocent, uninformed and juvenile fantasy? This Mr. Dosson was a person of the simplest composition, as James declared, complacently. He was a character "as cipherable as the sum of two figures:

He had a native financial ability of the finest order . . . which had enabled him, without the aid of particular strength of will or keenness of ambition, to build up a large fortune while he was still of middle age. He had a genius for happy speculation, the quick unerring instinct of "a good thing" . . . And he had grown rich not because he was ravenous or hard, but simply because he had an ear, not to term it a nose. He could make out the tune in the discord of the market-place; and he could smell success far up the wind.

Now this summarized the whole line of earlier Jamesian millionaires. But it had nothing to do, obviously, with the realities of a

Jay Gould, a Rockefeller I, a "Commodore" Vanderbilt, a Jim Fisk or a Jay Cooke. It had nothing to do even with the whole host of minor or lesser economic potentates — the newly arrived "princes and kings" of coal, oil, lumber and real estate, of minerals, transportation and utilities who were buying and selling the politicos of the period (as Matthew Josephson and Gustavus Meyers have demonstrated), and who were just then shaping up a new American Oligarchy — or Empire — of hardness, cleverness, shrewdness; of material power and sociomoral corruption.

Where did the Jamesian Mr. Dosson fit into this new American scheme? Innocence, indeed — it was all Henry James's. Nor was this rich hero ever guilty of "pecuniary malversation," said James — and his language itself was patently unfit for his theme — about the historical period when the embezzler or the defalcator were only the less successful types of the financial wizard. William Dean Howells knew all this by the 1880's, and was writing about it; but to Henry, his great American friend, editor and supporter was only another limited American provincial.

The age of American "innocence," which James proclaimed and celebrated in the first half of his career, was actually the age of the greatest moral corruption in the history of the democracy. And of sexual license, too, in the upper brackets of these vulgar, greedy, cunning, physicomaterial, both puritan or pagan alike, but predominantly amoral new American millionaires. (The true literary chronicler of this period, which was both repellent and fascinating, was Theodore Dreiser.) And the new age had spelled the doom of the old-fashioned American republic of James's own childhood which — from his own earliest memories and pubescent notions — he was still using for his "social" and cultural model. Just as "The Reverberator" was a popular variation on the international romance of *The American* — and *that* sweet, good, purehearted native financier! — so it was also a kind of postscript to *The Princess Casamassima:* because it revealed so transparently the Jamesian ignorance of the social-economic-political area not only in his adopted England but in his own native America, and not to mention the Latin cultures of his fondest fancy. This silly (though "warm" and "entertaining") "Reverberator" was illuminating for just these reasons. Its false premises, false values, false base and superstructure alike, all contrived and fabricated to establish the "Romance of Europe" in the Jamesian mind, made the outlines of the whole international theme all too clear. The literary craft of this writer, the talent, the powers of his singular gift for illusion, were all designed to make "real," by a kind of esthetic magic indeed (I don't really mean to say a brilliant kind of hokum), a subject which was obviously artificial — and highly personal with Henry James himself.

In a great writer, or even a serious one, this ignorance of a major part of human activity and social organization would have proved fatal — just as it was among the *other* temperamental limitations and inhibitions which effectively barred James himself from the first order of artists. But in a writer who existed, after all, almost completely in a "made up" world, a world of pure make-believe from the beginning, a world of illusion and "entertainment" from James's earliest origins, his social-historical, or economic and political, ignorance and indifference only became an embarrassing (or, say, amusing) weakness in James's work — *but* a weakness or limitation which must be understood and accepted, rather than ignored or glorified as a Jamesian virtue by the euphoric commentary of the Jamesian cult.

Let it be clear too that James himself, in his own grudging, apologetic, evasive, and equally euphoric manner, did come to acknowledge this central weakness in his craft, which his modern critics have chosen to ignore. In the later Prefaces to the New York edition of his work, he stated — quite explicitly if you can follow his circuitous style — his own lack of knowledge as to that "down-town world" of American business whose representatives he had made into such artificial symbols of either crude masculine "virility," or of sweet, genial and usually parental impotence. Yet even here the Jamesian terminology was hopelessly old-fashioned and ignorant. It was no longer "business" in the United States of his own lifetime — it was finance capitalism at work. And that "downtown world" was in reality very much "uptown," since it was the governing center, the real source of power in the modern U.S.A. which was no longer even Henry James's "America." "The comparative state of innocence of the spirit of my countryfolk," this later, older James of the Prefaces insisted upon repeating even in this context. But those "countryfolk" also represented the "innocence," at best, of the Transcendentalist epoch rather than that of the Gilded Age; if indeed the earlier epoch had ever existed in such "pure" terms except in the youthful Jamesian fancy.

And if all these premises of the Jamesian "international" fiction were untrue — or at the very best only a *little* bit true — what did remain of his writing except an entertaining, an ingenious (and also ingenuous) kind of literary romance, or fictioneering? Hopeless and fatal indeed, the Jamesian case; and also in its own esoteric way, so peculiar, so idiosyncratic, so patently fictitious as to be interesting and illuminating in *other* ways than James himself intended.

Among other things, he had made the mistake of leaving his country at a crucial turning point of its own history, its destiny. But Henry James was a writer with almost an inherited, a biopsychological, a "built in" time lag. And now moreover, towards the close of the 1880's, as in "A London Life," even the real outlines of that superior European "sophistication" — or the true nature and reality of that ancient, noble, virtuous, rich and cultivated British aristocracy towards which all good Americans aspired — were becoming a little more clear to James. (This was also a notion of noble European sophistication and culture which represented mainly James's own arrivist, parvenu and rentier-class — or shall we say "haut-bourgeois" — fantasies.)

Yes, the international theme had been a good commercial item for its own period of the new-rich democracy just beginning to

thirst for foreign culture and the tags (and furnishings) of antiquity. It was enhanced for Henry James by his own particular
fascination with this theme both as a method of personal salvation and, as he believed, of cultural indoctrination. But if one
pole of this argument (the American) was now patently false,
and the other pole (the English) was beginning to fail on him —
what then? At the close of the 1880's, plunging downward to the
nadir of a literary career which had opened with such bright
intimations of the fame, glory and success which James had always
deeply craved, he was working intensely, to recoup his failing
fortunes, on still another massive, ponderous "social" novel —
which was to turn out as thin in content, repressed in feeling,
elaborately overdone in structure and style.

After this he would turn even more desperately, and almost with
a sense of fanatical compulsion, to the one area of art he had
always been most deeply involved with: an area of "entertainment"
indeed, even more than art, for which it seemed all his verbal
talent, his penchant for illusion, enchantment and literary magic
were expressly designed. I mean the Stage itself, the glamorous
Theater of his childhood and youth — that area of natural make-
believe, as it were, which would subsequently provide the worst,
the most humiliating, wounding and traumatic episode in all of
Henry James's career.

The Nineties

4. La Crise du Drame

THE DECADE of the eighties, which had spelled the decline of Henry's popular literary position, was also one of personal loss. His mother had died in 1882; his younger brother Wilky (Garth Wilkinson), sick and disturbed since the time of his Civil War experience, a year later. His father, Henry Senior, who no longer wished to live, it appeared, without his wife's presence, died in December, 1882. "Thank God we haven't another parent to lose," Henry wrote to William, in a somewhat curious vein for a writer whose whole body of work revolved on the psychological renunciation — or the displacement — of his parents.

William, in addressing a farewell letter to Henry Senior, had written: "Good-night, my sacred old Father . . ." (This letter from Europe had arrived too late; just as Henry deliberately or unconsciously delayed his own return to the States until after the father's death.) In speaking of these parental losses both brothers took on something of the father's own exalted, mystic, suprasensory Swedenborgian idealism, so that, beneath their lofty tones, it was difficult to know what they felt. Except that in the family letters of this period William was always open, easy and affectionate with the mother on whom the father almost utterly depended — and to whom he gave his complete, and obviously physical, love — while Henry was typically formal, evasive, reticent. If the younger brother had the symptoms of an arrested oedipal development — the "pure" mother physically from whom no doubt all the virtuous Jamesian heroines descended; and then the adolescent or preadolescent fantasy of "pure" love — he was careful to give none of the overt evidence. It was more likely completely unconscious with him. And he was obviously ashamed of his mother's "inferior" social presence. (In their Boston visit, Henry Senior wrote his wife's social letters. She was not accepted by some of the Boston ladies of the period; and from here, in part, derived the young Henry's animus against New England.) Now what do you do with a mother-figure whom you may be fixed on emotionally when your father quite frankly enjoys all her physical charms, warmth and love — and when, moreover, this same mother-figure is a humiliating obstacle to your own social progress?

This, and the brother-rivalry with the brilliant, sophisticated young William, who had overshadowed Henry throughout their youth, were the decisive elements in Henry's move toward expatriation. But perhaps in his own psyche, the *social shame* was just as important as the oedipal love. And there were other curious elements here. For Henry James was also a classic case of "arrested development," or of Ernest Schachtel's "embedded infant," in the history of world literature; and a case in which the demands and needs (as we'll see) of his own insulated, armored and omnipotent ego dominated every other consideration. If society — that is, "high society" — was superior to Eros in the depths of the Jamesian temperament — just so, the power drives, vanity, egotism of the Jamesian self-image conquered and subjugated his other human needs, desires and satisfactions. The Jamesian answer to all the crushing burdens, defeats and demands of life was that man can live by ego alone. Well, Ego and Art — an art, based on this immaculate, infantine, and devouring egotism, which also precluded or actually denied all those typical human wants and responses which had been the central content of life and literature alike until the magical Jamesian wand transformed their central orbit, their hitherto accepted purpose and function.

Meanwhile, after the tragic series of family deaths, William had taken the big house in New Hampshire, from which he took, also, a dim view of the literary brother who had established his English residence only to live "hidden in the midst of his strange, heavy, alien manners and customs." Yet, as William added, with his customary generosity, all these alien coverings were at base "protective resemblances," under which "the same dear old, good, innocent, and at bottom very powerless-feeling Harry remains . . ." A brotherly generosity which also carried the usual brotherly thrust of amiable superiority! For William was shortly to publish his famous *Principles of Psychology* (1890), and meanwhile the invalid sister Alice — whose life had fallen apart with her parents' death, or with the advent of her own maturity — followed Henry to England, where she lived in seclusion and pain until her own death in 1892. There is still more to be said about these intricate family relations of the Jameses. (Henry was to portray them in various aspects, always shifting, always ambiguous, in the course of his own work.) This was a highly gifted but physically and psychologically delicate family group. Well, say neurotic, say even morbid, beneath their Victorian innocence and high moral principles. And the sequence of these family illnesses and deaths had filled Henry himself with an overwhelming anxiety about his own life and career.

As far back as the early eighties, imprisoned in his Boston hotel room, he had noted that he was soon to be forty years old, and what had he to show? "I shall have been a failure unless I do something *great*." During the composition of *The Princess Casamassima* he had written a more hopeful, but equally revealing, apostrophe to art and himself —

Oh art, art, what difficulties are like thine; but, at the same time, what consolations and encouragements, also, are like thine? Without thee, for me, the world would be, indeed, a howling desert. The Princess will give me hard, continuous work for many months to come; but she will also give me joys too sacred to prate about.

Was he still obsessed, or *more* obsessed, by his youthful visions of fame and glory in the literary life — in this personal prose which moved from archaic "romance" to an almost religious intensity? In 1888, at least, after the publication of the *Princess* in the *Atlantic Monthly*, and the frigidity of its reception, he wrote his famous letter of despair to Howells. "I have entered upon evil days . . . I am still staggering a good deal under the mysterious and (to me) inexplicable injury wrought — apparently — upon my situation by my last two novels . . . from which I expected so much and derived so little. They have reduced the desire, and the demand, for my productions to zero."

There was a familiar element of auctorial self-pity in these lines, of course. There was an element of commercial concern about his literary market in the popular magazines of the day. But there was genuine despair about his total literary position. Mark Twain, the universally acknowledged master of humor, had seen nothing funny in the satire of *The Bostonians*. Oscar Wilde had pointed out that James wrote fiction as if it were a painful duty. Thomas Hardy had added (as Dupee's study reports) that James had "a ponderously warm manner of saying nothing in infinite sentences." And perhaps James *wasn't* really a novelist at all. At least he had little or no interest in the depth or diversity of human character and of human relations which have always been at the core of serious fiction; or in the range of human experience which the later James admitted he had never known. For this staple of novel writing, he substituted the dramatic projection of his own *points of view*. And when his novels began to drag towards the middle (what James correctly called his "missing centre," though he never quite understood, or said, why) he simply added his typical romance melodramas, towards which, then, all of his characters adjusted their behavior. This was the central pattern of all his "big" novels to this point: *The Portrait of a Lady, The American, The Bostonians* and *The Princess Casamassima*. And it is in the light of both this Jamesian craft (which was an esthetic rationalization of his own temperamental weaknesses) and of the psychological crisis towards the middle of his career — in terms of his own life, his family heritage, and the decline of his literary fortunes — that we must consider his celebrated essay, "The Art of Fiction," whose official book publication was in the *Partial Portraits* of 1888.

This was an interesting document, historically and personally, if it isn't at all the supreme esthetic document that it is now considered to be.* First, James bewailed the lack of "theory" in English literary criticism in general: a lack which he more than compensated for. Oddly enough, this master magician of literary illusions also attacked the prevailing view of the novel as entertainment only, or "make-believe." He made a plea for a "wider realism" in the dawning age of literary realism. "The only reason for the existence of a novel is that it does attempt to represent life." He attacked the puritanism and moralism of Anglo-American fiction in an art, said James, whose very existence demanded moral freedom. The motive of "selection" in the novel, said he, was simply to convey "the strange irregular rhythm of life . . . whose strenuous force keeps Fiction upon her feet —

In proportion as in what she offers us we see life without *rearrangement, do we feel that we are touching the truth; in proportion as we see it* with *rearrangement do we feel that we are being put off with a substitute, a compromise and convention.*

Eloquent lines indeed; and here James was apparently aligning himself with a whole series of literary manifestoes for realism in the latter part of the nineteenth century, from those of Howells and Mrs. Wharton to Stephen Crane and Frank Norris. Just as in the portrait of the "American poet" Jeffrey Aspern, "The Art of Fiction" contained a fine vision of the great American writer in the vein of Emerson, Hawthorne and Whitman — though James could hardly resist his familiar allusions to a native land which was "nude and crude and provincial"; and which lacked, apparently, all such

* The essay, first published in the middle eighties, was written as a rejoinder to Walter Besant, the exponent, not very bright, of a kind of Victorian morality in fiction. Robert Louis Stevenson also took part in the debate.

typical writers as Emerson, Hawthorne and Whitman. "Humanity
is immense and reality has myriad forms," he said again; and,
"Experience is never limited, and it is never complete." And this
was James's own link with the American age and spirit which
William James, among others, was also to proclaim and celebrate:
the pragmatic age at the turn of the century which lay behind the
whole naturalistic and realistic movements in the American fiction
of the twentieth century.

Yet the central argument in this Jamesian essay was more complex than this, more enigmatic, personal and ambiguous. Up to
this point perhaps "The Art of Fiction" was a glorification of the
artist Henry James *wanted* to be, rather than the artist he was.
But then, as usual, he began to project *another* view of fiction
which became at base a rationalization of his own temperament:
his own lack of experience with that "immense humanity" and
myriad-shaped reality he had described; his own kind of Victorian
moralism, less obvious but no less rigid and binding than that
which he had attacked; and his own dependence, precisely, on that
"principle of selection," of fictional "arrangement" which, as we've
already noticed in his case, was in fact a substitute for, an evasion of
both truth and life in art.

For, in addition, he balanced his demand for freedom of subject
matter with an insistence on literary form which almost appeared
to make the *kind* of subject matter immaterial. In the essay it becomes increasingly evident that by "experience" James meant the
experience of the mind itself, or the mind of the artist, rather than
the general human experience he had stressed earlier. This artistic
mind, said James, was "an immense sensibility, a kind of huge
spider web," which was suspended in "the chamber of consciousness" and which caught "every air-borne particle" in its tissue. "It
is the very atmosphere of the mind; and when the mind is imaginative — much more when it happens to be that of a man of genius
— it takes to itself the faintest hints of life, it converts the very
pulses of the air into revelations."

Thus it was that the Jamesian notion of the "consciousness" of the artist became the equivalent of experience itself. And the workings of this "artistic mind" were, for James, the whole meaning and purpose of art:

The power to guess the unseen from the seen, to trace the implication of things, to judge the whole piece from the pattern, the condition of feeling life in general so completely that you are well on your way to knowing any particular corner of it — this cluster of gifts may almost be said to constitute experience . . . If experience consists of impressions, it may be said that impressions are experience.

But are they really? Or are they impressions *of* experience? For the writer, above all, isn't it just those "particular corners" of experience — which James here dispensed with under the guise of "feeling life in general" — which are the true material, the real test, of his craft? Through a brilliant kind of verbal sophistry, indeed, James simply reversed all the familiar concepts of major fiction to suit his own capacities, his own limitations. It becomes apparent that "The Art of Fiction" is proclaiming only a specific kind of Jamesian "realism" — a conceptual realism, as it were, which was altogether new and special in our literature, and which would remain so. Moreover, this new brand of "psychological" realism — wholly contained in the artist's *mind*, and confined only to his *consciousness*; using only those air-borne "particles" or those "faintest hints" of life, those "impressions" which were substituted for any full experience, and those "very pulses of the air" which became the Jamesian "revelations" — was repeatedly compared with painting, among the other arts, or with the act of "seeing," rather than that of living and feeling. Or rather, with the act of seeing those *ideas* about life which were, in this new Jamesian esthetics, to permeate and penetrate the work of art itself; to inform and animate it "so that every word and every punctuation point contribute directly to the experience."

Well then — is this the essay which has been celebrated, in recent years, as the great, pioneer document of the new realism in American literature? In fact, "The Art of Fiction" established a concept of the novel altogether different, perhaps, from the Victorian realism which James found so wanting — but also even farther away from what became the "real" American realism of the early twentieth century. It marked a turning point only in *James*'s own craft; and it indicated only *his own* future direction. No wonder that this critic had found so distasteful the Walt Whitman with whom he might have been linked in certain respects: the rude, barbaric poet of the New World, I mean, who had also defied the black and white universe of the Transcendentalists by stressing all the yearnings of the flesh, and all the varied colors and conditions of human experience. For Whitman's great volume of verses in 1865, so James had said in a review which he reprinted as late as 1908, was "an offense against art" which was also an outrage to good taste. "It is not enough to be rude, lugubrious and grim." Maybe this was one of the most famous "shocks of non-recognition" — to reverse Edmund Wilson's title — in our letters.

No; if the revolt against New England on the part of both James and Edith Wharton appeared in some respects to be so early and so bold; if it can be constrained, as it has been, to appear to anticipate the famous "Revolt of the Flesh" in the Chicago of the teens; it was also a "revolt from above" — a rebellion of the palace guard in our literature which had nothing in common with what actually took place later on. And the true meaning of "The Art of Fiction" becomes even more apparent when we compare it to the novel with which Henry James opened the new decade.

The idea of *The Tragic Muse*, in 1890, came from Mrs. Humphry Ward's anecdote (air-borne, or dinner-born) of the young actress who had gone far beyond the man who had loved her and taught her. "The interest, I say, would be as a study of a certain particular *nature d'actrice*," so James confided to his *Notebooks* in 1884. And while writing about his "ignorant, illiterate Rachel," in the novel which was serialized in the *Atlantic Monthly*, he had more to say:

*It is this time really a good subject, I think: save that it's too pale a one.
I have undertaken to tell and to describe too much — given my data,
such as they are — one of the reasons being that I was afraid of my
story being too thin. For fear of making it too small I have made it too
big. This, however, is a good fault, and I see my way out . . .*

Now *The Tragic Muse* was too pale and thin in its central content,
as James felt. But whether it was a "good fault" or not to make
something too small into something too big, it was certainly a typically Jamesian fault of which this novel was a perfect example.
There is the high English background of the narrative; and perhaps
James was almost too much at ease in describing the patrician chatter of his contrived British aristocracy. At least, after his uneasy
excursion into the "anarchism" of *The Princess Casamassima*, he
was back home in those upper echelons of English political life,
too, where Julia Dallow could offer her "borough" to Nick Dormer
on a platter, along with her fortune. For after all, if Nick should
run for office, he is the son of a famous father. He carries a "great
name . . . One of the greatest, simply."

This was really an upper class romance, *à l'Américain*, and
laid on thick for the tourist trade. Nick Dormer and Peter Sherringham ("old boy," "old fellow") are cousins. Their families are intimately involved, since the "good Bridget," who is Nick's sister,
would make a perfect wife for Peter; while Nick's mother, the
impoverished Lady Agnes, who urges on this match, also prods
Nick himself towards a high political career and a perfect (rich)
marriage. This was again the leisure-class world of the inheritors,
whose main activities are long walks and long talks. (And tea!)
No wonder that Nick, a perfect dilettante (whose last name suggests "sleeper," or sleeping artist), is appalled by "the humbug of
the hustings," even in such gentlemanly British politics; and that
the entrance of Miriam Rooth is a definite intrusion upon this
genial, easy, pleasant (if slightly unreal) scene of aristocratic country life.

For Miriam is partly Jewish (as Hawthorne's Miriam was in *The Marble Faun*). She is a lower class type who is struggling towards a career on the stage. That is to say, she is of dubious middle class parentage; and perhaps her Jewish strain was in accordance with a certain vulgarity which James also associated with the *"nature d'actrice."* She is determined to become "the English Rachel," ignorant and illiterate as that great actress might be in James's private thought — and Miriam's advent also brings *The Tragic Muse* at least momentarily to life. Shrewd, witty, ambitious, histrionic, and pretending passion at least, she is in fact one of James's attractive and promising heroines, bolder than Christina Light, far more vital than Isabel Archer. Though her father is only "a Jew stockbroker in the City" (another glimpse into the lower depths of the Jamesian social arrangement), Miriam's maternal heritage — like almost all these Jamesian "outcasts" — includes "the great ones of the earth." She even becomes a "tremendous lady," according to the bohemian philosopher of the novel, Gabriel Nash (who is himself a gentleman, for all that). But Nash's values, of course, are vague and hyperbolic; and Miriam is not really a lady to James himself, which may be one reason why she is so good a portrait at the novel's start.

Of the two counterplots in *The Tragic Muse* — Miriam's theatrical career and Nick's artistic career — Nick's is much less interesting. He is in fact a bore, and his conflict between politics and fame, and art and solitude, is tedious. Yet even this innocuous hero is offered another one of those "illegitimate" or fairy-tale fortunes by his foster-uncle, or foster-father in the narrative, old Mr. Carteret, if he will marry Mrs. Dallow. For in English politics, and that is to say in the House of Lords, "the manner of the real English lady is a force not to be despised." And if it is Miriam who gives the novel its only vital interest, it is Peter Sherringham's hopeless, jealous, frustrated (and typically Jamesian) infatuation for her which is the central emotion in the story. The point is, however, that *all* the love affairs here are those of adolescent frustration, just as all the love scenes are only talk — or are the "analysis" of love, or rather the analysis of the renunciation of love. Perhaps *The Tragic Muse* is the most impotent of all the Jamesian novels of spiritual or physical impotence.

And as I say, the most talkative. "My improprieties are all of the mind," Miriam says, and the central triangle of lovers in this story — as conceived by the Jamesian vision — made the development of the novel very difficult. Both Peter and Nick are more or less in love with Miriam; but Nick stands aside partly for Peter's sake, while Peter will not interfere with Miriam's obvious preference for Nick. True love was made impossible again in this Jamesian chronicle — but even more so, for, after all, Miriam was attractive but vulgar. What was obvious here, instead, was the theme of "cousinly affection." All these impossible loves were shared by an ingrown and vaguely incestuous group of characters. In this respect *The Tragic Muse* foreshadowed certain major themes in James's later work (as it reflected certain brooding preoccupations in his own temperament); and there were intimations of the later Jamesian manner. When Peter and his sister Bridget are studying Nick's painting of Miriam — and James drew all these tangled threads of emotion together through his typical (and voyeuristic) device of "the portrait" — Biddy watches Peter's eyes for his "impression" of Miriam's picture, while he in turn measures "her impression of his impression."

Those impressions of experience, which James had equated *with* experience, are already getting pretty complicated. The second half of *The Tragic Muse* simply fell apart under these disadvantages, or was dissipated into idle chatter and "fine writing" to conceal the lack of fictional development. And its failure, both in critical and popular reception, as the third of the three large, "realistic," social chronicles of this period — coming after *The Bostonians* and *The Princess Casamassima* — put an end to this phase of James's career. His early triumphs and popularity had led into an abyss of silence. Thus *The Tragic Muse* was a turning point in his career; even while it also pointed to an even more disastrous Jamesian obsession with the stage itself — and with "that great childish audience" which Miriam, who has become a little coarser, a little harder, a little more Jewish perhaps, finally learns to conquer and dominate.

Maybe the real failure in the novel was the author's own betrayal of his gifted and entertaining heroine. What was curious in the later Preface which James wrote for the New York edition of the *Muse*, however, was that this implication was never mentioned. What was curious indeed, and typically Jamesian, was that he rationalized all of the obvious defects in this weak novel into a series of hidden virtues. Looking back at it from the vantage point of the 1900's, he could not forget, to be sure, the disaster it had brought to his career:

What lives not least, to be candid, is the fact that I was to see this production make a virtual end, for the time, as by its sinister effect — though for reasons still obscure to me — of the pleasant old custom of the "running" of the novel. Not for many years was I to feel the practice, for my benefit, confidingly revive. The influence of "The Tragic Muse" was thus exactly other than what I had all earnestly (if of course privately enough) invoked for it, and I remember well the particular chill, at last, of the sense of my having launched it in a great grey void from which no echo or message whatever would come back.

James was not one to forget such wounds to his vanity, his integrity, his career and his pocketbook; and one notices the romance melodrama of the prose which rehearsed this old trauma — the "sinister" effect, the particular chill, and the great gray void from which no echo returned. But were the reasons for the novel's failure really so "obscure" to this high priest of estheto-metaphysics; and was this debacle almost, by implication, the result of some kind of sinister, or even anarchistic, "plot" against James? Well, at least, he invoked a "special tenderness of charity" in his parental and auctorial breast for the novel which he compared to "the maimed or slighted, the disfigured or defeated, the unlucky or unlikely child."

That was the infantine figure, in life and art alike, which always drew down James's special charity: this figure was himself. And he insisted that *The Tragic Muse* had its own special sustained, preserved *tone*. It had "its constant and doubtless rather fine-drawn truth to its particular sought pitch and accent." It had its inner harmony "that I perhaps presumptuously permit myself to compare to an unevaporated scent." He was aiming, in the *Muse* — and in this later tone of hardly a rigorous self-criticism he had by implication achieved — at the kind of literary "composition" which would equal that of "certain sublime Tintorettos at Venice."

These were the statements, and this the dominant tone, of the later Jamesian "criticism" which was promulgated as esthetic law by the Jacobite circle of critics. But how could you be, as James certainly was here, so obviously wrong, so deliberately blind, so unctuously self-flattering? As though half conscious of this, too, James went on to even more astounding generalizations in the Preface to *The Tragic Muse*. Compared with *his* ideal of form, as exemplified in this novel, he added, such previous literary works as *The New-comes*, or *Les Trois Mousquetaires*, or Tolstoy's "Peace and War" [sic] were definitely found wanting. Oh yes, they had *life* perhaps. But: "What do such large loose baggy monsters, with their queer elements of the accidental and arbitrary, artistically *mean*?" And the fact that Henry James could compare the other two novels with *War and Peace* wasn't as astounding perhaps as his sublime conclusion as to their *artistic* lack of meaning. But of course, as he said, he now delighted only in "a deep-breathing economy and an organic form." A *form*, that is, which had life; rather than the life which is given form in the great novels such as, at least, one of the three which he mentioned for the sake of comparison.

Now it is quite possible that the later Jamesian strictures on those "large loose baggy monsters" did apply to most Victorian novels, as they apply in fact to all the major novels of world literature. Perhaps the elements of "the accidental and arbitrary" are just what do contribute their decisive weight to the great novels — for, while perhaps "formless" in the Jamesian sense, they are never really so accidental and arbitrary as they appear: since they come out of the depths of the artist's unconscious. But didn't these elements apply precisely to *The Tragic Muse* itself, with only the reservation that this wasn't even a good novel? Well, no matter. The later euphoric esthete (James, I mean) did concede the *Muse's* "misplaced centre" — a euphemistic term for the novel's lack of organic development — and the collapse of the voluminous, talkative, second half:

The moral of all which indeed, I fear, is, perhaps too trivially, but that the "thick," the false, the dissembling second half of the work before me, associated throughout with the effort to weigh my dramatic values as heavily as might be, since they had to be so few, presents that effort as at the very least a quite convulsive, yet in its way highly agreeable spasm. Of such mild prodigies is the "history" of any specific effort composed!

And thus James used his own literary lapses as the occasion to expound his own later literary "principles" — as the glorious springboard, indeed, from which to vault so sublimely into the esthetic empyrean — just as he exposed his own failures only to twistedly applaud them.

Even this later *style* of the Jamesian criticism was hardly an impressive example of "deep-breathing economy" — of words, at least — or "an organic form" of sentence structure. Well, it is a marvelous style, in its own way, for its exotic shadings of meanings, once you have learned to follow its odd convolutions; and for what it reveals all so innocently as to the author's true meaning, as well as his formal "Principles of Art." How can you really criticize an artist who proclaims the failure of his own work to be "a quite convulsive yet in its own way highly agreeable spasm" of art? Or one who then proceeds to "generalize" that particular spasm of *The*

Tragic Muse as the "mild prodigy" which accompanies the "history" (but *what* history?) of all creative efforts?* Henry James really was incomparable, though hardly in the way which the Jamesian cult has presumed him to be incomparable. The Preface to the *Muse* (which has been praised as another Jamesian literary manifesto comparable to "The Art of Fiction" itself) is one of the most illuminating of all the later James Prefaces, in which he rationalizes an "esthetics" based so largely on his own idiosyncracies — even on his literary failures. For here he admits only to conceal (just as what he is concealing becomes his unconscious admission); and he "criticizes" only in order to justify. Here most plainly he "half-sees" so much of what was peculiarly his own talent, his own achievements, his own limitations — only to leap blindly over them in these grand general "conceptions" of art which concern themselves with everything but the specific work of art he is "analyzing."

Similarly, he admitted in this exotic Preface that he had always had a desire to "do the actress" and to touch the theater — "to meet that connexion, somehow or other, in any free plunge of the speculative fork into the contemporary social salad." (And how much of the overwrought imagery of this late Jamesian style centered around *food:* just as here a fork was described as "speculative," and a social environment was a salad!) But James's yearning for the stage — as with a whole line of puritanical and sexually inhibited American writers, from Howells and Twain to Ring Lardner — was tempered by his notion that the stage should be "purified" and spiritually elevated. And besides, if he had told Miriam Rooth's story *as it really was* no Anglo-American magazine of the

---

* James then went on to discuss the inadequate central plot of *The Tragic Muse* in terms of the alternation of "scenic" and of "dramatic" occasions; of the "precious" central unity of an "objective" Miriam surrounded by the "exposed subjectivity" of her two inadequate lovers; of a "logical, analytical structure" composed of dramatic symbols, and patterns of weights and forces, etc. In esthetic terms, that is to say, which approach those of modern abstract painting, or the New Criticism itself, and which completely ignore the inadequate, trivial content of the novel.

time would have printed it. Yet with this last restriction about *The Tragic Muse* (all of which James admitted in curiously muffled, orotund and circumambulatory terms), James was still highly pleased by *The Tragic Muse:*

The appeal, the fidelity to the prime motive is, with no little art, strained clear (even as silver is polished), in a degree answering — at least by intention — to the air of beauty. There is an awkwardness again in having thus belatedly to point such features out; but in that wrought appearance of animation and harmony, that effect of free movement and yet of recurrent and insistent reference, "The Tragic Muse" has struck me again as conscious of a bright advantage.

Now there was indeed an awkwardness in pointing out the "bright advantage" of a novel which lacked all the possible merits of its composition; a novel which had in fact, through its obvious failure, forced the author to turn to other fields of fiction. Wasn't there? But the Henry James of the late Prefaces, the master technician who could discern those hidden charms in the weakest of his works, delighted in just such feats of the critical imagination, such verbal tours de force of "self-criticism" — even while he also, in the same breath, appeared to applaud his own verbal ingenuity. And meanwhile, after the debacle (or the popular misunderstanding) of the *Muse*, he had turned, in the despair of that period which he rationalized so brightly in his later phase, to the more promising medium of the short story and the "blest nouvelle" itself. *The Lesson of the Master*, in 1892, was the first of a series of collections of these tales which James devoted himself to during the new decade.

Among the stories, there was one which later received what I can only describe as a peculiar, an impossible notoriety — "Brooksmith," the portrait of an "ineffable butler." Matthiessen and Murdock of *The Notebooks* apparently accept Pelham Edgar's view that this butler "was the only representative of the servant class whom James ever thought worthy to commemorate." Moreover, the story re-

vealed "the dilemma of the highly sensitive intelligence frustrated
and starved by lack of fit material and proper environment for its
development."

A serious theme indeed; and one that was later developed by a
whole school of native American realists. But what was this "sensitive intelligence" in Brooksmith himself; and what type of frustration did it suffer from? Well, his master's drawing room was surely
the happiest of happy salons, a rare garden of the muses which the
ineffable butler tended amidst the tinkling teacups and the *best*
conversation. There was never a crowd; and

always the right people with *the right people — there must really have
been no wrong people at all — always coming and going, never sticking
fast nor overstaying, yet never popping in or out with indecorous familiarity.*

A wonderful spot in truth for a sensitive and aspiring member of
the servant class; and this story conveyed the essence of the highest
Jamesian aspirations for "society," and "the best people," and
"good talk." This was a lyrical extravaganza of the perfect salon;
in which all the sofas were so *convenient,* as the Jamesian narrator
remarked: "the accidents so happy, the talkers so ready, the listen-
ers so willing." This was indeed a little cosmos of "culture," à la
James, into which poor Brooksmith, by the happiest turn of fate,
had stumbled.

But he has been rigorously trained for the perfection — and the
ardors — of this leisure-class paradise. The Master (Mr. Offord)
reads passages from Montaigne and Saint-Simon to his beloved
Brooksmith, while the fortunate butler carries the precious volumes
to and from the library shelves. "A certain feeling for letters must
have rubbed off on him from the mere handling of his master's
books" — though it is implicit that Brooksmith has never dared to
open these books. This is the final touch to the perfect salon.
Luxury, leisure and literature are the holy trinity of this Jamesian

vision of civilization, while, to be sure, Brooksmith has reached the
point where he can discern *"malentendus* in French." "Quite an
education, sir, isn't it, sir?" says this blessed butler to the sympathetic narrator of the tale — perhaps revealing the perfection of his
training by the two "sirs" in one short sentence. But then, "to what
was this sensitive young man of thirty-five, of the servile class, being
educated?" as the narrator asks himself solemnly. For with the
illness and death of Brooksmith's master, the butler's own life has,
in effect, also ended. He is unsuited for lesser salons. He faces
ruin. The end of the story describes his slow disintegration in
the "lower depths" (dirty, greasy, illiterate, uncultivated) of the
less fortunate servile class.

Was this a true reflection of the facts, an accurate portrait of
even the best-trained British butler? It was at least the butler's
vision of paradise which existed so deeply in James's *own* psyche.
It was the objective drama of the central fantasy of wealth, comfort, books and talk which had possessed his mind from so early an
age, and whose culmination *had* to be in British society. If not for
English butlers, at least for Henry James, it was a world of polar
extremes between the salon and "downstairs" — or vulgar ruin.
"It can't be fireworks *every* night," says poor Brooksmith, while
after his inevitable disappearance the narrator reflects that perhaps, after all, he was now "changing the plates of the immortal
gods." So that, in this tragicomedy of the servile class, or of James's
notion of the English servant class, we are left with a presumption
of a strict social hierarchy extending even unto the gates of heaven.

"The Lesson of the Master" — title story of the volume — was a
far more valid thing which was also concerned with a typical and
recurrent theme of James's. Dealing with the effect of marriage on
an artist, the deterioration of his work through overproduction and
the need for money, it reflected the underlying fear of love and of
women in the Jamesian temperament. Henry St. George is the
popular novelist, or the "Master" of the story — and James was
now beginning to see human relationships in an almost feudal

pattern of masters and disciples — while the background was again a sort of eighteenth century royal British elegance. At the estate of Summersoft, young Paul Overt, the disciple, meets the St. Georges and the bright young Miss Fancourt. Somewhat as in "The Author of Beltraffio," Mrs. St. George has never interfered with her husband's work except once — "when I made him burn up a bad book."

The wealthy, respected and admired St. Georges represent just that literary position and "success" which James himself had yearned for, but which now, from the depths of his own failure, he described with a more cutting satiric edge. For Overt soon discovers the real truth. The great popular novelist is chained to his writing desk, in his prison cell, in order to support his social position. Mrs. St. George has given him a study without windows, a good big cage for going round and round. "My wife invented it and she locks me up here every morning." There is the familiar "revelation scene" between master and disciple; but St. George is remarkably honest about his position, and his wife's "influence." He warns the young writer to avoid such dangers to his craft as embodied in the alluring shape of Miss Fancourt. "I refer to the mercenary muse whom I led to the altar of literature. Don't, my boy, put your nose into *that* yoke." And here occurs one of the most notable, if unintentional, passages in James's work: "It must be delightful to feel that the son of one's loins is at Sandhurst," says Paul Overt enthusiastically . . . "It is — it's charming," says St. George. "Oh I'm a patriot!"

Still, he warns Overt away from his own path, since the writer must heed not the chatter of society, but "the incorruptible silence of Fame" — a fine phrase that *was* intended. And the faithful, worshiping, devout and naïve Overt abandons Miss Fancourt in order to take "a long trip abroad" — always the Jamesian formula for frustrated love affairs, if hardly the recourse of the less comfortably situated broken heart. He profits by the "advice of the master" — only to discover on his return to London that Mrs. St.

George has died, that St. George is to marry Miss Fancourt, and that they are both blooming, happy, and "stupid." The older novelist even tells the younger one that he has stopped writing altogether, and will content himself by reading Overt's masterpieces. "He *was* the mocking fiend."

It is just this ambiguity in the master's "lesson" which makes the story so entertaining.* If James was dealing with obsessional themes in his work — the temptations of the world, the dedication to writing, the lure and the trap of women — here the balance of emotions was still maintained. The tone of this little parable of life and art was excellent, and life, however "stupid," won out. Both "the great misguided novelist," St. George, and the devout and dedicated young apostle, Overt — who was hardly capable of seizing or enjoying a creature like the story's heroine — were described with ironic insight. And perhaps the best story in the volume, the nouvelle called "The Pupil," maintained the same mixture of warmth and comedy, while it was based on deeper levels of emotion.

This was the tale which was centered on the relation of an impecunious young tutor and a gifted child, and set against the background of an eccentric and possibly evil family of expatriated "bohemians." The account of the Moreens as vagabonds, outcasts and "gypsies" was one of James's most effective pieces of satire. What is more, with Morgan Moreen, this extraordinary infant, diseased, perceptive, and tender, James accomplished the literary feat of making a child prodigy attractive. As for Pemberton himself, the young tutor, who gradually discovers the truth about the Moreen family, including the fact that it is a "privilege" for him to

* But not so, according to Matthiessen and Murdock in *The Notebooks*, who state that the ironic twist at the end of the story "blurs the main point by raising an ambiguity, and distracting the reader into conjectures about how far St. George's advice to Overt was sincere and how far it was dictated by his selfish wish to drive away a rival in love." But aren't these "conjectures" just the effect that James was trying to establish — the real point of the story? In this case the Master, James himself, was smiling at his own "religion of art," which his modern disciples, like poor Paul Overt, take so literally.

tutor Morgan — a privilege that requires no salary — and who is trapped little by little into staying on through his affection for the boy, and his sense of the boy's helplessness in this ménage of genteel scoundrels: this was a study of the dangers of compassion. "Beware of pity," in Stefan Zweig's phrase.

But was it only compassion? There is the growing "understanding" between tutor and pupil — an understanding in which the pupil is actually the tutor. There is their developing emotional affinity, with its concurrent physical affection. The boy yearns to leave his dreadful family and live with his tutor. The dream of escape occupies the tutor's mind as well as his small friend's. Thus "The Pupil" was a pioneer, Freudian study of a covert kind of homosexual affair — according to those critics who also saw in Henry James the first of the "modern" psychological novelists.

Well, we can only note that there are no overt signs of any deeper or "perverse" relationship between the two masculine figures in the story. Just as James converted the potentially oedipal relation of father and daughter in *Washington Square* to a matter of cash and (paternal) cunning, so here there is no doubt he *consciously* intended a study of his familiar orphan princeling, who had the good fortune to gain an older and protective filial guardian. Perhaps this was what William James *should* have been; or what Henry himself wanted — but still how these curiously incestuous if not directly homosexual and potentially perverse relationships hovered around his unconscious! This was at best the picture of an adolescent crush on the tutor's part — just as James was only depicting a feminine crush in *The Bostonians* — and it was a common, popular and romantic Victorian notion of friendship. Perhaps indeed only a totally *unconscious* writer could have described, in all innocence, and with such a glow of sentiment, what appears so suggestive to the modern mind in "The Pupil." (It is even safe to say, on the part of a writer so inhibited as James was about heterosexual love, that he would have been horrified at the suggestion — in print at least — of homosexuality.) What James himself was concerned with, on the conscious level of his art, was the case of a remarkable, or even supernatural, child genius, and his outrageous family.

The story was effective because again it projected and dramatized this artist's deepest conviction about himself, surely, and very likely — if rather oddly — about his own family. Young Morgan was the royal child — whom the mother, disgraceful yet pathetic woman that she is, was even afraid to touch physically. It is particularly the disreputable *social position* of his family that distracts the gifted child whom they exploit. By comparison with his "migratory tribe" (and *this* was true, at least, of the Jameses as a family), young Morgan has a "homebred sensibility." The tutor speculates on the mysteries of biological transmission, "the far jumps of heredity" which separate the princeling from his disreputable family; while Morgan blushes for his relatives. And the tutor becomes a hero to his small charge, whose note of shame quivers with a ring of passion. "like some high silver note from a small cathedral chorister." The strangest thing in Morgan's "large little composition," we are told, was "a temper, a sensibility, even a private ideal, which made him as privately disown the stuff his people were made of." It was as if, the tutor-narrator meditates again, "he had been a little gentleman and had paid the penalty by discovering that he was the only such person in his family." Now this was surely not the truth about Henry James's own family; but it *was* the deepest personal fantasy which the wounded little Henry had cherished in his childish heart.

But what other major writer in world literature — as Henry James is reputed to be — had ever aspired, first of all, to be "a little gentleman?"

And what young Morgan demands from his outrageous family is that, at the very least, they should save "a little reputation." "You *do* know everything," says the tutor-brother figure Pemberton to this marvelous little prodigy. "No I don't after all," answers Morgan; and this was because —

*"I don't know what they live on, or how they live, or why they live!
What have they got and how did they get it? Are they rich, are they
poor, or have they a modeste aisance? Why are they always chiveying
me about — living one year like ambassadors and the next like paupers.
Who are they, anyway, and what are they? I've thought of all that —
I've thought of a lot of things. They're so beastly worldly. That's what
I hate most — oh I've seen it! All they care about is to make an appearance and to pass for something or other. What the dickens do they
want to pass for? What do they, Mr. Pemberton?"*

And there is no doubt that this anguished lament corresponded
both to young Henry's vision of his odd, eccentric "gypsy" family,
and even somewhat to the facts about the senior Henry Jameses,
who did indeed have their *"modeste aisance,"* on which they lived
the good life of art, culture, travel, and other-worldly Swedenborgian mysticism.

But what then did this prodigious young Jamesian child spokesman mean by this weird, outcast family's being so "beastly worldly"
— which he hates most of all; and what has he *seen?* What dreadful crime or sin of theirs, apart from their rather amusing antics in
"The Pupil" itself, existed in the infantine Jamesian fancy?

Well, the ways of genius were inscrutable in the remarkable case
of Henry James at least. And notice that the figure of the all-loving
and all-understanding tutor himself was a composite father-brother
symbol: a brother who was willing to sacrifice all for the sake of the
unrecognized young prodigy; an imaginary father who had appeared
from nowhere — an "illegitimate father," as it were, who had come
to rescue the princeling from his purely circumstantial and uncomprehending parents . . . *That* was the real meaning of, and the
myth behind, "The Pupil," as we'll see it appear recurrently in
James's work, and clearly in his own memoirs of childhood and
youth. And that is the reason for the story's emotional impact,
down to the very end almost; until the weak heart of this noble little
orphan-prince finally gives way for good at the shock of his parents'
final infamy.

James was to use this convenient heart malady again in the case of another gifted and exploited (if not contaminated) child hero in "The Turn of the Screw." Meanwhile, however, the year 1893 marked another burst of Jamesian books, though mainly of minor significance.* He was struggling desperately to regain his popular position. But the title story in *The Private Life* (another volume of light fiction which James published as two books in the United States) was an interesting *jeu d'esprit* in a typically Jamesian vein.

It was based on the personage of Robert Browning, so we are told — or on the concept of his public and private personality being so different. To this notion James added the fictional counterpart of a fashionable English painter who had no "private life" — or hidden creative force — at all. Thus the story contains two protagonists, balancing each other off, and two "observers": the English actress, Blanche Adney, who is a rather good character; and the narrator himself, who is a literary failure and a would-be dramatist. The story becomes rather complicated in its development; but one realizes that the obsessive, or obsessed narrator-observer of "The Private Life" — who is determined to ferret out the secret existence of the two central figures, and who might be called the Jamesian snooper — is a descendant of the scholar-spy in "The Aspern Papers" and also foreshadows the series of future "voyeur-analysts" in James's work. And this narrative also ends on a rather baroque and fantastic note, in the twilight world of James's "mad" tales.†

---

* The title story in the volume called *The Real Thing* was a pretty parable of life and art, while "Greville Fane" was another satire on the successful lady fictioneers of the period whom James thought he could not compete with . . . *Picture and Text* was a collection of essays on some painters of the time. *Essays in London and Elsewhere* contained more essays on such figures as Flaubert, Loti, the Goncourts and Ibsen. As a critic of painting James was highly conventional; as a literary critic he was both sharp and curiously — or quite naturally as we've already seen — limited, though extremely well read.

† Among the other things in *The Private Life*, "Owen Wingrave" was a ghost story of a beautiful British youth, from a distinguished British family of martial heroes, who dies like a soldier and a patriot (if quite mysteriously) in his single-handed protest against the army and war . . . "The Wheel of Time" was a romance

But with this flurry of versatility, James found himself on the brink of another crisis which would preoccupy his mind, his whole creative being, through the last half of the decade. As early as 1891, he had issued a privately printed stage version of *The American*, as "A Comedy in Four Acts," to which he had also added a "happy ending" for the sake of a stage hit. The actor Edward Compton had asked James for a stage version of the novel, and the *Notebooks* contain a fascinating record of the Jamesian reflections during this period. "I had practically given up my old, valued, long-cherished dream of doing something for the stage," so he wrote —

for fame's sake, and art's, and fortune's; overcome by the vulgarity, the brutality, the baseness of the condition of the English-speaking theatre today. But after an interval, a long one, the vision has revived, on a new and very much humbler basis, and especially under the lash of necessity.

"Of art or fame *il est maintenant fort peu question:* I simply *must* try, and try seriously, to produce half a dozen — a dozen, five dozen — plays for the sake of my pocket, my material future. Of how little money the novel makes for me I needn't discourse here. The theatre has sought me out — in the person of the good, the yet unseen Compton. I have listened and considered and reflected, and the matter is transposed to a minor key. To accept the circumstances, in their extreme humility, and do the best I can *in* them: this is the moral of my present situation. They are the reverse of ideal — but there is this great fact that for myself at least I may make them better. To take what there *is*, and use it, without waiting forever in vain for the preconceived — to dig deep into the actual and get something out of *that* — this doubtless is the right

---

of two frustrated lovers whose children also end up as frustrated lovers; all of this in a kind of diagrammatic "square" of opposing forces which may be symmetrical but is hardly credible.

way to live. If I succeed a little I can easily — I think — succeed
more; I can make my own conditions more as I go on. The field is
common, but it is wide and free — in a manner . . . And if there
is money in it that will greatly help: for all the profit that may
come to me in this way will mean real freedom for one's general
artistic life: it all hangs together (time, leisure, independence for
'real literature,' and, in addition, a great deal of experience of *tout
un côté de la vie*). Therefore my plan is to try with a settled resolution — that is, with a full determination to return repeatedly to
the charge, overriding, annihilating, despising the boundless dis-
couragements, disgusts; *écoeurements*. One should *use* such things
— grind them to powder."

Very good in terms of moral fervor; and *The American* ran for
two months in London, and by the time of its production James
had completed four other plays, *Tenants, Disengaged, The Album,
The Reprobate*, though, as Matthiessen and Murdock tell us, "none
of these reached the stage." For this was also a peculiarly Jamesian
and egocentric way to regard the complex, highly skilled craft of
playwrighting. Despising the English and searching for something
closer to classical French drama, to which James had always been
drawn, since it was both "theatrical" and respectable, he yet saw
in the stage the chance both of elevating its tone and of refurbish-
ing his pocketbook. "For fame's sake, and art's, and fortune's" —
and he had no hesitation in dashing off the "half-dozen, dozen,
five dozen" potboilers, it must be, which would be an immediate
success and procure his freedom for real literature. Of such ambiguity (and childlike fantasy) was Henry James's approach to the
stage; a mixture of old, deep yearning and overwhelming disdain
and hard-cash necessity. And his notes on the play version of *The
American* were equally illuminating as to James's notion of *how*
this was to be done;

His proposal is that I shall make a play of the American, *and there is
no doubt a play in it. I must extract the simplest, strongest, baldest,*

*most rudimentary, at once most humorous and most touching one, in
a form whose main* souci *shall be pure situation and pure point combined with pure brevity. Oh, how it must not be too good and how
very bad it must be!* À moi, Scribe; à moi, Sardou, à moi, Dennery! —
Reduced to its simplest expression, and that reduction must be my play,
The American . . .

And then James proceeded to outline the purely melodramatic plot
of his novel with a vengeance; and with a new twist. "The hero,
injured, outraged, resentful, feels the strong temptation to *punish*
the Bellegardes, and for a day almost yields to it. Then he does the
characteristically magnanimous thing — the characteristically good-
natured thing — throws away his opportunity — lets them 'off' —
lets them go. In the play he must do this — *but* get his wife."

With such an approach, arrogant, cynical, mercenary, obtuse,
could he ever have written a good play? He published his unwanted and unheeded stage dramas in *Theatricals* and *Theatricals: Second Series*, both in 1894. *Guy Domville*, "for private cir-
culation only," appeared in the same year.

This play was not published elsewhere during James's lifetime,
according to the Edel and Laurence bibliography. Its first book
appearance was in *The Complete Plays of Henry James*, edited by
Leon Edel in 1949.* But behind this poor drama lay another
tormented Jamesian debacle. During the time of writing his hasty,
potboiling and unproduced plays he had written to his brother
William in high spirits. "I feel at last as if I had found my real
form, which I am capable of carrying far." He had even succeeded in instilling a similar excitement in the mind, and in the
Journal of Alice James, then in an English sanatorium, and Henry's closest confidante. What matter that his "light comedy," "Disengaged," based on a meretricious short story called "The Solution,"

---

* This volume is a useful scholarly enterprise — provided that one doesn't really
believe, as the editor of the volume wants to persuade us to believe, that James's plays
have any intrinsic literary or dramatic value. They don't; while, on the other hand,
his serious, nondramatic or nontheatrical, literary works do lend themselves surpris-
ingly well to theatrical adaptation — perhaps too well.

and rewritten for the actress Ada Rehan, was withdrawn after the rehearsal period? He pinned even more of his hopes on *Guy Domville*, a full-blown stage romance about a royal young Catholic hero, destined for holy orders, and inheriting a large fortune, who must take upon himself the moral responsibility of administering this great wealth in the worldly scene of the late eighteenth century. But failing in this "noble enterprise" (with which James undoubtedly identified his own sense of failure in the literary world), the revealing fantasy-hero of the play returns, in the third act, to a life of religious asceticism. The theme, the tone, the setting of *Guy Domville* were hardly conducive to its success. It was in fact a flat failure where the dramatist himself, as well as the drama, was hissed and booed from the stage.

What this meant in terms of James's private sensibility, not to mention his public vanity, or the crashing, amidst all the vulgar laughter, of his highest illusion of becoming a professional playwright, was revealed in his letter of January 9, 1895, to William. "Even now it's a sore trial to me to have to write about it — weary, bruised, sickened, disgusted as one is left by the intense, the cruel ordeal of a first night that — after the immense labour of preparation and the unspeakable tension of suspense — has, in a few brutal moments, not gone well:

In three words the delicate, picturesque, extremely human and extremely artistic little play was taken profanely by a brutal and ill-disposed gallery which had shown signs of malice prepense from the first and which, held in hand till the end, kicked up an infernal row at the fall of the curtain. There followed an abominable quarter of an hour during which all the forces of civilization in the house waged a battle of the most gallant, prolonged and sustained applause with the hoots and jeers and catcalls of the roughs, whose roars (like those of a cage of beasts at some infernal "zoo") were only exacerbated (as it were) by the conflict. It was a cheering scene, as you may imagine, for a nervous, sensitive, exhausted author to face — and you must spare my going over again the horrid hour, or those of disappointment and de-

pression that have followed it; from which last, however, I am rapidly and resolutely, thank God, emerging. The "papers" have, into the bargain, been mainly ill-natured and densely stupid and vulgar.

Were there curious accents of both a semi-paranoia and the most devout self-deception in this account of what amounted to a battle between civilization and the brute hordes of London theatergoers over the mangled corpse of *Guy Domville?* The only two dramatic critics who counted, so Henry assured William — W. Archer and Clement Scott — had done him more justice, while all *private* opinion was one of extreme admiration for his play. "I have been flooded with letters of the warmest protest and assurance . . . Everyone who was there has either written to me or come to see me — I mean everyone I know and many people I don't." Yet the Jamesian bitterness and hurt, the sense of a personal betrayal, and of a personal indignity, persisted. "Obviously the little play, which I strove to make as broad, as simple, as clear, as British in a word, as possible, is over the heads of the *usual* vulgar theatre-going London public." Wasn't that just the trouble — that this broad, simple, clear, little "British" play was patronizing and inept, esoteric in its theme, amateurish in tone; and obviously condescending to the usual "vulgar" theatergoing London public?

If so, Henry James never quite suggested this to his brother William, or, apparently, to himself. He affirmed his faith in himself while he lauded the misbegotten drama. "Don't worry about me: I'm a Rock. If the play has no life on the stage I shall publish it; it's altogether the best thing I've done." Yet he still brooded on the *external* causes of his defeat. "The thing fills me with horror for the abysmal vulgarity and brutality of the theatre and its regular public, which God knows I have had intensely even when working (from motives as 'pure' as pecuniary motives *can* be) against it . . . Doubtless, moreover, the want of a roaring actuality, simplified to a few big *familiar* effects, in my subject — an episode in the history of an old English Catholic family in the last century — militates against it, with all usual theatrical people, who don't want plays (from variety and nimbleness of fancy) of different *kinds*, like books and stories, but only of one kind, which their stiff, rudimentary, clumsily-working vision recognizes as the kind they've had before. And yet I had tried so to meet them! But you can't make a sow's ear out of a silk purse. — I can't write more — and don't ask for more details."

Thus the famous letter to William James, and the "details" were particularly unpleasant. According to H. G. Wells, who was present at the opening night of the play along with such other celebrities as Shaw and Arnold Bennett, the popular actor in the title role of *Guy Domville*, George Alexander, had deliberately exposed the play's author to the ridicule of the audience. "A spasm of hate for the writer of those fatal lines must surely have seized him. With incredible cruelty he led the doomed James, still not understanding clearly how things were with him, to the middle of the stage, and there the pit and gallery had him." F. W. Dupee's *Henry James* also correctly states that this was the worst moment of James's mature life. "His inward sufferings, his nightmare pursuers, were temporarily objectified in this scandalous scene — the kind of scene from which he had always sought to spare not only himself but his characters; for, courageous though he was in so many respects, a humiliation of this kind was for him the unspeakable."

Unspeakable. It was also the clue to the curious, eloquent, despairing entry in the *Notebooks* of January 23rd, 1895:

I take up my own old pen again — the pen of all my old unforgettable efforts and sacred struggles. To myself — today — I need say no more. Large and full and high the future still opens. It is now indeed that I may do the work of my life. And I will . . . I have only to face my problems . . . But all that is of the ineffable — too deep and pure for any utterance. Shrouded in sacred silence let it rest . . .

For one notices the almost religious dedication (and language) of the middle James to his own art now; the high resolve which surmounts and transcends the sacred silence — that silence which surrounds the failure, the debacle, the scandal of his visionary and misbegotten fantasy of wealth and fame on the stage.

But can you really *face* your problems, as James promised himself here, if you also shroud them in sacred silence; make them too deep and pure for any utterance? The process of the Jamesian "self-analysis" and the Jamesian "salvation" is interesting to follow.

For there was an element now of almost hysterical compulsion in his constant admonition to himself: "Produce again — produce; produce better than ever, and all will yet be well." And the point was that James, in his deepest heart, still clung, tenaciously, blindly, to his own immaculate vision of the stage. Conceding outrageous defeat, he would not concede his own failure. (In 1895, also, he wrote another play, "Summersoft," for Ellen Terry, who kept it, as James later wrote to Wells, "for three mortal years.") He was determined to salvage *something*, if only his wounded pride, from this humiliating theatrical experience; and what he actually brought forth from the catastrophe was his famous "literary principle" of the Dramatic Method or the Divine Scenario. Meditating upon his "large and confident action, splendid and supreme creation" (in terms of esthetic hyperbole, if not religio-esthetic exaltation, which also betray their uneasy psychological sources), and, as early as this, gathering his notes together for *The Wings of the Dove* and *The Golden Bowl*, James also made one of his most fantastical jottings in the *Notebooks* of that period. Everything about the idea of *The Golden Bowl*, he said, qualified it for a Harper's serial "except the subject — or rather, I mean, except the adulterine element *in* the subject. But may it not be simply a question of *handling* that? For God's sake let me try: I want to plunge into it. I *languish* so to get at an immediate creation . . .

"*Voyons, voyons*: may I not instantly sit down to a little close, clear, full scenario of it? As I ask myself the question, *with* the very asking of it, and the utterance of that word so charged with memories and pains, something seems to open out before me, and at the same time to press upon me with an extraordinary tenderness of embrace. Compensations and solutions seem to stand there with open arms for me — and something of the 'meaning' to come to me of past bitterness, of recent bitterness that otherwise has seemed a mere sickening, unflavoured draught. Has a *part* of all this wasted passion and squandered time (of the last 5 years) been simply the precious lesson, taught me in that roundabout and devious, that cruelly expensive way, *of the singular value for a narrative plan too* of the (I don't know *what* adequately to call it) divine principle of the Scenario? If that *has* been one side of the moral of the whole unspeakable, the whole tragic experience, I almost bless the pangs and the pains and the miseries of it. IF there has lurked in the central core of it this exquisite truth — I almost hold my breath with suspense as I try to formulate it; so much, so *much*, hangs radiantly there as depending on it — this exquisite truth that what I call the divine principle in question is a key that, working in the same *general* way fits the complicated chambers of *both* the dramatic and the narrative lock: IF, I say, I have crept round through long apparent barrenness, through suffering and sadness intolerable to that rare perception — why my infinite little loss is converted into an almost infinite little gain. The long figuring out, the patient, passionate little *cahier*, becomes the *mot de l'énigme*, the thing to live by. Let me commemorate here, in this manner, such a portentous little discovery, the discovery, probably, of a truth of real value even if I exaggerate, as I daresay I do, its *partée*, its magicality. Now something of those qualities in it vivifies, backwardly — or appears to, a little — all the horrors that one has been through, all the thankless faith, the unblessed work. But how much of the precious there may be in it I can only tell by trying . . ."

Such was the origin, too, of another self-admonition which James was to use almost compulsively or ritualistically, in his later period. "Dramatize! Dramatize! Dramatize!" — as if a novelist should not in his blood know this. But James meant this in a very special way. And here surely was the vocabulary, the tone, the mood, the personal source and ideological framework — the *meaning* (if I dare use *another* italicized word) of what was to become most typically Jamesian in the later period of this enigmatic artist. Now this celebrated esthetic "discovery" of James's, this intense, absolute, exalted application of the "dramatic method" to the older, the familiar, narrative form of the novel — was it really the key to modern fiction as the Jacobite cult has claimed? (And how many "academic novels" are turned out each year, based on this false principle which is in effect a detective story of the intellect, or a murder mystery of the heart!) Or was this exalted and hushed Jamesian "discovery," however portentous you like, simply a kind of personal salvation for the wounded and defeated Jamesian ego? A magical catharsis indeed for the blows incurred in his own theatrical failure, just as the Jamesian art itself was now to become a kind of religio-esthetic "transcendence" for the deep defeat (as he believed, at least) of his whole literary career to this point.

These are the questions — like James's "precious little theory" which he could only answer by testing — which are to dominate his later career, and his so-called Major Phase. But there is no doubt that the "crisis of the drama," this traumatic experience with the stage, was the turning point in his mature career; and that in his own way James would now use, or rationalize, what was almost a fatal tragedy — or even worse for this sensitive psyche, a lurid debacle — for his own esoteric literary purposes. From here came not only his "religion of art," as I say, but the studies of all the defeated "masters" in the literary craft; and the whole chain of often brilliant, nightmarish, or quite mad stories of human frustration in general.

During these years too — as another reaction to the failure of his long social novels, such as they were; and then to the flat failure of his plays — James had become absorbed in the long short story, in the manner for him mainly of Turgenev's "small, full perfect things." This wish and dream, he had said even at the start of the 1890's, had grown stronger than ever in him: "the desire that the literary heritage, such as it is, poor thing, that I may leave, shall consist of a large number of perfect *short* things, *nouvelles* and tales," which were to be "fine, rare, strong, wise — eventually perhaps even recognized." After the crisis of the stage James was to have an even more intense, exalted worship of "the beautiful and blest nouvelle" — and here indeed he was to do perhaps his best and most memorable work.

5. Terminations — and "Reconstruction"

THE TITLE of James's next volume of tales in 1895 was significant: *Terminations*. And the four best stories in the collection were dramatic projections of a single state of mind. Failure, death, the irony of popular success, the farce-tragedy of "outcast genius"; these were the themes which James now developed, and this was the brooding preoccupation, whether presented as tragedy or comedy, of Henry James himself at the nadir (so he felt) of his own career.

"The Death of the Lion" was the parable of a neglected writer who is suddenly elevated into "fame" by the popular press. Again the story's design was that of the lonely master and the adoring, self-abnegating disciple — ranged against the fickle "outside world" of society. (A central Jamesian theme which was later on to encourage the charmed circle of Jamesian cultists upon whose lips nothing could be discerned but reverent praise for *their* outcast master.) But here the neglected Neil Paraday was resigned to defeat, illness and obscurity. He is even content to live without the services of a butler — that is to say, he has only a timorous parlormaid about his "modest mahogany."

His journalistic disciple (who in this typical Jamesian pattern has abandoned his own career in order to pay homage to the arts) accompanies the great writer to the British estate of "Prestidge" just at the moment that Paraday suddenly becomes "proclaimed" and "anointed" by the popular press in what was now, in James's

own England, "this horrible age." The conscience of these people — meaning the "modern" and fashionable British nobility —
"is like a summer sea." Thus Paraday's newest manuscript is lost
because it has been handed by somebody's butler to somebody
else's personal maid. And when the Master himself, in the midst
of his new "fame," lies neglected and ill (the dying "lion") because two newer celebrities have replaced him on this callous social
stage, there is another colloquy, almost sacred in tone, between
the artist and the faithful disciple. "It would have been a glorious
book," says the disciple. "It *is* a glorious book," says Neil Paraday,
reproachfully. "Print it as it stands — beautifully." " 'Beautifully!'
I passionately promised."

This was the baroque estheticism of the Jamesian "religion of
art." And one notices the narrow-based, ego-centered and somewhat martyred tone of this Jamesian critique both of the "modern
age" and the modern press. In America, a rising generation of
realists were to attack the "free press," hardly so much for its de-
grading treatment of "art" as for its broader social failure: its bias
and its moral corruption in dealing with unpopular ideas and
causes in the labor wars of the period, or with the radical dissent
against a primitive and inhuman stage of finance capitalism. That
was a critique which went much deeper, and was far less personal
than James's, whose "modern age" had only become so horrible
after he himself had been rejected and "defamed" by it in both his
fiction and his plays.

Immured in the sanctity of the pure art which James now
stressed were, all too obviously, the sour grapes of his own sense
of failure. The goal of fame and of literary "success," which he
was now satirizing and parodying, was just the goal which he had
patently yearned for. It was the wounded vanity of the defeated
novelist, of the frustrated and rejected dramatist, which was at
the center of this "social criticism"; just as the typical form of these
art tales, the reverent and adoring worship of the Master by the
dedicated disciple, revealed certain oedipal and perhaps homosex-

ual components. And then there was James's curious notion of
what literary failure, obscurity, and "poverty" really meant! In
part "The Death of the Lion" was an entertaining kind of satire.
But how could it possibly be the "minor classic" which contemporary Jacobite criticism has proclaimed it to be?

The group of English society people who adored "culture" at the
typical great country house of Prestidge (the visionary English castle
of the earlier Jamesian fantasy) were particularly well done. But
did their literary lion of the moment have to die in the story?
Did their fickle and flittering adoration really have to destroy him,
as James envisioned the plot in his notes? The ending was too
heavy a blow for what was essentially social comedy; just as there
was both sentimentality and melodrama in another "famous"
story in *Terminations*. In a more serious vein, indeed, "The Altar
of the Dead" has received even more fervent praise from the circle
of Jamesian critics. The story's title had come to its author in
1894, along with the idea of a hero who really respects and worships the dead. Here was another rebuke to the modern age, where
even these dead "are forgotten, are unhallowed — unhonored, neglected, shoved out of sight." James lamented the rudeness and
coldness which, he felt, surrounded their memories; while *his* hero
sets up a spiritual altar in a convenient church, where are in-
stalled the burning candles which mark his own departed friends.
"The essence of his religion is really to make and keep such a
place." And the altar is not to be completed until his own taper
is lighted there.

Now that was a conceit, of course, a tricky fantasy, as James
realized; while, to complicate the plot, he added a heroine of sorts
who joined Stransom in his private worship; and then he added an
even more improbable trick ending to the story. What was clear
about this rather lugubrious parable of candle-worshiping was simply that it was another psychic projection of James's own dark
mood of these years. Or of his sense of a living death, where he,
too, was forgotten, unhallowed; dishonored, neglected — where

he was, therefore, raising his own private shrine as a public rebuke. This was another esthetic death fantasy, complete with its semi-Catholic decor, to mark his own neglected literary career, and this time the artistic projection was more revealing than effective. And what is curious is the solemnity of tone, not merely in the story, but in the later criticism of it.

According to Matthiessen and Murdock, for example, the puzzling thing was only that in James's *Notebooks* he appears to have thought of the story as slight and empty. (He was right.) "Possibly the passage represents no more than a momentary discouragement," these critics say. "Certainly his inclusion of it as a title-story to a volume in the New York edition, and his preface to it, suggest no dissatisfaction, and it has often been counted among the best of his tales." Has it been? That is just the point. In sober fact, it is among the weakest of the Jamesian stories.

Yet even such a peripheral Jamesian critic as Clifton Fadiman (standing on the edge of the charmed circle, and, rather cautiously, bowing to its edicts) selected the same story for its "cultural criticism." "Of all the short stories of Henry James, 'The Altar of the Dead' administers the quietest and gravest rebuke to whatever is spurious, whatever is quotidian, whatever is vulgar, in the reigning taste of our time." Tut-tut. You almost begin to believe such unanimity of contemporary criticism — until you read "The Altar of the Dead" again. No, this is a complete hoax of so-called Jamesian criticism, which James himself, who evaluated the story more correctly, might have used as the germ of another satiric fable on literary vogues.

There is firmer ground for critical praise in the two last and best stories in *Terminations*. The theme of "The Middle Years" was also that of failure and spiritual crisis. "The idea of the old artist," so James wrote in his notes, "who, at the end, feels a kind of anguish of desire for a respite, a prolongation — another period of life to do the *real* thing that he has in him — the things for which all the others have been but a slow preparation." Now again the story was highly personal in origins, but the emotions were both felt and projected. The central figure of Dencombe, the melancholy and defeated writer, was a sympathetic one, and here were some of James's most eloquent statements on the bitter illusions of life. The dying writer is "happy in the conceit of reasserted strength." He was better, he thinks, but "better," after all, than what? "He should never again, as at one or two great moments of the past, be better than himself. The infinite of life was gone, and what remained of the dose was a small glass scored like a thermometer by the apothecary. He sat and stared at the sea, which appeared all surface and twinkle, far shallower than the spirit of man. It was the abyss of human illusion that was the real, the tideless deep."

Beautiful lines; and a familiar disenchantment which appears in the work of almost all writers, famous or neglected alike, who have penetrated close to the meaning of life.* (And we shall compare this fine statement of middle-aged melancholia to the almost euphoric "ecstasy" of the still later, or the late-late James.) Dencombe, in fact, fingering the cover of his latest volume, is conscious of a strange alienation. "He had forgotten what his book was about." He is overcome by the sense of ebbing time, of shrinking opportunity. "He had done all he should ever do, and yet he hadn't done what he wanted." And then: "Illness and age rose before him like spectres with pitiless eyes: how was he to bribe such fates to give him the second chance? He had had the one chance that all men have — he had had the chance of life."

Yet even this Jamesian parable of human frustration is impaired by the narrow base of the artistic desire and the almost rigid form of its expression. "The Middle Years" was cast again in the

* See, for example, Dreiser's lament in the short story "Chains." "There is something cruel and evil in it all, in all wealth, all ambition, in love of fame — too cruel." Or see Scott Fitzgerald's "Babylon Revisited" for an elegy on all the false hopes of the past. Or note Willa Cather's comment, in *The Song of the Lark*, that "the unexpected favors of fortune, no matter how dazzling" can never compensate for the loss of those things "which in some way met our original want."

mold of master and disciple; or the familiar neglected master, the solitary, "discriminating" and worshipful disciple. In this case, too, it is a medical or "scientific" disciple; a young doctor who rather implausibly abandons his other patients, his whole medical career, even his hope of wealth, for the sake of the dying Dencombe. There is the same religio-esthetic tone. "This servant of his altar had all the new learning in science and all the old reverence in faith." There is the same fairy-tale quality in this tale of worldly despair, right down to the language of the story and the imagery. For the dying writer finds his last strain of eloquence in pleading the cause of "a certain splendid 'last manner,' the very citadel, as it would prove, of his reputation, the stronghold into which his real treasure would be gathered." While his disciple gives up his morning to listening, and even the ocean is described as "ostensibly waiting," the Jamesian artist-hero has "a wondrous explanatory hour."

Even for himself he was inspired as he told what his treasure would consist of; the precious metals he would dig from the mine, the jewels rare, strings of pearls he would hang between the columns of his temple.

And Doctor Hugh, in turn, assures the fatally ill but still entranced artist that the very pages he has just published "were already encrusted with gems."

Now these citadels, strongholds, and treasures, which are revealed in these wondrous "explanatory hours" while Nature herself waits in homage; this whole storehouse of precious metals, and rare jewels, strings of pearls, temple columns or relatively simple "gems" — this is to become a familiar mode of expression in the later James. It is almost as though, in the face of an increasingly oppressive reality, he had returned even more directly to the fairy-tale romances of his childhood — and had encrusted, or armored, his fantasy with such infantile images. Towards the close of "The Middle Years," there are scenes where the tragic Dencombe be-

comes almost insufferable, and the adoring scientific disciple intolerable, as well as implausible. We begin to suspect that even the
earlier statements about life's disappointments are confined to an
esthetic frame. Or rather, they are statements about the art which
James had now almost completely identified with life; while life itself is viewed as only the "gathering of materials" for the sake of
art. The "gathering" is more important than the living, in the
Jamesian view (as though living were not essential for gathering, as
though living was not gathering itself). And again, Dencombe's
deepest regret is not even for his art, purely, but for his lost reputation, his missed "position," his ebbing literary fame! Admirable as
is "The Middle Years" in its own genre, it *is* that genre, rather
than a transcendence of its type. It is still the Jamesian view of
human existence; it is the artistic life that is being hailed here,
rather than human experience. Moreover, as with the best of
James's work, the story was a curious mixture of reality and illusion, of knowledge and fantasy; even while it projected, under the
guise of a common or universal truth, a curious set of half-truths
about life and art.

But the esthetic absolute, around which "The Middle Years"
was really centered, is a dangerous basis on which to gain any true
knowledge of human character or experience. Thus the celebrated
final quotation from this story —

*A second chance — that's the delusion. There never was to be but one.
We work in the dark — we do what we can — we give what we have.
Our doubt is our passion and our passion is our task.*

— even this eloquent statement, which should apply to the whole
vista of human experience, was qualified by its final line. "The rest
is the madness of art." For the true "rest," as our major writers
have always said, is the madness of *life*.

But here at least James had brought over his increasingly self-
enclosed, rigid, armored and quite authoritarian little esthetic king-

dom closer to the boundaries of that surrounding, and larger, more general and infinitely more complex universe of common humanity. Proclaimed as a "masterpiece" by the Jacobites, "The Middle Years" is *almost* a good story. And James, returning to the satiric vein in the final nouvelle in *Terminations*, projected another entertaining study of outcast genius. "The Coxon Fund" was a comedy-farce (where James met, on a certain level, the best vein of Edith Wharton's work) of English society and the "Coleridge-type" of eccentricity. The nefarious hero, Saltram, comes from a Dissenter background. He has deserted his wife, he drinks heavily, he accepts all favors, loans, sacrifices as his due. He has had several "natural children" in his wanton youth, and his only solid achievement is that of brilliant conversation. But in such talk he is like "a great suspended shining crystal — huge, lucid, lustrous, a block of light flashing back every impression of life and every possibility of thought." The question is: does he really deserve the financial support of the Coxon Fund which is being raised for him?

There is again the familiar Jamesian stress on "good conversation," as the highest accomplishment or achievement of civilization — but the story's stress is satiric. The scoundrelly Saltram; his virtuous and abandoned wife; the surrounding cast of British socialites and the "good" young American heroine; the whole question of raising the Coxon Fund for this great, neglected philosopher-artist who is utterly unworthy of it — all this is excellently done. Here indeed James was reaching out towards the confines of the eccentric, the mad, the illegitimate, even the fraudulent aspects of "genius" in a new vein which also derived, no doubt, from his own sense of the "massive monstrous failure" at the midpoint of his own life and career.

"You'd like to see that scoundrel publicly glorified — perched on the pedestal of a great complimentary pension?" asks the solemn politician Gravener in "The Coxon Fund." "I braced myself," says the ironical narrator of the tale. And: "Taking one form of public recognition with another, it seems to me on the whole I should be able to bear it. When I see the compliments that *are* paid right and left I ask myself why this one shouldn't take its course." And here the Jamesian self-revelation — which is ultimately what James's art consisted of — was really objectified enough, was "dramatized" correctly, and directed outward into an entertaining parable. A year later, *Embarrassments,* in 1896 — though mainly a selection of lighter things — also contained stories of both personal and esthetic interest.

The best-known of these, "The Figure in the Carpet," was written in the same ironical, ambivalent tone as "The Coxon Fund." The plot involved another great artist (neglected, misunderstood again) who confides the "secret" of his work to a friendly critic — or, that is, he discloses the fact that there *is* a secret pattern in his work. The critic-narrator of the story then confides this "secret" — or the secret of the secret — to another young friend, who in turn reveals it, or the fact that he has "discovered" the secret pattern, to the young woman whom he marries. This "revelation" occurs shortly before his own death; and the original narrator, who has never learned the "secret," is driven by his compulsive curiosity almost to the point of marrying the widow of his young friend in order to find out the "truth" of the matter. Do you follow this so far? And wasn't this another perfect example of the Jamesian tease-technique? Well now, still another critic — and this was a world of Jamesian critics! — marries the bereaved "heroine" who, however, never does reveal the "secret" to her new husband; as the original narrator discovers at the story's end, through his persistent, indignant, and frustrated questioning, or inquisition, of the second husband. How far can you go with such twists on a theme; and was there indeed any "secret" at all to be discovered — and if so, was it worth all this exotic, involved exposition; and all the tormented existence on the part of these singular figures who are created, apparently, only to fill out *their* roles in James's own figure in the carpet?

This was a kind of intellectual voyeurism prolonged and rampant. And the original narrator — obsessive and obsessed, to the

point of a controlled mania; determined to discover the "truth" by
fair or foul means; a truth that may or may not exist; or that may
be imagined by the narrator himself — this singular Jamesian
hero goes back of course to the "scholar" of "The Aspern Papers"
(not to mention the prying dramatist of "The Private Life") and
forward to a whole series of similar "observers" whose intellectual
curiosity will reach a point of emotional pathology in seeking for a
"knowledge" which is always dubious, shifting, evasive, or non-
existent. "The Figure in the Carpet" was a beautiful take-off on
this type of mental activity; a story that, however, betrayed a curious kind of mental sadism, through which all the central characters, the whole fabric of their lives and relations, are really sacrificed to the series of ingenious Jamesian "twists." "For the few
persons, abnormal or not," said the later James of the Prefaces,
"with whom my anecdote is concerned, literature was a game of
skill, and skill meant courage, and courage meant honour, and
honour meant passion, meant life." But wasn't this a resounding
moral for what was at best a *jeu d'esprit* — just as a whole generation of later Jamesian critics followed the Master's verdict on this
story, rather than the story itself?

Now of course literary critics like stories about literary critics.
But just how do you proceed from "a game of skill," through courage, honor, passion, and the rest, to "life" — which, like serious
literature itself, is certainly not a "game" in the Jamesian sense?
One almost suspects that the later James, like the alienated artist
of "The Middle Years," had forgotten what his own story was
about. Yet among the modern Jacobites, Matthiessen and Murdock (*The Notebooks*) affirm that "The Figure in the Carpet" was
an ironic protest against the general numbness of Anglo-American
sensibility. "Through Hugh Vereker's plea for perception of the
animating design of his work James again took his stand against 'our
so marked collective mistrust of anything like close or analytic appreciation.' His own prefaces were to be his ripest demonstration
of the value of such analysis."

These Jamesian disciples have become even more pontifical, orotund and pretentious than the Master himself. We have already noticed the kind of "analysis" — or sublime rationalization — which
is at the core of the Jamesian Prefaces; and there is more of this
to come. But wasn't the real point of "The Figure in the Carpet"
precisely in the story's original ambiguity which also stressed the
almost pathological frustration (which James again coyly admitted
in his "few persons . . . abnormal or not") of the demonic search
for all such "animating designs"? This particular fable can be
used either as an argument for "close analytical appreciation" —
or more likely against it. It is an ironic little parable of intellectual
morbidity which hardly deserves, and was certainly never intended
to gain, the solemn moralizing of the late James himself or the
Jacobite cult.

Among the other stories in *Embarrassments* (and the title of
the volume indicated the prevailing tone of its fiction) "The Next
Time" was another entertaining satire about a writer who couldn't
descend, though he tried, to the level of "vulgar popular success";
to which James added the countertheme of a highly successful lady
fictionist who craved only to be "an exquisite failure." The personal sources of this story were obvious again; and here too the
"blighting critic" — a role which James took on after what he
presumed to be the popular failure of his fiction — was the familiar
observer-narrator of the story. "The worst he could ever contrive,"
said James or his spokesman about the "condemned artist" Ralph
Limbert, "was a shameless merciless masterpiece." And this fancy
of a talent inaccessible to vulgarity, popularity, or corruption,
while unfortunately not true either in life or in Henry James's own
career, made a pretty tale.

There are indeed passages of farce and satire in "The Next
Time" which almost bring this story up to the level of "The Figure
in the Carpet" in the Jamesian vein of social comedy. And certainly
these nouvelles or stories were far superior to the play-novel, *The
Other House*, in 1896, upon which James again lavished so much

of his time and talent, and the still-recurrent, and never-quite-to-be-relinquished hope of his own theatrical success and fame.

"Ah, divine principle of the 'scenario'! — it seems to make that wretched little past of patience and pain glow with meaning I've waited for!" So James had written about the final story in *Embarrassments.** But if he had carried over the techniques of stage writing to literature, he was still unable to bring over literature to his stage dramas as such. Unlike the writer-hero of "The Next Time," James could indeed, consciously or not, debase his art to what he thought was the level of the popular play. If he was now beginning to concentrate on the "drama of consciousness" in his serious work, his theatrical writing constituted something close to the melodrama of consciousness.

In a sense the stage dramas of James are most revealing. They illustrate the lowest levels of his literary work where his prevailing values are most clearly shown: the fairy-tale base, the histrionic finale. They are the worst that James could do, and did do; and in a curious way they humanize all the Jamesian metaphysical and esthetic theorizing, which was to such a large degree also an elaborate intellectual process of apology, evasion, and self-glorification under the guise of "analysis." Even the prose of *The Other House* was wooden, and reminiscent of the Victorian romances which James had read in earliest youth, or in childhood, and from which so many of his notions about "life" and "art" were drawn. (There were also Shakespearian echoes, solemnly commented on by the scholars, such as "Hark ye!" along with Exits and Exeunts.) All the famous Jamesian standards of criticism were in abeyance here, and what came through was simply the glittering

---

* This story, "The Friends of the Friends," was an odd melodrama of the supernatural which involved the heroine's passionate and destructive jealousy of her dead friend who, so she is convinced, is meeting her own fiancé daily, or nightly. While the plot is deliberately implausible, the study of the heroine's hysterical emotions is impressive — and James was now beginning to identify himself with these sexually frustrated, hysterical, destructive feminine types, as a sequel to — or a natural development of — his earlier heroines.

world of theatrical make-believe, of popular success and cash: a stage world which also objectified James's deepest psychological strain of voyeurism or exhibitionism in most unsatisfactory literary terms. Perhaps the *New York Journal* of the time was close to the truth, for once, in headlining "Henry James's New Novel of Morality and Crime: The Surprising Plunge of the Great Novelist into the Field of Sensational Fiction."

But what was remarkable in the farcico-pathetic tragicomedy of Henry James and the stage was the depth and intensity of his persistent and obsessive illusion about his own stage dramas. As late as 1910, quite oblivious to the inferior quality of his play-novel, he could still exclaim in the *Notebooks*: "Oh, blest *Other House*, which gives me thus at every step a precedent, a support, a divine little light to walk by . . ." It was this Jamesian illusion, so obvious, so meretricious, which lay behind his fatal adaptation of the "dramatic method" to the narrative form. And surely this was a supreme and shining example of the most devout and intense kind of rationalizing. It illustrated the determination, above all, of this artist's wounded and frustrated vanity, ego, or self-image, not indeed to learn from past errors, but to extol and exalt those errors, those failures, those shameful disgraces, into the most sacred kind of "success." For James later revised the fictional form of *The Other House* into yet another play, which hardly fared any better; and this still-recurrent crisis of the stage was the background for the nouvelle of the period called *The Spoils of Poynton*, in 1897.

This story, too, was written in play form, in three acts, as though it could be diverted, easily, into either literary form; as though it were a "secret play," which might be snatched from between the book covers by some discerning and ambitious stage producer. (Among the series of later writers who tried the same literary device, it was John Steinbeck who best proved, in the 1950's, that it couldn't be done; and perhaps the basic form of the play-novel, uneasy, ambivalent, double-focused, or, as it were, literarily cross-eyed, was fatal in itself.) Among James's nouvelles, at least, *The Spoils* was one of the poorest things he wrote. Starting out as a parlor comedy, ending as a moral sermon; ambulatory and tedious in its development; divided in its technical focus, with one eye on its material and the other on the stage "effect," it was also based on an improbable conceit — and a conceit or a plot which made all the personages and relationships of the story possess a dubious value.

And yet — once again — there is nothing in the whole circle of Jamesian criticism in the United States during the 1940's and '50's to suggest this fundamental flaw. *The Spoils of Poynton* has become instead another "rediscovered" and "famous" Jamesian nouvelle, much argued about and over as to its levels of meaning, its "symbolism." Right here indeed, on a relatively — I mean definitely — minor work, the Jacobite commentary reaches some kind of peculiar apogee of indiscriminate praise, and laudatory unctuousness.

Much is made, for example, of the point that old Mrs. Gereth's delight in "fine things," her collecting mania, around which the story's plot is based, is an example not of greed, but of "good taste." The Jamesian exposition of this theme is contrasted with Balzac's — as though greed, a major emotion in literature, were vulgar; and "good taste," a minor virtue, was a superior theme for a novelist. The story derived from "a small and ugly anecdote" which James had heard one evening at dinner at Lady Lindsay's about the "situation of a mother deposed," under English law, by a son who had married an obnoxious wife. James then emphasized, so we are told, how the "first tiny prick" of suggestion was all that the imagination needed. "He made his well-known discrimination between life 'being all inclusion and confusion, and art being all discrimination and selection.'" For his purposes, we are very solemnly told, "the conclusion to his companion's anecdote was both clumsy and sordid, another 'full demonstration of the fatal futility of Fact.'" (The companion was a certain Mrs. Anstruther

Thompson; the sources of James's anecdotes were carefully stated in his *Notebooks*, as though the more elevated the source the better the story.) But what Messrs. Murdock and Matthiessen do not say here is that, while the capacity to create an illusion is a writer's first requisite, the *nature* of that illusion is all-important. The highest literary illusions — those that affect us most directly and profoundly — are also those which contain the highest degree of lived and acknowledged human experience, and which therefore must also contain a large element of "fatal or futile fact."

What else indeed is life really made of; and what else is great literature but shared life? And how, really, could such eminent critics as F. O. Matthiessen and Kenneth B. Murdock accept this outrageous Jamesian precept of the immaculate vision; or, let us say the immaculate perception? We are told, moreover, that the Fleda Vetch of *Poynton* is one of James's best embodiments of "imagination, taste and renouncing sensibility" — and that is precisely what is the matter with this heroine. She is all imagination and taste, and very little of a person. As a sort of governess-companion to Mrs. Gereth, she is not only "without property" (a prime Jamesian sin) but also — as her name indicates — she comes from a lower middle class background. Miss Vetch (Vetch; vegetable?) has little of the charm with which James usually endowed his aristocratic or semi-aristocratic heroines. She is, for this writer, a kind of proletarian figure; and if James endowed her, belatedly, with a superior moral consciousness, he neglected, for three quarters of the story, to establish her as a woman. And that "renouncing sensibility," all scruples, qualms, and fastidiousness, hardly made her more so.

One notices also in the later preface to this story the familiar Jamesian vocabulary of the artistic parlor sport. There is "the little law under which my story was to be told." Or "the nobler parts of our amusement." Or "my prime loyalty was to the interest of the game." Or "the very flower of the performance" (another semi-theatrical phrase), or "the real fun of the thing . . ." And so on. So how could a reputable and distinguished early student of James, Joseph Warren Beach, come to the conclusion that "For swift, unhalting, onward movement, there is nothing in James — there is perhaps nothing anywhere — like 'The Spoils of Poynton' "? This could perhaps be said about "The Aspern Papers." It might be said, in a sense, about "The Turn of the Screw" — though James was never noted for swift, unhalting, onward movement even in his most melodramatic pieces. (Perhaps the single virtue of his "dramatic method" was that it imposed a kind of artificial form upon the natural garrulity of his narratives — his tendency always to expand, develop, reverse or qualify his plot line: to add still another twist.) One can only come to the conclusion that these Jamesian critics have become self-intoxicated with the incense of James's art; or they are bewitched by the verbal legerdemain of the great magician.

It was another distinguished critic, R. P. Blackmur, who followed up this astonishing comment of Beach's by stressing the "economy" of the later James's work — an economy not indeed fitted for the stage, as Blackmur added. (An "economy" that I, for one, can find only in his deliberately contrived shortest short stories; an economy of plot or "effect" rather than of character illumination or of the realities of experience.) About *The Spoils of Poynton* directly, Mr. Blackmur does concede that "James was uncertain of his intention." The first hundred pages are drawing-room comedy in which everybody, even the heroine, is seen pretty much as a type or character part. "The thing reads like a well-made novel trying to be a well-made play about trifles, about manners, with the men and women left out."

An "economy," that is — or a "swift, unhalting, onward movement" — in which the first hundred pages of the play-novel get nowhere at all; and are, apparently, to be dismissed! But there too is a familiar and disarming trait of the Jacobite cult — that of making a critical concession to the obvious truth about the literary work — or a critical feint — which serves only as a pretext for seizing upon the hidden splendors of all these Jamesian masterworks.

Now F. W. Dupee, by contrast, doesn't accept Blackmur's classification of Mrs. Gereth as "a witch," or the wastage of Fleda's "indestructible human goodness" under the "open vampirage of unspecified evil." Mrs. Gereth, says Dupee, is only "a persuasive example of enlightened egotism," with much charm, force, and a "frank happy humorous habit of self-interest." Yet both critics agree that the burden of *The Spoils of Poynton* is perfectly clear. "To exercise the moral sense, as Fleda insists on doing," says Dupee, "is frankly to risk the loss of natural happiness, which is shown to depend on just the kind of compromises she refuses to make." As in James's next novel, "the disparity between exciting the moral sense and enjoying animal happiness" is the real subject. But why "animal" and not ordinary human happiness (that is, sensual pleasure), and what is the real moral of all this, except that Mrs. Gereth is a rather nasty old woman who treasures her possessions above her son, and who tries to manipulate Fleda and everybody else around her? Or that Owen Gereth himself — half in love with Fleda, but put off rather naturally by her succession of qualms, compunctions, moral scruples and lofty stipulations — finally succumbs to Mona Brigstock: a woman who knows what she wants and uses her feminine charms, or her physical vitality, to get both the man and the property?

That could be the real point of *The Spoils of Poynton*, if it were seen, let's say, through the naturalistic realism of Dreiser — and with the addition that the play, or the nouvelle, as it stands, is hardly worth the attention of a first-rank artist. For Fleda's "human goodness" is about all she has. A brighter heroine would have seen her trap much sooner. A more forceful woman would have acted more directly, either to get out entirely, or to take over and control the situation which is dragging her down. If Fleda's "created conscience" is the Jamesian solution here, it is a conscience which is created by an almost disembodied woman; which is singularly unappealing when it is not downright tedious. And if

Fleda's "renunciation" is the final point of the nouvelle, it is that all too familiar Jamesian renunciation and flight when the demands of life become too intimate or too pressing. Both the Gereths and the Brigstocks of the story are equally vulgar and stupid, in plain fact. But Fleda herself, such a "good," humble, lower middle class heroine, is hardly much better, reminding us perhaps of the similarly "noble," conscience-stricken and self-destructive little bookbinding hero of *The Princess Casamassima*, where James had again descended into the "lower depths" of society for his central figure.

And what about the lurid fire at the close of the story, which destroys all the precious old things at Poynton in a highly moralistic way, even while it adds the final touch of melodrama to James's drama of moral sensibility? "It is quite fitting and right — it is poetic justice, it is the created justice of the free spirit," concludes the exuberant Mr. Blackmur, "that when Fleda is brought by a last temptation to redeem at Poynton, in symbol, some one of its spoils, at the very moment of her coming all the spoils should have been lost or saved in flame." To which lofty and moralistic rhetoric, one can only retort that perhaps Mrs. Gereth should have had a larger insurance policy — and that *The Spoils of Poynton*, considered artistically at least, is still a poor if not an absurd story. And to take one more point, consider the prose itself. "How came you to know my house?" says Fleda when Owen seeks her out in her own humble exile and refuge. "Ah, all the while you *cared*?" he cries when she is forced to acknowledge her love for him. "I cared, I cared, I cared!" she wails. "But you mustn't, you must never never ask! It isn't for us to talk about" — although there then ensues an interminable dialogue about their tragic plight. "You must leave me alone — for ever," Fleda proclaims finally. "For ever?" Owen gasps, while the reader is more likely to yawn.

That was the overtly romantic and "dramaturgic" expression for the type of renunciation scene that James could do far more eloquently in his serious work. *What Maisie Knew*, in the same year, also 1897, falls into the same class of "theatrical literature," but, for its illumination of the Jamesian psychology, is a far more interesting work than *The Spoils of Poynton*, which, if anything, was a dubious morality play about the perils of collecting *objets d'art*.

James was still brooding about the composition of the ill-fated *Guy Domville* when he was entertaining the first "germ" of *Maisie*, in 1892. ("He was the last *rejeton*," said he about Guy. "It was absolutely *necessary* for him to marry . . .") And then: "Surely if I attempt another comedy for Daly, and a 'big part' for A.R., as I see myself, rather vividly, foredoomed to do, the subject can only be (it is so designated, and imposed, by the finger of opportunity) the American woman in London society." By 1897, of course, these accents of infantine conceit — arrogant, fatuous, and mixed with a kind of pathetic innocence — had been altered somewhat. The "finger of opportunity" had inscribed a vivid chastisement upon the foredoomed playwright. Yet *Maisie* too was first conceived of as another play, based on a situation told to James by Mrs. Ashton — Mrs. (Lord) Bryce's sister — of a child divided by (or among) its divorced parents. In the case of this novel also, the surrounding paraphernalia of commentary — the Jamesian explication before, during and after the work — is almost as interesting as the literary work itself. James was thinking of some kind of sequel to "The Pupil" when he wrote: "Might not something be done with the idea of an odd and particular relation springing up 1st between the child and each of these new parents, 2d between one of the new parents and the other — through the child — over and on account of and by means of the child? Suppose the real parents die, etc. — then the new parents marry each other in order to take care of it, etc." His restless mind, playing with this plot situation, began to develop his "symmetrical set of complications," all with the innocent child in the midst.

In August, 1893, he added yet another twist to the subject of the *partagé* child and the divorced parents. "The little *donnée* will yield most, I think — most *ironic* effect . . . if I make the old parents, the original parents, *live*, not die, and transmit the little girl to the persons they each have married *en secondes noces.*" Still conjuring up his theme through these troubled years, he decided that for the sake of his symmetry, the second of the original parents should marry *again.* And then, working on the story for Henry Harland's *Yellow Book* in December, 1895, he reached the core of his concept. "*Voyons un peu* — what little drama *does* reside in it? — I catch it, I catch it: I seize the tail of the little latent action *qu'il recèle* . . . Make my point of view, my *line*, the consciousness, the dim, sweet, scared, wondering, clinging perception of the child . . ." And then came a Jamesian "scenario" of the story, covering every detail, every twist, possible in this already intricate plot, during the course of which the original story with eight or ten "little chapters" became thirty-one chapters in the novel.

Even so, only when he began to write, add the editors of *The Notebooks*, did he discover at last the real "essence" of his subject. "He was fascinated by the vision of the child's charm and innocence, which influenced the relations, often evil, of the other characters; and by the technical problem of presenting the whole through Maisie's consciousness, even when she was unable to understand the meaning of what she saw and heard." Was this really the theme of *What Maisie Knew* — difficult and perhaps even impossible as was the technical development? At least the later James of the Prefaces, as distinct from the earlier James of the Notes — and quite distinct also from the James who wrote the odd novel — supported the thesis, generally accepted, that the point of the story, as in *The Spoils of Poynton*, was the development of Maisie's "moral consciousness"; while her immaculate innocence pervaded a social environment of loose and evil sexuality. This tale was another instance, said the last and third Henry James, of the growth of a "great oak" from the little acorn. It was a tree that had spread beyond any provision which "its small germ might on a first handling have appeared likely to make for it." He stressed the idea of the "wretched infant," practically disowned, "rebounding from racquet to racquet like a tennis-ball or a shuttlecock." Odd imagery, perhaps, for his child-heroine; nevertheless, as James added, even the earliest elements of the novel had possessed "the vague pictorial glow" which signified a living subject to the painter's consciousness. "But the glimmer became intense as I proceeded to a further analysis."

Those Jamesian "glimmers" are always subject to the celebrated Jamesian process of "further analysis" — which, however, often omitted the ostensible subject of the "analysis," and avoided its real meaning. So here James rhapsodized over his own "further analysis" which he declared "is for that matter almost always the torch of rapture and victory, as the artist's firm hand grasps and plays it." It signified the artistic delight which is naturally "the smothered rapture and the obscure victory, enjoyed and celebrated not in the street but before some innermost shrine." And what in the world *was* he talking about? More seriously, however, he was only using that somewhat comic religio-esthetic vocabulary (with its curiously sexual, and here perhaps almost masturbatic imagery) of the worst phase of his own "art" tales. But underneath all this exotic verbiage, James finally declared that the real theme of *What Maisie Knew* — was Maisie herself:

To live with all intensity and perplexity and felicity in its terrible mixed little world would thus be the part of my interesting small mortal; bringing people together who would at least be more correctly separate; keeping people separate who would be at least more correctly together; flourishing, to a degree, at the cost of many conventions and proprieties, even decencies; really keeping the torch of virtue alive in an air tending infinitely to smother it; really in short making confusion worse confounded by drawing some stray fragrance of an ideal across the scent of selfishness, by sowing on barren strands, through the mere fact of presence, the seed of the moral life.

Wonderful prose, isn't it; and this later James, again rhapsodizing so grandiloquently on what was in fact one of his weakest heroines, only revealed the self-infatuated and euphoric "self-critic" in his most rhetorical vein of self-praise and self-congratulation.

Because the Jamesian concept of Maisie's role in the novel would be a rather difficult proposition for any little girl; and this one hardly lives up to it. Yet among the later Jacobites, compare F. W. Dupee's rehearsal of James's own "vision" to the effect that Maisie Farange "is obliged to acquire a conscience at an age and under circumstances which make survival itself difficult." The universe of Maisie's elders, this same critic said, is "entirely propelled and disintegrated by passion." And when Maisie at last "knows" that she is "an instrument of badness" among these adults, she abandons them. But Mr. Dupee never really questions the validity of the Jamesian thesis, or the authenticity of its projection — or the real meaning of the story on a different level of interpretation, less noble than that of "moral awakening," but in its own way just as curious and interesting.

For the whole concept of an immaculate infantine "innocence" shining forth in the midst of all this adult "corruption" — and even redeeming it — was sentimental and implausible; and also highly questionable. In the story itself Maisie is another one of the improbable Jamesian infants who in fact serves mainly as a "voyeur-glass," so to speak, for the obliquely reflected sexual antics of her elders. There were still deeper levels of meaning beneath the resonant moralism of the novel, and the highly applauded "technique," which may explain James's real fascination with the theme of innocent girlhood hovering on the fringes of what he almost considered to be sexual perversion. Wasn't this heroine too, quite like the orphan prince in "The Pupil," another abandoned infant — an orphan princess surely — far superior to the adults who use her, exploit her, and even try (vainly) to corrupt her? Which indeed was the more personal or more profound of these closely intertwined themes in the depths of the Jamesian ego-psychology? There is the fantasy of disinheritance reaching back to his first tales of the American claimants to royal British titles — and property.

In another guise this is the fantasy of the orphan child who is exploited by his "evil" (or "false") parents. In another guise still, this is the same child-hero who hovers all innocently, or even sublimely, around the secret, mysterious, gay but inevitably corrupt world of adult "intimacy" — or sexuality. This last notion was the dominant one in *What Maisie Knew*, and that was why James, stressing his "ethical" approach, was so involved with the story.

And that technical virtuosity which he also kept stressing and admiring: wasn't it really another psychological screen for this child-heroine both to "know" and yet not to know all about the world of adult sexuality? (And perhaps not only for the novel's heroine; but for its author, too.) Thus the fantastic elaboration of James's "symmetrical relations" — the series of ever new "parents" who surround Maisie's innocence — was another method of increasing both her orphanhood and her sexual frustration. We shall see this theme developed in several Jamesian works of the nineties, culminating in the sexual ring-around-a-rosy of *The Sacred Fount*. Little wooden heroine that she is, Maisie herself, subjected to such an overwhelming burden of infantine virtue in the midst of such widening rings of adult "corruption" (and that is to say, of adult sexuality): poor little Maisie's chief trait is the systematic repression of her own intense curiosity. "Everything had something behind it: life was like a long, long corridor with rows of closed doors. She had learned that at these doors it was wise not to knock — this seemed to produce from within such sounds of derision." And thus the real world of "within," from behind those closed doors, the private and hidden and mysterious adult world of "intimacy" and gaiety, appears to be directed *against* — or it mocks at — the lonely, "good," innocent and outcast Jamesian infant.

The friendly, noisy little house of Miss Overmore, Maisie's first governess, comes to include Maisie's first father, Beale, in its circle of "lively gentlemen." Maisie's mother, the first Mrs. Farange, is about to be married to Sir Claude, while Beale Farange himself is the victim of Miss Overmore's "flushed beauty." (The tone of

What Maisie Knew is social comedy rather than tragedy, however, and James changed the original name of Maisie's parents — "Hurter" — as being perhaps too revealing.) "He's my husband, if you please," the former governess explains to the child-heroine, "and I'm his little wife. So *now* we'll see who's your little mother!" These are shifting, deceitful, confused images of parenthood indeed, in what was for James a kind of brutal and hard satire. And Maisie's new mother also carries with her that "clatter of gaiety" which again leaves the heroine with the impression which "from her earliest childhood, had built up in her the belief that grown-up time was the time of real amusement and above all of real intimacy."

This "intimacy," and this "amusement," always surrounding the exploited, bewildered, but ever curious and ever inquiring little Jamesian protagonist has now become an obsessional concept with the writer himself. In the novel there is the rather vicious battle of the ex-governess, or the "new mother," and the new governess, Mrs. Wix, whose implacable virtue is set against all this alluring but corrupt adult intimacy. But Sir Claude soon tires of the impossible Ida Farange — who also has *her* group of gay blades — and, following Beale's example, comes to join the circle of the second Mrs. Farange, whom Beale, by now, has also deserted. Do you follow? In this case it can be said that life could never imitate the intricate Jamesian art. The next twist in *What Maisie Knew* is the triangle repeated of Sir Claude, Mrs. Beale and Mrs. Wix; while Maisie is the wise but "impotent" child-observer, or child-victim, always pinning her hopes falsely on each new combination of impossible, and inevitably disappointing parental symbols. But this Jamesian duplication of the original triangle also reduces the central feeling of the play-novel almost to the level of a stage farce rather than a serious or tragic chronicle. (And wasn't James in fact still toying with this secondary use of the novel as a stage vehicle, almost to the point of making it the hidden *primary* purpose?)

Well, at least he was guilty of manipulating his innocent child-heroine for the sake of his own "moral," which becomes here mainly a series of more and more ingenious and intricate twists of the plot. Still another triangle, that of Sir Claude, Mrs. Wix and Maisie herself, becomes rather tedious; perhaps also James could only redeem his lagging narrative by a further series of improvisations, or by new sets of "step-parents." (But all these "parents," including the original Beale and Ida Farange, are actually viewed as wicked, selfish, sex-ridden stepparents.) Moreover, if all the vices and evils, as well as the pleasures of passion are continually suggested here, it was a curiously cold, artificial and abstract kind of sex which James described. In this series of impossible or fantastic love affairs, the true anguishes, or the true rewards, of physical love are never mentioned; and passion itself is never described, or felt either by the Jamesian characters or by the Jamesian reader of *What Maisie Knew*. There are only the continuous vistas of human selfishness, weakness and cruelty persistently revealed to the bright, hopeful, ever trusting and ever betrayed child-heroine.

What is left for her but the endless rebirth of illusion endlessly destroyed in this peculiar childhood state of a perpetual disenchantment, surrounded by all these shifting, transient, uncertain and falsely parental figures? Life is a series of desperate and cruel "jokes" for this infantine Maisie; of recurrently broken fantasies of a "good" parent — over which her pure love and her unquenchable innocence are still bound, by the plot line, to triumph. Even at the point where the child has become the victim of so many contrived and artificial disasters that it hardly matters any more, there is still another "revelation." "You know your mother loathes you, loathes you simply," Maisie is told by her "first father," Beale Farange — hardly a consoling explanation. But Beale is now being supported by his "brown Countess," while Ida is going around with a certain Mr. Tischbein who, we are to infer, is the worst Jew of all. We have reached the extremes of degradation in this Jamesian parlor-comedy world.

For Mrs. Wix also tells the child that both of her actual parents are now engaging in these horrid affairs simply for the sake of *money*. This is apparently the last recourse of the leisure-class protagonist — the worst blow of all; but anything perhaps is preferable to *working*. *What Maisie Knew* ends on the flat note of the cash payment for sex, rather than on the more venerable and respected, and earlier Jamesian chord of inherited wealth and love — or love renounced.

To this later James also, it almost appeared that Jews, Negroes and Lovers were the worst culprits in his *fin de siècle* scene of bohemian decadence. When Maisie hears the word "amour" in a French café, she asks the incorruptible and virginal Mrs. Wix: "Is it a crime?" — and one really wonders what James himself thought about it here. The "brown Countess" is described as "a clever frizzled poodle in a frill, or a dreadful human monkey in a spangled petticoat." (Is it possible that she is an *American* Negro?) Earlier in the novel, also, we have been introduced to another of Ida's rich friends, Mr. Perriam, who has a bald head, a black mustache, eyes like "polished little billiard globes," and a large diamond of dazzling luster. "He's quite my idea," says Mrs. Wix, "of a Heathen Jew." But he will be immensely rich. "On the death of his papa?" asks the bright little Maisie. "Dear no — nothing hereditary," answers the refined and well-informed governess. "I mean he has *made* a mass of money."

We see both the consequences of this modern scene, and its typical practitioners in the curious farrago-melange with which the "Faranges" of *What Maisie Knew* bring the novel to its close. False parents, cheap sex, hard cash. These were the combination of "modern values" through which Maisie's enchanted innocence was all imperturbably intended to shine — to illuminate, to redeem. But in fact this implausible little play-novel brought to the surface of James's art certain recessive traits in his own temperament which were to become dominant in his later work. The central action and the true meaning of this fiction indicate something very different, as you see, from the moralistic burden which both James and his later critics stressed so insistently. (Perhaps Henry had his own reasons, again, for obscuring the real point of *Maisie*.) And it was just this underlying psychological pattern which was to become almost a complex, an obsession, in the subsequent Jamesian fiction around the turn of the century.

6. The Outcast Child —
the Omnipotent Infant

So THE PHASE of the Jamesian "Reconstruction" after the Terminations of the nineties was rather curious in its inception, both in its reliance on the dramatic method in fiction as a personal salvation, or solace, for the disturbed and suffering Jamesian ego, and in its intimations of an even odder kind of "sexual breakthrough" for this previously inhibited, if not altogether constrained artist.

This was the background for *The Two Magics*, in 1898, which included the now famous "The Turn of the Screw" and the lesser known "Covering End." The second of these two nouvelles was simply the elaboration of the American-woman-in-England theme which James had thought of as a play for Daly and the actress Ada Rehan. He wrote the play (called "Summersoft," or "Mrs. Gracedew") and submitted it to Ellen Terry instead. The plot concerned a rich American widow who saved a beautiful old English estate by paying off its debts and then marrying the handsome if "radical" heir to the estate. Romantic and theatrical enough, perhaps, for the vulgarest member of the vulgar stage audience — perhaps *too* romantic and theatrical to be produced at all — and yet James then insisted upon turning the ill-fated play back into a long story. "I had simply to make up a deficit and take a small revanche," James said in his letter to Wells. "I couldn't wholly waste my labour"; although both in the stage drama and in the nouvelle itself, his vindication was as dubious as his labor.*

* "In the Cage" (1898), now also considered as an "important" and neglected work of James's, was another nouvelle about the postal-telegraph service in London

In his scenario for *What Maisie Knew* James was still possessed by the hysteria of the stage. The *Notebooks* are baroque if not bizarre in these details. Scribbling his lurid passages, James was the mad dramatist incarnate. "I realize — none too soon," he wrote, "that the *scenic* method is my absolute, my imperative, my *only* salvation." But why, why, why? one is tempted to ask in return; for such hysteria is catching. And we remember James's dominant comparison of literature to *painting*, and to the merely visual area; another limitation, arbitrarily, of the established novel form, which had always *included* the visual area, but was not restricted to it. Yet James continued: "The *march of an action* is the thing for me to, more and more, *attach* myself to: it is the only thing that really, for *me*, at least, will *produire* L'OEUVRE, and L'OEUVRE is, before God, what I'm going in for . . ." This was also the backdrop for what became the most celebrated mystery story, lurid and bizarre, in the Jamesian canon.

With "The Turn of the Screw," however, we enter another area of critical debate and controversy. What may be defined as the "Freudian sector" of the James critics has put forth the proposition — innovated by Edna Kenton, popularized by Edmund Wilson — that the "ghosts" in the tale are hallucinations in the mind of the hysterical governess, who is ostensibly a "good heroine," but in fact an evil woman. On the other hand, at the opposite extreme of Jamesian criticism, the royalist and reversionary New Critics have advanced the counterthesis that the ghosts are indubitably real; and that indeed, unless you believe in the reality of ghosts, you lack the proper sense of evil to appreciate Henry James at all.

The first proposition is plausible, but not true. The second is manifestly absurd, if you know the work and temperament of

---

where the "caged operator" becomes involved in the love affair of two members of the upper class set, and rescues their illicit romance through her zealous pursuit of a misplaced telegram. The plot was fabricated; the story is notable mainly for James's peculiar notions of the telegraph system and for the underlying pattern of voyeurism. The heroine, of lower middle class origins, *lives* in the telegrams she sends (and reads). Her triumph is that she "knows" all about the secret romances of the nobility whom she worships.

James; while in between these extremes a more balanced group of Jamesian commentators suggest still other possible interpretations of "The Turn of the Screw." But both in the *Notebooks* and in the later Prefaces James himself was curiously aloof and enigmatic about this work. "Note here," he wrote in January, 1895, "the ghost-story told me at Addington (evening of Thursday 10th) by the Archbishop of Canterbury . . . the story of the young children . . . left to the care of servants in an old country-house, through the death, presumably, of parents. The servants, wicked and depraved, corrupt and deprave the children; the children are bad, full of evil, to a sinister degree. The servants *die* . . . and their apparitions, figures, return to haunt the house *and* children, to whom they seem to beckon, whom they invite and solicit from across dangerous places . . . so that the children may destroy themselves, lose themselves, by responding, by getting into their power. So long as the children are kept from them, they are not lost; but they try and try and try, these evil presences, to get hold of them. It is a question of the children 'coming over to where they are.' "

That is actually the literal plot of "The Turn of the Screw," and on this basis Matthiessen and Murdock are quite correct in denying the Freudian fantasy which is supposed to be conjured up by the neurotic governess who is the outside observer of the events. F. W. Dupee also points out that in this "most celebrated of all James's ghost stories," those who stress the hallucinations of the sexually repressed governess point to only one "of the large possibilities" of the story. And another bright spirit in this charmed circle, Philip Rahv (in *The Great Short Novels of Henry James*), utters an even more resounding blast of the critic's trumpet:

For sheer measureless evil and horror there are very few tales in world literature that can compare with The Turn of the Screw.

Well, this is a very large claim indeed, and one which commits this otherwise severe commentator to further excesses of hyperbole.

Did James himself describe the tale as "an inferior, a merely *pictorial* subject and rather a shameless potboiler?" He was being deliberately reticent, says Mr. Rahv, because of the morbid sexuality of the story which he was concealing from "the prudishness of his Anglo-Saxon public." And: "It is the sexuality expressed through the machinery of the supernatural that makes for the overwhelming effect."

Now the overwhelming effect of "The Turn of the Screw," like its "measureless evil and horror," is a matter of opinion. And one wonders, incidentally, just why supernatural sexuality should be more effective than natural sex. What *is* supernatural sexuality? And are we really to take it seriously? Nevertheless, Rahv's central point is "that the 'badness' of the prowling demonic spirits is of an erotic nature is shown by everything we are allowed to learn about them"; and that to interpret the story "in terms of the *reality* of Peter Quint and Miss Jessel's 'badness' enables us to take it *as given*, and at the same time to take it as a study in abnormal psychology." This is a neat evasion of the central problem of esthetic judgment about "The Turn of the Screw," since to state that supernatural evil is "real" simply because it is "given" — that is to say, because the author framed the story in these terms — is to abrogate any true critical function. Why, for example, did James find it necessary to conceal the abnormal psychology of the story — either from his audience, or from himself — through the device of the supernatural? And can a story based on such a device achieve *any* place in world literature?

However, Mr. Rahv proceeds to accord to James a post-Freudian rather than a pre-Freudian status. "Attempts to explain away the ghosts are but a fallacy of rationalism," we are told — as though James himself were not the most rational of writers — far too much so! — and as though he had not deliberately employed the device of the "ghosts" as another sophisticated parlor trick in the magic game of literature. And besides, continues Mr. Rahv blithely, the Freudian thesis "is so elementary as to make the story less rather

than more interesting. It lets off, so to speak, too many of the
agents — the servants and the children." And so far as the intention of James in the story goes, "we should keep in mind that in
James we are always justified in assuming the maximum."

Are we, indeed? The last statement is a typical example of the
whole burden of the Jacobite commentary in the mid-century
United States, where "to assume the maximum" about *every* work
of Henry James's became the critical norm.

But James himself, in the later Prefaces, described "The Turn of
the Screw" purely in terms of the ghost-story genre; and he specifically repudiated the psychological ghost story which was being
developed in the nineties by such contemporaries as Edith Wharton and Howells:

*The new type indeed, the mere modern "psychical" case, washed clear
of all queerness as by exposure to a flowing laboratory tap . . . the new
type clearly promised little, for the more it was respectably certified, the
less it seemed of a nature to rouse the dear old sacred terror.*

That "dear old sacred terror," deliberately roused by this master
magician in his game of literature, is rather remote, isn't it, from
Mr. Rahv's "measureless evil and horror." And so, clearly, was
James opposed to the new "scientific psychology" of the period,
from which emerged the Freudian precepts themselves, and on the
periphery of which hovered the spiritualism and other mystic movements of the nineties that had followed the decline of established
religion, and that were attempting to combine all the dark magic of
human history with the new learning. In another recent contribution to the Freudian sector of the Jamesian criticism, Professor
Oscar Cargill argues that during Alice James's long illness in her
asylum and her home near Henry, James would certainly have studied
the psychological literature bearing on the subject; and that *this*
was the real background for "The Turn of the Screw."

An interesting speculation; with the exception that there is nothing in Alice James's *Journal* to indicate that she realized the psychological sources (which are patently there) of her illness. And that James himself again rejected the notion of psychic or psychological ghosts as being suited for an "action," and his story was "an action, desperately, or it was nothing." (That is, it was a plot story, a drama, or a melodrama.) Those "recorded and attested ghosts," said the later James of the Prefaces, "are in other words as little expressive, as little dramatic, above all, as little continuous and conscious and responsive, as is consistent with their taking the trouble — and an immense trouble they find it, we gather — to appear at all." Again and again indeed, before, during and after "The Turn of the Screw," James repudiated both the notion of actual ghosts and of psychological ghosts. What he was after was simply the old-fashioned ghosts, so to speak, of magical literature — those quite objective presences, or supernatural villains, as he said, to be construed in the vein of goblins, elves, imps or demons, as they were in the old trials for witchcraft.

He talked instead of the haunted children and the "prowling servile spirits" at the center of his sinister romance. They were *Jamesian* ghosts, all right, and right down to their inferior social status. And thus "The Turn of the Screw" was intended to be "a fairy tale pure and simple" — except indeed, so the later James added, as to its springing "not from an artless and measureless, but from a conscious and cultivated credulity." The story was "a piece of ingenuity pure and simple, of cold artistic calculation, an *amusette* to catch those not easily caught . . . the jaded, the disillusioned, the fastidious." And it was written as a purely commercial Christmas item for a popular magazine.

But then — is there an inference that all the modern Jacobite critics who proclaim the measureless evil and horror in the same story, and its place in world literature: do *they* belong to the ranks of "the jaded, the disillusioned, the fastidious" who have indeed elevated an *amusette* into another masterpiece? In this controversy between James himself and his contemporary cult, there is the familiar discrepancy between the witty, slippery and ambiguous artist and his devout and solemn disciples. Or, on the other hand, between the urbane, sophisticated, worldly mind of James himself, which had little concern with religious values other than their esthetic appeal, and less concern with "real" ghosts except as pawns in a literary game of make-believe — and those contemporary neo-theological critics, disillusioned and jaded indeed, who are currently attempting to re-establish our lost sense of evil, or of original sin, through obsolete religious or magical symbols. (As though there isn't a sufficiency of evil in the modern world, and a rich store of fresh and appalling symbolism of social inhumanity, without recourse to primitive, infantile or obsolete rituals for "explaining" this!)

Meanwhile it was quite clear that in James's own mind, Peter Quint and Miss Jessel were intended to be real figures in the story — "my hovering, prowling, blighting presences, my pair of abnormal agents," so he described them in familiar, even personal tones — and not mere figments of the governess's imagination. The peculiar interest of "The Turn of the Screw" comes from another source. For those most "charming" of the Jamesian infants in this tale, as they have been described — could they really have been so corrupt? (Perhaps this was the real reason James was reluctant to discuss the story; since he had been charged with "a monstrous emphasis . . . of all indecently expatiating" — or of breaking the Victorian taboo about the sexual innocence of children.) At the story's outset Master Miles has been sent home from school for an unspecified reason; but Mrs. Grose, the solid, sensible, earthy housekeeper — "grows" rather than "gross" — swears by his innocence. Yet despite the old-fashioned English charm of Bly itself, the nameless young governess still feels "that hush in which something gathers or crouches. The change was actually like the spring of a beast." (This was a familiar anxiety-dream symbol of James's, recurrent both in his life and in his stories.) Even after her first vision of Peter Quint, the governess still clings to the pu-

rity of the children, and particularly of Miles. "My conclusion
bloomed there with the real rose-flush of his innocence; he was only
too fine and fair for the little horrid, unclean school-world." But
the nature of this heroine's first view of the "apparition" has its
own interest.

"Was he a gentleman?" asks Mrs. Grose about the ghostly figure
of Peter Quint staring down from the tower (just as in *The Mysteries of Udolpho* and the other Gothic novels which James used as
a model). "I found I had no need to think. 'No,' " answers the
governess. (The servile prowler indeed wears no hat.) "He's tall,
active, erect," adds the governess, "but never — no, never! — a
gentleman," and Mrs. Grose recognizes him instantly. "A gentleman?" she gasps, confounded, stupefied, "a gentleman, *he?*" Peter
Quint has been in fact the master's valet, and now dead, wears the
master's clothes. He is and was indubitably a villain who has been
"too free" with young Master Miles. "It was Quint's own fancy,"
says Mrs. Grose, "to play with him, I mean — to spoil him." "Too
free with *my* boy?" says the indignant governess. "Too free with
everyone," says the housekeeper. And when the specter of Miss
Jessel appears before little Flora at "the Sea of Azof," we learn the
further details of the "crime" of these two evil spirits which is
apparently as heinous socially as it is sexually.

Miss Jessel was handsome, wonderfully handsome, but infamous.
"They were both infamous," says Mrs. Grose. "There was something between them?" asks the governess. "There was everything,"
says Mrs. Grose. "In spite of their difference— ?" "Oh, of their
rank, their condition . . . *She* was a lady." This was the governess's predecessor's true abasement ("and he so dreadfully below").
Although, poor woman, she paid for it, we are told, by her suicide
after her love affair with a base menial. The governess herself, in
her series of encounters with the ghosts, begins to beat down the
spirit of Peter Quint and to conquer him. But meanwhile she becomes possessed by the mystery of the "evil" in the children themselves — and the fatal fascination of the supernatural figures for

them — to the point that she hounds and pursues, spies upon, interrogates her small charges who all the while defeat and elude her, and keep their own secret. She is indeed like one of those fanatical inquisitioners seeking out sin, as in the old witch trials. She is herself almost witchlike, while the charming children, in their interlocked "sweetness," taunt her, and drive her to the edge of madness.

That was the central human situation in "The Turn of the Screw," and the source of the Freudian assumption that the whole drama takes place only in the governess's mind — that *she* drives the children mad. But when she discovers Flora with Miss Jessel at their swamp rendezvous, and when Flora, becoming ill, refuses to see the governess any longer, there is another key scene with Mrs. Grose. Mrs. Grose has not "seen" the ghost (how James keeps torturing us with his series of twists!) but she has decided to leave Bly with Flora. "I can't stay . . . I've *heard* — !" "Heard?" "From that child — horrors! There! . . . On my honour, Miss, she says things — !" "Oh, thank God!" the governess says. "Thank God?" Mrs. Grose repeats. "It so justifies me!" "It does that, Miss!" And then the governess adds: "She's so horrible?" "Really shocking." "And about me?" "About you, Miss — since you must have it. It's beyond everything, for a young lady; and I can't think wherever she must have picked up —" "The appalling language she applied to me?" cries the governess triumphantly: "I can, then!" While Mrs. Grose again corroborates her. "Well, perhaps I ought to also — since I've heard some of it before!"

That is to say, from the lips of Peter Quint and his paramour, Miss Jessel, during their stay at Bly. The governess is triumphant. "Then, in spite of yesterday, you *believe* —" "In such doings?" says Mrs. Grose, "I believe." And it was just this "belief" in the ghosts on the part of a sophisticated credulity that James, following Coleridge's "willing suspension of disbelief," was seeking to achieve in "The Turn of the Screw." There remains only the final and quite lurid scene in the story where the governess *must* prove that Miles is guilty in order to save both her own sanity and his soul. "Leave us, leave us," cries the governess to Mrs. Grose, "I'll get it out of him. He'll meet me — he'll confess. If he confesses, he's saved. And if he's saved —" "Then *you* are?" says the good Mrs. Grose: "I'll save you without him!" This was indeed the Puritan strain in James, through its Victorian filter, and all adapted consciously to the make-believe melodrama of his horror tale. For it is to Miles's "intelligence" that the governess finally appeals, much as it is the superior mind of the Pupil which dominates that story. And when this new little condemned angel admits his crime, and no longer can see the ghastly visage of Peter Quint peering in through the window — that "white face of damnation" still seeking its innocent victim — he is "saved," and he dies. For Miles tells the pressing governess that he has "said things" at school. "Was it to everyone?" she asks. "No — only a few. Those I liked."

That is his poor crime, in truth; and to James "saying" appears almost as important, in this connection, as "knowing" or "seeing" in other areas — these spectator sports, as it were, at the apex of the literary life which preclude all possibility of mere vulgar "doing." And does poor Miles's overburdened little heart really stop beating because the governess has pressed him too far; or because he is tainted with a sexual guilt which admits no other solution but death; or simply because "The Turn of the Screw" had to have a horrifying and melodramatic finale? "We were alone with the quiet day, and his little heart, dispossessed, had stopped." The governess is the real figure here, of course, and it is the question of her motivation which has given the story its modern importance. But isn't she simply another addition — portrayed as well as she is — to the whole line of possessed and half-mad "narrator-observers" in this period of James's work? There is the fanatical voyeur in "The Aspern Papers"; the puritanical and demented mother who allows her child to die in "The Author of Beltraffio"; the morbid jealousy of the nameless heroine (almost a preliminary sketch of the governess here) in "The Friends of the Friends," who destroys her lover for the sake of a dead woman — and we shall see more of these particularly Jamesian figures in stories to come.

Perhaps the mental tragedy and death of Alice James had something to do with this particular line of heroines in James's work. But he himself was identified with such figures early and late in his career — they are among his favorite spokesmen — and he himself shared their particular, and often sexual, compulsions. The forms of psychological anxiety and of morbid fear which are objectified in "The Turn of the Screw" — and the prevailing tone of hysteria — are very close indeed to the tone of James's own *Notebooks* during the period which followed the fictional and dramatic crisis of his middle career; just as some of the "ghostly" material was derived directly from his own dreams.

There was no doubt, too, in the period from *What Maisie Knew* to *The Sacred Fount*, that James was beginning much more directly to snoop around the area of "evil sexuality" which "The Turn of the Screw" projected in terms of the "innocent" — if victimized — children and the virginal governess. But the modern concept of childhood sexuality was unknown to, and would have been abhorred by James, who accepted and even, for his own reasons, embraced the Victorian view of angelic and unspotted infancy. If the later Freudian interpretation of "The Turn of the Screw" had been at all correct, the story might well have been among the prophetic and great fictions of world literature. But this claim is wholly false. From all the internal evidence, and all the surrounding facts about the narrative which James himself gives us, it is simply a very tricky ghost story done very well. Once again James's real talent consisted of making the unreal real — or of creating an effective illusion based on an altogether artificial premise. And world literature is not comprised of ghost stories.

Yes; no doubt; but with all these facts about "The Turn of the Screw" so plainly visible, why does the little *amusette* continue, in its way, to haunt or at least to plague our imagination? What is the final inner mystery that lends its own added weight to the tale, despite the patently artificial form of this ghost story; and despite James's own flat statements as to his literary intention? The real issue here is of course the extent of the artist's own consciousness.

To what degree was James aware of the governess's true temperament when he projected her portrait as a superior form of entertainment? To what degree was he aware of the deeper levels of *his
own* temperament now breaking forth — in almost classic Jungian
fashion in this trauma of his middle life; or even let us say during
this menopausal mood — into a series of such disturbing, provoca-
tive, enigmatic literary creations? The artistic form for these emotional projections was always artificial; the artistic resolution was
usually "moral," high-minded, sentimental, and melodramatic. But
there is no doubt as to the recessive, intertwined emotions of infantile, and often quite incestuous sexuality which James, all so
innocently, poured *into* these narratives. And the latent content of
"The Turn of the Screw" will be more apparent a little later on in
his career.

Meanwhile, *The Awkward Age*, in 1899, was another curious
play-novel. He could not leave the drama alone. He was compulsively forced to incorporate the "laws of the theatre" — which had
led him to such disaster — into the novel form. If he had thought
of *Maisie* as "a succession of acts," what else was the new novel
but another succession of scenes and acts, all written in straight, if
highly mannered dialogue, with no narrative — that is to say, no
novel — at all? But within this strange new form, imposed by the
peculiarly Jamesian ego-psychology which he had elevated into his
esthetic discovery, he was concerned with the decline of manners
in English society at the turn of the century. This was his second
great "discovery" of this period; even if it only signified that James
had finally discovered that the British aristocracy was not quite as
noble, purehearted and aristocratic as he had always, from childhood, imagined it to be.

The plot of the novel was that of "the little London girl who
grows up to 'sit with' the free-talking modern young mother . . .
And, though the conversation is supposed to be expurgated for her,
[she] inevitably hears, overhears, guesses, follows, takes in, becomes acquainted with, horrors." Well, what horrors? But wasn't

this Jamesian statement itself a variation on "The Turn of the Screw" — if now the sexual horrors which he surmised everywhere were to be rendered in the natural, rather than the supernatural sphere; and if this Jamesian infant only *listens* to them. The hero of the story "hesitates" (as so many Jamesian heroes hesitate) because he thinks the heroine "knows" too much. "But all the while he hesitates she knows, she learns more and more. He finds out somehow how much she *does* know, and, terrified at it, drops her." Now again, wasn't this outline for the novel the essence of Victorian puritanism on James's part, plus the familiar underlying pattern of infantile voyeurism. The outcast or orphan child is now partly "let in" upon the horrid mysteries of adult sexuality through the medium — so vital to James — of "talk." She is contaminated, as it were, through her ears. *The Awkward Age* was another literary failure in its own time; but the later James of the Prefaces, pointing out the denseness of the audience of the time, accorded this novel also his highest praise.

Among all the Jamesian Prefaces indeed, this one was perhaps the most involved, the most "technical," and the most self-laudatory. James positively abounded in new conceits and new terms of esthetic appreciation and "analysis." There was the "artistic rage" and "the artistic felicity" and what he described as "the saving virtue of treatment," which included the Jamesian "row of circles," the different "aspects of the situation," the "series of lamps" which he so consciously used to illuminate these different circles and aspects — and "the exhaustive treatment of angles," and those even *larger* dramatic scenes which James now labeled as "Occasions":

I revelled in this notion of the Occasion as a thing by itself, really and completely a scenic thing, and could scarce name it, while crouching amid the thick arcana of my plan, with a large enough O.

Was this large "O," glimpsed by the mad dramatist crouching amid the thick arcana of his metaphysical conceits, another artistic triumph? At least James stressed the "objectivity" in *The Awkward Age* which came from "the imposed absence of that 'going behind' " to encompass explanations and amplifications. The same "going behind," I mean, which he had first denied himself in *The Tragic Muse* — and which simply meant the omission of the novelist's traditional use of exposition to define his subject; or the change of the novel form itself from the novel to the play. And even though, in fact, James could himself never *stick* with this enforced limitation of his craft, and had to find new ways to get out of the iron box which he had made for himself!

Nevertheless:

Something in the very nature, in the fine rigour, of this special sacrifice (which is capable of affecting the form-lover, I think, as really more of a projected form than any other) lends it moreover a coercive charm . . .

And so on. And a "coercive charm," one supposes, which is rather like binding oneself down with artificial ropes, in all this mumbo-jumbo realm of esthetics — and then slipping out of them all triumphantly. (I refrain from using the deeper symbolism implicit also in this "special sacrifice" of the artist, which is almost a form of imposed punishment, of masochism or mutilation simply to demonstrate the final power, the skill, the agility, of the "coerced" — the castrated? — artist.) For was there really any singular virtue, as Edith Wharton asked at the time, despite her own admiration and affection for the Master, in writing a novel as though it were a play? Wasn't the merit of the novel form precisely that it was *not* a play — that in its looseness and even laxness, as it might be, was also the latitude and freedom of the novelist to express depths of complexity, levels of meaning, a multidimensional view of his subject which rarely, if ever, emerged from the dramatist's straitjacket; and from the dramatist's necessity to create stage "effects" rather than aspects of reality. From this Preface to *The Awkward Age* came much of the Jamesian esthetics which was to be propounded and expounded by the modern group of Jacobite critics, deluded by and infatuated with such singular concepts and such resounding terminology. Yet that "going behind," which James sacrificed here with such delight (and which he didn't, really) was in fact the historical and the true function of the novelist as novelist. His illuminations, his *real* analyses of real experience, are just what make him a novelist, rather than a showman, a photographer, or a phonograph.

F. W. Dupee is probably right, then, in saying that *The Awkward Age* is "the most elaborate expression of James's preoccupations in the '90's." But was this mannered play-novel "almost one of his masterpieces and clearly the chief work of the period"? Well, each of these Jacobites also, while bowing politely to all the other Jacobites, has his favorite Jamesian work, his secret masterpiece, or almost-masterpiece. It is a matter of personal preference, since it is implicit that *all* of these Jamesian works are almost masterpieces. *The Awkward Age* was in fact one of James's most exasperating novels — a masterpiece of irritation, if you like — and a novel which was alternately brilliant and tedious, entertaining and boring.

In terms of Henry James himself, however, it is another revealing document. The setting is that of the highest ranges of the leisure-class novel. In the opening scene, which may not quite be an Occasion, but is the prelude, surely, to an Occasion, the aging and old-fashioned Mr. Longdon ("Long-done," or "Long Ago," and also the "London" of long-ago, that is now done with) discusses the corrupt "modern world" with the restless, cynical Gussy (Gustavus) Vanderbank — the true aristocrat of this modern London set. (Now it really couldn't be, could it, that the original literary source of James's enchanted vision of the British aristocracy was the opera of Gilbert and Sullivan, which these Jamesian scenarios come increasingly to resemble.) The opening tone of the play-novel is slow, stylized, teasing, evasive, while these two clubmen, representing two different "historical" epochs, gossip, and pace around the room, and exchange cigarettes and "ideas." For the legendary London society has become "a huge 'squash,' as we elegantly call it," Van says; "an elbowing, pushing, perspiring mob" where true friendship, or true love, or true human relations are no longer possible. "Oh, we're past saving, if that's what you mean!" Van admits, laughingly. "You don't care, you don't care!" answers Longdon, perceptively.

This light banter contains some of James's most bitter reflections about the same British society to which he had always aspired, and had viewed, from his earliest origins, as the apotheosis of "civilization." While the two clubmen discuss Nanda, the virginal young female presence hovering around the edge of all this "liberal" conversation, Van also remarks that beauty in London —

staring glaring obvious knock-down beauty, as plain as a poster on a wall, an advertisement of soap or whiskey, something that speaks to the crowd and crosses the footlights, fetches such a price on the market that the absence of it, for a woman with a girl to marry, inspires endless terrors and constitutes for the wretched pair (to speak of mother and daughter alone) a sort of social bankruptcy.

But what "endless terrors," what "social bankruptcy," what "wretched pair," to speak only of mother and daughter (which was mainly what Henry James always did speak of), was James thinking of here if he wasn't still involved with the old-fashioned Victorian notion of a "proper marriage"? Wasn't there a special ring of bitterness too in the description of a vulgar type of beauty which "crossed the footlights"? At least James's own semi-theatrical dialogue now harried and scourged the crass and commercial "New Age":

London doesn't love the latent or the lurking, has neither time nor taste nor sense for anything less discernible than the red flag in front of the steam-roller. It wants cash over the counter and letters ten feet high.

Well, this was also the frustrated dramatist who lurked and crouched in the latent, one supposes, arcana of his own fictional craft — and who, incidentally, was himself beginning to specialize in "cash over the counter" (as in *What Maisie Knew*) as regards the delinquent sexuality of the new age. But wasn't he also "going behind" his subject in this highly personal moral sermon which was strained through Vanderbank's mind and lips — which set the stage for James's social comedy of fast, free, loose modern life? "Lady Julia" (who is Nanda's aristocratic grandmother, and another symbol of the glorious past) is the title of the first Occasion — I mean Book, I mean chapter — in *The Awkward Age*, while "Little Aggie" (or the modern child) formed the second Book, or chapter. And here there is a quite brilliant scene between the ostensible heroine of the novel, Mrs. Brookenham, and her delinquent son Harold. For Harold is already a liar, a grafter, a petty thief, and a social gigolo, all of which he attributes to his mother's selfishness and sublime indifference to her own children. Mrs. Brook, a callous beauty — who in a sense might be considered as the portrait of a lady in reverse — is in the bosom of a very strange family. "You're always wanting to get me out of the house," says Harold. "I think you want to get us *all* out, for you manage to keep Nanda from showing even more than you do me. Don't you think your children good *enough,* mummy dear?" And then: "How you *do* like to tuck us in and then sit up yourself! What do you want to do, anyway? What *are* you up to, mummy?" And here, of course, so boldly expressed by the already corrupt and impudent son of Mrs. Brookenham, who however blames all his own moral failings upon his supposedly amoral mother, are the two dominant and intertwined Jamesian themes of this period: the outcast child (the orphan prince) and the voyeuristic approach to adult — or parental — sexuality which is embodied by the curious, snooping "observer" of these stories.

As a counterpart to this view of upper class English domesticity, James posited the "Duchess" of *The Awkward Age*, who has

brought up her Little Aggie in Continental seclusion and severity
— that is to say, until Little Aggie's "proper marriage" has been
consummated. "It's all a muddle, a compromise, a monstrosity,
like everything else you produce," says the Duchess about modern
English manners. "I see but one consistent way, which is our fine
old foreign way, and which makes — in the upper classes, mind
you, for it's with them only I'm concerned — *des femmes bien
gracieuses.*" So spoke the Madame Grandoni of *The Princess Casamassima* about *her* "upper classes"; so spoke Henry James himself
in his own deepest heart about the proper education of young
ladies — though he neglected to mention what often happened to
these "*femmes bien gracieuses*" after their virginal and proper marriages. Meanwhile, in the play-novel, while the Duchess and Mrs.
Brook exchange their barbs, the red-haired footman directs the
servingmen at the tea-table: an occasion indeed. And the Duchess
is also involved with Lord Petherton, a hideous old ruin — "whose
robustly symmetrical proportions gave to his dark blue double-
breasted coat an air of tightness that just failed of compromising
his tailor."

In the Drama of Furnishings, which has been intensified to suit
the leisure-class decor of *The Awkward Age*, a compromised tailor
is the symbol of social — or moral — failure. Petherton is poor,
coarse and cynical; and he lives off Mr. Mitchett's generosity. Then
there is the drama of Mitchie's clothes — "in the systematic dis-
agreement, above all, of his coat, waistcoat and trousers." But
Mitchie, son of a shoemaker, whose great wealth helps to support
this whole dubious upper class social set, is frankly a comic hero —
whose obvious commonness proclaims him to the elite as "secretly
rare." Making no pretense of being a gentleman, he has almost
learned to behave like one. He is perhaps James's *best* proletarian
figure; compared with the ennobled and tormented little bookbinder of *The Princess Casamassima*; or the "ineffable butler"
Brooksmith; or the goodhearted if slightly stupid, the high-minded
and renunciatory Fleda Fetch . . . no, Vetch, in *The Spoils of*

Poynton. Here, moreover, there is even the drama of Mitchie's facial expressions: his high color and "his queer glare" at tense moments. For James added a rather lurid physiognomical background to his parlor comedy of the conscious mind. Then there are the obscure breaks or elisions in the monologues or dialogues or group conversations of these high personages: the "arrested points," the "sliding away" from what was to be, but what isn't said, but what everybody apparently "knows," and takes to be said, or not said.

There is something you might call the decor of gossip, which is mainly the elaborate variations of the verb "to say." "It possibly chilled his interlocutor, who again hung fire . . ." we are informed at one point. (And this new interlocutor is a more virile observer, as it were, who now *takes command* of the "questioning" which is the prime activity, or counteractivity, of the later Jamesian narratives.) "She wound up," or "she rang out," or "she lightly moaned," are some of the typical descriptions of Mrs. Brook's utterances; while "she wailed" is another favorite tag of James in what also might be called the Drama of the Dixit. *The Awkward Age* marks an apogee in James's attempt to enhance what he must have felt instinctively to be the thin stream of the drama of consciousness — now relegated to the even more confining medium of stage dialogue. What verbal theatrics there are in these pages. The thinner the subject, the more confining the medium of expression, the more violent became the verbal forms, the verbal "action."

The artist was in fact working in two directions at once. There was the necessity, apparently, to constrain his subject; and the necessity to elaborate the form or the language of this constraint — until the climax of communication among the members of this exotic drawing-room group in *The Awkward Age* actually becomes that of "vibrations":

It was a place in which, at all times, before interesting subjects, the unanimous occupants, almost more concerned for each other's vibrations than for anything else, were apt rather more to exchange sharp and silent searchings than to fix their eyes on the object itself . . .

But how far can even a great virtuoso carry such a virtuoso affair? To the drama of shifting facial expressions; or of static faces and shifting eyes; or of static eyes, and changing irises or tense pupils? There is a limit, even to an art which grows increasingly more minute. And the underlying theme in *The Awkward Age* — just as in *What Maisie Knew*, and as in "The Turn of the Screw" — was that of the orphan children, in this case Nanda, Little Aggie, and the delinquent Harold, who are exposed to the "evil" of sexuality; even if, as here, it is merely a "verbal" (or visual) evil. Or perhaps, for James, it was worse, more dangerous, just because it was verbal, or visual, or auditory; and he singled out, in Mrs. Brookenham and her friends, the cause of this as being the whole group of selfish, self-absorbed, callous and "sex-ridden" (though ever so politely, so suggestively, so talkatively) mothers. Here again are the whole group of "modern" — that is to say, sexually loose — parents who nevertheless "have fun" in their secret intimacy, or enjoy themselves in some mysterious, hidden, delightful area from which they laugh at the outcast and victimized, although still curious and snooping, children.

This was the real and "secret" theme of the story; the subject, during this period, of James's own deepest preoccupation; but the vehicle he used, the play-novel of chatter, was almost designed to conceal, or dilute this theme, rather than to convey it. *The Awkward Age* becomes talky, ingrown, precious, and ultimately tedious. Beneath its continuous chatter, it is a voyeur's dream of sexual promiscuity — but again a promiscuity that is so *verbal* as hardly to leave any time for the "acts" which are hinted at or suggested so continually. And with this small, conversant, ingrown group of high-society characters, all of them snooping around each other's affairs, all of them discussing endlessly themselves and their friends, *The Awkward Age* was also a kind of dialogue of incest. Van, who is or was apparently Mrs. Brook's lover, has been singled out by this aberrant mother to marry her daughter Nanda; though he has never and never will "come to the scratch," as Mrs. Brook "resolutely quavers" — while one wonders to just which "scratch."

Is Mrs. Brook really the "moon-goddess" of this strange set, as Van says, which is governed everywhere by her, "in our mysterious ebbs and flows"? Then indeed what a distortion of nature is here. The central flaw in *The Awkward Age* is just that "liberty of talk" which was its proclaimed theme, and which takes the place of any real life. In all these tangled love affairs, which are heaped one upon another with a kind of insatiable, boundless and unappeased fancy, there is no feeling of love, just as there is, apparently, no actual behavior of love. These are all empty, sterile people involved only in their own gossip and scandals. And the book is certainly not a novel of "ideas" in any sense, since this little elite in-group has no concern with anything happening outside of its own small and select circle.

Is that what Mr. Dupee calls the "genial tone" of the satire which proved that James, at last, no longer felt himself the "outsider" in contemporary British social life? *The Awkward Age*, in fact, proves quite the opposite; just as all of James's work before and after this novel indicates that his own psychic state was a reversionary return to the central mood of the alienated infant. This was a world of evil sexuality, again, beneath the satiric and sometimes entertaining surface of parlor comedy; of sexual manipulation; and very likely of sexual impotence. And it was the dramatist Henry James who had created and was directing every mood and every word of this imaginary literary world. But, extending his drama beyond its proper limits, draining off its vitality by imposing more and more bizarre "twists" of the plot line, James also, in the conclusion of *The Awkward Age*, became careless about his own technique. Vanderbank "smoked and smoked," so we are told. Mr. Longdon indulges in what is surely an inordinate play of his "nippers." Mitchie specializes in his "wide, prolonged glares" — and all three of these characters steadily, continually, obsessively keep on consulting their watches.

Was it time that was running out — or Henry James's verbal ingenuity? The flashing dialogue, the elaborate amplification of the "drama of furnishings," the ingenious twist-upon-twist of the plot line no longer matter in the novel, because the people and human relations no longer matter: because we realize that all the characters and all their thoughts and behavior are being twisted and turned according to the dictates of dramatic "effect" — surprise upon surprise — rather than of their own temperaments and true needs. *The Awkward Age* is a remarkable example of purely verbal histrionics, or of that ostentatious display which Veblen found in every other area of the newly rich American "upper classes." In James's case it was a conspicuous consumption of talent.

At "Tishy Grendon's" (she is another of those profligate modern women in the later Jamesian exuberance of sexual fantasy), poor Vanderbank discovers that "the footman, opening the door, mumbled his name without sincerity." For if the morals of the British nobility have disintegrated to this point, what can you expect of the servile class? Here, too, James bore down more heavily on what had been only the prevailing and "polite" anti-Semitism of his class and his period. "The Jew man, so gigantically rich," says Mrs. Brook ("quite wailingly"), "Baron Shack or Schmack — who has just taken Cumberland House and who has the awful stammer — or what is it? no roof to his mouth — is to give that horrid little Algie, to do his conversation for him, four hundred a year . . ." Quite wailingly. And this "Jew man," who is also physically deformed, figures in the works of the American literary imagination increasingly strongly from Henry James and Edith Wharton to T. S. Eliot and Ezra Pound — from the dispossessed, alienated side of the "Old Republic," I mean, which is hardly ever mentioned as such in the criticism of the Jacobite cult; and from a diseased literary spirit which was projecting its own impotence upon an obvious scapegoat.

Certainly *The Awkward Age* marked the end of the fairy tale of British society for Henry James, which once again, as in his earlier period in America, had suddenly turned into a nightmare. (And wasn't the concept of the Jew-man himself, "so gigantically rich,"

another nightmare symbol?) But the dream of England was the
deepest, dearest, most profound and clinging obsession of the Jamesian ego: a dream which was as artificial and imaginary from its
earliest origins as was its nightmarish projection at the end. For
whenever did James really "know" either American or English
society, with his preconceived, romantic view from the start, his
"horrid" and "monstrous" conclusions at the end? Both his premises and his conclusions were inadequate; were the product of an
extreme, an intense, an obsessive and obsessed imagination which
was untempered by any adequate sense of reality. Possibly from
this uneasy realization of his own central weakness came Henry
James's special and insistent stress on "knowing" as the highest
goal of human endeavor — since he knew, perhaps, that he did not
know.

The drama of cigarettes in *The Awkward Age*, of clothes, of
furnishings, of physiognomical expressions, of "looks" which "exhausted the possibility of looks"; the drama of horology or of the
restless watches which kept appearing and disappearing towards
the close of the rarefied play-novel: what was all this excessive
elaboration of minutiae but the Jamesian attempt to fill up the
vacuum — not only in the stream of his characters' limited consciousness, but also in the range of his own limited experience,
both as to any kind of realistic and adult sexual behavior and, even
more important, as to the real nature of the English aristocracy
itself. Furthermore if this sexual and social corruption now existed
in the highest circles of British noble life (as to some degree it
surely had from the outset of Henry James's English career) why
did he attribute it only to "modern times" — that is to say, after
1895, and after his last great hope of theatrical fame, wealth and
glory had been so rudely dispelled? (Yes, of course, the Edwardian
age had succeeded the Victorian; but hardly in the exaggerated
and fantastical manner with which Henry James viewed the
change.) For it was only *then* that James once again felt himself
thrust back, and he himself reverted to his old familiar role of the

"innocent" but also now quite fanatical voyeur (or outsider) who ferrets out the mysteries of sexual and social corruption.

No, the "genial environment" which Mr. Dupee stressed in *The Awkward Age* was at base rather ugly, vicious and cheap. It held in it the elements of a revenge taken by the outraged Jamesian psyche, all of whose lost hopes, indeed, were embodied in the old-fashioned and quite heroic figure of Mr. Longdon. Here was the true ghost from the past; as the child Nanda (the "future") also conveyed the Jamesian rebuke to modern society through her withdrawal from it. And James in turn had been rebuked, and rejected, by the decadent modern spirit of the stage, at least. The dramatic form of his last novel in the nineties still betrayed his dominant compulsion — as did all his private esthetic formulations, "laws" and "principles" of this period. He was still determined to make his theatrical debacle pay off, almost at any cost, and certainly at the cost of the traditional novel form.

In short, then, the Jamesian "shift of view" in the mid- and late nineties was too extreme, too sudden, too personal. What he so abruptly "saw," and "knew," and "understood," had been there all along. His world had not really changed so much as he had. And still confined within the strict, narrow boundaries of the British "nobility" — the only social environment which James, like his Duchess, was really concerned with — he had simply turned the rosy, enchanted vision of such a fortunate elite upside down, or inside out. And wasn't the Jamesian notion of the lower classes — or of the lower middle class, which was as far down as he could penetrate in the social labyrinth — equally notable? Those lower classes who, in the works we have already mentioned, or as in "In the Cage," existed merely to admire, to ape, and to enhance the Jamesian upper classes. With such a view of "society," was it possible to have any valid view not only of "modern times," but of human existence itself?

Now this social-historical limitation of Henry James was of course even further complicated by his peculiar notions of the psychosexual elements in human behavior. Most certainly the Jamesian crisis of the nineties, professional and temperamental alike, led him backward to the childhood orbit of *What Maisie Knew* and *The Awkward Age*. His particular infantile and outcast literary vision is probably unique in the annals of letters. His overflowing, undefined, all-pervasive concern with "evil" or "corrupt" sexuality appears even in the typical terminology of the later James; such as the "mouth of the cave" for which the morbidly curious and perpetually frustrated observer hero of the "The Figure in the Carpet" seeks in vain. This is voyeurism of the mind gone mad in James, and culminating in his peculiarly personal orbit of prurient sexual "curiosity."

But wasn't that always, so far back as "The Aspern Papers," the real meaning — or the latent concern — of the Jamesian fiction? We have also noticed, from the very start of James's writing, and particularly in *Washington Square* and "The Pupil," the recurrent and dominant theme of the orphan prince (or princess); or of the outcast child who is invariably superior to a mysterious and shifting set of parental surrogates, and almost inevitably condemned to suffering, pain, renunciation or even death through the machinations of the callous or cunning, or positively vicious adults. In the works of the nineties, more directly, we get the Jamesian descriptions of the adult "intimacy" around whose mysterious perimeter the dispossessed infants prowl and snoop: still tormented by the fact that all this hidden "gaiety" and laughter is directed at *them*. In *Maisie* and in *The Awkward Age* alike, the parental symbols rotate in even a faster and dizzier (and more sexually corrupt) cycle; just as the Jamesian "lovers" follow the same pattern.

In very few writers has the concept of adult love derived so obviously, so directly, so clearly from the earliest emotional sources (or fantasies) of the family, the parents. (But then, what *other* experiences of even adolescent love or passion did Henry James ever have? — while very likely, in turn, this bizarre early emotional pattern kept him *from* having any further experiences.) And wasn't this a very odd infantile base indeed, of self-imposed "exile," of indignation, of outrage at such adult behavior; of an inherent "mental" superiority, at least, to those parents who treat one so badly, who mock at one, who have their own mysterious modes of pleasure, whose laughter comes from behind their closed doors — who are not really then, after all, one's *true* parents? The core of this Jamesian concept was the embedded infant, as we shall see in the later periods of his work. But meanwhile we should note that during the more directly "sexual" period of this infantine emotionalism, the outcast children of the nineties have come gradually both to "know" the meaning of adult sexuality — as Maisie does, as Nanda does — and hence, finally, both to condemn and to *dominate* the wicked parents, or the loose lovers. Quite similarly, the Jamesian observer, in the technical area of his craft, has gradually become the interlocutor — who already *knows* the answers he is seeking to discover from all these uneasy accomplices of passion.

This odd strain — or is it really the center? — of James's work will come to even more exotic climax in *The Sacred Fount*; but meanwhile it is in *this* context that the "inner mystery" of "The Turn of the Screw" also becomes clear. For James was not only "identified" with the nameless governess; he *was* the governess, in the sense that her snooping, prurient, obsessive sexual curiosity was his own. But this time, quite logically, it is the children who "know" all the dark, mysterious, hidden life of sexuality. (Quite logically, I mean, in the retrograde Jamesian development of this period from the outcast child to the omnipotent infant.) But then, in a curious twist of the narrative, it is the brother and sister of the story who have become the figureheads not of childlike but of *parental* sexuality and "corruption." There is no doubt that they are the married couple of "The Turn of the Screw," with all their secret knowledge and secret pleasure — while the governess, in effect, has become the peeping and prying child who finally forces them to "reveal" and to abandon their sinful, hidden pleasure.

This could be described as a form of "hysterical conversion" in terms of modern depth psychology, and in terms of a story which describes so accurately the innocence, the inhibition, the final hysteria of the heroine herself. (It wasn't a far jump for James — always identified with *feminine* symbols on the adult level — from the sexually terrified Isabel Archer to the prurient governess who is now simply paying the price, as it were, for the defensive "purity" of James's earlier heroines.) But on another level of this childhood fantasy or ego-rationalization, wasn't it quite obvious that these Jamesian children, moving more and more closely to the dark, hidden core of adult sexuality, always "knowing" more and more about it (in their own, or in James's devouring need) should finally know it *all?* And that is to say that they not only come to "know" and to dominate the parents — but that they themselves *become* the parents. But then also, if they are the parents, it is inevitable that the "guilty father" (Miles) should be condemned to death for his mysterious and corrupt pleasures; while the guilty mother (Flora), more tenderly treated, is only sent off, in the midst of a complete nervous breakdown, to some infantile-oedipal netherland. Odd, or even fantastic as it may sound — as it surely was — this explanation of the "mystery" of "The Turn of the Screw" is the reason for this little tale's abiding fascination, and it is supported by all the surrounding evidence of James's work both before and after it.

A "ghost story" indeed of the most intimate and recessive fantasies of the unformed, prelogical baby-soul. And one notices, incidentally, how the Jamesian descriptions of parental or fatherfigures (starting out, mainly, with wicked, or cunning or "evil" figures) develop steadily into ever more diminutive terms and symbols — until we get the Adam Verver of *The Golden Bowl*, the "first father" himself, who is described as a kind of adorable, innocent, sweet little child-parent whose whole life — powerful financial titan that he is! — is managed and controlled by his daughter Maggie. This was to be the final phase — or the final revenge — of the omnipotent infant who now was at the center of the Jamesian vision of the universe. (Does it account also for another part of the increasing stress on *minutiae* of the Jamesian craft: the increasing use of the diminutive terms of childhood?) But no wonder that the orthodox or conventional Freudian interpretations of the governess's "hallucinations" in "The Turn of the Screw" are so inadequate; or that James himself was so reticent — so unconscious, apparently, and perhaps yet "half-conscious," of the latent content of his contrived little "*amusette.*"

Well, haven't we said enough about the different facets of the baroque Jamesian temperament during the trauma of his middle career? It is something altogether special as I say, in the annals of literature, both as to artistic vision and artistic method. And here again, the method and technique of the artist were the direct reflection, or even result, of his peculiar inner temperament. (To study *only* the craft, which the New Critic sector of the Jacobite cult proclaims as its purpose, is not even to understand the craft itself.) And wasn't there something illuminating as well as bizarre in this peculiar retort of the defeated, the wounded, outraged Jamesian ego to all the heavy blows of his later life: to his whole thwarted and "misunderstood" literary career? To convert such failure into a self-proclaimed "success," even into his religio-esthetic salvation, was in its own way a triumph of will; if not altogether of intelligence or insight. Very much like his mad governess, there was something compulsive, panicky in James's repeated admonitions to himself to "produce, produce, produce!" and all yet would be well. And he did produce — if his typical productions during the crisis of the nineties were rather strange — and he would indeed continue to produce, if at times much too fast and too much.

He was moving into the period of what has been called "the major phase" of his work; and that work would become increasingly odd, exotic, idiosyncratic. Really most singular! For the last half of Henry James's career — upon whose threshold we have paused to summarize his talent — was to become an even more remarkable case of an absolutely private world, an altogether bizarre literary vision and production.

The Nineteen Hundreds

7. The Psychology of the Keyhole

WHAT SHALL WE SAY, too, of James's half-conscious awareness of his own paucity of knowledge and experience — which he then rationalized and glorified into more than a method: into a mystique?

"This shadow of a shadow," he said about the original "anecdote" for "The Turn of the Screw": "My own appreciation of which . . . was exactly wrapped up in that thinness . . . On the surface there wasn't much, but another grain, none the less, would have spoiled the precious pinch." He was beginning to commemorate just that "thinness" which was his chief human and artistic lack; and to pad it out, all serenely, happily, with the elaborate convolutions of his "fancy," the intricate turns of his "technique." Even in the mental or intellectual sphere, into which James also prided himself upon channeling all the other human feelings and reactions, we have already noticed his lack of interest in, or real concern with, not merely socioeconomic or political issues, or science (the odd medical disciple of "The Middle Years"), but even philosophy or history (apart from its romantic or noble pageantry), or indeed any field of knowledge outside of his total and absolute and self-contained kingdom of pure art.

But what then does literature mean, if it is not conjoined with, if its "laws" and "principles" are not operating upon, the whole varied, rich, and complex scene of our natural and our social behavior? (Perhaps James really was a "pioneer," as he is claimed to be in so many other respects, in the development towards a purely abstract art, which may be feasible, if not always commendable, in the field of modern painting or music, say; which is a vogue in the "modern" or "new" criticism — but which can't, by the nature of things, have much future in the development of fiction.) Yet Henry James now pushed away, with something like indignation and anger, even the literal details of the second- or thirdhand verbal anecdotes which supplied the precious "germs" of his literary inspiration. Very often the Jamesian glorification of the *lack* of source material; of the "purity" of method, of the artistic "imagination" which was used to supply all the other missing elements, may seem — well, what? But what is really odd is the modern phase of Jacobite scholarship which in turn has accepted, has even further elaborated this dubious Jamesian approach to fiction into a universal, or a transcendent "esthetic."

The Jamesian scholars are also evasive or enigmatic about the central crisis in James's middle career; and the curious, almost monomaniacal resolution of his failure. "He was absorbed first with salvaging what he could from his recent experience," we are told by Matthiessen and Murdock in *The Notebooks of Henry James;* but they don't describe the nature of this salvaging." Dupee in turn stresses the "strenuous work of reconstruction" on James's part during the later nineties; but this critic also accepts the Jamesian "reconstruction" as an esthetic achievement rather than a mode of personal salvation — of restoring a shattered self-image — through very dubious and completely idiosyncratic esthetic "principles." "I have only to *face* my problems," James said after the debacle of his dramas; but what he did instead was to *make* these problems into the rationale of a new artistic vision and method. Just as his failure as a popular playwright led to the invention of the "scenario" form, and to the "play-novel," so he rationalized his own meager stock of knowledge and experience alike into the "law" of the artistic imagination which in essence repudiated as "gross" the notion of any reality, or factuality.

This was in fact the exotic catharsis, the baroque "reconstruction," of a wounded and rejected, an enraged and "unconquerable" egotism. In the *Notebooks* of this period, just as in the later Prefaces, the underlying Jamesian principle of the orphan prince approached the paranoiac limits of the One against the World: the solitary, great, neglected artist who will yet "show" the universe which has so badly misunderstood him. Just as in James's early and recurrent nightmare dream of the threatening figure whom *he* suddenly attacks and pursues and conquers, the Jamesian ego itself now bounded after the demon failure in full pursuit of its final victory. How James "used" (that is to say, manipulated, rather than understood) his dramatic failure in his subsequent literary works to the point of obsession, disaster and literary loss, in the play-novels themselves, is a notable episode in his career. The manner in which he so brilliantly rationalized and "objectified" this whole curious phase of ego or vanity redemption through the simple process of making the world, or the literary world, conform to *his* notion of the world; and then how his modern critics not only failed to perceive the true nature of this artistic "reconstruction," but accepted, expounded and glorified it — this is another remarkable chapter in literary history as a whole.

What real advantage was there in constraining the traditional novel form into the theatrical straitjacket — except the fact that James was still proving to himself that he *could* write plays; or that he could turn novels, nouvelles, stories — anything — into those play-novels, play-nouvelles, play-stories? Yet we are solemnly told by Messrs. Murdock and Matthiessen that James had now arrived "at the acquired mastery of scenic presentation" — as though all the great novels before James had not had their "big scenes," and as though there was some mysterious advantage in writing a novel composed *only* of such scenes. But James's own true state of mind during this period was revealed more accurately in some of his letters. Writing to Howells in the mid-nineties he already felt that a new generation, "that I know not, and mainly prize not," had taken "universal possession" of the literary scene. He was rejected and unwanted.

"The sense of being utterly out of it weighed me down, and I asked myself what the future would be," he had written to his goodhearted if "provincial" American editor friend when he had found himself equally cut off from the magazine world of popular fiction, the glittering world of theatrical fame. "All this, I needn't say, is for your segretissimo ear. What it means is that 'production' for me, as aforesaid, means production of the little *book* pure and simple . . . It is about the distinctness of one's *book-position* that you have so substantially reassured me; and I mean to do far better work than ever I have done before. I have, potentially, improved immensely and am bursting with ideas and subjects — though the act of composition is with me more and more slow, painful and difficult. I shall never again write a *long* novel; but I hope to write six immortal short ones — and some tales of the same quality. Forgive, my dear Howells, the cynical egotism of these remarks — the fault of which is in your own sympathy."

He was indeed bursting with ideas and subjects; he *had* produced, almost feverishly and frantically. He was writing his short novels and tales, though still with one eye on the stage, as we have seen; and he was just on the eve of composing the famous, last and very long novels which he had sworn never to write again. He urged Howells to visit him in England that summer. "I shall probably not, as usual, absent myself from these islands — not be beyond the Alps as I was when you were here last. That way Boston lies, which is the deadliest form of madness" — hardly a tactful closing line, which James balanced off with an effusive series of personal messages for his Boston friends. Dictating another letter to Alice James (Mrs. William James; not his sister Alice), he reveled, however, in his new, *less* painful form of dictation, which was also to shape, in part, his later style — as the letter itself already showed. The reason he had not written to her sooner, James said here, was that "I have been driving very hard for another purpose this inestimable aid to expression, and that, as I have a greater loathing than ever for the mere manual act, I haven't, on the one side, seen my way to inflict on you a written letter, or on the other had the virtue to divert, till I should have finished my little book, to another stream any of the valued and expensive industry of my amanuensis. I *have*, at last, finished my little book — that is *a* little book, and so have two or three mornings of breathing time before I begin another. Le plus clair of this small interval 'I consecrate to thee!' "

Charming in its way, and revealing as to the pressured schedule of the Jamesian production. The "little books" (and note the affectionate, if also rather patronizing diminutive for his own work) were now emerging steadily, almost remorselessly, as though from some conveyer belt of the conscious mind. The style certainly had changed too, even in the most personal communications of James. This was the advent of his famous "later style." And how much did the process of dictating, the relinquishing of the odious "mere manual act" of writing, the presence of the valued if expensive amanuensis-secretary, the sound of that loud, booming, resonant Jamesian voice which filled, as we are told, the halls of De Vere Gardens in London: how much did all this compensate James for the loss of the larger audience which he felt so keenly? At least it may partly account for the curious sense, which we often have in his later work, of a completely private and solitary world of pure language in which the Jamesian observer-narrator-actor-manager-interlocutor now controls every minute detail of the story, of scene, of character, of relationships, of plot — in order to achieve his mysterious, secret, singular literary "effect" against a background of universal silence.

In the same letter to his sister-in-law James, however, professed to be even more than serene. He was almost lyrically ecstatic at having just acquired Lamb House in Rye — which he described in the terms of the "hopeless passion," "the sudden chance of acquisition," the "pride of possession and ownership," which other men might have used about a mistress. He went into complete detail about his precious new home (his two rooms of complete old oak, his "landscape-painter" Alfred Parsons, his distinguished architect Edward Warren) and the care he was taking to rebuild it and to refurnish it in "not too-delusive Chippendale and Sheraton"; and particularly:

The "King's Room," so-called by reason of George the Second having passed a couple of nights there and so stamped it forever . . .

Outwardly rejected as he felt himself to be, James had yet realized, in his new English domicile, the final and most cherished wish of his childhood years for royalty, legend, pageantry; and here indeed he revealed the patience, the cunning, the calculation, and even the fulfillment of the lover which was apparently denied to him everywhere else. (There was also the collector's mania for "fine old things" with which he had endowed the Mrs. Gereth of *The Spoils of Poynton* among the other Jamesian figures who shared this trait.) And seven years later, writing to Edmund Gosse from William James's house in Lenox, Massachusetts, he echoed the same sentiments.

Enjoying as he did "these really admirable little Massachusetts mountains," he was still, he said, "at the back of my head and at the bottom of my heart, transcendently homesick, and with a sustaining private reference, all the while (at every moment, verily,) to the fact that I have a tight anchorage, a definitely little downward burrow, in the ancient world — a secret consciousness that I chink in my pocket as if it were a fortune in a handful of silver."* And his tight anchorage, his definitely little downward burrow in the ancient world, like the consciousness of a secret treasure in chinking silver coins: this was the background for another of

---

* These statements of James's are taken from the group of letters in Morton Dauwin Zabel's *The Portable Henry James;* a useful anthology edited by a discerning critic who, however, also tends to abandon, or to jettison, all his critical values and his critical detachment when confronted by the imperial art of Henry James.

James's celebrated tales in the volume of stories called *The Soft Side* in 1900.

"The Great Good Place" is consistently praised throughout the canon of Jamesian criticism; but why did Clifton Fadiman, for example, stretch this praise to the utmost, to the limits of lyricism? Any gloss or commentary on "this beautiful story," said this normally intelligent critic, would only be "a tactless challenge" to James's calculated effect — which seems to dispose of the critic's role entirely. Yet Fadiman went on to invoke such epics as *Pilgrim's Progress* and *The Divine Comedy* in discussing the tale. Like those works, said he, "The Great Good Place is a criticism of a whole culture, though developed on a miniature scale —

In this tiny bit of ordered dreamwork James points, however obliquely, to the essential vacuity of modern living. Only those infatuated with the twentieth century, only the gadget-men, the accumulators, will fail to make some response, however feeble, to "The Great Good Place." But it will haunt the others like a dream which, despite its oddity, seems to offer the serene answer to our deepest and most desperate prayer.

To which fervent eloquence one can only respond, after reading the story itself, Dear God, what has happened indeed to "man's rational mind" (or Mr. Fadiman's rational mind) which this same critic described as the victim of modern civilization? But the enchanted circle of "received opinion" on all of James's work in the mid-century United States was rather like Circe's island where good men were turned into swine; or perhaps in the Jamesian case, into cooing doves.

For "The Great Good Place" was, after all, one of James's minor pieces of entertainment. Admitting certain limitations obliquely as Mr. Fadiman did, he was only stimulated to rise to new heights by adding that this story, like Mozart's music, was "all beautiful with omissions." Just like his critical judgment perhaps; and this critic went on to add that, while the Place is no ethereal heaven — James is almost devoid of any religious sense;* nevertheless:

The Place is what our civilization could be if we did not persist in taking wrong turnings, if we divested ourselves of things . . . if we had not forgotten the know-thyself of the Greeks, if we could rediscover the private life.

And more: "To my mind, 'The Great Good Place' is, of the seventeen stories in this collection, the one most densely charged with contemporary application." Thus the contemporary social critic Fadiman on the famous old social critic Henry James, even while we know that James was, of all writers, most intimately involved with "things"; that he lacked precisely the know-thyself of the Greeks or of all major artists since the Greeks; and that the "private life" of these later stories was in such large part a defensive reaction to the "wrong-turnings" which he himself felt he had made, not so much in modern civilization, but in the timeless, enchanted kingdom of art.

It is remarkable, too, when good critics, like good writers, are betraying their own instincts, how the truth of the situation always emerges obliquely despite all the convolutions of the conscious mind or the perfervid pen. But yielding to Mr. Fadiman's eloquence for the moment, for the sake of the literary game, as it were, what is "The Great Good Place" really about? It is a rather nice, entertaining, minor tale of an eminently successful English writer, George Dane, who is weary of all his social and literary life, his endless appointments and dates, his lunches with celebrities and mediocrities, and the deluge of fashionable new books, including

* Here Mr. Fadiman is entirely correct; while I believe it was the Anglo-American critic Spender, or perhaps his colleague the poet-critic Auden, who solemnly reconstructed "The Great Good Place" precisely *into* a religious allegory; an almost impossible feat for anybody except a confirmed and highly imaginative disciple of James's . . . But once a body of criticism has been based on the assumption that there are no limits to James's talent, there can be obviously no limits to the critical interpretations, or fantasies.

his own. The story is a lesser variation on "The Lesson of the Master," or "The Death of the Lion," or "The Middle Years." The central focus is again the Jamesian fantasy of the weary and overwhelmed *popular* artist versus the defeated and unpopular literary masters of this period of his work. The story's familiar theme is "the punishment of success."

But the artist-hero, meeting his new secretary, falls asleep, and awakens, as he believes, in what is really the perfection of an English gentleman's club. There are "religious" overtones to be sure, just as there were in "The Altar of the Dead" — and with the same element of comfortable, respectable, upper middle class estheticism. The place is like some "great cloister" or some "mild Monte Cassino, some Grande Chartreuse" — but the story really concerns itself with a kind of high-class salvation extended as a balm for the weariness of "those who can no longer meet the pressure of social engagements." (James didn't mean "social conflict" either, and was this the reason perhaps why the story appealed so immeasurably to the popular, successful Mr. Fadiman?) But this idyllic semi-cloister has nothing else religious about it; and everything in it is paid for in good solid English sovereigns and shillings, "just like those of the world." Thus the Jamesian Utopia, or maybe the Jamesian Heaven itself, was run on a solid financial basis, and the cash payment was quietly removed by those "unobtrusive effaced agents" who constituted Henry James's notion of perfect (or heavenly) servants.

If "The Great Good Place" is really so densely charged with contemporary application, as Mr. Fadiman reports, you should notice that this is the peculiar Marxism of the leisure classes. The Place has indeed been created by some "wise mind" which is the equivalent of a leisure-class God. There is excellent food here also, "where the soundless simple service was a triumph of art" — or at least of the culinary art. This little fantastic fable, hailed as it has been throughout the canon of the Jamesian critics, is surely one of the oddest, most self-centered, luxury-loving and utterly selfish "utopias" ever dreamed of. It is "unique" indeed to the point of being ludicrous, for again even the climate has been taken care of, and this perfect "serenity" entails no hint of any self-sacrifice. "Yes, that's the beauty, that it isn't, thank goodness, carried on only for love," Dane reflects as he girds his spirit, and all his "refreshed" and "reconsecrated" faculties, to return to life, "with all its rage."

Well, what rage? And seldom before, perhaps, has such a semi-spiritual and lofty vocabulary been used to describe such a materialistic vision. We also realize that the cash basis for this Jamesian utopia is simply to preclude the possibility of even the most casual human relationships, or the most trivial human emotions. If this Great, Good Place isn't carried on for love, indeed, it is a triumph of narcissistic self-love. "It's all right," says Dane's new secretary as the famous writer awakes from his nap — his dream — to find himself back in his familiar study, with his tactful servants. "It *was* all right," James added at the story's close — but was it?

In James's favor it must be added that he had written the story as another *amusette*, and could hardly have anticipated the solemn and extensive claims of his latter-day disciples. *The Soft Side* as a whole was a volume of lighter tales when compared with the best work of James's. " 'Europe,' " for example — now also critically acclaimed — was another tour de force: an ironic parable of the fatal impact of the "dream of Europe" upon a family of New England spinsters. Was this tale really notable "for its penetrating study of the Puritan mind"? The family relations of the mother and three daughters were well done, but James actually knew very little about the Puritan mind beyond his earliest convictions that American "provincial life" (i.e., New England, Boston, Harvard) was meager, barren and starved. He had also convinced himself that the primary ambition of all these "provincial souls" was, like his own, to visit Europe; and that such a visit, or such a trip, would compensate for all the other varieties of human experience which presumably did not exist in the Brookbridge-Cambridge scene of

" 'Europe.' " In the Jamesian case one might revise the old apho-
rism that all good Americans go to Paris when they die to: "All
good Americans were dead unless they went to London."

In *The Soft Side* also, "The Tree of Knowledge" was another
tricky but entertaining anecdote about a dubious Euro-American
sculptor (based apparently on the career of Horatio Greenough in
Italy) whose faith in his own work and fame is sustained — somewhat as in "The Liar" — by an adoring and hypocritical wife. But
following directly after this collection of minor stories, *The Sacred
Fount*, in 1901, was one of the most perplexing, difficult and revealing nouvelles that Henry James ever wrote. ("The Turn of the
Screw," by comparison, was child's play in mystification.) This
was also one of James's worst-selling books, and no wonder in terms
of a popular audience; and it is still one of the few works in the
Jamesian canon about which a real, rather than a nominal difference of critical opinion exists. The *Fount*, as we are told, derived
from Stopford Brooke's anecdote about the marriage of a young
man and an older woman which had the effect of reviving the
wife's youth, and of causing the husband to appear much older.
"Don't lose sight of the little *concetto*," James reminded himself
later, "that begins with fancy of the young man who marries an old
woman . . . Keep my play on idea: the *liaison* that betrays itself
by the *transfer* of qualities . . . from one to the other of the parties to it. They *exchange*. I see 2 couples. One is married — this is
the *old-young* pair. I watch *their* process, and it gives me my light
for the spectacle of the other (covert, obscure, unavowed) pair who
are *not* married." But *The Sacred Fount* was in fact more complex
and byzantine than this bare outline of the plot suggested.

"Some critics have maintained the novel to be a serious study of
the sexual 'fount' of personality; to others it has seemed an over-
elaborate working out of a device in which any possible symbolism
is pretty well swamped by the detail with which the observer's relentless inquiry is displayed." So the editors of *The Notebooks*
comment, rather sourly. To Mr. Dupee in turn, *The Sacred Fount*,

"evidently a self-satire that misfired, seems pretty clearly to associate the unrestrained moral sense with mere snooping and malice on the part of its author-hero, who is given to discovering far-fetched perversities among his friends." This is getting warmer; while to Edmund Wilson the same story was "mystifying, even maddening. But I believe that if anyone really got to the bottom of it, he would throw a good deal of light on Henry James" — and this is getting hot, as usual with this larger-minded and more discerning commentator. (It was also the older American novelist-critic, Howells, who commented on the book's publication that he had discovered its "secret" though for the present he wouldn't reveal it.) But upon these sharper critical intuitions, Mr. R. P. Blackmur threw what amounted to another wet blanket of inflated and obscured rhetoric. To this metaphysician of modern criticism, *The Sacred Fount* — "not a novel at all but a vast, shadowy, disintegrating parable, disturbing, distressing, distrait, indeed distraught — remains in the degree of its fascination quite ineluctable. It is the nightmare nexus in James's literary life, between the struggle to portray the integrity of the artist and the struggle to portray, to discover, the integrity of the self."

Well, there was a certain glimmering of truth even here, although the point of the novel had little to do with the moral integrity which this philosopher was always seeking to discover. Does indeed morality have anything at all to do with that nightmare nexus which Mr. Blackmur did perceive here? There was a deeper level of thought and feeling which had created and colored the quite lurid scene of *The Sacred Fount*, and which takes a certain amount of human insight — and humor — to appreciate. The earlier Jamesian critic, Wilson Follett, was closer to the real thing when he described the book as a witty extravaganza "and one of the most stupendous parodies ever concocted . . . It is Henry James deliberately turning a searchlight on Henry James," while it was also an extreme illustration "of how one intrusion of raw reality at the wrong point can shatter the coalescing work of art." Why then did the contemporary James biographer Leon Edel describe Follett's comment as being couched "in the sensational terms of journalism rather than the more sober evaluative terms of criticism"? Mr. Edel was distressed at the thought that James could ever satirize James, simply because "he took the art of fiction too seriously ever to burlesque or parody his own practice of it."

But did he? Or rather, didn't he? Isn't it just the mark of a larger talent that it can regard itself, or its most cherished preconceptions, in the light of irony, satire, even farce; while the mark of a lesser talent is the emotional rigidity, the basic insecurity, the fear of just such "humor"? If Mr. Edel were correct, he would almost automatically remove James from the first category of writers (or human beings). But we have noticed in James's own work, from "The Aspern Papers" to "The Coxon Fund," a capacity to satirize (to the edge of farce) his own most serious or solemn convictions. It was his latter-day critics, rather than the artist himself, who espoused and expounded the Jamesian laws and principles without a trace of his own humor. There is no doubt that *The Sacred Fount* started out as another *jeu d'esprit* (as James himself said); as a satiric take-off on his own celebrated Method, and on his own line of possessed or demented observers. But the novel extended itself in a curious way, and the real question (and main reason for the story's obscurity) is to what degree James himself was conscious of all its implications beyond those of satire and self-satire. How much is parody, indeed, and how much is a kind of nightmarish, half-conscious form of revelation?

For this was one of the oddest of all the odd English house parties in the Jamesian orbit. There is first of all the dream-world atmosphere of a house party with no hosts to speak of, with almost invisible servants (as in "The Great Good Place"), with empty rooms where one notices strolling, gossiping couples engaged in mysterious tête-à-têtes usually after midnight — couples who change, shift or vanish as in a nightmare sequence. Who are they, what are they really doing, or at least talking about; what are the "real," innermost, secret, and most "intimate" relationships beneath their fashionable chatter? That is the secret to be divined by the Jamesian observer-narrator in *The Sacred Fount*, whose curiosity has reached the point of real obsession, mania, and a limitless passion for speculation in the sexual area. The elderly Grace Brissenden has become positively young and beautiful, while poor Briss himself has aged immeasurably. (Of all the hypotheses raised about this young-old couple in the story, the obvious one that Mrs. Briss has been revived by love — either of her husband or of another — or that Mr. Briss may simply be sick, or dying, or, say, destroyed by jealousy of his wife: this is never really entertained either by James or his "analytical" spokesman.) While, to balance this equation, there is the parallel case of the mediocre, inarticulate Gilbert Long who has suddenly become a supreme conversationalist, and a remarkable critic. Which woman then, of all the guests and couples at Newmarch, has nourished his conversational gift at the expense of her own wit, just as Mrs. Briss has regained her physical vitality at the cost of poor Briss's health and life-span?

That is the very odd "plot" of *The Sacred Fount*, in essence. That is the mystery which the Jamesian voyeuristic spectator sets out to discover through his characteristically oblique method of questioning all the major and minor participants in the drama. Of questioning, and then evading and blocking the questions which are in turn put to him; since along the way he has picked up Mrs. Briss as a fellow snooper, and the painter Ford Obert as a fellow hypothesizer. They are assistant observers, as it were, who must however be put off the trail when they come near the truth. Also, are Obert and Mrs. Server making love, possibly? And how does this affect Obert's view of Mrs. Server as the true source of Gilbert Long's eloquence? And: "for Long to have been so stamped, as I found him, how the pliant wax must have been prepared, the seal of passion applied!" Of course, "these things," as the Jamesian narrator admits in a rare moment of humility — "the way other people could feel about each other, the power not in one's self, in the given instance, that made for passion — were of course at best the mystery of mysteries; still, there were cases in which fancy, sounding the depths or shallows, could at least drop the lead."

And his fancy runs wild. There is the satiric portrait of Lady John, who first is, and then isn't the lady who is servicing Gilbert Long. But then, at whose sacred fount are all these men — and all these women — *not* drinking? Poor Briss, defeated, beaten, looks at least sixty years old. "It was as if he had discovered some miraculous short cut to the common doom." And "intimacy, of course, had to be postulated" in the marriage of the Brissendens. But the blooming Mrs. Briss (rather like the Mrs. Brook of *The Awkward Age*), handing out the worst kind of sexual gossip, scandal and "information" to the eager observer, is also not to be dismissed as Gilbert Long's helpmate. Meanwhile they trade observations about what, but for the refinement of the Jamesian vocabulary, would be a sexual sewer. "My companion, once roused, was all there." "I see. You call the appearance a kind of betrayal because it points to the relation behind it." "Precisely." "And the relation — to do that sort of thing — must be necessarily so awfully intimate." "*Intimissima.*" The word "intimate" is recurrent throughout the narrative of *The Sacred Fount*, and what awful, delightful, terrifying visions doesn't it conjure up to the remorseless searcher after sexual secrets who is the novel's "hero." This prurient gossiper, still searching for Gilbert Long's mysterious mistress, gathering up Mrs. Briss as the main source of his information — his own sacred, if verbal fount — also declares that they will "burn, as they say in hide-and-seek" when they come near the right answer. But is this "burning" only from the pleasure of intellectual validation? And there is a succession of false alarms. They do indeed witness Long "in the act of presenting his receptacle" at the very fount itself — but it turns out only to be the Comtesse de Dreuil, who is obviously a "screen" for somebody else.

The Jamesian language is interesting, again, with its obvious

sexuality, and its curiously feminine imagery. But what an even
more curious world of adult "love" is described by this language in
the plot and the theme and the tone of *The Sacred Fount.*

It is a world of "liaisons" gone mad in the later Jamesian repressed and spinsterish world of sexual fantasies. But these liaisons
and secret affairs are "experienced" only in talk, in gossip and in
speculation. There is nothing direct, nothing physical ever described
here, or experienced firsthand by the spying, curious, fertile mind of
the observer-hero; just as there are no pleasures of the flesh, or of
sexual love, no rewards, no satisfactions, ever described beyond those
of an increased mental cleverness on the part of Gilbert Long, a re-
newed physical vitality on the part of Mrs. Briss at the expense of
her suffering and devitalized sexual mate. The myth of Egeria, from
which the title of *The Sacred Fount* was derived, is that of the ves-
tal virgins who served the gods by anointing their disciples with
the holy water. But we know that these "religious rites" were pagan
and directly sexual in their content, as offerings to the fertility of
nature itself. In James's view the "Fount" contributes at best to
verbal eloquence, at the minimum to social poise. This is a world
not indeed of passion, but of sexual manipulation — of human
passion being *used* for the leisure-class graces and virtues which
James considered dominant. And this manipulation goes on mainly
in the mind of a hero who apparently sees no other values in sexual
love, and no harm done by a continuous shifting (in his own fancy)
of the human lovers.

"But I maintain, none the less, that so far as they *can* go, they do
go," says the observer to Mrs. Briss about Gilbert Long and his
mysterious lady. "It's a relation, and they work the relation." But
what *is* the relation, and how does it work? It is the relation "exquisite surely, of knowing they help each other to shine." And "to
shine" is to shine socially, in the art of conversation. If sexual love
is viewed here as the sacred fount of true personality, if it is described as a kind of hidden natural resource, a secret deposit of
shining golden ore, there is after all nothing "vulgar" in the use to

which it is being put, just as there is, at base, nothing sexual in this love. But what of the opposite side of this curious concept: the price which is paid by the "victims" of such passion? Was *The Sacred Fount* a pure conceit, as James implied, or did he really believe that in any human relation — or rather, sexual relation — one partner had to pay, one partner had to sacrifice his deepest vitality, one partner had to lose all, in order for the other partner to bloom, to thrive, even to "shine"? What a rigid and fearful base for all these strangely shifting and nonsexual sexual love affairs! Wasn't it conceivable to the questioning, fanciful and analytic Jamesian mind that through the process of both lovers giving themselves wholly and completely to their passion, without stint and without ego, each might be mutually nourished and enhanced? Or that in the normal course of human passion, the price of love — yes, the sacrifice, the giving, even perhaps the destruction of personality — had something to do with the pleasure of love?

In real life, of course, lovers do destroy each other; but this was far, far away from the Jamesian concept in *The Sacred Fount*. According to Leon Edel's essay on the novel,* the theory of "cannibalism" in the story was one of Henry James's earliest and abiding convictions not only in literature but in his own life. It originated with the young Henry's idea that his mother had sacrificed her own personality and life in order to support and strengthen his erratic philosopher-father. It included the tragic early death of the one woman he had dared remotely to love, the beautiful, bright cousinly Minny Temple, whose "sacrifice," so James wrote at the

* In Mr. Edel's Introduction to the Grove Press edition of *The Sacred Fount*. This critic *is* perceptive, both here and in what has been called the definitive biography of Henry James. But since Mr. Edel refuses to follow out his own psychological perceptions, since he always rationalizes them in James's favor, and is fearful of any real criticism, his own conclusions are curiously muffled. One might say that this Jamesian scholar, learned as he is, reveals James's temperament exactly as *James* saw himself, whereas it is the duty of a critic or biographer to see around and through his subject — to reveal that subject from both within and without. Volumes II and III of this exhaustive biography, published in 1962, suffer even more severely from the same biographical and critical limitations, while the "game of James" becomes more apparent. Exhaustive — but *not* definitive.

time, coincided with — and was responsible for? — the growth
and release of his own literary powers. Yet this is hardly a satis-
factory answer to the central enigma of *The Sacred Fount*. Henry
James's family relations, both parental and sibling, were much
more complex than this. And we know also that the "cannibalism"
at the base of the love affairs in *The Sacred Fount* is related, on the
psychological level, to a very early and primitive infantile fancy —
pre-oedipal, and pre-sexual — of the child "eating" the mother who
is nursing him, and hence possessed of the equivalent fear of also
being "eaten up." We see something of this same fantasy in the
phobias of Swift and Lewis Carroll, about which the psychoanalyst
Phyllis Greenacre has written a discerning study; not to mention
Jack London's deep oral complex in which the Darwinian law of
the jungle becomes mainly a matter of the gastric juices.

In the Jamesian case, however, this fear of love, and particularly
sexual love, also precluded any chance of the artist himself being
involved in a serious human relationship, masculine or feminine,
and contributed in turn to that self-enclosed, all-sufficient, armored
and embedded Jamesian ego. (And wasn't *that*, the desire to de-
vour, quite as important as the fear of being devoured in the deepest levels of this writer's psyche?) In the case of *The Sacred Fount*
itself, the underlying concept of love as food was accompanied by
other equally childlike and pre-sexual obsessions. The symptoms
of the infantile-oral in the basic concept of the novel are matched
by the symptoms of the infantile-anal, as though the giving or withholding of love were like the giving or withholding of bowel movements; or by the equally juvenile fantasy that the loss of human
sperm impairs the health and vitality of the human organism. The
central concept here was that of "hoarding" love — as though love,
and sexual love, were not infinite, as though love did not replenish
love, as though love did not create love in an inexhaustible cycle;
while James indeed viewed the sacred fount of sexuality not as a
boiling spring of human creativity, but as some exotic, expensive,
mystical fluid, to be treasured in tiny, precious vials.

It is clear, too, that the fanatical observer of all the peculiar sexual antics in *The Sacred Fount* is directly in the line of the Jamesian children, as in *What Maisie Knew* or *The Awkward Age*, who stood outside the charmed circle of adult "intimacy," or who, as in "The Turn of the Screw," had to be punished — or even killed — as a result of their contact with the mysterious, sacred, evil force. But here the typical Jamesian hero — this spy in the house of love — has made a momentous step forward. It is in his own *mind* that he has created these transient, shifting, slippery love affairs. It is his own mind which now even invents and *controls* these love affairs; it is his own mind which, as he admits, is in the end far superior to love. It is the pure Jamesian ego, in short, cut off and constricted from all normal human relations, self-enclosed, so heavily inhibited and surrounded by this chain network of unfortunate "lovers," which emerges triumphant in *The Sacred Fount*.

Meanwhile, the "germ" of sexual curiosity is very catching indeed, and we have a series of "multiple observers" (which James had suggested earlier in "The Private Life"), each with his or her own theory which the obsessed advocate of "pure reason" also has to control or manipulate. For it turns out that May Server must be the logical victim of Gilbert Long's rise to conversational brilliance. She is the true fount of his suddenly acquired critical acumen and eloquence. She is on the edge of hysteria and collapse, and she has completely lost her own "conversational gifts." Is the omnipotent analyst of *The Sacred Fount* absolutely positive about this? He admits his own ignorance about certain facts of love. "It would have been almost as embarrassing to have to tell them how little experience I had had in fact as to have had to tell them how much I had had in fancy . . ." Yet there is Long, "the transfigured talker," and there is Mrs. Server, flitting, distraught and mum. The novel's hero puts forth a bold front, even while he feels a certain condescending "sorrow" for the victims of his relentless curiosity. When poor Briss raises "his pathetic old face" to inquire: "You 'know'?" the hero responds: "Ah, I know everything!" But this is to a certain degree a paranoid kind of pity, and a false compassion. Briss pleads with him (as he thinks) not to tell. "I felt as if he were now, intellectually speaking, plastic wax in my hand."

Does this sexual "researcher" remind us at times of the hysterical governess in "The Turn of the Screw"? But the governess was a true heroine — made mad by circumstances — while this hero only serves to make everybody else go mad. He is what James was so fond of presenting — "the other side of the case." And now, as he pursues Mrs. Server in order to force a confession out of her, in order to prove to himself "the beauty of having been right," the nightmare atmosphere of *The Sacred Fount* thickens and darkens:

I scarce knew what odd consciousness I had of roaming at close of day in the grounds of some castle of enchantment. I had positively encountered nothing to compare with this since the days of fairy-tales and of the childish imagination of the impossible. Then I used to circle round enchanted castles, for then I moved in a world in which the strange "came true." It was the coming true that was the proof of the enchantment . . .

And that is to say that the fairy-tale enchantment which had possessed James's own mind from his early youth; which had quickened his first vision of medieval England as the true home for his outcast soul; which had remained as the real base and ideological (or emotional) framework for all his literary work, was now being used — "with an evening sky above and great lengthening, arching recesses in which the twilight thickened" — to overpower an innocent soul. May Server is a ruined woman, owing to her passion — "voided and scraped of everything, her shell was merely crushable" — and the narrator-inquisitor is nevertheless determined to get the last secret out of her broken spirit and miserable body alike.

In one sense, this is perhaps the oddest "punishment" for the strangest love affair in the annals of literature. And in another twist, the Jamesian observer — now "hot" on the trail, now turned implacable interrogator — almost ignores Mrs. Server's own plight in his overwhelming compassion for all such victims of love. "Who of us all could say that his fall might not be as deep? — or might not at least become so with equal opportunity. I for a while fairly forgot Mrs. Server, I fear, in the intimacy of this vision of the possibilities of our common nature." Now these possibilities of common nature must at all costs be avoided. "She became such a wasted and dishonoured symbol of them as might have put tears in one's eyes." And "wasted" and "dishonored," naturally, because in the Jamesian lexicon of love, such a total sacrifice of tragic womanhood implied no possible returns, no satisfactions, even no merely transient rewards of a passion which simply encompassed and destroyed the whole personality of the lover. Or, on the other hand, implied the bland, self-serving, self-enhancing, purely narcissistic "gifts" of love which are accompanied, which are covered, by the lifeblood of the other partner. May Server is "the absolute wreck of her storm, accordingly" — a ruined, devitalized, dishonored woman to whose passion-wracked frame "the pale ghost of a special sensibility still clung."

Only now the Jamesian interrogator-inquisitor, having plumbed the final depths of love, is covered indeed with a kind of terrible shame and horror. It is almost as though that prying, peeping child, who is at the psychological core of all these morbidly and sexually curious observers during this period of Henry James's work, had at long last gained entrance to what has been called "the primal scene" of his parents' sexual intercourse. (But why "primal," why even sinful or shameful, except of course in the Victorian framework of western European or American culture of inhibited sexuality in which James, like Freud, had grown up.) At least this narrator blames himself profusely. "Nothing need have happened if I hadn't been so absurdly, so fatally meditative about poor Long . . ." And now even Gilbert Long, the brilliant critic and conversationalist, the bland recipient of May Server's total passion and total being, is also to be pitied. The victors and victims of love alike are to be mourned, just as the Brissendens are also the tragic results of our common human nature. The narrator sees this clearly — "I had puzzled out everything and put everything together" — even while he staggers under the burden of his knowledge, and his guilt. "Nothing could have been stranger than for *me* so to know it was while the stricken parties themselves were in ignorance."

Thus *The Sacred Fount* was a key document to Henry James's peculiar notions about human relationships and the human psyche. (Edmund Wilson was correct in his intuition about this esoteric document, although he lacked the patience to follow it up.) But having revealed so much about the central content of his fiction, and the peculiar if logical form which his craft then followed, it was almost as though the writer hastened to cover up, to mystify and conceal what he had just expressed and exposed. For May Server summons up her last bit of remaining personality to deny flatly the narrator's great "discovery." "What makes you have such a fancy," she asks; while the painter Obert and Mrs. Briss also retreat from their assistant or collaborative roles in his gruesome theories.

The mental manipulation of all these secondary characters by the omnipotent observer — complacent, smug, perhaps mad — is the final twist in *The Sacred Fount*. He becomes the perfect proto-Freudian analyst, as it were, who is always right, who always understands the peculiar behavior of the "patients" who may oppose or flatly deny his speculations; the analyst who can rationalize away any action which contradicts his own "conclusions." That is also the final enigma of the novel. For the terrible, devouring Jamesian desire to discover, to understand, or to see all these mysterious, evil, fascinating and secret love affairs is matched by the Jamesian instinct to place "screens" before his observer's eyes — or not to see.

That is the psychological pattern of *The Sacred Fount* which the Jamesian critics have evaded through the application of the moralistic or metaphysical theme of "appearance versus reality." "Psychologic evidence" is honorable and intelligent, says James's literary spokesman here. "What's ignoble is the detective and the key-hole." But isn't his whole method of psychological observation, pursuit and interrogation simply a somewhat veiled, and perhaps more dubious sublimation of the detective and the keyhole? A keyhole psychology, as it were, in which the prurient observer himself is not only covered with guilt at what he has finally "seen," but also becomes the victim, in part, of the speculations he has set going in the minds of all his assistant snoops? The final section of the novel, at least, becomes a kind of mad farce of psychologic theory and countertheory, finally exploding into nothingness.

The chief sexual investigator is still absolutely certain of his own results. "I could toss the ball myself, I could catch it and send it back, and familiarity had now made this exercise — in my own inner precincts — easy and safe." (And this was James's own notion of a creative fancy pure and inviolate within the artist's own mind, not to be contaminated by any further "facts," or the intrusion of reality.) In the novel, alas, Lady John's "clumsier curiosity made me tremble for the impunity of my creation." It is Lady John who takes him to task, very sensibly, for his intellectual omnipotence. "Well, all the same, give up, for a quiet life, the attempt to be a providence. You can't be a providence and not be a bore. A real providence *knows*; whereas you . . . have to find out." (There is also, of course, the simple explanation, for all this Jamesian sexual complexity, that Mrs. Server is having a nervous breakdown of sorts, owing possibly not so much to "love" as to lack of love, while Gilbert Long has been taking instruction in the art of parlor conversation.) In the face of these facts the observer retreats a few steps: "It comes back to me that the sense thus established of my superior vision may perfectly have gone a little to my head." But only to advance even more triumphantly in his own mind! "If it was a frenzied fallacy I was all to blame, but if it was anything else whatever it was naturally intoxicating. I really remember in fact nothing so much as this confirmed presumption of my impunity had appeared to me to mark the fine quality of my state —

I think there must fairly have been a pitch at which I was not sure that not to partake of that state was, on the part of others, a sign of a gregarious vulgarity; as if there were a positive advantage, an undiluted bliss in the intensity of consciousness that I had reached. I alone was magnificently and absurdly aware — everyone else was benightedly out of it.

Now this was the familiar cry of the typically Jamesian orphaned and outcast child; the wise child who "knows all" about the mysterious world of adult intimacy; the child observer who has developed into the "outside-narrator" but who nevertheless dominates the aristocratic (if corrupt?) "insiders" simply by his intensity of consciousness, his superior mental power. This was indeed very close to the tone and manner of the later James of the Prefaces; or maybe it was the real key to the celebrated Jamesian "method," and his elaborate esthetic rationalizations.

There is the admission on the narrator's part of his own need of his theories as a compulsion or an opiate to cope with the blank or boring "reality" of ordinary life. Suppose that May Server should suddenly return to her normal self! Then he would be "free" to leave Newmarch, but —

Was this now a foreknowledge that, on the morrow, in driving away, I should feel myself restored to that blankness? The state lost was the state of exemption from intense obsessions, and the state recovered would therefore logically match it . . . My liberation was in a manner what I was already tasting. Yet how I also felt with it something of a threat of a chill to my curiosity! The taste of its being all over, that really sublime success of the strained vision in which I had been living for crowded hours — was this a taste that I was sure I should particularly enjoy?

So it isn't the truth or the reality of a human situation that the Jamesian spokesman seeks, so much as his own state of intensity resulting from these "obsessions," or the sublime pleasure "of the

strained vision," which obviates the fear of solitude, loneliness or
the chilled curiosity. This is surely again something like the description of an artist's imagination, but carried to the point where
the intensity of the imagination (or the fear of the nonimagination)
takes precedence over any sense of factuality; or over the *kind* of
content with which this imagination is dealing. In the novel itself,
Mrs. Server does return to normal, and Ford Obert repudiates his
own connection with the narrator. "Well, I'm afraid I *can't* take
any more —" the painter says. "*Mon siège est fait* — a great glittering crystal palace," says the narrator-hero: "How many panes
will you reward me for amiably sitting up with you by smashing?"
"How on earth," answers Ford Obert, "can I tell what you're talking about?"

How indeed? Has the whole novel been a prolonged fantasy on
the part of its "hero"? Or has the psychological process of "devouring passion" à la James — of cannibalistic love — begun to reverse itself, perhaps? Or is the narrator's hypothesis *so* accurate
that the chief personages in this narrative are withdrawing in order
to protect themselves from it? Here begins, at least, the frenzy of
the frustrated "psychologist" to flatter, to charm, to force, to coerce,
if need be, his assistant observers not to destroy his "theories,"
during the course of which he teases, begs, lies, cajoles, threatens,
with every weapon, every wile of his superior intellect. But Obert
remains stubborn in his common sense. "Oh, I've watched *you*,"
says the painter in his turn, in this drama of voyeurism in which
everybody has been spying on everybody else. And just at this
point "poor Briss" appears to bring the message that Mrs. Brissenden has to speak with the narrator. "I trod with him, over the vel-
vet and the marble, through the twists and turns, among the
glooms and glimmers and echoes" — of Newmarch, that is. And:
"He let me keep his hand while things unspoken and untouched,
unspeakable and untouchable . . . were between us again."

There is another fairytale-nightmare episode within the English
country house, the "enchanted castle" with its great corridors, its

long series of brilliantly lighted empty rooms, its complete absence
of servants and of guests alike now; and with its wandering spy
awaiting his final encounter with the great lady who best represents
this dreamlike aristocracy. The narrator leaves Obert, with a polite
lie, and proceeds to meet his doom. For Mrs. Briss, too, has turned
against him; and rejects not only his "theories" but the narrator
himself as a suitable member for their select company. The ending
of *The Sacred Fount* is overextended, overwritten, overdone. As
in a play, the two protagonists match wits with each other in a series
of long, elaborate, formal "set speeches."

But now the narrator is a confessed liar, sneak, voyeur and
trickster, in the best tradition of the hysterical or possessed Jamesian heroes. He is a trifle "menaced." "Things *had* to hang together . . . and now they don't." Mrs. Briss, moreover, is "under
arms" for this final battle. Her beauty, her tone, her authority, all
certify her as the legitimate spokesman for her group, her circle,
her "race." The narrator — uneasily aware of the chinks ("the
thing I had not thought of") in his wall of pure reason, or his
crystal palace of sexual hypotheses which is about to become a
house of cards — is aware of a number of things "that occurred in
these stayed seconds of our silence":

But they are to be perhaps best represented by the two most marked
intensities of my own sensation: the first the certitude that she had at
no moment since her marriage so triumphantly asserted her defeat of
time, and the second the conviction that I, losing with her while, as it
were, we closed, a certain advantage I should never recover, had at no
moment since the day before made so poor a figure on my own ground.

For the narrator, despite his egoism, vanity, and complacency —
"If I didn't fear to seem to drivel about my own knowledge, I
should say that she had, in addition to all the rest of her 'pull,'
the benefit of striking me as worthy of me" — despite all his
"me-rooted" verbal skill, the narrator has already lost the battle.

Mrs. Briss is "in the mystic circle," and even "her looks around" at the empty chambers of this so intensely nocturnal palace, are "immense." Then at least, so we are told, "she charged." "It's nonsense. I've nothing to tell you. I feel there's nothing in it and I've given it up." "You've made out then who *is?*" the narrator asks eagerly; if, that is, the sacrificial woman is *not* May Server. "Oh, I don't make out, you know," says Mrs. Briss, "so much as you!" Just as in the preliminary interview with Ford Obert, and just like a pleading child who has the gift of a marvelous sophistry, the narrator, even at this point, will not admit the defeat of his singular superiority of mind; or of the rigid, closed circle of his intellectual vanity; or of the armor of his ego-bound temperament. (He is indeed horrified by, and placates and flatters the "huge egotism" of Mrs. Brissenden.) There comes to him, with the click of a sudden intellectual connection, the further "hypothesis" that Gilbert Long and Mrs. Briss, the two "victors" of love, have combined forces to pretend normality, and hence defeat his whole concept of the devouring passions. "I had achieved my flight into luminous ether and, alighting gracefully on my feet, reported myself at my post."

What a scene; what a grand climax to a mad novel! Perhaps nowhere else in his work did James reveal so clearly, so brilliantly, with so much self-insight and wit, the arrogance of pure reason; the follies, grandeurs and disasters of the superior intellect; the abounding faculty (and facility) of both James and his spokesmen to rationalize all the disasters and debacles of life into a consuming image of self-aggrandisement: to strain all the truth of reality through the screen or the sieve of self-serving "theory." Whether in parody or self-revelation too, the narrator of *The Sacred Fount* not only has the view and tone of the later Prefaces; but he is very close to the possessed or obsessive author of the *Notebooks* also, asserting his own will and talent against the world's indifferent verdict.

This was the monomania of the intellect. But it is of no use. Like Obert, Mrs. Briss clings stubbornly to her own conclusions.

"I'm afraid I know nothing," she insists, while noting that her interlocutor "abounds in traps." "I stick . . . to my ignorance," she says again, and then even repeats Obert's phrase. "How can I tell, please . . . what you consider you're talking about?" And then: "You talk too much!" she repeats. "You build up houses of cards." And then: "The trouble with you is that you over-estimate the penetration of others . . . How can it approach your own?" She is not without an irony to match the fevered appeals of the narrator. "I don't at all feel comfortable about your new theory," cries this narrator, to whom even her present *lack* of any theory is a theory, "which puts me so wretchedly in the wrong." "Rather," says Mrs. Briss, almost gaily. "Wretchedly indeed in the wrong!" "You flatly contradict me?" he cries, "You deny my miracle?" "I don't believe in miracles," she says. And then he feels some intensification — "not quite, I trust, wanton" — of her suspense. (And how James uses the terminology of the flesh for this purely cerebral exchange. Mrs. Briss has also "panted," not to say "wailed," during this encounter.) And then she gives it to him. "Do you know what I think," says Mrs. Briss. "Well . . . I think you're crazy." "Crazy?" he says. "Crazy."

There is still more of this in the climactic scene of *The Sacred Fount*, convolution upon convolution, for the narrator is willing to debate even his own lunacy, and wants to know how Mrs. Briss has made up her mind, of a sudden, that she "has been steeped in the last intellectual intimacy with a maniac." He is still convinced that if this aristocratic circle of British lovers is now cruel to him, it was he, after all, who has *caused* their cruelty. And he gives up hard. " 'Remember,' I pleaded, 'that you're costing me a perfect palace of thought!' " Yet his frail, "but, as I maintain, quite sublime structure" has already crashed on the rocks of Mrs. Briss's indifferent disdain; her rejection not only of the narrator's "theory," but, along with this, of the narrator himself. Finally, "with her negations arrayed and her insolence recaptured," Mrs. Briss has the last word. "My poor dear, you *are* crazy, and I bid you good night!" And then there is the narrator's final confession of defeat, and of flight. "Such a last word — the word that put me altogether nowhere — was too unacceptable not to prescribe afresh that prompt test of escape to other air for which I had earlier in the evening seen so much reason. I *should* certainly never again, on the spot, quite hang together, even though it wasn't really that I hadn't three times her method. What I too fatally lacked was her tone."

Thus the final note of *The Sacred Fount* is the ignominious flight of the "outsider" — one who in his own mind has dominated the charmed set of the British aristocrats (and evil, incestuous lovers), but who finally proves unacceptable to them precisely *because* of his superior intellect which threatens their social (and personal) security. Was there something familiar about all this, a recurrent Jamesian notion, cast in a somewhat new light, with a new, and rather unpleasant ending? Was it indeed a variation on the fantasy of the orphan and outcast child, cut off from the charmed and mysterious circle of adult (sexual) "intimacy," now transformed into the omnipotent "observer" who is nevertheless still rejected by precisely the same royal English society which the younger James had claimed as his true ancestral home and his definitive literary orbit? How many stories and novels had he not erected on the theme of the vulgar American outsider, rich as he might be, who could not yet enter the "palace" of ancient European culture; while he himself, as the true chronicler of the international scene, could see both sides, and held all the keys, and was perched securely apart from, or on top of, the battle! Yet it was the same Anglo-American artist whose most revealing spokesman now confessed his failure to dominate the charmed society, European or English, even by the utmost power of mind or talent — who was so clearly sent packing by them; who slid down again — *himself* — the slippery moats of the old-world castle of culture.

Earlier in *The Sacred Fount* the Jamesian observer had hinted at this impending doom, because of his own "imagination":

I think the imagination, in those halls of art and fortune, was almost inevitably accounted a poor matter; the whole place and its participants abounded so in pleasantness and picture, in all the felicities, for every sense, taken for granted there by the very basis of life, that even the sense most finely poetic, aspiring to extract the moral, could scarce have helped feeling itself treated to something of the snub that affects . . . the uninvited reporter in whose face a door is closed. I said to myself during dinner that these were scenes in which a transcendent intelligence had after all no application, and that, in short, any preposterous acuteness might easily suffer among them such a loss of dignity as overtakes the newspaper-man kicked out . . .

Now one notices the curious ambiguousness in this passage, where the glittering halls "of art and fortune" have no real use for art, or where the symbolic artist himself, though endowed with his aspiring poetic sense, his transcendent intelligence and sublime acuteness — still, that is, superior to the group which casts him out — is nevertheless compared with the "uninvited reporter," or the newspaperman kicked out. In the Jamesian fantasy the fairy-tale myth of noble British society still persisted. "We existed, all of us together, to be handsome and happy, to be really what we looked — since we looked tremendously well; to be that and neither more nor less, so not discrediting by musty secrets and aggressive doubts our high privilege of harmony and taste." The narrator even inquires, rather plaintively, if *he* doesn't look as good as the rest of these fortunate folk. "Was I not very possibly myself, on this ground of physiognomic congruity, more physiognomic than anyone else?" Yet no woman here seeks him out for anything but conversation. He is alone with his esoteric fantasies of their sexual secrets. And in the end James linked his protagonist in the tale to just that loathsome symbol of the newspaper reporter (or the "damned publishing scoundrel" of "The Aspern Papers") who had been held up to such ridicule and contempt in James's own work.

Had he not then, in his own secret heart, also recognized himself, as well as his present spokesman, to be hardly more than a superior gossip columnist — this singularly talented artist! — in the cultivated British society whose anecdotes he gathered and developed for his unread books, his hissed-at plays? In this sense *The Sacred Fount* was a kind of parting, a farewell to the earliest, most prevailing and profound Jamesian dream of an English home. But in the same breath, it was also a realization of, and a partial catharsis for, his own deepest illusions, obsessions, or perhaps even psychological hallucinations on both the sexual and social levels. If indeed *The Sacred Fount* started out with the fertile sexual fantasies of the outcast child, it ended, grimly enough, on the note of the mature artist cast out of British "society" because of his own superior but unwanted talent. Well, there was still an infantile element, never to be lost by Henry James, in this ironical conclusion, too. But meanwhile by this sliding-down again, in the fantasy life of his fiction, the high, slippery moat-wall which surrounded his European castle of fortune, culture and art — by being in short kicked out of the castle — he had perhaps gained another ironic perspective as a writer. (Or at least any artist *but* Henry James might have gained this perspective.)

The Sacred Fount, then, under the guise of parody and self-parody, was a kind of disguised, and even deliberately obfuscated spiritual autobiography which, in a typically Jamesian manner, both displayed and hid its real content. Very likely the levels of meaning in the nouvelle-novel could hardly have been faced by this writer unless they had been masked in satire, farce and ambiguity. But in a measure, if they were not completely faced here, they were expressed and revealed. And Henry James was already composing and writing those big novels of his final phase which — with all their obvious shortcomings, and maybe just *because* of their increasingly exotic mannerisms, their increasingly singular vision of experience — would be among his most complex and most curious works.

And meanwhile we have seen clearly enough, haven't we, the true fantasy life and the secret nightmares of Henry James himself. I mean the haunted and terrified visions of failure, impotence and rejection which lay behind that massive, portentous, ponderous social façade of "omnipotence" which he had constructed as his official literary personality — and which, in turn, he hid behind during his daylight life.

8. False Gold

"THE WINGS OF THE DOVE," published in 1902, was written directly before (or at the same time, psychologically, as) Henry James's excursion into "parody" and self-revelation in *The Sacred Fount*. It was the first of the three "major novels" — including *The Ambassadors* and *The Golden Bowl* — in a burst of the Jamesian virtuosity which greeted the new century.

Nor was this the end of it. There were still to appear ten-odd volumes in the years from 1905 to 1915, and at least six more posthumous books; not to count the scores of new volumes which were fashioned out of the body of his work by the indefatigable and zealous Jacobite critics and editors in the great revival of the 1950's. It was almost as though this writer continued to "produce, produce!" more books at the close of his long life — and after it — than he had during the four full decades of his "apprenticeship."

In the Jamesian canon, too, the *Dove* is generally assumed to be the great tragic novel of his major phase. And there is even more than the usual amount of critical paraphernalia, both from the writer and from his disciples, surrounding the novel. There is the autobiographical element of Minny Temple, the orphan cousin of James, and apparently the one deep romantic attachment of his youth. Her beauty "in her fatal illness" deeply impressed the early writer, as he stated, and she is the prototype of the stricken American heiress, Milly Theale, in the *Dove*, as well as a source of Isabel Archer in *The Portrait of a Lady*. (Her image, her name, or her

initials occur elsewhere in James's work; we shall come to this relationship in the context of the James family.)

There is the first entry about the novel in the *Notebooks*, dated
November, 1894, at 34 De Vere Gardens. (Even James's London
address had a certain fairy-tale quality of long-ago romance.) "She
is in love with life," so Henry wrote about the novel's heroine, "and
she clings to it with passion, with supplication" — and in this case
the origins, the "germ" of the novel as the writer visualized it, were
of particular interest. The hero was initially "to take pity" on the
rich, beautiful and diseased American girl through an impulse of
kindness or indulgence. But the young hero was to be also entangled with another woman — "committed, pledged, 'engaged' to
one" — and he must expect no "reward" for his kindness. For the
novel's stricken heroine, "even if he loved her, has no life to give
him in return —

*no life, and no personal, no physical surrender, for it seems to me that
one must represent her as too ill for that particular case. It has bothered
me in thinking of the little picture — this idea of the physical possession, the brief physical, passional rapture which at first appeared essential to it; bothered me on account of the ugliness, the incongruity, the
nastiness, en somme, of the man's "having" a sick girl; also on account
of something rather pitifully obvious and vulgar in the presentation of
such a remedy for her despair — and such a remedy only. "Oh, she's
dying without having had it? Give it to her and let her die" — that
strikes me as sufficiently second-rate.*

"If I were writing for a French public the whole thing would be
simple," so James added. "The elder, the 'other,' woman would
simply be the mistress of the young man, and it would be a question of his taking on the dying girl for a time — having a temporary
liaison with her. But one can do so little with English adultery."
But was it only a question of English adultery? For passages like
this one are often quoted by the Jacobite critics to refute the charge
that James was incapable of describing the primary passions.

Certainly he was at last "conscious" of them — but wasn't the *manner* of his consciousness just the point here, as it is in *The Sacred Fount?* That "brief physical, passional rapture" — and why was it necessarily so brief, in a novel like *The Wings of the Dove* which extended itself for over seven hundred pages in two volumes? Why was it described as ugly, incongruous and nasty, *en somme,* simply because the heroine was sick or dying? Certainly a later generation of major writers, from D. H. Lawrence to Thomas Mann, felt differently about the kind of physical passion which was engendered precisely on account of the physical disease of tuberculosis in their heroes or heroines. And that which was truly obvious and vulgar in the Jamesian presentation of such a remedy — and why such a remedy "only," as though physical love absolutely precluded any form of spiritual love? — was not the dying girl's not "having had it." (And what was the "it" that James meant?) What was obvious and vulgar and second rate indeed was the whole Jamesian concept of sexual love described in this passage of the *Notebooks.*

Wasn't it a perfect example, not so much of James's "acknowledging" the physical passions, but of his true view of them, and of his curious process of refining them away, of converting the primary human drives into a sublimated sort of idealism, an ethereal sensibility? "Doesn't a greater prettiness, as well as a better chance for a story," he asked himself, "abide in her being already too ill for that, and in his being able merely to show her some delicacy of kindness, to let her think that they might have loved each other *ad infinitum* if it hadn't been too late." And "prettiness," "delicacy," in the prevailing Jamesian notion of a hopeless, tragic lost love — of love denied *ad infinitum* — took over the place of the passions again in *The Wings of the Dove.* But there was, to be sure, the subplot of the curiously named hero, Merton Densher, and of Kate Croy, whose initial crime was simply that of poverty. If James refined away the sexual elements of his narrative, he grounded himself firmly again on a solid base of cash. "From the moment a young man engages himself he ought to have means," he said here, rather sententiously; "if he hasn't he oughtn't to engage himself" — just as if he were echoing the sentiment of all his respectable, Victorian, middle class maiden aunts.

In the *Notebooks* he outlined the drama, or melodrama, of Densher's attempt to marry Milly Theale, in order to get her fortune for himself and Kate Croy. "I had asked myself if there was anything in the idea of the man's *agreeing with his fiancée that he shall marry the poor girl in order to come into her money and in the certitude that she will die and leave the money to him* — on which basis (his becoming a widower with property) they themselves will at last be able to marry." The italics are James's. On the matter of inherited fortunes he was as definite as ever — though now what he envisaged was the idea that a woman in love would "lease out" her lover to another woman for the sake of the fortune; although now what he was imagining was a kind of unnatural human behavior, as well as a kind of moral, if not legal, crime. "Then the sequel to that?" he added. "I can scarcely imagine any — I doubt if I can — that isn't ugly and vulgar: I mean vulgarly ugly." And notice how James, in respect to both sex and money in *The Wings of the Dove*, was almost obsessed by the fear of the ugly and the vulgar: of vulgar sex that can be dispensed with, and of vulgar money that can't be.

But then came the idea of Milly Theale's "sacrifice." She will give her fortune to Densher *despite* the fact that she knows he has never really loved her, that he has been plotting to get her fortune for the sake of Kate Croy. "Some rapturous act of that sort — some act of generosity, of passionate beneficence, of pure sacrifice, to the man she loves." In this carefully plotted "scenario" for the *Dove*, what one realizes, of course, is how James was weaving his way between two extremes of human behavior, both of which were essentially false, or highly improbable: between the woman who would "lend" her lover and the woman who would reward him for his deceit — between the moral crime and the rapturous act of idealism; between — still, and always — the nightmare and the fairy tale.

Besides this, however, the plot which James finally evolved for the *Dove* had several contributory virtues. The generous gesture of Milly Theale's sacrificial offering of her fortune to Densher directly before her death "would obviate all 'marriage' between *them*, and everything so vulgar as an 'engagement,' and, removing the poor creature's yearning from the class of egotistic pleasures, the dream of being possessed and possessing, etc., make it something fine and strange." Thus, any notion of physical love was not only vulgar but "egotistical." The dream of being possessed meant to James the idea of "possessing," just as in *The Sacred Fount* the relationships of love meant either devouring or being devoured. And there was still another variation on his theme. The woman who had lent her lover for the sake of the illicit fortune was also to be frustrated. "She is eager, ready to marry now, but he has really fallen in love with the dead girl . . . In the light of how exquisite the dead girl was he sees how little exquisite is the living." Just as the lack of money had originally prevented Kate Croy and Densher from consummating their passion (in or out of marriage), now the presence of money would equally prevent it; and just as Densher was unable, really, to give his love to the living Milly Theale, now he would give it only to the dead Milly Theale.

What a complex of ambiguous frustrations! And there was still the final twist upon all the other twists of this projected scenario for *The Wings of the Dove.* For James had originally conceived this story also to be a *play.* "I seem to get almost a little 3-act play — with the main part for a young actress. I get, at any rate, a distinct and rather dramatic *action*, don't I?" As indeed he did; while the late Jamesian impulse for rather lurid melodrama — which paralleled, which supplemented his almost "actionless" drama of consciousness, or the silent play of intellect or sensibility — found its rationale, its "authority," so to speak, in his impenitent yearning for a popular play, and his sense of the necessary *stage action.* Just as the dominant theme of the narrative was the repression, or the "sublimation" of all the primary and vulgar physical passions, the final note was to be that, again, of the resolution of the illegitimate fortune which Densher has inherited from the dead Milly Theale. "Does he want to keep the money for himself?" Kate Croy would demand of her former lover.

There is a very painful, almost violent scene between them. (How it all — or am I detached? — seems to map itself out as a little 3-act play!) They break, in a word — he says, "Be it so!" — as the woman gives him, in her resentment and jealousy (of the other's memory, now) an opening to break — by offering to let him off. But he offers her the money and she takes it. Then vindictively, in spite, with the money and with her father's restored countenance, she marries Lord X., while he lives poor and single and faithful — faithful to the image of the dead.

How noble, how lurid, how sentimental, how improbable, how "touching" and how hammy, in fact, was this projected Jamesian stage drama of *The Wings of the Dove;* and he was moreover quite willing to add a "happy ending" for his great tragedy if only it could reach the stage!

Yet the Minny Temple-Milly Theale story was, according to Matthiessen and Murdock, based on James's deepest feeling: "the stored-up accumulation of one of the primary emotional experiences of his youth." In Milly, James "probed the deep connection between love and the will to live," while in the *Dove* itself, "his accumulated resources of pity and terror enabled him to produce his principal tragedy." Well, we have already noticed the Jamesian concept of "primary experience," the deep connection between love and the will to live which is based on the renunciation of any physical or passional love at least, and those "accumulated resources" of pity and terror which are also predicated on financial accumulation. Moreover, in his *Henry James: The Major Phase,* F. O. Matthiessen himself, so often elsewhere a discerning critic with sound values, described *The Wings of the Dove* in such terms as James's "masterpiece." Or "that single work where his characteristic emotional vibration seems deepest." Or the novel in which "we may have the

sense, thereof, that we have come to 'the very soul' of the artist";
and of which "the dominating beauty" was in its heroine, Milly
Theale. Now Matthiessen wasn't unaware of certain limitations in
this masterpiece. His whole study of the novel, originally given as
a lecture, is an attempt to explain away, to "understand," and to
prove the hidden merits of what are precisely James's most patent
deficiencies.

As a result, the historical and cultural observations in Matthiessen's essay on *The Wings of the Dove*, based on the false premises
of the Jamesian fiction itself, lead to very dubious conclusions.
(This critic was also blocked psychologically, as we shall notice
shortly; and accepted the Jamesian "morality" as given, without
questioning its real meaning.) The superstructure of Matthiessen's
analysis, based on the Jamesian sand, totters uneasily; the tone of
his "critical study" is sentimental, uneasy, apologetic, evasive. By
comparison, F. W. Dupee is more acute about the obvious shortcomings of the *Dove*. The writing in this novel, to be sure, reaches
"some kind of high water mark in English prose," says this critic,
though he neglects to specify what kind. The two girls, Milly
Theale and Kate Croy, are "magnificent," Dupee also admits, but:
"As Milly is mortally ill, so Kate is mortally poor" — a sharp observation, which again fails to state that Kate is only too poor to
marry Densher in middle class circumstances. Within the same
aura of veneration for the novel, Dupee argues that Kate is the real
heroine, if an evil one, while he quotes Edmund Wilson to the
effect that there is some kind of "cloudy integument" around Milly
— that cloudy integument which Matthiessen converted into a triumph of "indirect presentation." Yet Dupee must add his own
paean of praise for this acknowledged Jamesian masterpiece, even
at the risk of being really quite incomprehensible.

For the dying heroine of the *Dove*, says Dupee, is a more exquisite Daisy Miller; and: "Milly is free to embody in a large way
the uncreated conscience of her race." And what this statement
means, borrowed as it is from James Joyce's *Portrait of the Art-*

ist, to be applied to the Jamesian narrative, I have frankly no idea.

Well, *if* James had really been writing about the daughters of the American robber barons who were marrying into European royalty during this period, and exchanging their new fortunes for the spurious patents of antiquity; and if James had understood the basic social-economic context of his own international theme, the Dupee statement might possibly have had some validity. But James was of course comparing the innocent American scene of his own youth — or the imaginary pre-Civil War scene of his own youthful ignorance — with his glorious vision of old-world culture. And even more than Matthiessen's perhaps, Dupee's study of the *Dove* accepts James's own view of history as a private kind of romantic, colorful, "noble" pageantry. So that, studiously avoiding any social-economic references in the contemporary fashion, Dupee ends up also with the Jamesian word "race" as a synonym for a nation, or a culture, or a limited upper class segment of a society. But now, after these typical, alas, critical commentaries on the *Dove,* what is the real import of this later Jamesian novel, and what is its true literary position?

It is, to begin with, another old-fashioned "romance" of Europe, a sequel to or a revision of *The Portrait of a Lady,* often rather glamorous and touching, if at times tedious; but refinished with a new technique (the late James), and refurbished with a subplot that is in essence a melodrama of lust and greed; while all this is viewed through the particular focus of the later Jamesian sensibility. No wonder the Jacobite critics had trouble in locating the particular source of greatness in this masterwork of James's later period, since it is such a peculiar mixture of literary parts.

The long, slow opening section of Book One (and James had now substituted "books" for chapters), which describes Kate Croy's evil heritage, is a familiar homily on middle class "degradation" — the lowest depths, to this artist, of poverty and spiritual confinement. The father, Lionel Croy, is a bankrupt dandy, whose heritage of mysterious "crime" has already influenced his beautiful, ambitious and outcast daughter. Kate's unhappy and unfortunate sister Marian, to be sure, has received "her scant share of the provision their mother had been able to leave them" — for none are so poor, even in this middle class netherland of the Jamesian social cosmos, as not to have a *small* inheritance. But she (Marian) has made the fatal mistake of marrying the parson of a dull suburban parish. She exists, in short, to show us the awful example of marriage without money — or with a little money, with four children, and with only a "small Irish governess" in a very small private house.

The opening sections of the *Dove* are thus a typical exposition of the "genteel poverty" which Henry James considered to be the lowest depths of social degradation. For after all even a suburban English minister can hardly be classified as among the slum dwellers, and there are lower class families who don't have *any* governess, even an Irish one. But from this peculiar background, Kate Croy emerges as a rather good portrait of an unloved, unwanted child who is being pressured to "make good" — that is, again, as always in James, to make a rich marriage — while unfortunately she has fallen in love with a dubious journalist (the Merton Densher of Book Two) who hardly offers her this prospect. Kate has consented to be "adopted" by her rich, brassy, vulgar Aunt Maud, the "Britannia of the Market Place," who is another satiric picture of "modern" or debased London society. "Mrs. Lowder *was* London, *was* life — the roar of the siege, and the thick of the fray." She too is determined that her handsome niece shall not marry Merton Densher; while Kate herself, impaled on passion's pitchfork, is equally adamant about having the best of her two possible worlds. Thus James really had introduced a new element in *The Wings of the Dove:* that of a consuming, illegitimate love between two social outcasts. The long talks of these lovers (Kate and Densher, I mean), and their long walks — and their "long looks" — also serve the technical purpose of elaborating the dubious social background of these illicit personages, and of foreshadowing their

dubious plans and plots in the novel's underlying melodrama —
even though these long walks and talks and looks are manipulated
so minutely by James himself for the purposes of his lurid plot that
any possibility of physical passion is drained off through the extent
of sheer verbal "analysis."

There are all the refinements of illegitimate love in the preliminary conversations between Kate Croy and Merton Densher, with
hardly a trace of physical affection. But notice the deliberate, enforced "indirection" of the later Jamesian narrative technique,
where ambiguousness is compounded by obliquity. There is Densher's reverie of his meeting with Mrs. Lowder — the whole elaborate scene of this — *while* he is walking and talking with Kate in the
park. *The Wings of the Dove* opens, indeed, in this dense fog of
reminiscence, introspection, speculation about both past and future
action; of thought and conversation which are equally complex,
veiled, enigmatic in the continual action of the lovers' *minds*, accompanied only by the perpetual flow of their words, or the use of
their larynxes rather than their lips. And then, into the midst of
this curious "old-world" scene, there is the sudden dramatic appearance of the American fairy princess, the "striking apparition"
of Milly Theale. She is "the slim, constantly pale, delicately haggard, anomalously, agreeably angular young person" (in Book Three
of the *Dove*) "of not more than two-and-twenty summers, in spite
of her marks, whose hair was somehow exceptionally red even for
the real thing, which it innocently confessed to being, and whose
clothes were remarkably black even for robes of mourning, which
was the meaning they expressed. It was New York mourning, it
was New York hair, it was a New York history . . ."

So James described her in curiously moving terms despite the
exaggerated flow of rhetoric, the dramatic attempt to make more of
Milly than she really was:

*It was a New York history, confused as yet, but multitudinous, of the
loss of parents, brothers, sisters, almost every human appendage, all on
a scale and with a sweep that had required the greater stage; it was a*

New York legend of affecting, of romantic isolation, and, beyond every-
thing, it was by most accounts, in respect to the mass of money so piled
on the girl's back, a set of New York possibilities. She was alone, she
was stricken, she was rich . . .

What a marvelous heroine of romance indeed; never forgetting, as
James never did, the last item of cash, or gold, on top of the human loss, or isolation. For Milly is a "real orphan," and wealthy,
while Kate Croy is the acquired, or self-made orphan, so to speak,
and poor. But even Milly comes to us in the narrative through
another technical "reflector," or perhaps reverberator; through the
mind of Mrs. Stringham, a rather dullish caricature of a New England spinster artist, who is Milly's companion, or semi-governess,
and whose reverie gives us the heroine's background.

Was this technique overdone by the later James, amounting in
The Wings of the Dove to a tour de force of oblique narrative, or to
something that might be called the circular novel? At least the
story's opening, up through the Fourth Book, is slow, heavy, verbose, extended, magnified, both in style and in structure. What
James called his "misplaced centre" really described his elaborate,
portentous, elongated openings, where there was no middle to the
narrative at all: but only the sudden gripping of the melodrama for
which he had set the scene. The formal structure of the *Dove* is
really that of "pre-analysis," in which the characters reveal themselves and their past while they reflect upon each other and speculate, sometimes coyly, about the impending event. Then there is
the "big scene" itself, in which we see them all functioning; or that
is to say, talking. And then there is the "post-analysis," where the
characters, reverting to their reveries, examine the event which has
happened, both in their own minds and in further conversations
with each other. And this baroque, complex structure which
James had evolved for his drama of consciousness — the multi-
circle or con-circular narrative of "analysis" — had even more elaborate developments.

But meanwhile, with Milly Theale's confrontation of English society towards the close of the first volume of the *Dove*, we have reached the point of impending melodrama and of the novel's real theme. Is it the familiar conflict of "appearance and reality" as the Jacobite critics insist? At Matcham, the great English country house where Lord Mark takes over Milly's education, where she has never felt life and civilization at so high a peak, where her vibrations, her sensibilities, are almost too tense and sharp for comfort, the Jamesian heroine feels that her quest has been achieved. But in James's own mind, of course, this modern English "society" of Mrs. Lowder and Lord Mark is no real social set at all; and moreover they are all conspiring to entrap the innocent, beautiful and wealthy American princess. The real conflict is that of illusion *and* illusion; or illusion upon illusion.

The American princess is false, or at least a romantic, improbable and rather thin embodiment of James's own pubescent concept of a heroine; without apparently any social, economic, or domestic reference at all. Her vision of English culture is false, since it represents James's own earlier (and now disenchanted) dream of the Old World. And the actual appearance, or materialization, of this dream in the smart British circle of *The Wings of the Dove* is not only false, but designed to be false — a deliberate lure and snare. In the novel's ever-widening and deepening circles of ambiguity, which are all constrained into a rigid pattern of deception by the plot line, there can be no sense of reality anywhere.

That was the central flaw of the "plotted novel," which, despite all the elaborate involutions of technique to hide, as it were, rather than to reveal the central action, James now clung to rigidly, and at the expense of any genuine literary realism. This was the novel of manipulation, rather than the novel of experience or revelation. Milly must become the pawn of all these glittering (and deceitful) English society figures; just as they in turn are the pawns of the plot, or of James himself. Moreover, while Milly possesses the early Jamesian vision of "Europe" almost intact — and how this vision, this obsession, or this fixed compulsion still haunted the Jamesian mind — so the "reality" of English society which is portrayed so glamorously and so villainously in the novel was simply his later disenchantment with "Europe." It is the obverse of the fairy tale, or the nightmare extreme of the artist's disillusionment; where the daylight world of solid, material factuality hardly can be represented. Thus the Jamesian manipulation of all these Jamesian characters (or embodied fantasies) is at the core of the novel; it is the real secret, and perhaps the real fascination of *The Wings of the Dove.* The plot action has completely superseded any chance of genuine character development, or of true human relations in the later narratives; but what they *do* reveal is what Henry James was thinking about Henry James.

These Jamesian "themes" (fantasies, illusions, notions, conceits) were, to be sure, dramatized with great skill. Under the spell of this magician's dusky enchantment, the characters, motives, relations are *almost* convincing — until you look at them in the cold light of day. In another famous scene in the novel, Milly becomes the "dove," and Kate the panther. (It is Kate who has described Milly in such terms.) "With which she felt herself ever so delicately, so considerately embraced; not with familiarity or as a liberty taken, but almost ceremonially and in the manner of an *accolade*; partly as if, though a dove who could perch on a finger, one were also a princess with whom forms were to be observed." And this imagery is elaborated and expanded in the story almost too heavily, in the manner of the later James — for this is the "embrace" of the panther which is stalking its prey. What one really becomes most conscious of at the middle point of this novel (or at the close of the first volume) is simply the high degree in which this whole cast of literary characters — who, except for the two women, are a rather mediocre lot — are "handling" and manipulating each other for their own purposes; or, more accurately, how James himself is handling and manipulating every one of them for the purposes of his own highly plotted melodrama. How, in short, this supposedly great novel, interesting as it is to read and speculate about, is centered around a series of tricks, angles and twists in the narrative.

What a curious middle-climax exists in *The Wings of the Dove*, where each character is plotting against almost every other character: where Kate is hiding her real relationship with Densher, even while she is planning to offer Densher to Milly. Where Milly, in turn, is concealing her own "secret" earlier relation with Densher, even while she may vaguely suspect, or may not suspect, the secret relationship (though how could it be?) of Kate and Densher. Where these leading characters, and the supporting cast of minor characters, snoop and spy continually upon each other's behavior, and "doings," from those hidden balconies or windows which are, as well as old-world decoration, the theatrical stage props of James's voyeurism. Or where these baroque literary figures actually *catch* each other walking with each other down the — it would seem quite public — aisles of the great British art museums!

Milly is the last good dead (or dying) American princess. All the other figures in *The Wings of the Dove* are conspiring to trap her; or to kill her, for the sake of her golden treasure — while the "dove" herself is not without her own dovelike secrets and stratagems. "The great debate" might be another title for the final sections of the first volume; but, when the melodrama begins to grip, when James, after the long, slow buildup of his plot, throws all his action into these pages of the novel — into these strange "talks" — what an odd debate of virtue and vice it really is. Thus we suddenly perceive "the onyx eyes" of Aunt Maud Lowder, with all the immensity of a literary revelation. There is also her own gossipy snooping; just as all the primary drives of these later James figures have been compressed into an overwhelming "curiosity" which this writer attributed so freely to his major and minor characters alike — replacing, in a curious contravention of the late nineteenth century Darwinian-Freudian world, the usual biological motives of food, fear, flight and sex.

Yet maybe curiosity *is* the dominant motive of the leisure-class novel at its peak, since it was elevated so far above the sphere of ordinary or typical human needs and desires. And Mrs. Lowder is another schemer and liar in the later Jamesian cosmos of schemers and liars. " 'Ah,' said Milly, 'I *don't* make out'; for again — it came that way in rushes — she felt an obscurity in things." What a marvelous, rich, calculated obscurity indeed! While in turn: "Aunt Maud took it in—took in, that is, everything of the tone that she just wanted her not to; and the result for some seconds was but to make their eyes meet in silence." With these typical Jamesian phrases and tags — "to make out" or not to make out, to "take in" or not to take in — to take in, perhaps, what is meant, and to take in, or not to take in, what is meant or what is not meant — and with this final silent meeting of eyes, or the mutual avoidance of the meeting of eyes — we have reached another climax of the drama of consciousness.

To speak or not to speak is the Jamesian question, while the hidden coil of the melodrama's trap is being slowly released. And human relations, in this esoteric literary orbit, are another synonym — or a euphemism — for human manipulation. There is Milly's stream of consciousness when Kate is "teaching" her the real truth about the shoddy, make-believe British "nobility" which Milly has considered to be the highest experience of her innocent life — and a "truth," of course, which will benefit Kate's plans for Milly rather than Mrs. Lowder's.

"She gave away publicly, in this process, Lancaster Gate and everything it contained; she gave away, hand over hand, Milly's thrill continued to note, Aunt Maud and Aunt Maud's glories and Aunt Maud's complacencies; she gave herself away most of all, and it was naturally what most contributed to her candour. She didn't speak to her friend once more, in Aunt Maud's strain, of how they could scale the skies; she spoke, by her bright perverse preference on this occasion, of the need, in the first place, of being neither stupid nor vulgar. It might have been a lesson, for our young

American, in the art of seeing things as they were — a lesson so various and so sustained that the pupil had, as we have shown, but receptively to gape. The odd thing furthermore was that it could serve its purpose while explicitly disavowing every personal bias. It wasn't that she disliked Aunt Maud, who was everything she had on other occasions declared; but the dear woman, ineffaceably stamped by inscrutable nature and a dreadful art, wasn't — how *could* she be? — what she wasn't. She wasn't any one. She wasn't anything. She wasn't anywhere. Milly mustn't think it — one couldn't, as a good friend, let her. Those hours at Matcham were *inespérées*, were pure manna from heaven; or if not wholly that perhaps, with humbugging old Lord Mark as a backer, were vain as a ground for hopes and calculations. Lord Mark was very well, but he wasn't *the* cleverest creature in England, and even if he had been he still wouldn't have been the most obliging. He weighed it out in ounces, and indeed each of the pair was really waiting for what the other would put down.

" 'She has put down *you*,' said Milly, attached to the subject still; 'and I think what you mean is that, on the counter, she still keeps hold of you.'

" 'Lest' — Kate took it up — 'he should suddenly grab me and run? Oh as he isn't ready to run he's much less ready, naturally to grab. I *am* — you're so far right as that — on the counter, when I'm not in the shop-window . . .' "

And so on. But is this typical Jamesian "moment of revelation" a little confusing, not only to the astonished and innocent Milly, whose whole glamorous world of British aristocracy has been swept away here, but to the Jamesian reader also? Well, really, not at all, if you understand that the description of Kate Croy's "lesson" in the verities of life (in indirect discourse) is being strained through Milly Theale's "consciousness" at first, and then through James's consciousness, in turn, to allow us to know certain things about Kate that Milly doesn't know, or that even Kate doesn't know yet, or at least doesn't choose to reveal. For this is the "stream of consciousness" quite literally; not the stream of the *un*conscious, as in the generation of writers who followed James. Every detail in the passage has been carefully selected by the artist to throw its light on Milly, on Kate, on the surrounding cast of characters in the novel (so falsely interpreted by Milly; so carefully characterized by Kate for her own advantage), and on the novel's plot action.

But what you do notice in this lesson on the art of seeing things "as they were" is the self-serving purpose of Kate's talk. What is clear is the description of Lord Mark (whom Mrs. Lowder has chosen for Kate), whom Kate is using as a cover for her passion for Densher, as weighing out his emotions in ounces, while both Mark and Mrs. Lowder are each "waiting for what the other would put down." What is inescapable here, even somehow to the innocent and thrilled Milly, is that while Mrs. Lowder has put Kate "on the counter" — how these Jamesian figures buy and sell each other — she is still also "keeping hold" of her — and how these Jamesian figures also toy and tease with their influence over each other! This was a curious application of the marketplace to the most intimate human relations. This was a kind of commercial sadism, if you like, where human beings are being bribed and corrupted by the cash nexus, where they are being "displayed" on the counter and yet not quite offered for sale; where the only force superior to the financial factor is not so much the will to power, as the will to tease by power. This remarkable passage, during which Kate has interposed her own power over Milly directly in the path of Mrs. Lowder's projected power, also ends with Kate's declaration that while Lord Mark has been intended for her, he has actually turned to Milly. And with Milly's enforced declaration that she will have no part of Lord Mark — which clears the way for her *to have* a part of Kate's Densher!

But whose hard commercial ethos, whose will to power, whose delight in teasing, is really triumphant here, if not James's own? It is Kate, too, who warns Milly against herself, Densher, Mark, and their whole crowd. "My honest advice to you would be . . .

to drop us while you can," which has the effect both of providing Kate with a moral "alibi," another Jamesian term which is increasingly sounded in this world of schemers, liars and manipulators, and of suggesting the dangers to come. Before this there is the scene where Kate is probing Milly as to the extent of her sickness, and where Milly proclaims her new "line" of going in for "pleasure." "But what kind of pleasure?" asks Kate. "The highest," says Milly. "Her friend met it nobly. 'Which *is* the highest?' " Which indeed; since this could be the Sixty-Four Thousand Dollar Question in James's work; though it is certainly not a question of sexual pleasure. And while these Jamesian puppets are chattering away, talking, thinking, analyzing, suspecting, handling, fixing and dealing with each other, around, above, beneath the double secret of Milly's fatal illness and of Kate and Densher's equally hidden, and perhaps equally fatal passion — there before us stands Volume Two of *The Wings of the Dove*.

Now we reach the moment of Densher's own self-revelation: this mediocre "hero," rather indefinable and weak-willed alike, who has been left dangling so long on the rope of Kate Croy's beauty, her passion, her ambition, her grand scheme. What is the meaning of Densher? (His name, while it conveys his dubious social background and character alike, has the added connotation of "dense," of course, and possibly dense "about her," and that is to say, about Kate.) Well, first of all, he is a *working* journalist, rare figure among all these leisure-class protagonists; even though he works mainly (and mysteriously) at night, and has the means somehow to follow Milly to Venice, and to dally there at his leisure. But unlike the equally lower class Hyacinth Robinson of *The Princess Casamassima* (a quaint little fellow if ever there was one), Merton Densher has no illegitimate noble parent. He isn't even *adopted* by royalty, or wealth, as Kate is by her rich aunt; his only connection with this upper world of privilege is through the handsome girl's yearning for him. Nothing in Densher's rather tedious stream of consciousness comes up unexpectedly or illuminatingly from the depths of his psyche. Perhaps in the Jamesian view nothing could come up.

What is interesting, nevertheless, in Densher's self-portrait is the description it contains of "passion." Through his suffering, Densher is almost about to give Kate up. "Their mistake," he reflects, "was to have believed that they could hold out — hold out, that is, not against Aunt Maud, but against an impatience that, prolonged and exasperated, made a man ill."

He had known more than ever, on their separating in the court of the station, how ill a man, and even a woman, could feel from such a cause; but he struck himself as also knowing that he had already suffered Kate to begin finely to apply antidotes and remedies and subtle sedatives. It had a vulgar sound — as throughout, in love, the names of things, the verbal terms of intercourse, were, compared with love itself, horribly vulgar.

There is that later Jamesian note of "vulgarity" again, as though it preyed upon the mind, or the spirit, of this genteel middle class writer now condemned to describe the illicit emotions he had begun to yearn for in this period of his work — but which he also scorned or was terrified of. Isn't the Jamesian "love" comprised here mainly of illness, sedatives and vulgarity? Now this passage was also describing the social rather than the unthought-of sexual "intercourse" of love. But the choice of the word was still interesting; and one also wonders *what* names of *what* things, in the verbal intercourse of love, were so horribly vulgar.

And isn't a writer so horribly obsessed by the notion of "vulgarity" itself — and to this novelist, perhaps, nothing human was *not* vulgar — isn't such a writer more than half aware of his own vulgarity? Meanwhile it is at this point in *The Wings of the Dove*, in Venice, that the "secret" of the melodrama, which everybody knows, is let out. "You're cryptic, love!" says Densher to Kate at Milly's triumphal party, while Kate retorts: "Don't think, however,

I'll do *all* the work for you. If you want things named, you must name them." (Are *these* the vulgar terms of love? Well, at least, in this case, they are lurid, criminal, and improbable.) "Since she'll die I'm to marry her?" Densher says. And Kate's lips "bravely moved: 'To marry her.' " "So that when her death has taken place I shall in the natural course have money." "You'll in the natural course have money. We shall in the natural course be free," Kate answers; since in the leisure-class novel freedom, like love, implies, above all, money. "Oh, oh, oh!" cries Densher. "Yes, yes, yes," says Kate. And while, from across the reception hall of the great party, Milly sends to them "all the candour of her smile, the lustre of her pearls, the value of her life, the essence of her wealth" — Densher agrees to the bargain if Kate will come directly to his rooms.

Rooms: for even this obscure, thwarted little journalist has to have, in the Jamesian scale of housekeeping, an adequate apartment with perhaps even a poor little butler. And their "bargain" is a bargain of future cash for Kate, a bargain of lust for Densher; a triumph of manipulation for them both. The sexual act in *The Wings of the Dove* is the culmination of the criminal plot against Milly.

Now Matthiessen's *The Major Phase* points to this scene as a refutation of "those inattentive critics who keep insisting that James is always flinching from physical passion." But this very attentive critic of James's neglects to give the context of the sexuality just described. There is no doubt, as we have already seen, that the later James was obsessed by sex, rather like a prurient old maid when he was not playing out the role of the infantile voyeur — but in what curious ways! Just as here, physical passion celebrated the triumph of restless poverty, thwarted power, unnatural behavior and a criminal plot, so we shall notice other lurid aspects of the thwarted, submerged, inhibited sexuality of Henry James himself. Meanwhile in the novel, Milly, having heard of Densher's perfidy from the scheming and corrupt Lord Mark, has turned her face to the wall in order to die. And Densher, refusing to see her (because he has been overwhelmed by Kate's embraces), flees from her presence, from Venice itself; only to discover, on Milly's actual death, that she has nevertheless, in spite of her knowledge of his treason with Kate, bestowed her great fortune upon him.

Just before his sexual embrace with Kate, Densher has allowed Milly Theale also to believe that he was falling in love with her. But what curious human motivation all this is, in the complicated narrative chronicle of the *Dove*. What fairy-tale generosity on the part of the betrayed and dying princess. And then, what a sudden sense of *noblesse oblige* on the part of Densher himself, whose "physical passion" for Kate is now balanced off, negated, and made totally ambivalent by his growing moral and spiritual love for the dead American girl. Just like the spiritualized, ex-revolutionary little bookbinder-hero of *The Princess Casamassima*, Merten Densher follows the Jamesian formula for the "common man" — the man almost from the lowest depths of the Jamesian social arrangement — who has glimpsed, however briefly, the aristocratic nobility of life, and whose whole spirit has been changed.

Is he really a weak and petty "criminal" of the heart — the leisure-class equivalent of a Clyde Griffiths — whose whole moral fibre collapses at the evidence of his double-dealing being known? Couldn't he, in fact, have "loved" both women at the same time (it has been done), particularly since one of them has conveniently died? And didn't this final guilty, self-tormented remorse on Densher's part towards the end of *The Wings of the Dove* follow, in reality, the still deeper, fixed and recurrent Jamesian pattern of the "impossible love" — of always loving the woman you *can't* have?

Densher, nevertheless, has been purified, ennobled and spiritualized through his "suffering." Back in London, he refuses to see Kate for a fortnight, consumed by his remorse over Milly, by his newly gained moral superiority, and by a kind of priggish hauteur. When he does finally see her at Mrs. Lowder's Lancaster Gate —

and the two lovers have a little talk "after the withdrawal of the
footman" — Densher has an altogether new tone with his former
(and that is to say, *one*time) mistress. "We *are*, my dear child . . .
I suppose still engaged." He is full of "honour," and middle class
morality while he lectures Kate on Milly Theale's "magnificence"
— hardly an endearing trait on the part of any male. Furthermore,
he has almost come to exonerate his own devious part in the
romance melodrama. "He understood . . ." Densher tells Kate
about the equally noble medico, Sir Luke. "But understood what?"
asks Kate. "That I had meant awfully well," says Densher.

He is really quite unbearable. But not apparently to Mr. Matthiessen again, who accepts and quotes approvingly James's own
view of Densher. "Something had happened to him too beautiful
and too sacred to describe. He had been to his recovered sense,
forgiven, dedicated, blessed . . ." (Which is probably just what
makes Densher the prig that he is.) Kate again tries to use her
physical power over him:

*She was once more close to him, close as she had been the day she
came to him in Venice . . . He could practically deny in such circumstances nothing that she said, and what she said was, with it, visibly, a
fruit of that knowledge.*

Yet he "winces" at her words; so vulgar does she now seem. He
takes refuge in the "aftersense" of Milly, which "day by day, was
his greatest reality." (This "aftersense" which, throughout the
work of Henry James, is always used to compensate for, or indeed
to prevent, the consummation of any present pleasure.) Now
Milly has also died, significantly, symbolically, shortly before
Christmas Day. And how the extended, complex, opaque narrative
exposition in *The Wings of the Dove* weaves back and forth,
around and about this event; what an interminable time Milly
does take to leave this world; what a long day's dying this is! And
so the solitary Densher, this suffering, atoning and regenerated

working-class hero of the Jamesian fancy, also attends the "splendid service" — the flocking, fashionable crowd, the glittering and resounding pageantry, the blaze of altar lights, the swelling chord of organ and choir — after leaving his club.

Well, of course, even the humblest Jamesian journalist has his club. We begin to see what James is after; but he is not yet ready to give it to us all. Isn't Kate Croy's "punishment" sufficiently indicated by the fact that she has voluntarily left Lancaster Gate — that she is now, "pale, grave and charming . . . a distinguished stranger," back again in the dingy scene of Marian Condrip's little private house, a residence which is ugly, we are told, "almost to the point of the sinister"? Yet Kate is stubborn; persistent; she won't let go. She is still waiting for Densher — and the cash. Two months later she visits Densher in "his own quarters" (perhaps a breach of decorum in itself) bearing the letter from Milly's New York lawyers which she has somehow received, and opened. And this final renunciation scene in the *Dove* (which James actually described twice; with a preliminary, anticipatory renunciation scene directly before this one) revolves around the fact that Kate has *broken the seal* of this legal and financial document. (She has read it, naturally.) It is the final proof of her complete perfidy.

Densher, however, remains aloof, superior, noble in his rebuke to Kate. " 'If the seal is broken, well and good . . . But we *might*, you know,' he presently added, 'have sent it back to them intact and inviolate. Only accompanied,' he smiled with his heart in his mouth, 'by an absolutely kind letter.' " Kate "took it," we are told, "with the mere brave blink with which a patient of courage signifies to the exploring medical hand that the tender place is touched." (The analytical medical hand, in this elaborate, extended imagery of the later James, which has so swiftly replaced the exploring hand of, let us say, sexual pleasure.) "You wanted," Kate says, "to measure the possibilities of my departure from delicacy." But Densher is steady, easy, sure of his moral superiority.

"Well, I wanted — in so good a case — to test you." His heart must indeed be in his mouth. (Although where is there any real heart in these two former lovers who are now probing and squirming so exquisitely; bound as they are are within the twisted coils of this extended, repetitious, "theatrical" denouement — which goes on and on in *The Wings of the Dove*.)

How these two "lovers" indeed circle around the opened envelope of the legal document which contains their lost fortune! "You mean," says Kate —

> *"You won't give up if I don't consent?"*
> *"Yes. I do nothing."*
> *"That, as I understand, is accepting."*
> *Densher paused.* *"I do nothing formal."*
> *"You won't, I suppose you mean, touch the money."*
> *"I won't touch the money."*

And so on. "You'll marry me without the money," says Kate finally. "You won't marry me with it. If I don't consent *you* don't." "You lose me?" Densher cries. And: "He showed, though naming it frankly, a sort of awe of her high grasp. 'Well, you lose nothing else. I make over to you every penny.' " Then there are the much quoted last lines of the novel. "I'll marry you, mind you," Densher cries again, "in an hour." "As we were?" asks Kate. "As we were." But she turned to the door, so James wrote in his famous exit line for Kate Croy, "and her headshake was now the end. 'We shall never be again as we were!' "

Well, naturally. Nobody ever is. But when were the two protagonists of a so-called major novel ever put in a box like this — for which "what they were," some seven hundred pages earlier in *The Wings of the Dove*, is merely the long build-up, laborious and meticulous alike, for what they come to be? Though Kate's ostensible reason for not marrying Densher (and not accepting the money?) is that he is now in love with Milly's "memory";

and Densher's for not marrying Kate is that she won't marry him *without* the money, there is no doubt that the final note in the last great tragedy of Henry James's is the dollar sign. But isn't the cash nexus, which is the one solid factor throughout the whole fabricated, artificial narrative — which has been the real core of the "evil" and sentimental romance melodrama: isn't the golden base for the *Dove's* esoteric superstructure also contrived? It is at least false gold. For what right has Densher to assign the fortune which he has never earned, which has come to him in fact as a direct reward (or rebuke?) for his moral perfidy; how can he assign this fortune, as a noble gesture, precisely to the woman whose own criminal plot has caused, or at least hastened, the death of the fairy-tale princess?

Yes, the Jamesian sense of theatrics — the dentured melodrama in the *Dove* — has triumphed over any real concern for human credibility; even on the stage. That was the real result of his much-vaunted fusing of the novel and play form in his scenario method. Furthermore we realize that the Jamesian wealth was always to some degree "illegitimate" in the leisure-class novel, in the sense that it was always inherited, or acquired by any means except that of *earning* it — and as far back as the case of Isabel Archer, who was given her inheritance simply for the sake of her charm. So now the Jamesian wealth is not only "inherited" quite improbably but even corruptly: simply to demonstrate Milly's peculiar generosity, Densher's newly acquired nobility, Kate's fundamental avarice. And if this last cornerstone of the Jamesian sense of reality (the cash motive, I mean) is removed from *The Wings of the Dove*, what else, really, is left?

Surely, among the supposedly great novels of world literature, this one is the most singular, fantastic, baroque and byzantine in its values and in its form alike. The calculated, contrived, altogether esoteric literary method merely reflects the artificial and fabricated human values — which, in part at least, as I say, this method was also designed to conceal from us.

This is a novel which proceeds from false premises to false conclusions; which constrains all of its character development to its own rigid, tricky form; which is based on a completely idiosyncratic vision of life always alternating between the make-believe extremes of the fairy tale and the nightmare; which is compounded of illusion upon illusion, with no possible sense of human reality or of true human experience in its increasingly complex, convoluted and, above all, numerous and abundant pages, chapters and books.

But then, can *The Wings of the Dove* really be classified among the great novels of world literature? No; of course not; naturally not — since the major novels always do bear on human destiny, while this one concerns itself with human daydreams of a very special order. The "noble end" which James proscribed for Densher destroys the possibility, even, that James was aware, conscious, or ironic about his own daydreaming fantasy life; on the contrary, he was completely immersed in it, to the extent that he saw no other reality except his own. Quite similarly, his Kate Croy, starting out as an interesting portrait of a powerful, ambitious and passionate woman, is also subordinated to the Jamesian notion of romance melodrama, rather than to life itself, and ends on an ignominious rather than a tragic note. Here, more clearly than in all his previous work, the deep repressions of James, acting upon the writer's natural flow of unconscious material, produce a curious kind of "psycho-morality" — as we have called it — where the "noble," the sentimental, the romantic, the theatrical emotions preclude any chance of depth psychology, or any true view of human nature.

The Wings of the Dove is high and unusual entertainment, if you like, rather than serious literature. Perhaps the real question is how James himself — working in such an artificial sphere of literature; using such elaborately contrived methods of art; giving us finally not a picture of any recognizable side of life but of a special and unique *fantasy* of society, civilization and "culture": how this Gothic Romancer (who looked down upon Hawthorne) can yet hold our interest to the degree that he does, and stimulate our imagination to the point, at least, of trying to understand what *his* literary illusion really means. That is the true Jamesian spell; the enchantment of an extraordinary magician of art, whose bag of literary tricks contains ever more astounding surprises. Very likely the *Dove* is an example of just that "magic hope" and "magic faith" which Ernest Schachtel has described in his study of early childhood called *Metamorphosis* — or of that period in infantile development when the child imagines that his wants, needs and fears really *do* dominate and control the outside world.

Yes, I suspect that the final "secret" of the *Dove*, a novel based on such spurious secrets, is just there: that it draws us back to that childlike fantasy world of how things "might have been," although we realize they never were, and never could be like that. Most artists, just like most people, draw their primary inspiration, it is true, from this buried, but never altogether abandoned, core of human illusion. But the great writers confront the infantine dreams of life with the hard reality of things as they are. The revelations of art all too often consist precisely in this stripping away of such primary illusions. By contrast the art of Henry James is not only magic hope or magic faith, or magic fear, or magic craft. It is, at its real center, a kind of magic-magic. What a series of pure, entrancing, inviolate visions this writer presents to us! And what an extraordinary kind of elite vision — or visions for the elite — he propounded at a certain period in the climax and flowering of the great American fortunes; in their transient hey-day of golden munificence — and in the face of the whole hitherto accepted literary record of common human aspiration and of general human suffering.

Thus *The Wings of the Dove* brings us a step closer to the true nature of America's first leisure-class novelist, who saw all history, all culture, all life within the rarefied and narrow confines of his own completely fabricated "aristocratic" values. This was a class-view of civilization so powerful, so intense, so absolute, and so confined as to make a Marxist blush.

9. The Achieved Life à la Henry James

OF ADDITIONAL interest (as though there wasn't already enough, or too much, both *in The Wings of the Dove* and about it) was the later James's Preface, or critical retrospect on the novel. Here he noted the technical problems of dealing with a sick heroine, who was in some respects as much related to Ralph Touchett as she was to Isabel Archer in *The Portrait of a Lady*. The illness of James during his own youth, which he attributed to purely physical causes; the beautiful and diseased cousin Minny Temple; a family which was surrounded and marked by sickness, orphanage and death, were embedded in this writer's consciousness.

But the American heiress of his novel, so James wrote in 1909, had "a strong and special implication of liberty, liberty of action, of choice, of appreciation, of contact — proceeding from sources that provide better for large independence, I think, than any other conditions in the world." Did he mean the special conditions of American family life, or (since Milly Theale had no family) simply more money *and* no family connections in this Jamesian concept of "freedom"? And despite his later disenchantment with British society, his earlier romantic notions of it still persisted. "To be the heir of all the ages," he said about his heroine, "only to know yourself, as that consciousness should deepen, balked of your inheritance" — and here he still meant the inheritance of European *culture.*

Well, that was the theme of the *Dove* in James's own view; and his business as an artist became merely that of "watching" the turns of his story "as the fond parent watches a child perched, for its first riding-lesson, in the saddle." And wasn't this a somewhat esoteric view of parenthood (and childhood) in the leisure-class romance? Much has been written about James's later imagery without mentioning its obvious social orientation. And then the tone of this Preface, as James described the problems incurred by so special and high a "vessel of sensibility" as Milly Theale, became positively euphoric. "If, as I had fondly noted, the little world determined for her was to 'bristle' — I delighted in the term! — with meanings, so, by the same token, could I but make my medal hang free, its obverse and its reverse, its face and its back, would beautifully become optional for the spectator." Did he mean the true nature of the plot against Milly, while she is being taken in so gloriously by the glamour of English nobility? And was the social area of childhood horseback lessons and of embossed medals hanging free the best source of literary imagery?

Yet James had more, much more, to say about this novel. "Preparatively and, as it were, yearningly — given the whole ground — one began, in the event, with the outer ring, approaching the centre thus by narrowing circumvallations. There, full-blown, accordingly, from one hour to the other, rose one's process — for which there remained all the while so many amusing formulae." Notice again the stress, in all these later Jamesian esthetic formulations, on the amusing, clever, entertaining "game of literature." And here again Henry praised, on the one hand, the artistic freedom he had gained in the *Dove* by *not* having had it serialized, just as elsewhere he had eulogized the "discipline" and "economy" which were necessitated by the fact of *being* serialized.

All things were grist for this artist's ingenious capacity for theoretical speculation: his ability always to "explain" himself, his work, his method. He mentioned those circling rings of his later narrative method; those "narrowing circumvallations" from which his heroine Milly was not only "superficially" (as he claimed) but literally and at great length absent. The ingenuity of the expert craftsman, so James claimed, delighted in being taxed by technical problems very much as the well-bred horse "likes to be saddled" — repeating and overdoing his equestrian imagery perhaps, and reminding us that this upper class view of life took as much liberty with animal as with human motivation. But then the Preface swung into its since-celebrated discussion of dramatic "centres" and of the Jamesian "points of consciousness," and of his latest esthetic discovery, the "discriminated occasion." He was positively enchanted by his own originality of technique, and asked himself disturbing questions about various phases of it only to answer his own critico-analysis with the most triumphant affirmatives. This Preface to *The Wings of the Dove* contained indeed the most finished formulation of what became the later Jamesian esthetics, both admired and expounded in the modern period almost as the only esthetics.*

Those celebrated phrases of technical method which the Jamesian virtuosity threw off here in a sheer pyrotechnical display of his craft: what do they really mean? We see that his famous "points of view" (the moving of the novel form towards a modern "subjectivity") were not exactly points of view at all, since "under degrees of pressure" these "registers" of individual consciousness become a represented "community of vision," in which all the characters merge in the later Jamesian "unity," the chorus, the community of like minds, which is used to bend the narrative into the form of the Jamesian romance-melodrama plot. In *his* terms, the "discriminated occasion" was used to unveil the "secret" of the story, to which all the characters must contribute, rather than to describe the secret or hidden depths of the individual

---

* See Percy Lubbock's *The Craft of Fiction*, for example, as an early "analysis" of James's craft which is then projected outward as the guide for *all* fiction. Lubbock has been followed up by a score of other books, and perhaps hundreds of articles, in a similar vein of esthetic adulation rather than true criticism. Mr. Leon Edel's steady stream of articles, essays, critical interpretations, editorial introductions, etc., on the work of James is the latest example of the same vogue.

characters themselves. The "Scene," in turn was perhaps just another name for this, which James took over from his unfortunate
stage experience as some kind of personal compensation or ret-
ribution, along with the equally impressive-sounding nomenclature
of the Scenario, or the Dramatic Method. What was the meaning
of the "Picture," by contrast, I frankly don't know — except that
it was a scene whose whole meaning was not divulged, a pre-
paratory glimpse, as it were, in this completely voyeuristic, altogether teasing, meticulously planned and plotted (although usually overexpanded and overwritten) narrative.

In the same Preface, didn't James go on to state even more
extravagant, and more revealing, esthetic "principles"? His "registers" and "reflectors" were other terms for the series of individual
consciousnesses which all pushed along his story. "My registers or
'reflectors,' as I so conveniently name them (burnished indeed as
they generally are by the intelligence, the curiosity, the passion,
the force of the moment, whatever it be, directing them), work, as
we have seen, in arranged alternation." (For "the force of the
moment," read "the force of the melodrama" in this elaborated
Jamesian rationale of his method.) The example of this which
James then mentioned was Kate Croy, who is, "for all she is
worth, turned on" in Venice. And how this writer unconsciously
admits his "turning on" and "turning off" his characters according
to the dictates of that "moment" which is never a moment of
pure life in his narrative, but of artificial and manipulated suspense.
"She is turned on largely at Venice, where the appearances, rich
and obscure and portentous (another word I rejoice in) as they
have by that time become and altogether exquisite as they remain,
are treated almost wholly through her vision of them and Densher's
(as to the lucid interplay of which conspiring and conflicting agents
there would be a great deal to say)."

Naturally. When James is speaking about James there is always
a great deal to say. But all that the present Jacobite can add is:
What marvelous, self-serving, and self-seeking fatuity on the part

of any writer talking about his own craft. All that we can say to this euphoric Henry James praising, admiring, rationalizing and generalizing about the esthetic subtleties of his own later literary method is: How nice, how wonderful! Well, to be sure, as if half aware of these self-laudatory commendations, the celebrated Preface to the New York edition of *The Wings of the Dove* turned to a rather uneasy note of self-criticism. As to Milly Theale's complete disappearance from the last quarter of the novel (just as she has been completely absent from the first quarter), James noted: "Heaven forbid, we say to ourselves, during all the whole Venetian climax, heaven forbid we should 'know' anything more of our ravaged sister than what Densher darkly pieces together, or than what Kate Croy pays, heroically, it must be owned, at the hour of her visit alone to Densher's lodging, for her superior handling and her dire profanation of." Meaning? Well, one can only assume that while Densher has refused to see the dying Milly Theale, for whatever peculiar reasons, and while she then refuses to see *him*, to add to the novel's general obscurity — that Kate Croy has in effect sold her body to Densher not in love or desire but merely "heroically," to further her "dire profanation" of the pure American princess. (And to James, very likely, the act of physical possession in love, or of being possessed, was equivalent to some kind of physical torture.)

He went on to mention "the author's scarce more than half-dissimulated despair" — and who is fooling whom? — at the *Dove's* "makeshift middle," and the inveterate displacement of its general center; and the "false and deformed" latter half of the novel; which he again blamed on the fact of having "quarters so cramped" in the narrative of over seven hundred pages. More, more, more was what this later James began to demand: more wordage yet, more space still — in a kind of insatiable oral sucking and spewing of rhetoric as the only solution for the limitations of his work which, at points, he was so uneasily and evasively forced to recognize. If he was really talking about the contrived, repetitious and dubiously "theatrical" ending of the *Dove,* the fault was surely not "the reduced scale of the exhibition," nor the necessity of "foreshortening at any cost" — but an inherent failure of his literary vision. Of space and wordage and rhetoric, there was no lack and no failure in that novel. Moreover, in this Jamesian self-criticism of the *Dove,* if the middle was makeshift, the latter half false and deformed, what was left of the story?

What we begin to realize in these much quoted passages of the Jamesian "esthetics" is that we can trust neither the fatuous and euphoric self-praise nor the sudden and curiously harsh intervals of self-criticism. For if James rather obliquely denounced almost three-quarters of *The Wings of the Dove,* he had recoiled upon himself in despair, as it were, only to make an even further, higher leap into the sublime and beneficent regions of self-congratulatory commentary. Thus:

I recognize meanwhile, throughout the long earlier reach of the book, not only no deformities but, I think, a positively close and felicitous application of method, the preserved consistencies of which, often illusive, but never really lapsing, it would be of a certain diversion and might be of some profit to follow.

What James was describing here was the long, involved, cunningly plotted — but actually rather tedious and purely verbose — early relation of Kate and Densher. On the face of things, it appears that the later James of the Prefaces made a point of praising — under the abstract, illusive guise of "Method" — just those phases of his fiction which were in fact the weakest.

Cunning indeed; disingenuous, whether deliberate and conscious, or sincerely self-deceived. For it was the *community* of Kate's and Densher's "understanding" which James praised, and which served very well indeed his "method" for outlining the impending romance-melodrama — at the cost, however, of the individual characters of the two lovers; or of the affection, understanding and conflicts of any *real* human relationship; or, as we've seen, of any possible indication of physical love. The abstract method of the later Jamesian fiction, the "game of literature" that James himself stressed, had taken precedence over the human content of *The Wings of the Dove*, and was becoming all-important in itself. Thus Densher's *memory* of the earlier scene with Mrs. Lowder at Lancaster Gate (so the later James again stressed in his celebrated retrospective Preface) was followed by Kate's "apprehension" of that scene — "her contributive assimilation of his experience; it melts back into that accumulation, which we have been, as it were, saving up" — in this notably oblique and subjective later Jamesian fictional approach to experience.

"Does my apparent deviation here count accordingly as a muddle?" so James then questioned himself with a kind of false modesty, a pseudo self-criticism, which was in fact the real salve for his true anxiety. (That is to say, had he sacrificed everything he had sacrificed in terms of Kate and Densher for the sake of the "dramatic exposition" of his plot?) And he happily answered himself: "No, distinctly not; for I had definitely opened the door, as attention or perusal of the first two books will show, to the subjective community of my young pair." Or in other words, he had gained what he had gained in his idiosyncratic romance melodrama; and he had not lost what he had lost in obvious human values. For what was James describing here but the technical method which created his peculiarly opaque kind of narrative, in these early books of the *Dove*, with all the dark hints as to "the trap of innocence" which was being laid through these long, long walks and talks of the two "lovers," and all those veiled and ominous "portents" of the oncoming melodrama which this Jamesian Method both suggested and muffled, and which James himself was attempting to tell and not to tell the reader? This was the literary method par excellence of what might be called "the strip-tease narrative," in which each level of meaning cast off by the artist brings us closer and closer to the "naked truth" of the preconceived plot. And "levels of meaning" which this artist first contrived to *hide* or cover the naked truth of his criminal plot.

In this new, unique, subtle, esoteric kind of literary game, indeed, what the later James also found most "striking, charming and curious," in his reperusal of *The Wings of the Dove*, was "the author's instinct everywhere for the *indirect* presentation of his main image." (So that was where Matthiessen got his clue as to the excellence of the *Dove*; and that was the Jamesian directive which was swallowed whole.) Now there was James's instinctive preference for the "indirect presentation" of all the human experience which he lacked, or gathered at second hand, which he then presented in the guise of the idealization of the "pure imagination" which needed only the germ — or the crumb — of the actual life episode. But besides, in *The Wings of the Dove*, wasn't Milly Theale herself — like the whole line of Jamesian innocent and virginal young American girls whom her portrait capped, as far back as Daisy Miller or Isabel Archer — wasn't it a fact that Milly, "charming" and touching as this romantic heroine was: that Milly Theale, I say, didn't, after all, have very much inside her? Yes; and add to this that James himself was not so much interested in the full development of her character, even for what it was worth, as he was in the dark melodrama of her entrapment.

He saw this differently himself, however; and from a curious angle in his retrospective "analysis" of the original narrative. The "straight exhibition" of Milly had resorted, "for relief," to a kinder and more merciful *indirection*, "all as if to approach her circuitously, deal with her at second hand, as an unspotted princess is ever dealt with . . .

All of which proceeds, obviously, from her painter's tenderness of imagination about her, which reduces him to watching her, as it were, through the successive windows of other people's interest in her. So, if we talk of princesses, do the balconies opposite the palace gates, do the coigns of vantage and respect enjoyed for a fee, rake from afar the mystic figure in the gilded coach as it comes forth into the great place.

Yes, and with these "unspotted princesses," these mystic figures in their gilded coaches, emerging so magnificently and mysteriously into their great *places*, we see quite obviously that towards the end of Henry James's career, just as from the very start of it, his mind dwelt in a fairy-tale limbo.

Yet this passage had other curious connotations. Just as *The Sacred Fount* was a primary document of a snooping, prurient sexual curiosity which formulated fantastic "theories" on the basis of second-, third- or fourthhand "facts," so here again the Jamesian approach to the unspotted princess was admittedly circuitous, second-hand: through the "windows" of other people's interest, through those "coigns of vantage" enjoyed for a fee. Was this really the painter's "tenderness," or was it also the primary mark of a kind of adolescent worship of women, indeed, which feared to get too *close* to its subject, which feared to really "know" — that favorite Jamesian term! — what a woman was like? The unspotted-princess ideal in the Jamesian imagination was matched by a fervent, unquenchable, terrible curiosity both to "know" and to really see, perhaps, what a *spotted* princess might be like; and by an equally fervent and "unstained" adolescent imagination which resolutely blocked this curiosity — and removed itself from the possibility by constraining itself to these balconies, coigns, mirrors and windows which served here as the Jamesian "reflectors."

This was a curious kind of voyeurism; refined, censored, diluted — rarefied into the esthetic abstractions of the Jamesian "method" where the "body" of the narrative, like the body of the heroine, was simply omitted; and where the singular failure of primary human values was always compensated for by the unceasing, compensatory flow of *words*. For James concluded the famous Preface with the same note of mingled apology and euphoria. "And as to what there may be to note of this and other supersubtleties, other arch-refinements, of tact and taste, of design and instinct, in 'The Wings of the Dove,' I become conscious of overstepping my space without having brought the full quantity to light." More, more,

more, as I say, is the Jamesian lament, yearning and exculpation. For still: "The failure leaves me with a burden of residuary comment of which I yet boldly hope elsewhere to discharge myself." And one can hardly fail to note, again, the somewhat masturbatic imagery, all unconscious, in these final lines of what we might call the paranoid fabulist of the late Prefaces: the ebullient verbalist of the Jamesian esthetics, caught up so fatally by the dictational sonority of his solitary, resonant, all-dominating vocal chords.

An undischarged burden of residuary comment indeed. And could these "laws," "principles," "ordinances" of the peculiarly unique, individual, esoteric Jamesian "esthetic" possibly apply — as they have been applied rigorously during the last decades of American literary criticism — to any other artist *except* Henry James? Meanwhile *The Better Sort* (1903) was another collection of virtuoso short stories, for the most part popular in tone and in a lighter vein.

The title of this volume was itself a reminder that James still clung to the snobbish values of the British aristocracy with which, at the same time, he had become so disenchanted. And most of these tales were examples of literary conceits or of obvious esthetic trickery.* Yet the volume contained three notable stories, too. "Mrs. Medwin" was another entertaining account of the same corrupt "modern" British society — of the decadent Edwardian set (to which James was more and more drawn) where sexuality again was viewed as a cheap and easy commodity, merely vulgar when it was not vicious. This was a world of fixing and squaring, of

---

* "Broken Wings" was the account of two popular artists who had lost their vogue and their following. "The Tone of Time" was another "meta-ideo" twist tale of two women who battle over the portrait of their mutual (and dead) lover. "Flickerbridge" described a rather improbable young American painter who abandons a rather obnoxious female journalist for the sake of an old English castle. "The Beldonald Holbein" was a clever tale of a faded English beauty who imported an ugly American companion to set off her own appearance. "The Story in It" was a pedagogical and moralistic parable of "passion" as mainly discussed by a purehearted heroine and a sophisticated man-of-the-world . . . This story was revealing again as to the basic Jamesian equation of moral virtue with emotional inhibition.

adventurers and promoters, of wanton British ladies and semi-American bounders. This was the moral corruption which followed, in James's mind, the decline of manners; and the lack of manners which marked (or which caused?) the sexual laxity. But the satire was sharp; and "Mrs. Medwin" is probably a better story, all in all, than the much better-known one in this volume, called "The Birthplace."

This story too has been up-rated during the last decade of Jacobite commentary into the position of a minor masterpiece; and among these commentators probably Clifton Fadiman again proves to be at once the least well informed about James himself and (therefore?) the most ecstatic about this particular example of the Jamesian art. Well, the story was a take-off, very well done of its kind, on the mumbo-jumbo of "popular" admiration for Shakespeare. The location is the supposed shrine of the Bard himself, now become a notorious tourist-racket; and the tale's modest hero, one Morris Gedge by name (and the Jamesian names are almost always revealing), discovers that there are no supposed Shakespearian relics in the highly dubious site of his birth. Morris is the official caretaker of the "Shrine," a comfortable job for him; but becoming more and more disenchanted by the obvious fraud which is being practiced under the name of culture, he takes to giving more and more lyrical (and unfounded) Shakespearian "lectures" — which bring in higher and higher tourist fees. Now this *was* an entertaining Jamesian conceit on his familiar theme of the vulgarity of fame, the debasing of genius. But still, does this make little Morris Gedge one "of the great perceptives" of world literature; and does this hero's insight, "humble as it is . . . link him to all the great sensitives who have ever lived"? (Mr. Fadiman.) He is in fact linked to the culture-haunted butler of "Brooksmith," the formerly anarchistic bookbinder of *The Princess Casamassima*, the belatedly noble journalist of *The Wings of the Dove*, not to mention the equally high-minded and renunciatory Fleda Vetch of *The Spoils of Poynton*. Morris is simply another one of Henry

James's "little gentlemen," and he is the central flaw in what is otherwise an entertaining if minor bit of literary satire.

Both this tale and "Mrs. Medwin" prepared the way in *The Better Sort,* however, for what is unquestionably the best story in the volume, and one of James's most revealing chronicles of "the unused life." The hero of "The Beast in the Jungle," John Marcher, finds a new meaning for his own existence in the belated "love" of May Bartram. "He had thought of himself so long as abominably alone, and lo he wasn't alone a bit." What draws Marcher to May (the names are again obviously symbolical) is her concern with his "secret destiny" — his lifelong problem, his mysterious fate, his vague but profound and consuming anxiety about himself. "It's only a question of the apprehension that haunts me — that I live with day by day," says this hero, and she in turn is all concern and sympathy beneath her delicate scruples and refinements of sensibility. "Is it a sense of coming violence?" May Bartram asks, quite in the all-sacrificing mood of the May Server of *The Sacred Fount.* "It will only depend on yourself," he answers, "If you'll watch with me." And the scene of their true "engagement" is in this bond, as it were, of a mutual, a double and shared voyeurism which revolves around this hero's odd destiny.

"You mean you feel how my obsession — poor old thing! — may correspond to some possible reality?" asks Marcher again. "To some possible reality," says May, comfortingly. "Then you *will* watch with me?" And again she asks him: "Are you afraid?" And Marcher admits that he doesn't know if he's afraid. "And I should *like* to know . . . You'll tell me yourself whether you think so. If you'll watch with me you'll see." "Very good then," says May, as they move across the room and pause at the door "for the full wind-up of their understanding." "I'll watch with you." She has acquired property, naturally, "to an amount that made luxury just possible," under her aunt's extremely complicated will, and now their odd love affair, their odd vigil, commences in earnest. They are, to Marcher's sense, "no longer hovering about the headwaters of their stream, but had felt their boat pushed sharply off and down the current." Down the current, that is to say, of *his* destiny; his mysterious, alarming fate which also prevents all thought of marriage. "His conviction, his apprehension, his obsession, in short, wasn't a privilege he could invite a woman to share" — though May Bartram does insist on sharing it. "Something or other lay in wait for him, amid the twists and the turns of the months and the years, like a crouching beast in the jungle." And scrupulous, modest, proper and decent as Marcher is about his terrible psychic burden, he knows that May is the perfect companion, almost the dream woman, in his ordeal, or "his unhappy perversion."

He, too, has his little office under the government, his modest patrimony which takes care of his library, his garden in the country, the social life in London "whose invitations he accepted and repaid." But he was detached from it all, so James wrote; it was all a long act of dissimulation. "What it had come to was that he wore a mask painted with the social simper, out of the eye-holes of which there looked eyes of an expression not in the least matching the other features." Was this close to describing the later James's own mood of disenchantment with the British society which had in effect rejected *him*; and weren't those eyes looking through the social mask marked, just like his hero's, by the deep intuition — early and late, naïve or disillusioned — of his own special destiny as an artist, or his terrible failure? It was this, in the literary projection which James offered in "The Beast in the Jungle," that "the stupid world" had never more than half discovered, and that alone of women and of people May Bartram understands; and for which Marcher worships her. (On her birthdays, to preclude any suggestion of selfishness on his part, he always provides her with a trinket, fine of its kind, and costing a little more than he can afford.)

But there are other curious undertones in this satiric tale of the devouring, self-enclosed masculine ego and the all-protecting, all-giving feminine ideal.

"I'm your dull woman," May tells Marcher, as they grow older together. "That covers your tracks more than anything." And she adds: "Considering what the danger is, I'm bound to say I don't think your attitude could well be surpassed." "It's heroic?" asks Marcher. "Certainly — call it that." And this is indeed what this hero would like to call it. "I *am* then a man of courage?" he persists, while he keeps up, as he feels, "his consciousness of the importance of not being selfish"; and the point that he makes, in his own mind, "by his not eternally insisting with her on himself." They go to the opera; they discuss literature together. Yet he still has qualms about the relation — that she is being talked about, that she may want more from him, that her life — her fine "curiosity" in sharing his watching and waiting — has been wasted. The relationship is indeed solely concerned with preserving, with nourishing, expanding, elaborating his sense of his own importance, his unseen but high or tragic destiny. But May Server Bartram appears quite content. "If you've had your woman I've had my man." All that concerns her, she repeats, is to help him "pass for a man like another."*

But isn't his "appreciation" of her generosity simply another manifestation of his rapacious, devouring, sucking, nursing narcissism? And isn't she in turn something of an "unnatural woman," a Jamesian dream woman indeed, to accept, to encourage, to validate, even, this consuming masculine vanity and egotism, without thought, through the years, of anything further than their "talks" about him? (She is, in fact, the feminine masochistic equivalent of his concealed masculine sadism — if we can separate these terms,

---

* Some lines in this story appear to have even odder connotations than those suggested in my text. Was this Jamesian hero guilty in fact of some overt manifestations of his "obsession," or his "unhappy perversion," for which May Bartram served as a conscious and sacrificial shield? In the third volume of his authorized biography of Henry James, *The Middle Years,* Leon Edel makes much of James's hitherto "secret" love affair with Constance Fenimore Woolson in Italy in the late 1880's. But it is more likely that Henry was using this affair as a cover mechanism for his perhaps increasingly homosexual tendencies — and that this was indeed the central human situation of "The Beast in the Jungle."

or these sexes, in this ambiguous and ambivalent tale of the double-watchers.) In "The Beast in the Jungle," too, the day inevitably comes "for a further sounding of their depths," and that is to say, of her unnatural devotion to his total self-absorption. (Since the alternative of physical or sexual pleasure, or of a full human relationship, is denied to them, both the "sacrifice" and the "vanity" of the story become almost intolerable. What "depths" are here really?) For Marcher is convinced that May "knows" something about his own "secret" which she refuses to tell him; even while he circles around her mind, if not her body, "at a distance that alternately narrowed and widened."

She suddenly looks older, "because inevitably, after so many years, she *was* old." She has a "deep disorder in her blood" — she is, in fact, dying. And he immediately thinks of "aggravations and disasters" — he considers her peril "as the direct menace for himself of personal privation." There is the threat of much personal inconvenience in her death. And he wonders if "the great accident" which he has always anticipated for himself, "would take form now as nothing more than his being condemned to see this charming woman, this admirable friend, pass away from him." Thus, even while her death will deprive him of the perfect audience for his special sensibility, it will also in turn perhaps help him to fulfill his destiny. It may even *be* his destiny.

Thus, too, more or less, had James "consoled" himself, in earlier years, for the loss of his own beloved Minny Temple — that her death was somehow necessary to fulfill his own life and fame. (In the dying scene of May Bartram here, given to us more directly than in the case of Milly Theale, James used the same "gliding step" for this heroine as he had used in describing Minny and Milly themselves.) But Marcher is still consumed by his anxieties. May's death will also revive his own uncertain status. "It wouldn't have been failure to be bankrupt, dishonoured, pilloried, hanged; it was failure not to be anything . . . He had one desire left — that he shouldn't have been 'sold.' " What one notices here, of course, is

the romantic accent in the use of such words as "dishonoured, pilloried, hanged," along with that worst of Jamesian fates — bankruptcy.
And by "being" this Jamesian hero certainly didn't mean the mere
enjoyment of life; he meant "being" something or somebody *in* life.
Achievement, not existence, is the real point of "The Beast in the
Jungle," just as the "experience" of the central relationship is a
purely mental one. In this story too the hero emerges clearly — for
all his superficial "decency," and "modesty" — as another of the
obsessed and hysterical Jamesian "supermen" of the spirit. He belongs to that whole line of similarly odd and possessed observers,
narrators, see-ers, knowers and interlocutors, gradually becoming
more and more omnipotent, who extend from "The Aspern Papers"
to "The Turn of the Screw" and *The Sacred Fount*.

"What do you regard as the very worst that at this time of day
can happen to me?" Marcher asks the dying and mute May, while
he adds that, after all, he has had fears of his own which he *hasn't*
told her about: still pressing as he is upon her attention, her sympathy, still "testing" her weakened consciousness, her emotional
capacity to support *him*. Even at the moment of her farewell, her
eyes hold for him "the high flicker of their prime," and the en-
couragement to him to ask her one more last time about "me, me,
me."

In the odd rhythm of their "intensities and avoidances," so James
wrote of their relationship (but an intensity that concerns itself
only with the hero's plight; an intensity which is in fact a lifelong
avoidance of any real human relation), he still harries her for one
last deathbed confession about his own "destiny." "You've done.
You've had your experience. You leave me to my fate," he accuses
her, just as an infant might accuse, if less articulately, or verbosely,
a dying mother for having "betrayed" him. May Bartram's funeral
is also a great disappointment to Marcher, since he feels himself
not only deprived of her support, but unattended by "the distinction, the dignity, the propriety, if nothing else, of a man markedly
bereaved." And at the graveyard he sees the "stricken lover" of the

story. "What had the man *had,* to make him by the loss of it so bleed and yet live?"

Marcher realizes suddenly that his great experience in life was to have had no experience — not even to have been in love. "The escape would have been to love; then, *then* he would have lived . . . *She* had lived — who could say now with what passion — since she had loved him for himself; whereas he had never thought of her (ah how it hugely glared at him!) but in the chill of his egotism and the light of her use." And there is the dream-nightmarish finale to the tale:

The horror of waking — this *was knowledge, knowledge under the breath of which the very tears in his eyes seemed to freeze. Through them, none the less, he tried to fix it and hold it; he kept it there before him so that he might feel the pain. That at least, belated and bitter, had something of the taste of life. But the bitterness suddenly sickened him, and it was as if, horribly, he saw, in the truth, in the cruelty of his image, what had been appointed and done. He saw the Jungle of his life and saw the lurking Beast; then, while he looked, perceived it, as by a stir of the air, rise huge and hideous, for the leap that was to settle him. His eyes darkened — it was close; and, instinctively turning, in his hallucination, to avoid it, he flung himself face down on the tomb.*

That was the famous closing passage to "The Beast in the Jungle," nailing down the description of an insistent, implacable egotism of the story's hero which was close to, which really *was* the description of Henry James's own egotism. Therefore this tale, rather than the evasive, apologetic, rationalizing later Prefaces, was the true example of the Jamesian "self-criticism" — and this story perhaps forms the real base for understanding the much lauded Jamesian "esthetics." What was remarkable, too, was how this completely autocentric writer (to use Ernest Schachtel's phrases) who saw the world only in terms of his own standards and values — romantic, "literary" and abstract as they were — could, in one leap here, move to an "allocentric" or objective view of his own deepest and primary drives, his own true failure as a human being if not as a literary spokesman. In this sense, "The Beast in the Jungle" was a Jamesian epitaph on Henry James.

Yet interesting as the story is, both in itself and as a kind of autobiographical illumination, there are still very curious and very typical Jamesian undertones in it. To what degree, here as in *The Sacred Fount*, was James *conscious* of the self-revelation which had poured forth in this parable of a hero who was incapable of life and love; of an impossible and overwhelming self-centeredness — a self-love, a beseeching and all-demanding vanity of spirit which negated all human experience; which demanded everything and gave nothing; which never could be satisfied even while it reduced the wide world to its own narrow claims? Just as in the sex-haunted novel, the central concept of love here was that of devouring or being devoured — this infantile-oral, pre-oedipal or pre-sexual fantasy of love and sex in terms of food and cannibalism. And James apparently, while illuminating fully the hero's selfishness, never questioned the whole nature of the story's love affair. In the picture of the "true lover" at the graveyard there is that "image of scarred passion," still bleeding over his true — and dead — love; just as Marcher only "loves" May Bartram after *her* death.

Perhaps this artist was as falsely romantic in his notion of "passion" as he was infantile and neurotic in his rejection of it. We notice also that May Bartram has "lived" because she has "loved" Marcher for his own sake — even though this life and this love were purely spiritual — and verbal. It was the spirit of love and not the act of love that James still praised; it was the sacrifices of love and not the rewards or pleasures of love he still commended — and these sacrifices were still purely mental. Moreover, even in the hero's final realization of his own frigid egotism, wasn't he still *not* the hero? — still marked off as *"the* man" of his time whose destiny — and it is still a destiny! — was to have nothing happen to him. The beast continued to crouch in the jungle;

the accents of a fatal narcissism mark even the failure of that narcissism. Here indeed all the inhibited yearnings of our normal
human biopsychic behavior have been "transcended" by a single,
enormous and appalling kind of spiritual self-interest, which persists in its magic-wish of the world on the very brink of desire's
grave. Whether consciously or not, "The Beast in the Jungle"
came straight from the depths, tormented and insatiable, of the
Jamesian temperament. And from James's own autobiographical
writing, we know how closely the story followed — projected, dramatized — the writer's own youthful visions of fame and his recurrent, terrible, anxiety-ridden nightmares of disaster and defeat.

Even at the very end, when Marcher is fully conscious — or as
conscious as he could ever be — of his own character, he thinks of
heroic personages as beings "who had been wondrous for others,
while he was but wondrous for himself." And those heroes of life
are still described in terms of having fought in their time "twenty
duels or been loved by ten princesses." The fairy-tale note of enchantment rose more strongly in James's later work as the hard
truth of "reality" — of his own disenchantment — pressed down
upon this writer. And even the Darwinian imagery of "The Beast
in the Jungle," deriving from the late nineteenth century world-
view of man's animal origins, was used here in an altogether special
Jamesian sense. For the lurking, savage "beast" in the jungle of
Marcher's failure was employed by James to symbolize his hero's
"destiny" or lack of destiny. But wasn't it also a curiously suggestive (if again utterly transformed) symbol of the animal passions
in man which Marcher had avoided — and of those human motives, needs, desires, both savage perhaps and affectional, which
James himself always consciously rose "above"; and quite unconsciously repressed in his fiction? And now the beast had charged,
in a sense which quite certainly James was not aware of.

The second of James's major novels in this period, *The Ambassadors*, in 1903, was also an amplification on the theme of the
wasted life. (Or more accurately, it described the "Achieved Life,
à la James.") This book had a curious history, too. Rejected by

Harper's Magazine as a serial, then accepted by the *North American Review*, and published as a book by Harper and Brothers, it took so long to appear that James had meanwhile completed and published *The Wings of the Dove* a year earlier. Moreover, in both the original American edition of the novel, and in the definitive Scribner's New York Edition of James's work, the 28th and the 29th chapters were in reverse order. The discovery of this error was made by an American scholar, Robert Young, in 1950; and the official bibliographers of James's work, Leon Edel and Dan H. Laurence, have formulated various theories to explain the Master's nod. "James seems never to have discovered the error," so we are told — but perhaps he was so irritated at the delay in the Harper edition that he never looked at the book. Yet in the New York Edition, with the famous Prefaces by this master craftsman about his own fiction, James himself stated that his editorial revisions were reduced to nothing "in the presence of the altogether better literary manners of *The Ambassadors* and *The Golden Bowl.*" These chapters were renumbered as the opening two sections of Book Eleven in this edition, which perhaps further contributed to the confusion.

The New Critic, Robert W. Stallman (*The Houses That James Built*, 1961), added another bit of unconscious humor to this comedy of publishing errors which is a sore blow to all the Jacobite technicians. "In my Introduction to the Doubleday Anchor Book edition of *The Ambassadors* (1958), I claimed" — so Mr. Stallman claims — " 'The present Anchor edition is a faithful copy of the text of the Methuen first edition' — only to discover, when the book was published and by then already distributed, that the Methuen text had *not* been used, and once again the two ill-fated chapters were produced in reverse sequence."* Now it almost appears that these two chapters *want* to be reversed; and it is an in-

---

* In the original version by James, the two chapters contain an evening scene and then a throwback to the afternoon before; and Harper's editor, perhaps confused by the Jamesian method, returned them to their logical or chronological order. Now we are assured that these two errant chapters will be straightened out correctly in the *New* New York Edition of James's work (Scribners, 1961 —). But a critic who has not yet seen *The Ambassadors* in this new edition may have some doubts.

teresting commentary on the novel that the wrong order of the two chapters was not really noticeable for almost fifty years, and hardly affects the story's development. The "scenario" of *The Ambassadors* also, as James transcribed it in his *Notebooks*, was wordy, pretentious and dull; perhaps *Harper's* turned it down with good reason. The germ of the little nouvelle — which James transformed into his usual two volumes of about six hundred pages, lay in William Dean Howells' attributed remarks to Jonathan Sturges in Paris: "Oh, you are young, you are young — be glad of it: be glad of it and *live*. Live all you can: it's a mistake not to . . . This place makes it all come over me . . . I haven't done so — and now I'm old." This was of course James's own later mood, as much as it was Howells'; and if the Lambert Strether of *The Ambassadors* was really meant to describe James's American friend, any resemblance was purely coincidental.

At any rate, so James added in the *Notebooks*, this statement of Howells', again heard at second hand, gave him

the little idea of the figure of an elderly man who hasn't "lived," hasn't at all, in the sense of sensations, passions, impulses, pleasures — and to whom, in the presence of some great human spectacle, some great organization for the Immediate, the Agreeable, for curiosity and experiment and perception, for Enjoyment, in a word, becomes, sur la fin, or towards it, sorrowfully aware . . .

Now this was a typical later Jamesian statement; but what in the world have sensations, passions, impulses, pleasures got to do with "some great human spectacle" or "some great organization for the Immediate, the Agreeable," etc. What then did James mean by sensations, passions or pleasure? "He has never really enjoyed," he said about the prospective hero of *The Ambassadors*. "He has lived only for Duty and conscience — his conception of them; for pure appearances and daily tasks — lived for effort, for surrender, abstention, sacrifice." Was this also a Jamesian self-portrait, all apparently unknowing here? — just as it may remind us of the later novelist Thomas Mann's description of the stricken hero of *Death in Venice*: the elderly Aschenbach who did indeed surrender himself to sensations, and was destroyed by them.

But James hastened to qualify his own outline of the hero in the *Notebooks*. "I don't see him as having battled with his passions — I don't see him as harassed by his temperament or as having, in the past, suspected, very much, what he was losing, what he was not doing." That was the point, and: "The alternative wasn't present to him. He may be an American." That was the reason. Obviously, to an American, there was no possibility even for a *choice* of the sensations and passions, of pleasure or enjoyment; and James went on to show why. "He has married very young, and austerely. Happily enough, but charmlessly, and oh, so conscientiously: a wife replete with the New England conscience." Now were there *no* New England wives who suffered, so to speak, a temporary remission of the New England conscience — even with their husbands? Late as early in his work, James could not really vary from his fixed, rigid, aversion to — his youthful literary scorn of — the New England spirit. At the conclusion of this preliminary profile of *The Ambassadors'* elderly hero there was the familiar Jamesian solution to this central human problem. "It is too late, too late now, for *him* to live — but what stirs in him with a dumb passion of desire, of I don't know what, is the sense that he may have a little super-sensual hour in the vicarious freedom of another. His little drama is the administration of the touch that contributes to — that prolongs — that freedom."

This dumb passion of desire for I don't know what, this little supersensual hour — and how James hovered around such terms — concludes only with the vicarious freedom of another. Was a man of fifty-five really too old to live? Or was it simply impossible for any Jamesian hero, at any age, to live the life of sensations and passions except through some grand organization for the immediate and enjoyable — whatever that may mean — and only then vicariously? If England had disappointed James, and he changed the scene of his illusion to Paris in *The Ambassadors*, "life" still meant Europe to him, for the constricted American temperament; and "Europe" meant a general sociability rather than any direct, personal, achieved human experience.*

And finally, *The Ambassadors* was, as James confidently reported in his later Preface, quite "the best, 'all round,' of my productions." We shall come to his own reasons, but meanwhile it is certain that the later Jacobites all more or less followed the Master's tip, as well as his nod.

In this group of critics, it was the Harvard professor F. O. Matthiessen who was largely responsible for the revival of "the later James," and whose essay on *The Ambassadors*, in particular, in *Henry James: The Major Phase*, set the tone for the received opinion on the novel. Working in the early 1940's from the as yet unpublished material in James's notebooks, all of which Matthiessen accepted quite literally in the first glow of a literary "discovery," this critic solemnly praised the scenario-laden dramatic method of James which we have already described. He accepted it all without qualms, and without qualification; even took over the euphoric tone of James himself in celebrating these great technical discoveries. *The Ambassadors* was one of the three crowning works of James, said Matthiessen. "After the strained virtuosity of *The Awkward Age* and *The Sacred Fount*, James expanded into a theme that was both opulent and robust." But the two earlier novels which Matthiessen dismissed here were particularly interesting, while the opulent, robust *Ambassadors* was at least partly a return on James's side to the old-fashioned, sentimental, popular Victorian serial.

Thus *The Major Phase* paid tribute to the novel's "roundness of

* Howells may have known only one woman, his wife (as James claimed, rather sententiously for a man who had known, apparently, no women) but the American novelist knew about marriage at least. "A happy marriage," said Howells, "is the peace of exhaustion." In point of fact, however, *both* of these writers had precluded from their lives, and mainly from their work, any varied experience with women and love.

structure," its "architectural competence," and its long-delayed, familiar Jamesian strip-tease introduction to the chief characters — if they can be really called that. This was narrative suspense, according to the Matthiessen argument, and he went on to even more peculiar critical judgments. "The portrait of the Pococks . . . is one of James' triumphs in light-handed satire, in the manner he had mastered in *Daisy Miller* and had developed further in that lesser known but delightful *jeu d'esprit*, *The Reverberator*." The Pococks we shall come to shortly; but the long short story, "The Reverberator," was surely one of the poorest and most contrived of all of James's light fictions. How far really can you go in this vein of Jamesian "criticism"? Such a statement, from a critic of Matthiessen's caliber, would be impossible to make except under the influence of some mad enchantment — some bewitchment, some literary love potion. But more: "The eleventh book rises to the most effective climax of all, Strether's glimpse of Chad and Madame de Vionnet together on the river, and his long-delayed perception of their real relationship." How can a climax reside in a "glimpse"? And wouldn't even a Boston literary man (such as Howells was presumed to be) have surmised from the start that long-delayed perception of Chad and his mistress?

In the novel Strether has been sent to Paris precisely to find out *what* this relationship is. If he doesn't already guess the truth, he is deliberately self-deceived. (The point is that James *makes* him obtuse for the sake of his plot, for the elaborate, portentous narrative suspense.) But Matthiessen is again overcome — that is really the word — by the Jamesian technique; by the use of Strether as "a centre of consciousness." "What Strether *sees* is the entire content, and James thus perfected a device both for framing and for interpreting experience." Thus *The Ambassadors*, according to Matthiessen, was noteworthy for its large unity, for a heightened singleness of vision, and it was perhaps "the most skillfully planned novel ever written." Now after such extravagant praise, one can hardly bring oneself to inquire just what is it, after all, that Strether does see (except two lovers sitting in a rowboat), or what *kind* of experience is it that James is framing and interpreting in his celebrated centers of consciousness?

Was the most skillfully planned novel ever written on the same order as that plot melodrama which regulated and controlled, which manipulated and twisted every character, every normal human impulse, in *The Wings of the Dove?* Well, Matthiessen went on to state that

> *there is a vast difference between James' method and that of the novels of "the stream of consciousness." That phrase was used by William James in his* Principles of Psychology, *but in his brother's novels there is none of the welling up of the darkly subconscious life that has characterized the novel since Freud. James' novels are strictly novels of intelligence rather than of full consciousness; and in commenting on the focus of attention that he had achieved through Strether, he warned against "the terrible fluidity of self-revelation."*

A remarkable and illuminating critical passage; for: Is *that* the real virtue of Henry James? which might otherwise be considered the barrier which separates James from the moderns, and marks him so clearly as among the last of the Victorian artists. We have already noticed too, particularly in the novels which Matthiessen snubbed, just how much of that darkly subconscious life did in fact well up in the work of James — as it must in any literary talent — even when the writer himself was unconscious, or at best half conscious, of its true meaning. That strain of James's work is just what gives it the interest that it does have — the terrible fluidity of self-revelation which is so revealing in the work of this writer when it does not simply mean that James is talking endlessly about James.

With this singular critical statement, Matthiessen established himself as the first of the non- or rather anti-psychological critics who embraced James deliberately as a rational and conscious artist, and who were then forced to ignore the "pre-logical," or "supra-logical," or the *true* psychological bases of his work.* Thus *The Major Phase* stressed the "trained eye" of James in *The Ambassadors*, while it completely ignored the deep, compulsive voyeuristic patterns in James's temperament which created indeed such a large part — that seeing and knowing about life, rather than living and sharing — of his esoteric technique. As to the rest of the Jamesian critics who followed both James's and Matthiessen's statement that *The Ambassadors* was quite frankly the best, all round, of the later novels, haven't they found it equally difficult to justify their praise in critical terms? And wasn't this because the novel was at best a rather charming light social comedy on the familiar international theme; and at worst a rather improbable romance based on the idea that a French love affair could educate and improve a man beyond all the possibilities of provincial American culture?

But to what lengths now didn't James go in his method of redoing the old-fashioned popular travel romances of his youth. This perhaps, rather than the somewhat implausible theme, or the generally weaker cast of characters in *The Ambassadors*, and the long-delayed and inadequate action, is the novel's real interest.

The aging Strether, who is merely middle-aged, is a rather weak and unconvincing hero (who could hardly have been flattering to the provincial and innocent Howells). James was also trying to prove, rather absurdly, that the French love affair of Chad's was not, naturally, a *carnal* but a spiritual one — a liaison of virtue rather than desire. This novel was indeed a sort of final justification of the international theme, which we have already seen to be artificial in its conception; and which James himself felt so disenchanted about in respect to its English conclusion. But how the international *fantasy* still persisted in James's imagination; how this

---

* Matthiessen was quite correct, as we've noted, in declaring that "The Turn of the Screw" was not a conscious Freudian story. But by ignoring the wealth of repressed emotional material even in this story; and by neglecting the whole infantine, ego-centered and fairy-tale base of James's literary cosmos, this academic critic made literary judgments which were, as in the treatment of *The Ambassadors*, simply not adequate.

illusion only needed a change of place, rather than of values, or understanding, to flourish again! "Mr. Waymarsh of Milrose Connecticut" (and now James also dispensed with the conventional comma between place names; while his later style fluctuated rather wildly between the "disappearing comma," so to speak, and the omnipresent comma) was again the taciturn Yankee lawyer who is Strether's foil; just as Maria Gostrey is his confidante, or a Jamesian *ficelle*. Like the Longdon of *The Awkward Age*, Strether carries his eternal nippers through the narrative (as a stage prop of vision); and the "sacred rage" of the obtuse Waymarsh is scattered about the novel.* The later James was becoming a little careless (perhaps through the habit of dictation) about the use of his favorite literary tags and tricks.

The names are still revealing, however. Waymarsh is obviously stuck in the morass of provincial American society. Maria Gostrey is a gossip (or a goose?), and very much so. Strether is stretching for new horizons, or a new breath of life; perhaps he is also at the end of his tether. Or at least he often makes the reader feel so. Strether's long analyses of his European experiences are tedious in the first half of *The Ambassadors*; there is again so much analysis of so little content in a narrative which might be described more correctly as an "anti-narrative" or a "non-narrative." (Now I am borrowing terms from Mr. Fadiman's review of William Faulkner's *Absalom! Absalom!*: just as Faulkner borrowed some of his style from James, no doubt, in the days before Mr. Fadiman had become a convert to the Jacobite cause.) Strether's is the stream of consciousness plain; since apparently he has no unconscious at all.

In the later Jamesian style, too, there is a curious use of the double negative as an apex to some kind of ultrarefinement:

* Unfortunately, Robert W. Stallman chose this phrase as the title for his study of "time" in *The Ambassadors*, without realizing that James first used the "sacred rage" for the dubious hero of *The Awkward Age*, and then used it indiscriminately thereafter. It has nothing to do with "time," in James; but perhaps it appealed to him as having a certain sexual undertone. Mr. Stallman's essay is a fine example of the "metaphysical approach" to James's work which avoids all the real issues of the novel.

Strether told Waymarsh all about that evening, on their dining together at the hotel; which needn't have happened, he was all the while aware, hadn't he chosen to sacrifice to this occasion a rarer opportunity.

Now what Strether has chosen to sacrifice is of course the chance to see Chad — who is not, as it turns out, in Paris at all. Like Milly Theale, like these later Jamesian royal figures in general, both Chad and Mme. de Vionnet must be glimpsed from afar at some length (or *not* glimpsed from afar) before they descend to the common scene. Meanwhile there is the sparkling Paris life of the novel: free, bohemian, artistic, cultivated, altogether charming to the provincial, or American hero. These Parisian esthetes show a candor and verve for life which is astounding to the ignorance of Woollett. "They were red-haired and long-legged; they were quaint and queer and dear and droll; they made the place resound with the vernacular . . . They twanged with a vengeance the aesthetic lyre — they drew from it wonderful airs."*

Now surely these were the banquet years of Parisian, French, and European culture, as Roger Shattuck has reminded us recently in an entertaining survey of the period which James was ostensibly describing in *The Ambassadors*. They were the years of the great European renascence in the arts, painting, writing, the stage; that high peak of western capitalistic culture just before the beginning of the end in the First World War. But where in James's whole work, not to mention his specific novel of Parisian culture, is there any real familiarity or concern with the modern French movements in art, music, or even the literature, which he read, to be sure, with a certain alarmed apprehension. Where are the great French Impressionists, say, whom James touched on very briefly near the end of his career; not to mention such really bohemian figures as Alfred Jarry, Erik Satie, Rousseau or Apollinaire? No, James's taste was still classical, academic; very close to the formal or antiquarian taste of the great American fortunes themselves. He viewed even

---

* These sections of the novel also resound with such phrases as "license," "freedom," the "irregular life, or "the fundamental impropriety," etc. — but Miss Barrace's smoking, or perhaps Mme. de Vionnet's elbows on the table while she dines, are almost the only examples we get of the bohemian life.

the paler, milder British equivalent of *fin de siècle* decadence and bohemianism with the same distaste (fear?) that he expressed about Zola, not to mention Huysmans. He was actually as remote from the contemporary French culture of his own period as he was from the contemporary American scene; or, with a certain difference, from England itself.

He was a writer with a built-in time lag of almost half a century. The cutting of his American roots appeared to have cut off his time sense everywhere. He dwelt still — and forever — in the imaginary fairy-tale world of his youth and adolescence at best; but then, as we shall see, perhaps the real roots of Henry James had been cut off, in a curious biopsychic phenomenon, almost at his birth — in his earliest childhood. Meanwhile what he described as the "great French culture" in *The Ambassadors* — that "great human spectacle," or that grand organization "for the Immediate, the Agreeable," etc. — was merely a little ingrown group of more or less ineffectual Franco-American expatriates and half-artists. It was in fact the same familiar circle always present in the leisure-class novel; but here even more cultivated, apparently, more charming, useless and idle.*

No, what we actually get of "art" in *The Ambassadors* are simply those familiar walks through the Louvre, those epicurean lunches and dinners, those scenes at the Comédie Française where finally, in the great "confrontation scene," Strether "sees" Chad standing alone at the back of the box. "They were in the presence of Chad himself." James repeated this portentously — although it was hardly so remarkable considering that, after all, Strether had come to Paris to meet Chad — and the novelist embarked on another of his purple prose passages when Strether reflects that

---

* So how could a critic of Dupee's quality also concur with Matthiessen and with James himself in describing this Parisian life in such terms as: "As distinguished from bourgeois Woollett, Strether's Paris is a city of artists and members of the nobility united in the pursuit of pleasure, enlightenment, and artistic creation . . ." Just what artists, what pleasure, enlightenment, and artistic creation are really *described* in *The Ambassadors?* Dupee, like Matthiessen, has swallowed the Jamesian donnée whole, even when James's own rendering of this scene was so inadequate.

*these were the accidents of a high civilization; the imposed tribute to
propriety, the frequent exposure to conditions, usually brilliant, in which
relief has to await its time. Relief was never quite near at hand for
kings, queens, comedians and other such people, and though you might
be yourself not exactly one of these, you could yet, in leading the life
of high pressure, guess a little how they sometimes felt. It was truly
the life of high pressure that Strether had seemed to feel himself lead
while he sat there, close to Chad, during the long tension of the act.*

This confrontation is actually a silence; another unique development in the bizarre extremes of the drama of consciousness. The
life of high pressure consists, apparently, of just sitting next to the
fabulous (if also to this point quite nebulous) hero of *The Ambassadors* during the course of an anonymous French play. But
what were the comedians and other such people doing in the presence of what James was certainly laboring to create as his own fabulous leisure-class royalty of these new literary kings and queens?

Maybe the uneasy tone of this complex, labored and hortatory
prose reflected the writer's own consciousness that he had not established the literary illusion he was trying for — that he really
could not. So that James tried again, in still more extreme terms, to
express Strether's enchantment and awe at finally meeting the legendary, royal, munificent Chad — this new vision of true life for
the naïve, elderly New Englander; this "remarkable truth" personified somehow by the solitary, silent hero sitting in his opera box:

*But oh it was too remarkable, the truth; for what could be more re-
markable than this sharp rupture of an identity? You could deal with
a man as himself — you couldn't deal with him as somebody else. It
was a small source of peace moreover to be reduced to wondering how
little he might know in such an event what a sum he was setting you.
He couldn't absolutely not know, for you couldn't absolutely not let
him. It was a case then simply, a strong case, as people nowadays called
such things, a case of transformation unsurpassed, and the hope was
but in the general law that strong cases were liable to control from
without. Perhaps he, Strether himself, was the only person after all
aware of it. Even Miss Gostrey, with all her science, wouldn't be,*

would she? — and he had never seen any one less aware of anything than Waymarsh as he glowered at Chad. The social sightlessness of his old friend's survey marked for him afresh, and almost in an humiliating way, the inevitable limits of direct aid from this source. He was not certain, however, of not drawing a shade of compensation from the privilege, as yet untasted, of knowing more about something in particular than Miss Gostrey did. His situation too was a case, for that matter, and he was now so interested, quite so privately agog, that he had already an eye to the fun it would be to open up to her afterwards . . .

Now here again, in the face of his spiritual impotence, as it were, the Jamesian "observer" takes his only comfort from "the privilege, as yet untasted," of "knowing" more about the apparently unknowable than do his less privileged friends. But what is the "too remarkable truth" that Strether, before he has spoken to Chad, suddenly perceives in this fabulous moment of enlightenment in that dark theater box: this sharp rupture that he feels about Chad's identity, this "case of transformation unsurpassed" that also throws light on Strether's own "case," that leaves him so privately agog with the fun of opening up the "secret" afterwards to his little French confidante?

"He had never in his life," so James added about Strether's ecstasy, "seen a young man come into a box at ten o'clock at night." Is *that* the secret of all this Jamesian excitement; of this overdone, extreme, rather foggy and euphoric hyperbole — where Strether, again, is also seized by a "wild unrest urging him to seize his chance" to say, finally, "hello" to Chad? What is this marvelous change of character, manners, personality, values, taste in the princely young hero? There is Chad's "wide-brimmed crush hat," his "strong young grizzled crop," his "inscrutable new face," his new "ripe physiognomy," his "identity so rounded off, his palpable presence and his massive young manhood." There is the hint of some new self-respect, we are told again (and again), "some sense of power . . . something latent and beyond access, ominous and perhaps enviable." Chad is "an irreducible young Pagan." But then also, Strether reflects in his first conversation with this hero, he is something more. "He had been wondering a minute ago if the boy weren't a Pagan, and he found himself wondering now if he weren't by chance a gentleman."*

But Lambert Strether's is, of course, a highly artificial, a contrived and perhaps altogether improbable "innocence." (The point is that neither Strether nor Chad is really convincing in this overwrought Jamesian rendering.) He still believes, Strether, that Chad's relation with Mme. de Vionnet is "pure." Maria Gostrey, whose silences "were never barren, nor even dull," has something of a silence at this juncture. "The fathomless medium held them — Chad's manner was the fathomless medium; and our friend felt as if they passed each other, in their deep immersion, with the round impersonal eye of silent fish," Strether also reflects about Waymarsh's withdrawal from the novel at this point. And here again, as in the *Dove*, the Jamesian puppets speak or don't speak, appear or withdraw conveniently, according to the dictates of the *plot line* (the romance melodrama) rather than according to any true development of character or human relations.

And just what is that "fathomless medium" of Chad's which is celebrated in such a portentous manner? Just as in *The Wings of the Dove*, James was at his old game of "appearance and reality," although both poles of his "illusion" were so forced, so manipulated and so abstractly theoretical as to leave little room for any decent reality. Strether's "innocence" and Chad's "sophistication" are equally implausible; they are merely the extremes of James's own illusionary yearnings. There is another fabulous Parisian party scene in the French garden on the Faubourg Saint-Germain where

* There is a curious resemblance, *autre temps autres moeurs*, between the later Jamesian glorification of Chad as the highest form of handsome, virile, polished masculinity and the virility-laden equally romantic and handsome sexpot heroes of Tennessee Williams in twentieth century American dramatic writing. Now these idealized portraits of youth, masculinity and virility reflect probably some kind of recessive homosexual yearning rather than any kind of mature realism — but with Henry James, of course, the *social* graces were as important as the purely sexual charms of his hero.

the sculptor Gloriani; but just a minute — I had almost forgotten.
There *is* an artist in these pages, the same sculptor Gloriani who
was the dubious Italian "master" of *Roderick Hudson,* about
twenty-six years earlier, but who is now, in this total (tricky) transformation of the later James, a truly great "master" — to Strether's
naïve eyes — an artist to beat all artists. But in this Parisian party,
as I say, where there are truly "ambassadors, cabinet ministers,
bankers, generals, what do I know? even Jews," as Little Bilham
reports to Strether, there are also just the right kind and right number of *femmes du monde.* Chad's history is equally "fabulous" on
this score, we are told. "They *never* give him up. Yet he keeps
them down: no one knows how he manages: it's too beautiful and
bland. Never too many — and a mighty good thing too; just a perfect choice." And how Henry James, or his Strether-hero, circles
around these mysterious, delightful (no doubt sinful but lifegiving?)
femmes du monde against the background of whom we get our first
direct view of Mme. de Vionnet herself.

Well, naturally, this view is not entirely direct. Mme. de Vionnet
is accompanied by her young daughter, with whom, Strether immediately assumes, Chad is really in love, in this "virtuous attachment." James has deliberately thrown another false lead across the
reader's path, as in all these later novels of tricks and stratagems
and manipulated personality: the so-called "perfectly planned
novel." And our first vision of Mme. de Vionnet is accompanied
by the high chatter of all these European sophisticates in what is
really another incredible scene of "Parisian life." Amidst all the
enchanting Poles, Turks, Portuguese, even Jews; those glittering ambassadors, duchesses, countesses; those "brilliant strangers" and cul-
tured Continental types with a "bold high look," and noble ladies
with gold bracelets and precious bangles beneath their fine black
sleeves, we get such comments as Little Bilham's: "That's half the
battle here — that you can never talk politics. We don't talk them"
— as another mark of high culture, pure art; or of the highest
ranges, at least of the emasculated leisure-class novel. But wasn't

this actually another part of the genteel society's view, in James's own American youth, of the "vulgar" American democracy's political organization: an upper class void, a social vacuum, as in Edith Wharton's work too, which the financial titans were happy to fill up?

It is curious how James displayed all the traits of the established "upper class" group of the older American republic confronted by the new power, the vulgarity, the materialism of the robber baron period. But also James *shared* certain values and tastes of the new American fortunes themselves; and in his last major novel of an aging "provincial" and European "culture," he revealed himself as perhaps the greatest provincial of them all in American literature. "Europe" — this yearned-for, imaginary identity of his youth — persisted forever and ever in an endless and untouchable dream of "art" and culture high above the mundane events of ordinary life. The same fantasy of James's childhood and adolescence, though now refurbished "for others" in *The Ambassadors*, persisted in his maturity and old age, and now in a heightened and even more fabricated form. "He's delightful; he's wonderful," both Miss Barrace and Little Bilham repeat in unison about the dour, uncomprehending, comic-opera "Yankee," Waymarsh, who is also not much removed from the small-town New England lawyer in *Roderick Hudson*. (Just as this whole Paris scene was a "retake," at best a "remake," of the glittering Roman scene in James's first novel, where the little Dickensian painter, Sam Singleton, and the "sophisticated" Miss Blanchard were the prototypes for Little Bilham and Miss Barrace.) Henry James was never one to be changed by experience. "Dear old Paris!" all these expatriated "artists" echo in their communal chorus, and: "She's charming; she's perfect . . . she's wonderful," they exclaim about Mme. de Vionnet herself. This was a kind of fairy-tale masque of Parisian life — of a glittering, marvelous, beautiful world of ambassadors and duchesses and artists — rather than any kind of realistic appraisal. But just as in *The Wings of the Dove*, or as in all the later

James novels, there is an added layer of deception. They are all
in the plot — this whole cast of cultivated European figures — to
deceive Strether (who hardly needs their help), to keep him in
ignorance about the obvious relationship of Chad and Mme. de
Vionnet.

Chad himself begins to hint ominously and mysteriously about
"the damnable terms of my sacrifice," and how much he owes to
Mme. de Vionnet. (She is beginning to age, she is almost forty.
He has grown tired of her anyhow; he will not risk his American
wealth and position for her sake.) In the novel there is hardly any
direct view of Chad and Mme. de Vionnet together; they barely
speak to each other in this "intimate" relationship. But meanwhile Strether has met her and he himself has fallen completely in
love with her feminine charm, her culture (she subscribes to the
Revue de Deux Mondes), her plight. It is Strether now, despite the
risk of his own career and his intended marriage to Mrs. Newsome,
who urges Chad to keep Mme. de Vionnet and to defy the puritanical American codes and conventions. "I understand what a
relation with such a woman — what such a high fine friendship —
may be. It can't be vulgar or coarse, anyway — and that's the
point," he declares, and then: "Let them face the future together."
And here, at the close of the first volume, *The Ambassadors*, in its
own odd way, despite all the implausible nonsense of its background, and perhaps the even more dubious nature of its "plot,"
does achieve a certain tension, sympathy and interest.

That is the familiar "secret" of the Jamesian literary magic; of
making the unreal, or the half real, seem real for the moment as we
read the novel, at least; or if not quite "real," at least "convincing,"
or if not quite convincing, somehow and someway interesting. This
is the special Jamesian "illusion" of literature and life, again,
spreading its own wings of artifice over our infatuated fancies; even
though so obviously based on such a transparent web of "magic
yearning" and wishful thinking. Mme. de Vionnet, worried and
anxious about Chad and his American family, persuades Strether

to help her case, just when the handsome young pagan is preparing to leave her; and to pay her off. Strether clearly faces the "truth" — "as with dormant pulses at last awake" — and stakes everything on his own belief. He concedes that Bilham, the poor little painter-man, is not good enough for Mme. de Vionnet's cultivated daughter, Jeanne, who has been the previous blind for Chad's "interest" in the French household.

There are curious psychological elements, of course, in the central relationships of the novel. Earlier Chad is almost viewed as a paternal figure seeking the hand of his mistress's daughter. Now Strether, in his own passion and enthusiasm, takes over the role of the father-surrogate who is persuading an unruly "son" to keep an aging mistress-mother symbol — a "pure" father-figure on Strether's part, but one who is also in love with the woman with whom the son is obviously on the most intimate terms. These shadowy and shifting familial and filial relations, centered around an unconscious or repressed incestuous triangle, accompanied, very often, by a sublimated homosexual or lesbian situation, are evident in James's work as far back as *The Bostonians* or *Watch and Ward*. They were even more explicitly developed in the novel which followed *The Ambassadors* — despite all the Jamesian critics who stressed his rational and conscious, or moral and metaphysical grandeur. How often indeed did the later James, increasingly obsessed by "sex," play so delicately with these "abnormal," or historically "primitive," or infantile states of the human psyche — and perhaps that, too, is almost unconsciously part of our concern with the Chad-Strether-Vionnet triangle in the novel.

One notes, incidentally, that Mme. de Vionnet's daughter Jeanne — but not Chad's — is cast in the familiar role of the child-orphan exploited by the callous adults. For Mme. de Vionnet forces her into a "suitable marriage"; partly, we are told, because Chad *has* had his eye on her, and also because Madame wishes to free herself entirely of any encumbrances Chad might object to. So not only is the attachment between Strether and the charming

French lady — sentimental and romantic as it is — another "impossible" love affair of James's; but Mme. de Vionnet's charm itself soon becomes questionable, and her character dubious. Here as in *The Wings of the Dove*, after the brief interlude of Jamesian enchantment, the central figures of the novel are soon transfixed by their "prearranged destinies." They are trapped again by the relentless coils of the romance melodrama. In one sense indeed the three main figures can be viewed as an aging, desperate and manipulative woman; a rich, slippery and callous young American bounder; and a perpetually adolescent, rather pruriently old-maidish and inordinately "innocent" middle-aged voyeur. For Strether also "spies out," with a kind of childish wonder, and a certain curious loverlike jealousy and envy, all the "intimate" sexual behavior of Chad and Mme. de Vionnet. In a more realistic chronicle, this after all barely more than middle-aged literary man, completely entranced as he is by the maturing French lady, might well have married her. And the well-matched couple might then have left their wealthy, handsome, cultivated and "pagan" young American friend to go his own idle way.

But this is impossible, of course, in the typical Jamesian view of reality, human behavior, or experience. It is much too sensible, possible and practical. If Mme. de Vionnet is "strange and beautiful" to Strether in "her quiet soft acuteness," we are shortly told that "the golden nail she had driven in pierced a good inch deeper." If Chad is "strong and sleek and gay, easy and fragrant and fathomless," he becomes all the more ambiguous about his future plans when Strether becomes more importunate. "Are you tired of her?" asks the infatuated intermediary of this odd triangle:

Chad gave him in reply to this, with a movement of the head, the strangest slow smile he had ever had from him.
  "Never."
  "Never?"
  "Never?" asks Strether again.

And: "Never," says Chad, "obligingly and serenely," in this typical later-James verbal interchange. But he is, of course. And he has already decided to leave her. Then there is the celebrated arrival of the Pococks in the novel (as the Jacobites proclaim) as the real emissaries of the vigilant, rich, powerful, threatening, puritanical and provincial (if always absent) New England mother-figure, Mrs. Newsome herself.

Yes, they do provide a kind of familiar and accomplished light-comedy touch in *The Ambassadors*. But Sarah Pocock also — with "her marked thin-lipped smile, intense without brightness and as prompt to act as the scrape of a safety-match," and "the protrusion of her rather remarkably long chin," and "the penetration of her voice to a distance," is the Jamesian stereotype of the angular, virginal, narrow and chill New England woman. Beneath the entertainment, Henry James's animus towards this area of American life was as persistent as his view of New England was fixed. As for Jim Pocock himself —

Small and fat and constantly facetious, straw-coloured and destitute of marks, he would have been practically indistinguishable hadn't his constant preference for light-grey clothes, for white hats, for very big cigars and very little stories, done what it could for his identity.

— he is another caricature of the American businessman: a pre-Babbitt or pre-Dodsworth figure, also in Edith Wharton's vein, who comes off less harshly perhaps because he is after all the victim and puppet of the dominating New England women. Less harshly, but not too convincingly, because *as* an American businessman there is nothing in him of the business world except an incurable, gaping tourist-type misunderstanding of "Europe."

What is curious, however, in the novel's big confrontation scene of Europe and America — of the Pococks and Mme. de Vionnet; where Strether finally declares himself as Europe's friend — is that neither side of this rather forced, artificial ideological debate comes out very well. If the Americans are stupid and vulgar, Mme. de Vionnet is obviously scheming, self-pitying and rather tactless. From this point on her character falls apart rapidly — the moves in "her game" become apparent. "Do I seem to you very awful?" she asks Strether; and even with the advantage of her "noble old apartment" which is "full, once more, of dim historic shades, of the faint far-away cannon-roar of the great empire," Mme. de Vionnet becomes, if not "awful," at least a selfish or even a stupid woman. And when this heroine collapses, the novel collapses. We suddenly become aware of the celebrated "method" of the narrative: the indirect presentation through a series of alternating conversations; the different points of view always centered around the meaning of the events rather than of personality; the "pre-anterior" analysis of events to come, the anterior analysis, the event itself, and then the series of "post-analyses." But we become aware of this intricate, elaborate and artificial method simply because the novel's content has ebbed away. In the "circular narrative" which constitutes the form of *The Ambassadors* — this "architectural roundness" which James considered to be at its height and perfection here — it is quite possible to omit several rings of the exposition without doing much harm to the story's meaning. These are really duplicating interpretations, or what one might call also "the skippable exposition." (Thus the famous "reversed" chapters, which are not really reversed at all.)

How far was James deliberate or unconscious, again, in charting Mme. de Vionnet's disintegration? Was this a measure of Strether's dawning European consciousness, his so-long-delayed social maturity? Was it also a necessary attribute of the plot line, in order to rationalize Chad's desertion of her, to make him a little less of a cad? There was still another, deeper, typically Jamesian reason, perhaps. In a climactic scene towards the novel's end, when Strether, too, abandons Mme. de Vionnet — for no reason that you can see, except that perhaps he has finally discovered, with a pang of jealousy and a blush of shame, "the deep, deep truth of the intimacy revealed" — with Chad, that is; and when James again invoked the glorious French past, not of the grand empire but this time of the Revolution itself to serve as the dying chord of his doomed heroine —

Thus and so, on the eve of the great recorded dates, the days and nights of revolution, the sounds had come in, the omens, the beginnings broken out. They were the smell of revolution, the smell of the public temper — or perhaps simply the smell of blood . . . His hostess was dressed as for thunderous times, and it fell in with the kind of imagination we have just attributed to him that she should be in the simplest coolest white, of a character so old-fashioned, if he were not mistaken, that Madame Roland must on the scaffold have worn something like it . . .

— in this dramatic or even somewhat melodramatic scene of Mme. de Vionnet's final ruin, we may come across the real reason for her decline.

James again stressed her "cultural value," her connections with an "old, old, old" race and tradition; her association with "things from far back — tyrannies of history, facts of type, values, as the painters said, of expression — all working for her and giving her the supreme chance, the chance of the happy, the really luxurious few . . ." And the Jacobite critics of *The Ambassadors* make much of the fact that here, somewhat as in *The Princess Casamassima*, this artist used the great moments of French history to add "tradition," "depth," "tone" to his condemned heroine. But consider for a moment just *what* view of French history James adduced in these passages of romantic rhetoric about the "grand Empire," the Revolutionary Terror, and Mme. Roland on the scaffold. After all, was it so unusual in French society for a wealthy young man to discard an older mistress? Did this really warrant the "smell of the public temper," which was equated, in this Jamesian "history," with the smell of blood?

No; all this was simply another dubious and metaphysical smoke screen of Henry James's, another adolescent-romantic "picture" of French history and culture as embodied in the doomed Mme. de Vionnet. And this heroine was not as "natural and simple" with the grandeur of condemned royalty as James here described her — as James himself then grudgingly admitted. Strether could "trust her," as we are told; but: "That is he could trust her to make deception right. As she presented things the ugliness — goodness knows why — went out of them; none the less too that she could present them, with an art of her own, by not as much as touching them."

But then what *was* this "deception," this "ugliness" and this art of omission which is also embodied in Mme. de Vionnet? For James finally did reach — after all the elaborate "counter-screens" so to speak, of her charm, tact, beauty, culture, art, simplicity — the flaw in Mme. de Vionnet. "Women were thus endlessly absorbent, and to deal with them was to walk on water," Strether reflects in an illuminating phrase:

What was at bottom the matter with her, embroider as she might and disclaim as she might [or as James might] — *what was at bottom the matter with her was simply Chad himself. It was of Chad she was after all renewedly afraid; the strange strength of her passion was the very strength of her fear; she clung to him, Lambert Strether, as to a source of safety she had tested, and, generous, graceful, truthful as she might try to be, exquisite as she was, she dreaded the term of his being within reach. With this sharpest perception yet, it was like a chill in the air to him, it was almost appalling, that a creature so fine could be, by mysterious forces, a creature so exploited.*

And Strether finally tells Mme. de Vionnet: "You're afraid for your life!"

Now there is a certain truth in all this eloquence with which James recurrently propounded his own deepest fear and suspicion of the "passions." They do indeed exact their toll — the hard vow of the goddess — upon their deluded and inflamed victims; they do exploit the finest creatures impaled upon these "mysterious forces"; while fear, anxiety, deception are their psychological concomitants, as the bards, the poets and the novelists of love have always told us. But is this the single medium of the passions? Is it love's *only* conclusion; its only premise and only reward — and was this Mme. de Vionnet's only true moment of revelation and sincerity in *The Ambassadors?* What was illuminating in this Jamesian passage was the deep tone of horror with which it regarded love and passion as the destructive agent of all human grace, dignity, and even beauty.

It was actually moreover as if he didn't think of her at all, as if he could think of nothing but the passion, mature, abysmal, pitiful, she represented and the possibilities she betrayed. She was older for him to-night, visibly less exempt from the touch of time; but was as much as ever the finest and subtlest creature, the happiest apparition, it had been given to him, in all his years, to meet; and yet he could see her there as vulgarly troubled, in very truth, as a maidservant crying for her young man. The only thing was that she judged herself as the maidservant wouldn't; the weakness of which wisdom, too, the dishonour of which judgment seemed but to sink her lower.

So now the secret was out. The Jamesian half-truth about the passions in the heroine of *The Ambassadors* was the same, familiar fixed fantasy in the Jamesian mind as to not only the destructive impact of passion, but its final cheapness and vulgarity. Mme. de Vionnet was the highest product of French culture, as James implied, whose whole merit was that she has reclaimed and re-educated the brash, provincial young American millionaire, whose whole mysterious sexuality has been employed, as it were, for a purely cultural and "social" purpose. But Mme. de Vionnet is punished in the novel because, after all, she *is* sexual. Or else why did James describe her passion as "mature, abysmal, pitiful"? And what "possibilities" has Mme. de Vionnet betrayed? Why is she suddenly so much older, and as "vulgarly troubled" in truth, as the

Jamesian maidservant crying for her young man? (Like the prurient Victorians in general, James apparently identified the "lower
passions" with the lower classes; or sometimes even, as we see in
the literature of this period, with "the lower races.") And was
James so certain that a maidservant *wouldn't* judge herself — about
what? — while Mme. de Vionnet's self-image now revealed only
the weakness of her wisdom, the dishonor and depths of her
shame?

If the handsome villainess in *The Wings of the Dove* showed
that sexuality was at base criminal, the enchanting, subtle and cultivated heroine of *The Ambassadors* showed that sex was still disastrous — even when there was a minimum of it in this "virtuous"
alliance; and when that minimum was used, in the Jamesian view,
for the noblest of social purposes. Now this whole tragedy of
Mme. de Vionnet's "ruin" simply reflected, in a somewhat less obvious way, the abiding Jamesian superstition that sexual love, just
as in the phobic fantasies of *The Sacred Fount*, was not a source
of life and pleasure, but was a hideous, devouring and destructive
process. Mme. de Vionnet is ruined, after all, because she has
made Chad what he is. (She is a literary cousin of May Server, of
May Bartram.) She has given everything to him; he has taken it
all without qualms and without reciprocity; and all that is left for
this heroine is abysmal and vulgar grief. Strether abandons her
in her deepest moment of need; though why? Chad abandons her
without even a farewell recorded in the novel. And the two men
have a final, quite euphoric (and illogical) post-mortem on this
suffering woman. "She must have been wonderful," says Strether.
"She *was*," says the young American mercantile prince.

But was she, really? The great Jamesian buildup of Mme. de
Vionnet's charm, grace, beauty, tact, wisdom now appears again
merely to be contrived, forced and strained in the light of its true
purpose in the novel, and the Jamesian moral she illustrates. Her
portrait is another technical "counter-screen" in large part, designed to hide her real meaning until the very end; and hence the
adolescent and exaggerated view of her charm on the part of

Strether — the contrived view by James himself. And thus we get those almost always enigmatic "glimpses" of Mme. de Vionnet, the reflections and refractions of her "charm" — and the one famous scene of her sitting in the rowboat with her lover; the "glimpse" indeed that condemns her — since to approach too closely to her character before the close of *The Ambassadors* would give the whole thing away. But then James never could approach any of his charming heroines too closely. It was his technical virtuosity that could create this "charm" on such an insubstantial base of knowledge, on such a partial innocent and fearful view of women in general.

If you remember Mme. de Vionnet's peers in the American literature of the period — the lovely, graceful and mature Mme. Olenska of Edith Wharton's fiction, for example; or even the practical, simple little Sister Carrie of Dreiser's — the Jamesian heroine is attractive, yes, but inadequate. She is inadequate precisely because she is attractive — and so unfulfilled as a woman even within her own terms. The final "revelation" of her plight also marks the wind-up of Strether's own career, entranced as he has been by this "happy apparition" of ancient French femininity. But what, after all, *was* his career? The novel ends with a familiar series of rather touching Jamesian "farewells" — to Strether, to Chad, to Maria Gostrey, whom Strether might also have married, in a more realistic chronicle, if Mme. de Vionnet had become out of the question. But this middle-aged "observer," still living out his life through all these other people, prefers to dwell alone with his new European sensibility. That is the only human gain in the novel, apparently; that is the familiar Jamesian "moral."

Is it enough, even for a lighter novel of social comedy on the international theme? Well, here as in *The Wings of the Dove*, the real base is that of solid cash. "Shall you give up your friend for the money in it?" Strether finally asks Chad directly, while the handsome young American pagan has become immersed, conveniently, in his new theories of "scientific advertising." As for Strether's own "ruin," he is not averse to renouncing the wealthy, dominating, puritanical American widow, Mrs. Newsome. He still has "a little money" of his own, while Chad assures him fervently that "he mustn't starve." That is what lingers with us, curiously, after we have finished reading *The Ambassadors*, interesting and entertaining as it is in parts — if also quite pretentious, overblown and tedious in other sections of its extended "analyses" of such meager content. Otherwise, after the spell of James's own literary magic has subsided — the magic-magic of illusion, artifice and pretense — we may wonder just what *is* in the novel, beyond the endless chatter of a group of fashionable expatriates and mediocrities, dwelling in an obviously inadequate and patently artificial "international scene."

What an esoteric fiction, in short, this was; and how James could still blow it up to such inordinate proportions. Perhaps his real gift lay in the immense fertility of trivia with which we are constantly beguiled under the pretense of importance. If *The Ambassadors* is at least highly readable (when it is readable at all), how thin, forced and superficial it appears upon any real reflection or analysis. (In this respect it anticipates J. P. Marquand's later blend of "romance" and innocuous social satire; perhaps Henry James helped to fashion that attractive but inconsequential literary genre.) This novel is probably the most ingenious of all the Jamesian "games of art," and the novel which is most clearly just a game. That is possibly the reason why the contemporary Jacobites, who followed James's dictum and Matthiessen's solemn explication that this was quite the best, "all round," of the later novels, have found it so difficult to make any case for their claim.

It is a false claim, and there is no case. Almost all "pre-action" and "post-post-analysis," the human content of *The Ambassadors* is limited; the view of human behavior is dubious; the moral is particularly Jamesian and arbitrary; the literary method is exotic, orotund and verbose. All that remains is a sentimental romance, an entertaining fiction in parts, which has a certain charm at the expense of credibility.

10. The Unholy Quartet

In the Preface to the New York edition of *The Ambassadors*, his last say on the matter, James was, as we've noticed, at his most self-congratulatory and condescending peak. How he did go on about his elderly hero Strether, the "dear man in the Paris garden," or the "rueful worthy, from the very heart of New England."

He was explicit that his novel was a "drama of discrimination"; of the mind, purely, and the ethical sense. For, as he noted, it was well known "that people's moral sense *does* break down in Paris." There was in fine "the *trivial* association" of Paris and sex — "one of the vulgarest in the world; but which gave me pause no longer, I think, simply because its vulgarity is so advertised." Now was this "vulgarity" to be deleted because it was so obvious, or because it was so sexual? Nevertheless it was clear that Strether's "revolution" — and what a revolution it proved to be — was to have nothing to do "with any *bêtise* of the imputably 'tempted' state."

He admitted that the technique of what was really his last old-fashioned Victorian romance, recast in his later method, had also to be adapted to the requirements of the magazine serial. (Just as the virtue of the *Dove* was that it did *not* have to be adapted to the requirements of the magazine serial.) But these limitations of commerce were simply another challenge to the Jamesian virtuosity, which he here acknowledged and commended. "Fortunately thus I am able to estimate this as, frankly, quite the best, 'all round,' of my productions." This was the famous claim, while: "Any failure

of that justification would have made such an extreme of complacency publicly fatuous" — and such a thought was unthinkable to
the prefatory James. Dismissing any literal connection with the
"real Howells" who had made the remark about living life fully,
James went on, even more lyrically, about his own creative process:

He *remains but the happiest of accidents; his actualities, all too definite,
precluded any range of possibilities.* [Hardly flattering to Howells perhaps? M.G.] *It had only been his charming office to project upon that
wide field of the artist's vision — which hangs there ever in place like
the white sheet suspended for the figures of a child's magic-lantern —
a more fantastic and more moveable shadow. No privilege of the teller
of tales and the handler of puppets is more delightful, or has more of
the suspense and the thrill of a game of difficulty breathlessly played,
than just this business of looking for the unseen and the occult, in a
scheme half-grasped, by the light or, so to speak, by the clinging scent,
of the gage already in hand. No dreadful old pursuit of the hidden slave
with bloodhounds and the rag of association can ever, for "excitement,"
I judge, have bettered it at its best.*

Now what was interesting, in this purple passage on the Jamesian
method, was of course the heavy use of childlike and fairy-tale imagery quite directly. The magic lantern and the white sheet, the
shadows of artifice, the suspense and thrill of the "game," the hidden slave, the bloodhounds and the "bloody rag of association" all
led directly back to the romance literature of James's own childhood and youth — not to mention the "teller of tales" who is
equated with "the handler of puppets." Yes, the earlier James had
charged the Victorian fictionists (who had a primary concern, at
least, with the creation of character, or even "characters") with
"not being serious" about their art; with intruding their own personalities upon their tales in the role of moralist-entertainer. But
now this writer himself, claiming to have replaced the old-fashioned,
obsolete "omniscient author" with his own modern, subjective
"points of view": now Henry James himself indicated quite openly

his own auctorial role as childhood magician, as fictional gamester, as a literary puppeteer. Removing the technical device of the artist as commentator upon the work of art which at least presumed to describe life, James had substituted — and here admitted that he had substituted — a much more arbitrary and contrived form of "art" which no longer even pretended to represent reality: which even rejoiced at its disassociation from life.

Well, to be sure, there were still those glimmers and "germs" of his stories which James picked up mainly in the conversation of fashionable English society at dinner. He admitted that "art deals with what we see" — rather than what we may feel about life, or experience. "It plucks its material, otherwise expressed, in the garden of life — which material elsewhere grown is stale and uneatable. But it has no sooner done this than it has to take account of a *process*." And it was this process of composition, rather than the vegetables, so to speak, from the Jamesian "garden of life" — and how this later imagery betrayed his real values! — that he now frankly delighted in.

It was his famous "dramatic method," which he elucidated again in *The Ambassadors'* Preface, that now gave him such pleasure and profit, and: "I blush to confess it, but if one's a dramatist, one's a dramatist." Judging from the novel itself, one might add that James was the oddest kind of dramatist; but in his own mind, at least, he had recapped his old, sad debacle. He had redeemed his great defeat. In his fancy at least he had exploited the "lesson of the stage" for the benefit of his fiction. Was Freud really correct in judging this kind of compulsive and repetitious rehearsal of past traumas as a sign of the organism's need for punishment, for pain, even for death? In James's case at least — and it was a prime example of this Freudian behavior pattern — it was simply the ego's need to escape from the trap of defeat, to arrive at a *better* sequence of events than what originally happened; to redeem the ego's soul, as it were, and save its face — to restore its happy self-image. And this was what James had succeeded in doing by the period of his last novels. This was the true "germ," also, of his later literary method; and this was its real meaning.

How full this fatuous Preface was with James's delight with James. Maria Gostrey's perfect essence was not in being herself a character. She is only "an enrolled, a direct, aid to lucidity." "She is in fine, to tear off her mask," said James proudly, "the most unmitigated and abandoned of *ficelles*" — that is to say, a literary trick or dodge. She almost becomes, instead of a suffering and slighted woman, one of the triumphs of his "art," achieving something of the dignity, so James expatiated, "of a prime idea."

Which circumstance but shows us afresh how many quite incalculable but none the less clear sources of enjoyment for the infatuated artist, how many copious springs of our never-to-be-slighted "fun" for the reader and critic susceptible of contagion may sound their incidental plash as soon as an artistic process begins to enjoy free development. Exquisite — in illustration of this — the mere interest and amusement of such at once "creative" and critical questions as how and where and why to make Miss Gostrey's false connexion carry itself, under a due polish, as a real one.

And this kind of fictional duplicity, exquisite as it may be, highly polished as you like, enjoyable *in extremis* to the infatuated artist; did it now appear to pass, for James, as the true artistic process? "Since, however, all art is *expression*," he added, "and is thereby vividness, one was to find the door open here to any amount of delightful dissimulation. These verily are the refinements and ecstasies of method . . ." So that in effect he equated again his process of "delightful dissimulation" with the curious thrills of his literary method. He confessed to the positive charm in producing an "ambiguity of appearance" in his fiction which was not also, "by the same stroke and all helplessly," an ambiguity of sense. And more. As if now not merely delighted with such contrivances of art, but almost obsessed by them, James went on quite explicitly to expatiate on the deceptive, the irrelevant, the wholly fabricated relationship of Strether and Miss Gostrey in *The Ambassadors*. This relationship was *not* a relationship at all, it turns out, since its only purpose was to illuminate the plot of the novel; but it was a relationship which was designed to "look like" a relationship in order to fulfill its purpose of not being a relationship —

To project imaginatively, for my hero, a relation that has nothing to do with the matter (the matter of my subject) but has everything to do with the manner (the manner of my presentation of the same), and yet to treat it, at close quarters and for fully economic expression's sake, as if it were important and essential — to do that sort of thing and yet muddle nothing may easily become, as one goes, a signally attaching proposition; even though it all remains but part and parcel, I hasten to recognize, of the merely general and related question of expressional curiosity and expressional decency.

Now this was surely the clearest Jamesian revelation of the true nature of the "plotted novel," in *The Ambassadors*, or of that "architectural roundness," perhaps, which so delighted him and the later generations of Jacobite critics. And wasn't this curious new concept of the purpose of literary expression very close, in turn, to the modern concept of abstract art? — where the creative delight lay solely in the forms and patterns of the literary work, the neat convolutions of literary design, which were developed not only at the expense of any sense of reality or human content — which were indeed developed to conceal, deform or destroy the human content for the sake of the deceptive literary form — the literary game. Only, what was so expressionally "economic," and so signally "attaching" to James, in developing this entire Strether-Gostrey relationship, in such detail, one might add, and at such length in the novel, simply to make it appear "important and essential," falsely, while it had absolutely nothing to do with the central matter of the novel's subject? This was an economy of abundance; if not an economy of pure waste — a kind of conspicuous consumption, again, in Veblenian terms, of literary trickery over and beyond the deliberate human loss. As to the related question, in the Jamesian mind, of "expressional curiosity," we have already noted the dominance of this single human trait in the Jamesian fiction at the expense of all the other primary human emotions; and a "curiosity" in the typical Jamesian characters which was now being exploited for the sake of his own singular literary designs. And finally, *what*, in this whole complex constellation of the contrived — in what we might call the methodically misleading novel — could really be described as "expressional decency"? Echo answers silence.

Well, there is the point in the novel's structure where Mamie Pocock — another example in the line of those impossible, omniscient Jamesian children, very much akin to Maisie or the Nanda Brookenham of *The Awkward Age* — where Mamie gave her

appointed and, I can't but think, duly felt lift to the whole action by the so inscrutably-applied side-stroke or short-cut of our just watching, and at quite an angle of vision as yet untried, her single hour of suspense in the hotel salon.

Do you follow? This was also for the late James a marked example "of the representational virtue that insists here and there on being, for the charm of opposition and renewal, other than the scenic." From the structural opposition of the "Picture" to the "Occasion," moreover, "it wouldn't take much to make me further argue that from an equal play of such oppositions the book gathers an intensity that fairly adds to the dramatic," James added happily. And: "I consciously fail to shrink in fact from that extravagance" — of making such grand claims for *The Ambassadors*, that is, on the basis of his *own* (James's) talent. "I risk it, rather, for the sake of the moral involved." Which was not, perhaps, that his own novel exhausted all the interesting esthetic questions it had raised, or that he had raised about it; or that the bewildered reader of this Preface was likely to be exhausted by such a dazzling and virtuoso series of esthetic speculations, theories and "principles." But only

that the Novel itself, to James, still remained "under the right per-
suasion, the most independent, most elastic, most prodigious of
literary forms."

Prodigious indeed; if not entirely, as we note, either independent
or elastic in any sense *other* than the Jamesian one here. And of
such was the Jamesian Kingdom of Art in its highest phases. While
to this new principality, too, each of the later Prefaces contributed
its own mite of illumination, of respect, or of reverence and worship. And yet perhaps, somewhere in the Jamesian unconscious —
which had become, at this point in his career, possibly the most remarkable unconscious in the national letters — the more uneasy his
critical sense was about the Jamesian work it was surveying, the
more hyperbolic, perfervid and prodigious was the "critical" estimate.

However, *The Golden Bowl*, in 1904, was the most interesting,
complex and puzzling of the later James novels.* By contrast,
The Ambassadors is revealed even more clearly for what it is: as
perhaps the *silliest* novel ever to be taken seriously in world literature. In the *Notebooks*, James's first entry for what became *The
Golden Bowl*, as far back as 1892, concerned the growing "divorce,"
which Edwin Godkin had described to him, "between the American woman (with her comparative leisure, culture, grace, social
instincts, artistic ambitions) and the male American immersed
in the ferocity of business, with no time for any but the most sordid interests, purely commercial, professional, democratic and
political." A notable line from the Master's hand on the true meaning of democracy as political and sordid; and James went on to describe this cultural divorce of the American woman as having become a gulf, "an abyss of inequality."

What he was really talking about, of course, or what Godkin was,

---

* *William Wetmore Story and His Friends*, a year earlier, was a Jamesian "biography" — anecdotal, nostalgic, verbose and diffuse in form — of the New England
lawyer who settled in Rome around the middle of the last century to become the
famous sculptor of his time. Story's statuary also figured in Hawthorne's *The
Marble Faun*, though it now appears quite conventional.

was the ascendant epoch of finance-capitalism; the barons and titans of big business; the new epoch of corporations, trusts and monopolies at the turn of the century. But James naturally equated this with "democracy" and with democratic politics. In the *Notebooks,* he joined this entry with a situation also told to him "about a simultaneous marriage in Paris . . . of a father and daughter — an only daughter. The daughter — American of course — is engaged to a young Englishman, and the father, a widower and still youngish, has sought in marriage at exactly the same time an American girl of very much the same age as his daughter." Say he has done it "to console himself in his abandonment," James added, "to make up for the loss of the daughter to whom he has been devoted —

I see a little tale, n'est-ce pas? — in the idea that they all shall have married, as arranged, with this characteristic consequence — that the daughter fails to hold the affection of the young English husband, whose approximate mother-in-law the pretty young second wife of the father will now have become. The father doesn't lose the daughter nearly as much as he feared, or expected, for her marriage which has but half gratified her, leaves her des loisirs, and she devotes them to him. They spend large parts of their time together, they cling together, and weep and wonder together, and are even more thrown together.

The reason for all this, James continued in his scenario for *The Golden Bowl* (after he had debated having his usual observer in the novel, or not having one "in the interest of brevity") was that the father-in-law's second wife had become much more attractive to the young husband than his own wife. *"Mettons,"* he cried to himself in these notes —

Mettons that this second wife is nearly as young as her daughter-in-law — and prettier and cleverer — she knows more what she is about. Mettons even that the younger husband has known her before, has liked her, etc. — been attracted to her, and would have married her if she had

*had any money. She was poor — the father was very rich, and that was
her inducement to marry the father. The latter has settled a handsome
dot on his daughter (leaving himself also plenty to live on), and the
young husband is therefore thoroughly at his ease.*

Well, there is the familiar Jamesian concept of cash: the money received so nicely by the two girls; and given by the father who still,
naturally, is comfortably off, while the young husband's main purpose in life apparently has been accomplished . . . This was the
perennial base and milieu of the leisure-class novel, which James
again sketched out almost mechanically, or immutably; adding
only the later twist that the young husband, at his ease, and the
father-in-law's pretty young wife become "very intimate."

"The whole situation works in a kind of inevitable rotary way
— in what would be called a vicious circle [he noted]. The subject is really the pathetic simplicity and good faith of the father
and daughter in their abandonment":

*They feel abandoned, yet they feel consoled, with each other, and they
don't see in the business in the least what every one else sees in it . . .
A necessary basis for all this must have been an intense and exceptional
degree of attachment between the father and daughter — he peculiarly
paternal, she passionately filial . . .*

And with this blunt statement of the underlying nature of the father-daughter relation in *The Golden Bowl*, what happens to the
whole array of modern critical studies which have stressed the incestuous nature of the novel — which have apostrophized James
as the precursor of the Freudian depths, as the first of the "modern"
psychological artists? Alas, in his customary vein, he made sure to
strain away the specifically sexual content of any possible sexual
implication, though there are curious undertones still to his "peculiarly paternal" father, and his "passionately filial" daughter.
Were the *Notebooks* themselves another of the Jamesian blinds,
another literary *ficelle*, indeed, which he used for the purpose of

not telling himself the truth about his own work? But the "intense and exceptional degree of attachment" between Maggie and Adam Verver, the "pathetic simplicity and good faith" between father and daughter which James stressed so definitely in his notes, has further connotations in the novel itself.

It is of interest too that Matthiessen, while stressing James's own conviction that no "abnormality" was intended in the father-daughter relationship in *The Golden Bowl*, had less sympathy for this novel than for the other works of "the major phase." Perhaps something underlying the involved if not incestuous human quadrangle in the story interfered with the critic's judgment. Here indeed he noted "how thoroughly James' imagination was imbued with the devices of the fairy story" — which elsewhere in the charmed circle of Jamesian devotees is hailed as "the myth-making faculty." The chapter on *The Golden Bowl* in *The Major Phase* stressed "the mingled images of beauty and wealth" in this novel, as though they were not always mingled, or inextricable, in the Jamesian vision of life. "When there is so much gold that it pervades even the vocabulary of love," noted Matthiessen, "is that a sign of life or of death?" — a good query, though this critic might have noted the same mixture, the same ultimate reliance on gold, rather than love, in *The Wings of the Dove* and *The Ambassadors*. Matthiessen also commented that though James "could understand Lesbianism without having to give it a name, just as he could understand the corruption of the children in *The Turn of the Screw*, he was elsewhere oblivious to sexual distortions which would seem an almost inevitable concomitant of the situations he posits." And this critic concluded, almost harshly, that: "What it comes down to, again and again, is that James' characters tend to live, as has often been objected, merely off the tops of their minds . . . This is what caused a representative modern psychologist like Gide to conclude that James 'in himself is not interesting; he is only intelligent.' And what bothers Gide most in James' characters is the excessive functioning of their analytical powers, whereas 'all the weight of the flesh is absent, and all the shaggy, tangled under-growth, all the wild darkness . . .' "

This was an interesting statement from the French novelist, himself a master of intellectual analysis; but one who had forced himself, as James could not, to acknowledge and even to defend the emotional and sexual variations of human behavior. What Matthiessen did *not* note, however, was that the picture of lesbian-ism in *The Bostonians* was still within the Jamesian framework of an adolescent, purely emotional, and peculiarly feminine "crush" — the "ultimate level," as it were, of James's identification with, or recognition of, sexuality. And the "corruption" of the children in "The Turn of the Screw" — and their harsh punishment unto sick-ness and death — was simply *because*, in some mysterious way, they had had contact with some form of servile sex. Matthiessen ended this essay, moreover, with the familiar disclaimer of the Ja-cobite critics, acknowledging some possible lapse in the Master only to enhance his esthetic triumphs. "Instead of belaboring fur-ther his social and psychological limitations, it is more revelatory to examine the positive values which he found in such a world."

Well, now, those "positive values" in *The Golden Bowl* were ap-plauded and eulogized indeed by the second generation of Jacobites who followed hard on Matthiessen's heels. There is first of all Stephen Spender's "notable study of the novel," in F. W. Dupee's phrase; and these two critics echo each other in what is almost a Jamesian chorale. In James's other books, so Dupee quotes Spender:

He has convinced us that a part of life . . . is the power to choose to die. The question James has not yet answered is whether it is possible in the modern world to live: and Maggie triumphantly answers it for him.

Well, "Maggie's triumph" is very dubious indeed, as we'll see: it is on the order of a popular thriller. And which of Henry James's

characters has really "chosen to die," outside of the fact that they
have all refused to live — and *what* "modern world" is Mr.
Spender talking about?

The Ververs, so Dupee adds, "hold in a kind of vassalage a
place beyond the Mississippi called American City, they have a
million a year, and Mr. Verver is said to be one of the world's
best-known collectors of art." Now this was the typical Jamesian
fantasy about the new American fortunes which he knew so little
about, and simply fashioned to conform to his own fairy-tale notions of "modern" American life. But set against "this great historical and geographical tradition," Spender reports in *his* turn:

> *there is the strangely insulated, shut-off life of the actors . . . The
> struggle of the Ververs is a struggle to make the picture fit the frame;
> they are constantly struggling to make their lives worthy of their dead
> surroundings.*

And this was a remarkable example of a modern "pseudo-liberal"
interpretation of what Henry James surely never meant. There is
no "great historical and geographical tradition" in the Jamesian
concept of western American wealth; while wealth, luxury, and art
collecting were never "dead surroundings" to this earlier and
baronial novelist. Quite to the contrary, these were the things in
life best worth living for. It was only a question, in the Jamesian
mind, of "educating" the new provincial millionaires, with their
familiar blank western culture, as James had described them over
and over again in his international fiction — of educating them
"up" to the approved standards of *inherited* wealth.

What one must conclude is that just as James knew nothing of
the robber baron class which he was trying to exemplify in the
Adam Verver of *The Golden Bowl*, so in turn Spender knew nothing about James's real values. He saw this novel through the focus of his own modern sensibility; and he attributed to James, as
the whole circle of Jacobites has consistently done, almost the di-

rect opposite of what the novelist meant. Dupee, to be sure, quali-
fies the Spender thesis somewhat. "Not all the American barons
of their time were robber barons, and this father and daughter embody the good faith of the best of them." But, while admitting
that the Ververs exemplify James's "ideal program for the class,"
this critic goes on, almost in spite of himself, to embroider the
Spender thesis even more:

*As Americans, above all Americans of the West, they have no society
proportionate to their wealth. They huddle together, even at first shrinking from attendance at London parties. On their respective sposi, the
worldly sociable Prince and Charlotte, they impose a curious quadrille-
like pattern of existence which consists in their regularly exchanging
partners and now and then coming together, the four of them, over
cards or dinner, with two trusted friends, Colonel and Mrs. Assingham,
usually present as spectators. Their being partners in solitude is for the
Ververs their distinction, their pathos, and their original sin. In the
scale of their money and the adventurous life it would seem to open
to them, they are shown as perennially shrunken and isolated. "The
word 'small' is constantly associated with Maggie," notes Mr. Spender,
"and it is she who in one of her moments of greatest exaltation realizes
that her father was 'simply a great and deep and high little man,' and
that to love him with tenderness was not to be distinguished, a whit,
from loving him with pride."*

And now this Spender-Dupee thesis on *The Golden Bowl* has
reached an Orwellian point of double-talk which can only be compared with Lionel Trilling's view of *The Princess Casamassima* as
a counterrevolutionary novel of the same type and class as Dostoev-
ski's *The Possessed*. Perhaps the kindest thing to say is that this is
pure nonsense; since Mr. Dupee must know: (a) that this isolated
life of wealth and sensibility corresponds completely to the later
Jamesian ideal of the good life; (b) that this view of provincial
American western society had marked James's work from the start;
(c) that the word "small" James now applied indiscriminately to

almost everything around him, including his own work; and (d)
that this form of the diminutive was also a revealing adjective as to
the childlike view of reality which was at the base of the whole
body of Jamesian fiction.

Thus the "great and deep and high *little* man" (italics added)
who is the millionaire father in *The Golden Bowl* illustrated
James's patronizing view of the new western wealth; and his fairy-
tale imagery of both fatherhood and titanhood. This was also and
obviously a form of childlike revenge upon both superior wealth
and superior paternal power, by reducing them both to the level of
childhood itself. This rich, powerful father-symbol is moreover described by James as sexually impotent or sterile. ("For James
spares us nothing," as Dupee adds; and indeed James didn't, when
it accorded with the fantasy sphere we are describing here.) As to
Adam Verver's "somewhat morbid intimacy with his daughter,"
Dupee also states, almost as categorically as the later James himself, "Yet James cannot be said to have been of the devil's party
without knowing it." But couldn't he? That is indeed the dis-
tinguishing trait of his work as Victorian fictionalist which we have
noticed most consistently; that is almost his true fascination: that
he continually belonged to the "devil's party" without *ever* knowing
it — while one must also ask both of this Jacobite critic and of
James himself, what really is the devil's party in any study of human character? And finally, as to Maggie's broken marriage with
the Prince, whose moral, according to Dupee again, is that

*Maggie, then, has only to assert herself, to make clear how much she
loves him, to re-establish the original order, for him to find her attractive once more . . .*

— as to this blithe verdict on the Prince's love affair and Maggie's
inadequate marriage, one can only conclude that Dupee, like Matthiessen, has swallowed the Jamesian potion (not to say magic or
trickery) whole.

For the "original order" of any broken marriage can never be re-established; just like the original order of any broken love affair, and just like the original order of life itself. It was after all James's Kate Croy who pointed out at the end of *The Wings of the Dove:* "We shall never be as we were before." Dupee is on safer ground when he quotes Glenway Wescott to the effect that the psychic content of the novel "is too great for its container of elegantly forged happenings; it all overflows and slops about and is magnificently wasted." Well, that "magnificently" — but then, putting aside all the standard Jamesian critiques of the novel, each expatiating upon the other, what is the real social meaning and the true psychic content of *The Golden Bowl,* which is nevertheless, and for very different reasons, still the most curious and interesting of the later Jamesian novels?

Certainly the element — the theme — of money, which was at the base of *The Wings of the Dove* and *The Ambassadors,* has become all dominant here. From the opening lines it is the absolute medium, so to speak, of *The Golden Bowl.* Directly before the marriage ceremony with Maggie, the first reflections of the Prince are that "the London lawyers had reached an inspired harmony with his own man of business, poor Calderoni, fresh from Rome" (page 5, New York Collected Edition). And that "inspired harmony" is of course the Prince's marriage settlement for having contracted his royal blood to the provincial American heiress. From this point the Prince's "career" is accomplished; he has completed his noble task. But Amerigo, whose name denotes either that he has discovered America, or that he is to be (as compared with the commercial and naïve Christopher Newman of James's early novel) the idealized international American: certainly Prince Amerigo is very flattering about his newly acquired father-in-law. "You know, I think he's a *real* galantuomo — 'and no mistake.' There are plenty of sham ones about. He seems to me simply the best man I've ever seen in my life."

It is not wealth alone that counts with this later Jamesian spokesman. There are true and there are sham millionaires. To which, when Maggie Verver retorts that *he*, the Prince, is also the real thing, Amerigo adds: "Say, however, I *am* a galantuomo — which I devoutly hope: I'm like a chicken, at best, chopped up and smothered in sauce; cooked down as a *crème de volaille*, with half the parts left out. Your father's the natural fowl running about the *bassecour*. His feathers, his movements, his sounds — those are the parts that, with me, are left out." *Good* money and good food set the opening tone of *The Golden Bowl*, and even James's imagery has moved from "the garden of life" to its fine sauces. But the Prince's own reverie centers around the veritable bath of gold, the sweet waters in which he now floated, as if "poured from a gold-topped phial, for making one's bath aromatic. No one before him, never — not even the infamous Pope — had so sat up to his neck in such a bath." This shows him "for that matter how little one of his race could escape after all from history," and it is precisely his race, his history, that Maggie delights in acquiring. The Prince is simply the best piece in the collection which Adam Verver is acquiring for the edification of his birthplace, American City. "You're at any rate a part of his collection," Maggie "explains" to the Prince in the first glow of their honeymoon — "one of the things that can only be got over here. You're a rarity, an object of beauty, an object of price. You're not perhaps absolutely unique, but you're so curious and eminent that there are very few others like you — you belong to a class about which everything is known. You're what they call a *morceau* de musée."

And she plies him with similar endearments of her love. Now was this curious opening really meant to indicate a satiric study of the new American western fortunes, as Dupee-Spender assume? Can it be compared with the ironic Dreiserian self-identification of the artist with the American financiers and titans of industry, as in the Cowperwood trilogy? And all this emphasis on "collecting" and objets d'art and rare museum pieces: was it the odor of death, as Matthiessen felt? No; for there is no doubt that in the whole context of the Jamesian fiction, and of the leisure-class novel, money meant life to this artist, not death; only provided that it was rightfully and lawfully acquired — and that is to say, that it was inherited, or freely given. *The Golden Bowl* is simply the apex of the Jamesian international theme which had always confronted American wealth with European culture. It is a sort of dream-world fantasy of *greater* wealth and greater "art." It is a kind of reversionary romance, towards the climax of James's own career, which is still centered around his familiar, fixed notion of immense riches and noble culture.

But the exotic tone of the novel's opening was false in another sense. If it represented the farthest extension of James's own values and beliefs, the note of hyperbole — as in the descriptions of Strether's European agitation in *The Ambassadors* — was also the Jamesian attempt to establish an artificial innocence, so to speak — a mask of the Jamesian illusion which was to be stripped away. In the early scene between the Prince and Fanny Assingham (who is another *ficelle*, like poor Maria Gostrey, designed to illuminate the future course of the novel rather than to be herself) we first learn of Charlotte Stant's previous love affair with Amerigo — and that she is coming to his wedding. (In a more realistic chronicle either Fanny or the Prince might have warned Maggie of her impending danger; then there might not have been any *Golden Bowl*. Meanwhile there is the scene where Charlotte buys the flawed bowl (symbol) as a wedding present for Maggie and the Prince. And here James even turned upon — for the sake of the higher trickery — his own familiar theme of "renunciation." "To have one hour alone with you" is Charlotte's ostensible reason for seeing the Prince at all, and: "What she gave touched him, as she faced him, for it was the full tune of her renouncing. She really renounced — renounced everything, and without even insisting now on what it had all been for her." And Charlotte declares again: "This is what I wanted. This is what I've got. This is what I shall always have . . ."

Very eloquent; and completely untrue, of course, since whether
Charlotte Stant knows it or not, James knows she has come to stay
with the Prince. What marvels of irony indeed, what pitches of
virtuoso eloquence, does this Jamesian anti- or non-narrative — the
narrative of traps, red herrings and false appearances — now contain. And again, as with Kate Croy and Densher, the fictional pattern is that of the scheming, devouring woman; the reluctant,
gradually compromised and weakish male. Charlotte buys the glittering bowl for fifteen pounds, and tells the Prince she has paid
but five. The Prince leaves the little antiquarian shop during the
actual purchase of the bowl, since he knows intuitively (racially?)
it has a flaw, which is also a portent.* "The danger — I see — is
because you're superstitious," says Charlotte. "Per Dio I'm superstitious! A crack's a crack — and an omen's an omen." "You'd be
afraid — ?" Charlotte asks, persistently. "Per Bacco!" cries the
Prince. "For your happiness?" "For my happiness." "For your
safety?" "For my safety." Charlotte "just paused," wrote James,
and then comes the key question. "For your marriage?" "For my
marriage. For everything."

This was the theatrical dialogue closing the first book or first
scene in the dramatic structure of *The Golden Bowl*; and one sees
pretty clearly where the novel is going, despite the protestations of
the Prince, Charlotte, Mrs. Assingham that nothing like that *will*
happen; and despite all the glittering falsehood that James himself
drags across the appointed trail of the narrative. Yet in these pages
Charlotte Stant, like the early Kate Croy, is one of James's most
attractive women in her desire, her audacity and her charm. (Although she too is destined by the Jamesian "morality" and melodrama alike to become a victimized puppet of the story line.) By

---

* The little "antiquario" is a Jew, of course, whom the Prince gazes at without
seeing, as a mark of noble bearing, and talks to without looking at — though it
develops that Amerigo is no mean bargainer himself. "You were splendid for beating down," says Charlotte admiringly about their earlier Roman days together. Thus
in the Jamesian domain of antique-collecting, it appears that the Jews *have* all the
valuable pieces, for which the noble Christians must "Jew them down."

comparison, however, the description of the great American financier himself, Adam Verver, at "Fawns," is a most peculiar piece of
romantic fantasy. Adam is of course the supreme "collector" of valuable art, one of "the great collectors of the world . . . Great people, all over Europe, sought introductions to him; high personages,
incredibly high, and more of them than would ever be known, solemnly sworn as every one was, in such cases, to discretion, high
personages made up to him as the one man on the short authentic
list likely to give the price."

Well, James's penchant for fairy-tale romance, along with his
portentous sense of those high and mysterious ruling-class personages all over Europe (the same combination of lurid emotions
which provided the background and milieu for the "Anarchist-
Revolutionary" movement in *The Princess Casamassima*), still
concluded on the hard note of the "authentic list," the clang of
the cash register.

And this hyperbolic verbal extravagance could be possibly applied, one might think, to such personages as statesmen, perhaps,
or scientists, artists, intellectuals. But in the diminishing boundaries of the leisure-class world, it is the dilettantish Italian prince,
and the retired financier turned art collector who are most worthy
of these purple passages of praise. Adam Verver — the primeval
American man; or the ancestor, with all his "verve" for doing things
in the world, of the new race of international types to come — is
an improbable portrait. James was never less at home in the
"downtown world" of American high finance than in this full-
length (verbose, empty and tedious) description of this Last Ty-
coon among his aristocratic and costly treasures of European art.
This was also setting the scene for the future action of the novel,
and could any acquisitive American financier, for that matter,
have been more abstract in his view of human beings and human
relations than the later James himself in these deceptive, tricky calculated romance melodramas? Henry James was all for acquisition
with appreciation. He represented here most clearly, if all uncon-

sciously and all complacently, the peak of the Veblenian ostenta-
tiousness in the culture of the robber baron period; and his Adam
Verver was meant to signify the highest point that great wealth
might reach as a patron of the arts.

But Adam's reverie was another piece of simulation and "effect,"
and here, no doubt, as in *The Ambassadors*, James exaggerated
his tone in order to dissemble his meaning. Then there is the picture of the perfectly self-enclosed private world of sensibility in
the later James fiction; the "daylight equivalent," as it were, of the
nightmarish evening scenes in *The Sacred Fount*. But the "attendance at tea" of four or five "selected persons" in "just the right
place" on the west terrace (which almost comprises the early "action" of *The Golden Bowl*) was also the ultimate and inevitable
destination of the leisure-class novel as a whole, which had increasingly withdrawn itself from a "modern world" described only
as "vulgar," "material," "gross," and "democratic" in both England and America alike. The snobbish little circle of "superior
sensibility," which had become the standard cast of characters in
the later James's fictional dramas, and which, increasingly isolated,
trivial and selfish, viewed with disdain all the common habits
and pursuits of humanity at large, was no longer even a form of
Jamesian social commentary. Rather, it was a mode of personal
refuge — a temperamental sanctuary more than a cultural symbol.

But wasn't this inevitable almost from the start of Henry James's
career? And was *this* the "evil of the modern world" which Mr.
Spender decried in his notable essay on *The Golden Bowl?* Moreover, Charlotte Stant's early role in the novel is precisely to bring
the Ververs into contact with a better and more aristocratic society
than that which they had known: to "educate them up," in the
familiar, fixed Jamesian notion of wealth and culture, to their
rightful social position. As the Ververs' secretary-housekeeper she
runs their dream house, their dollhouse, perfectly, at the novel's
start at least. But surely Adam's subsequent "courtship" of Char-

lotte must be counted among the most esoteric of the later Jamesian fictional sequences. It is at Brighton, "during the three wonderful days he spent there with Charlotte," that Adam finally understands "the merits of his majestic scheme." This scheme is simply to marry her for his own convenience, that is, and in order to remain close to Maggie without being a burden upon her. And all this takes place while these two "lovers" are in mutual pursuit of some Damascene tiles owned by a certain Mr. Gutermann-Seuss.

Against this background of Jewish antiquarianism, again, or of Oriental fertility, duplicity and guile; surrounded by the "collective caress" of all those dark, shining ancient eyes and by the rich food — which add to the Damascene quest "the touch of some mystic rite of old Jewry" — Adam makes his careful, complex and highly verbal marriage proposal to Charlotte; and she, with the Prince's wire of consent in her hand, assents.

This ancient, mysterious tribal scene at the Gutermann-Seusses' (with its barely veiled connotations of moral corruption) was another extended form of imagery, of the portents of danger, to balance off the recurrent symbolism of the broken bowl itself. And in the elaborate, discursive, "analytic" discussion of Adam Verver's engagement, each of the two partners of the impending marriage probes the motives of the other while carefully concealing his, or her, own. This is the marriage of convenience, in the heightened Jamesian European style — and not merely of convenience, but of calculation and of a kind of mutually agreed-upon deception — and not merely a deception of each other, but of self-deception too. This was another climax in the Jamesian view of "passion" — and not only is physical contact of the slightest, but there is hardly the faintest word of affection, not to mention love. "I do like you, you know," says Charlotte to Adam, almost as an afterthought. "What my child does for me — !" says Adam. "It isn't Maggie. It's the Prince," Charlotte returns. "I say!" Adam "gaily rang out." "Then it's best of all." "It's enough," says Charlotte.

But is it really? Throughout this dialogue of deceit and exploita-

tion — both of human beings and of emotions — we notice once
again the ambiguous nature of the Jamesian human relationships.
The father binds himself more closely to the daughter by marrying what is in effect a daughter-image. Charlotte, the best friend
of Maggie, marries her friend's father — also a father-image for
herself — in order to become not only the Prince's mother-in-law
(stepmother? mother?) but his mistress. We have already described the pattern of these shifting, ambiguous parental relations
in James's work, usually centered around the orphan child or orphan prince, as in "The Pupil," with his set of unworthy or false
parents; or as in *What Maisie Knew*, with an actual, "real" set of
shifting and "loose" parents — those anonymous, fluid, disappearing, nightmarish relations which appear again as the central focus
of *The Sacred Fount*. In addition, in *The Golden Bowl*, Verver
has two "false wives," both Maggie and Charlotte; and Charlotte
herself is a false daughter as well as a false wife, and a false sister-
image to Maggie.

Of such was the Jamesian kingdom of human relations.* Then
there is the great ceremonial London party in which both the
Prince and Charlotte celebrate the triumph of their scheme, and
where Fanny Assingham gets her first strong conviction about the
Prince's and Charlotte's love affair. "You live with such *good* people," she says pleadingly to Charlotte, and —

"Ah *don't talk to me of other women!*" *Fanny now overtly panted.*
"*Do you call Mr. Verver's perfectly natural interest in his daughter* —?"
"*The greatest affection of which he's capable?*" — *Charlotte took it up
in all readiness.* "*I do distinctly — and in spite of my having done all
I could think of to make him capable of a greater. I've done, earnestly,*

---

* There never was a writer so immersed in personal relations, according to Philip
Rahv; but again this Jacobite critic neglected to mention what *kind* of personal relations James had immersed himself in. Haven't we seen that the case is exactly the
opposite: that throughout James's work both his characters and personal relations are
always manipulated for the sake of his abstract plots? James had *no* sense of real
human relations either in his life or his art.

everything I could — I've made it, month after month, my study. But I haven't succeeded — that has been vividly brought home to me to-night."

During this Jamesian interchange, we may recall Kate Croy's similar "lesson" to Milly Theale on the way "things really were" — an argument designed to bring Milly out of her Aunt Maude's orbit of power into Kate's. So here, at the termination of Charlotte's ingenious, even brilliant "confession" of her failure to seduce Adam Ver-ver's affections from his daughter (a confession designed to allow Charlotte her complete freedom with the Prince), Mrs. Assingham recoils in despair. "I can't conceive, my dear, what you're talking about!" And neither, at points, can we.

But just to make the point clear, James repeats the same argument, in almost the same scene with Fanny Assingham; but this time from the Prince's "point of view." And then the Assinghams together go over the same material from *their* point of view. This is in the best vein of the concentric, the refracted, the dispersed, the splintered narrative: the extraordinary bedtime conversation of the Assinghams in which we suddenly have a new set of "double analysts," and a conversation in which alternatively both Fanny and her Colonel take the lead in "speculation" during some forty-odd pages of dialogue. (There were some advantages in the old-fashioned method of direct auctorial exposition which James had eliminated from the modern novel.) Now this astounding bedtime talk goes on while the Assinghams slowly wend their way from the front door of their deserted, dark house, to their separate bedrooms in a period of perhaps an hour — or at least an hour's worth of reading.

But Fanny's ringing "Good-night!" to the Colonel is altogether premature in what might also be called the concircular Jamesian narrative. For their talk, summarizing the first volume of *The Golden Bowl*, is also a "pre-plot" of the real meaning of the second volume. The "real meaning": well, that is always the most difficult thing to get at in Henry James. The occult elaboration of his "points of view" (which were not really points of view, but angles of vision, so to speak, in the plot line of his novels) suited his own fundamental ambiguity, even while it was an admirable technique for both displaying and concealing the "action" of these psychic melodramas. For, as I say, this is the strip-tease plot. The question always is: how much are the Jamesian characters *allowed* to know; how much are they deliberately falsifying for their own sake — or for James's sake, or his plot's sake; and to what extent indeed was James himself fully aware of the real meaning of the material he was using? In the later Jamesian world of illusion upon illusion, of illusion for the sake of illusion, it is always difficult to grasp the sense of a fundamental reality which the author does believe in. Surmounting the general web of deceit which is the common and prevailing medium of life itself, James now placed his own special, artificial, even more intricate and elaborate web of literary deceit. The imprint of artistic belief and of a fundamental human integrity which is at the core of great literature is altogether missing in the exotic Jamesian "game of art."

Meanwhile, just before the second half of the *Bowl,* we get our first direct view of the love affair itself. (If it *is* a love affair, since the drive of passion, on the part of Charlotte mainly, is almost wholly obscured by the maze of manipulation and maneuvering.) There is a throwback in which we learn just what the Prince has wired to Charlotte about her marriage to Adam Verver; which is also the Prince's permission for Charlotte to be *his* mistress. There is another throwback to one of the (smaller) empty salons in Portland Place, where the Prince, deserted again by his wife Maggie for her father's company, is walking about moodily when Charlotte drops in upon him. "*A la guerre then . . . à la guerre,*" the Prince has written to Charlotte, in what is apparently a Jamesian invitation to love, and she returns: "What else, my dear, what in the world else can we do?" After their preliminary talk in the luxurious chamber, the Prince offers her "a good stiff cup of tea," and they discuss the angelic but inexplicable behavior of their *sposi,* and how they are pledged to respect, cherish, guard from all harm the virtuous Ververs. "It represents for us a conscious care —" says the Prince. "Of every hour, literally," says Charlotte, "And for which we must trust each other —!" "Oh as we trust the saints in glory," confirms the Prince:

With which, as for the full assurance and the pledge it involved, each hand instinctively found the other. "It's all too wonderful." Firmly and gravely she kept his hand. "It's too beautiful." And so for a minute they stood together as strongly held and as closely confronted as any hour of their easier past ever had seen them. They were silent at first, only facing and faced, only grasping and grasped, only meeting and met. "It's sacred," he said at last. "It's sacred," she breathed back to him. They vowed it, gave it out and took it in, drawn by their intensity, more closely together. Then of a sudden, through this tightened circle, as at the issue of a narrow strait into the sea beyond, everything broke up, broke down, gave way, melted and mingled. Their lips sought their lips, their pressure their response and their response their pressure; with a violence that had sighed itself the next moment to the longest and deepest of stillness they passionately sealed their pledge.

Now this passage too is cited by the Jamesian specialists as another example of love and passion in the Master's work. And it is in its own way not only effective but even elegant. But please note that this solemn pledge and seal of sexual love is another ironic scene of hypocrisy and duplicity, in which the two "lovers" are trying, probably without success, to dupe each other by the pretense of moral righteousness even while it is obvious that, through their physical yearning, they are betraying their lawful spouses. What indeed was so "sacred" in this first post-marital embrace on the part of Charlotte and the Prince; what was too "wonderful," too "beautiful" — except the embedded Jamesian notion that sexuality was always linked with crime and sin?

Then there is the great party at Eaton Square which marks the "coming out," so to speak, of Adam Verver himself; in which "Maggie's anxiety had conferred with Charlotte's ingenuity, and both had supremely reveled, as it were, in Mr. Verver's solvency." That element is certainly clear and solid in the narrative, while Maggie quite bristles "with filial reference" and "with little filial recalls of expression, movement, tone," simply to make the occasion a success for her father, who appears to be more and more her child as well. "He was meagre and modest and clear-browed, and his eyes, if they wandered without fear, yet stayed without defiance; his shoulders were not broad; his chest was not high, his complexion was not fresh and the crown of his head was not covered; in spite of all of which he looked, at the top of his table, so nearly like a little boy shyly entertaining in virtue of some imposed rank, that he *could* only be one of the powers, the representative of a force — quite as an infant king is the representative of a dynasty."

But what kind of "infant king" was the American titan really supposed to be? Was this curious description of him at the very moment of his social triumph in England merely to ensure once more the domestic innocence of his relation with Maggie? Was it an extension of the Jamesian "affection" and patronizing concern for these naïve western millionaires who needed so desperately his own European culture and training? But one notes — though James hardly intended such a reference — that this pure and childlike father-image is also being betrayed by his adopted son, the Prince himself, about to take the liberty of sleeping with Adam's wife; the wife whom Adam himself, for whatever reasons of his own, has so obviously neglected. Was there indeed a deeper level of biopsychic yearning or *revenge* in this Jamesian fantasy of the infant-father: the good, pure, childlike and rich "infant king," whose wife was obviously immaculate so far as the father-image was concerned, but whose *son* indeed had replaced the father in the "mother's" affections, and even in her embraces? This late vision of James's Adam Verver was euphoric, certainly, and at base another variation of infantile fantasy. And then James returned from this poetic excursion to the cash nexus. At this high festive social table, Adam regards the Prince with much the same quality "as any glance directed, for due attention, from the same quarter, to the figure of a cheque received in the course of business and about to be enclosed to a banker. It made sure of the amount — and just so, from time to time, the amount of the Prince was certified."

But hardly a flattering gaze for such a real galantuomo as the Prince is. Amerigo's smoldering resentment — his own increasing state of being the orphan prince — reaches a climax at Matcham during the Easter days.* He is insulted at the thought of going about "with such a person as Mrs. Verver in a state of childlike innocence." In his wounded heart the Prince now considers the whole range of British nobility to be somewhat like the Ververs themselves: as "good children" and "the children of good children." He becomes altogether impatient with "the fathomless depths of English equivocation." He feels snubbed and rejected by this "ambiguous race," with the result that "he was in the last analysis, among all these so often inferior people, practically held cheap and made light of." But who was really puzzled, wounded, angry, resentful here: this princely hero of James's, or James himself, now admitting through this "superior" and outcast protagonist both his own incapacity to understand the British nobility, and his rejection of their rejection. Shades of the theatrical debacle in James's middle career; and of his subsequent literary trauma, too. Just as he had selected his visionary Parisian society as the "true" instrument of culture for the provincial hero of *The Ambassadors*, so he was now using his ancient, "pagan" Italian Prince to show up the deficiencies of both American and British civilization.

The same noble, ancient English culture, I mean, to which the

---

* Yes, the same Matcham as the "great historic house" where Lord Mark launched Milly Theale into British society in *The Wings of the Dove*. But there is no mention of Lord Mark in the Matcham of *The Golden Bowl*; and James may have simply repeated this name, unconsciously or carelessly, as the symbol of fast, loose, "modern" British nobility. There has been no Jacobite study written yet, that the present writer knows of, to prove James *intended* this repetition; but no doubt one will be written.

self-orphaned and self-exiled young American writer had aspired, from his earliest visions of wealth, leisure and "art"; and in the very highest reaches of which, now, James's last prince still feels himself — though still obviously "superior" — to be only another orphan, exile and outcast. And that rootless, or rather self-incisored and self-enclosed, restless and relentlessly devouring Jamesian id-ego which had never yet, whether through external circumstances or more likely its own incapacity for fulfillment and satisfaction, found itself a true home.

The Jamesian wound, at least, lay behind the portrait of the Prince in *The Golden Bowl:* and this was the real background of the "golden day" which Charlotte and the Prince spend together — of that one assignation which is apparently, despite all the "freedom" for which Charlotte has plotted with so much devious ingenuity, the only complete sexual experience in their relationship after the double marriage. (As in *The Wings of the Dove*, with Kate Croy and Densher, "once" is apparently enough — or too much — in the later Jamesian love affairs; it represents the outer, fatal limits of the Jamesian sexuality.) Now the harm has been done; and the point of view, mainly the Prince's in the first half of the novel, shifts to Maggie's in the second half. Maggie, that is, who now "knows all" — like that whole line of omniscient Jamesian children — or suspects all; who is determined to punish Charlotte and the Prince for their crime, while hiding it from her good, sweet, innocent, little father (who is also quite aware of everything, as we learn). For no word of the hidden struggle is ever to be breathed, in typical Jamesian fashion, between the two — or even almost among the four — protagonists of the novel; though Maggie Verver is also determined to reclaim her own lawfully wedded royal husband, the Prince. Here the novel picks up its momentum. This unspoken battle of wits, of "moral fervor," and of spiritual control and manipulation, is at the center of the last half of *The Golden Bowl*, and is announced in Maggie's first direct reverie, or dawning of true consciousness. If Charlotte has told the

Prince he is too fearful of the "crack" in the golden bowl (and of "the little swindling Jew" who sold it to them), now indeed it is Maggie — in James's recurrent and heavy use of symbolism — who declares to the Prince: "That's what happened to my need of you — the cup, all day, has been too full to carry. So here I am with it, spilling it over you." (Hence, too, Glenway Wescott's image of the psychic content of the novel spilling over everything so "magnificently.")

Suddenly we learn that Maggie has "admired and missed and desired" her Prince; even while in her own mind she is working out "her lucid little plan" — of reacquisition, that is — which is never to be mentioned. As the first step in the process of her "finding herself," Maggie has realized that Charlotte and the Prince are "treating" her — "that they were proceeding with her — and for that matter with her father — by a plan that was the exact counterpart of her own." In the midst of these plots and counterplots of human "treatment" and "countertreatment," James was in his happiest milieu. Maggie, of course, must *learn* how to deal with people; she is only starting. "She had flapped her little wings as a symbol of desired flight" — those same wings, perhaps, which the golden American princess of the *Dove* had spread, in her dying agony, over the conspiring protagonists of the earlier novel. And Maggie's first plot is to have her famous dinner party of the Matcham people who could bear witness to the golden day. "Each of these persons had for Maggie the interest of an attested connexion with the Easter revels at that visionary house."

Is she, perhaps, like the mad Prince of Denmark, planning to confront and to torture the guilty pair with the symbolic "play" of their crime? In the first moment of her revenge, her triumph, she is almost overcome by a mania of manipulation, a joy in "detection" which matches, which more than equals the period of her misery, her fear, her suffering. For she has begun "to break the ice" where that formation was thickest. "They're paralyzed, they're paralyzed!" she cries out to herself about her false friend and her faithless husband, who are confronted at the dinner table by the select group of mute witnesses to their assignation. She has indeed "captured the attention" of Amerigo and Charlotte, as James remarked even while "at neither of whom did she so much as once look." That is the point of the dramatic little climax in Maggie's Matcham party — the accusation, the imputation, the leveled charge without *words*, without even a glance, now, when the drama of consciousness has reached another peak of subtlety. For the immediate effect of this dinner-party confrontation upon Amerigo and Charlotte, as Maggie "secretly," as she now "almost breathlessly measured it," was prodigious. "Everything now so fitted for her to everything else that she could feel the effect as prodigious even while sticking to her policy of giving the pair no look. There were thus some five wonderful minutes during which they loomed to her sightless eyes, on either side of her, larger than they had ever loomed before, larger than life, larger than thought, larger than any danger or any safety . . ."

This was indeed prodigious, in the later James scale of values, when the inordinate stress on "seeing" in his work led finally to seeing through "sightless eyes"; and when the triumph of *detecting* the crime, and of acquainting the sexual criminals with the fact of her knowledge of their crime, looms larger to this Jamesian heroine than life or thought. Was Maggie the center of "the novel's peculiar atmosphere of horror," as Mr. Dupee claimed? Was *The Golden Bowl* as a whole James's greatest chronicle of "suffering," as this critic went on, triumphantly himself, to state? The "horror" is a peculiarly Jamesian one, as we see; the "suffering," of Maggie (who does illustrate the familiar mood of James's own neurotic fear and anxiety) is at base the suffering of wounded vanity, of a deflated self-image, a humiliated egotism. The accents of true suffering, of wounded passion, of thwarted desire, of tormented jealousy — of all the depth emotions which center around the various modes of human love — are entirely missing in *The Golden Bowl*. But the single, entwined passion of "knowing," and then

of Maggie's mental *power* over the unfortunate lovers: this dominant and typical intellectual passion of Henry James's later fiction
more than compensates, apparently, for any other sense of personal
loss. Now this too is presumably what Mr. Spender meant by Maggie's "triumphant answer" to life in the novel. But just like the
entire circle of Jacobites, Mr. Spender does not specify what kind
of "life" James was describing; or what kind of "affirmation"
Maggie Verver really embodied.

The novel is almost a classic study of the wounded ego (in the
conventional, non-Freudian terms of ego psychology); of the desperate manipulations of the self and of others in order to restore the
favorable self-image — and of the heedless, blind "triumph" of this
formidable type of self-love. The Prince, scenting danger, uses his
proclaimed powers of sexual attraction in order to quell his wife's
suspicions. But Maggie, drawn as she is, apparently, to Amerigo's
physical presence in the second volume of *The Golden Bowl*
(though she has apparently scorned and rejected him throughout
the first volume): Maggie will not yield to his embraces for fear of
spoiling her "plan," and that is to say, her plan of obtaining
revenge and power over both the Prince and Charlotte. But this
naked use of power, for power's sake, in the later Jamesian fiction
is both curiously limited in its goal and remarkably elaborate in its
"method," since the drama between Maggie and the two lovers
must also be a triumph of subtlety, tact, indirection and evasion.
Maggie strikes back — indeed! — in the second half of *The Golden
Bowl*; but the whole point of her revenge is in the tortuous (rather
than tortured) manner of it. Moreover, atoning for her earlier
"sin" in deserting the Prince, Maggie has also decided she must
abandon her darling, her precious, her beloved and childlike father
himself:

*"Sacrifice me, my own love; do sacrifice me, do sacrifice me!" Should
she want to, should she insist on it, she might verily hear him bleating,
like some precious, spotless exceptionally intelligent lamb. The positive*

*effect of the intensity of this figure however was to make her shake it
away in her resumed descent; and after she had rejoined him, after she
had picked him up, she was to know the full pang of the thought that
her impossibility was made, absolutely, by his consciousness, by the
lucidity of his intention: this she felt while she smiled there for him
again all hypocritically; while she drew on fair fresh gloves; while she
interrupted the process first to give his necktie a slightly smarter twist
and then to make up to him for her hidden madness by rubbing her
nose into his cheek according to the tradition of their frankest levity.
From the instant she should be able to convict him of intending, every
issue would be closed and her hypocrisy would have to redouble. The
only way to sacrifice him would be to do so without his dreaming what
it might be for. She kissed him, she arranged his cravat, she dropped
remarks, she guided him out, she held his arm, not to be led but to lead
him, and taking it to her by much the same intimate pressure she had
always used, when a little girl, to mark the inseparability of her doll —
she did all these things so that he should sufficiently fail to dream of
what they might be for.*

Now isn't this something, as a typical later Jamesian passage?
For despite all these gilded assurances, and the redoubling, in Maggie's mind, of her superhypocrisy, Adam Verver does know exactly
what is going on. Henry James knows it, and we know it, too. And
amid this conspicuously contrived infantile setting — this father
image now viewed as an intelligent if sacrificial lamb, as an in-
separable doll — Maggie does have her brief moment of genuine
emotion, of affection, remorse. But why? Was James so intent on
establishing the "innocence" of this father-daughter love that he
risked the most ridiculous imagery; not to mention the other reasons that we have noticed for the devirilizing, the unmanning and
the defathering, as it were, of the father image in general? Or was
it that Henry James himself, like his present and revealing heroine,
could only release this emotion *within* a childlike or at best an
adolescent framework of feeling? The latent content of *The Golden
Bowl* is perhaps even more interesting than the overt action.

At any rate Maggie's devotion to her father is the pure, innocent, lamblike and doll-like affection for the lost childhood that she must renounce in order to gain her own "maturity." "Maggie, of all James's characters, is the most vividly susceptible to the presence of evil," adds our Jamesian Mr. Dupee — but to him, this evil, for what it is worth, is *outside* Maggie rather than, as it really is, also within her. If the ostensible and conscious theme of *The Golden Bowl* was the "sentimental education" of a self-made American princess, according to James himself, it is really quite obvious that this noble and idyllic heroine also belongs directly in the line of the Jamesian "obsessed observers" who have gradually turned into interrogators, inquisitors and finally complete spiritual manipulators.

In turn, the pagan Prince and his scheming Charlotte are another variation on the Jamesian "evil couple" — always contaminated by sexuality rather than, of all things, Mr. Spender's peculiar social "evil" of the modern world. (Peculiar, I mean, to read into such an unlikely source as Henry James.) The Prince is an example of the noble outcast too, as we've seen, while Adam Verver also takes on the qualities of the Jamesian type of innocent child-hero who has been mortally wronged by his wicked "adult" companions. *The Golden Bowl* is the climax and the epitome of the *Jamesian* literary world, which had nothing to do with the modern world (even of James's own time); which had nothing to do, indeed, with any conceivable world of social reality which ever really existed in the long chronicle of human history. Moreover, the development of Maggie's "consciousness," so devoutly stressed by the whole Jacobite circle, is simply the growth of her watching, her spying, her planning and plotting — her "detection" and her manipulation again — in the typical Jamesian mode. Her growth as a woman is reduced to the enticement of the "chase" in a detective story of the obsessed psyche, rather than in any true narrative of the heart.

She even begins to wield her newly won power over the guilty and worried Fanny Assingham — who also, of course, lies steadily to Maggie in this chronicle of obliquity, even more than of opacity. While Fanny, in turn, confides to her Colonel that she knows Maggie has decided "to keep up *her* lie so long as I keep up mine." This was an elaborate and calculated world of deception in every corner, which also exaggerated the Victorian world of pretense and "appearance": the maintaining of the pretense and the appearance of respectability or propriety at whatever cost of the true feelings and true facts of human experience. The whole purpose of *The Golden Bowl*, in this sense, is the evasion of the novel's real issues. Then there is the shared "communion of knowledge" between the two charming liars, between Fanny and Maggie, I mean; and a further "intensity of intimation" in the higher reaches of the drama of consciousness — and then there is the sudden appearance of the Prince himself, as Fanny dashes the cursed golden bowl to pieces. (Another theatrical coup; another, sudden magical apparition, as though by the Jamesian wand.) And there is another typical Jamesian confrontation scene between husband and wife — a confrontation of two people who are "furiously thinking," of these two marital protagonists who are "watching" each other so intensely, while each knows what the other is thinking, and each of them utters evasive commonplaces. Maggie's "triumph" is again that of *not* telling the Prince what she knows, and what he knows that she knows. "It's you, cara, who are deep," acknowledges the Prince respectfully. But this abstruse heroine, who lacks all the common hysteria and jealousy and sympathy of a betrayed woman, is chiefly concerned with the difference it would make for herself: "My possession at last, I mean, of real knowledge."

Here *The Golden Bowl* takes a real twist, as it describes the psychological punishment of Charlotte, who doesn't know even what the Prince now knows — namely that Maggie knows — who (Charlotte, that is) knows *nothing*, since her former lover doesn't deign to tell her anything. Is this princely behavior; is it even decent? Well, at least Maggie feels she is having "the time of her life." . . . "She knew it by the perpetual throb of this sense of possession, which was almost too violent either to recognize or to hide" — a sense of solitary, calculating, mental "possession," almost akin to a kind of mental masturbation, which is enhanced, on Maggie's part, by the knowledge that Charlotte will also attempt to force her, Maggie, to tell the "truth," which Maggie, of course, will *never* do:

Even the conviction that Charlotte was but awaiting some chance really to test her trouble upon her lover's wife left Maggie's sense meanwhile open as to the sight of gilt wire and bruised wings, the spacious but suspended cage, the home of eternal unrest, of pacings, beatings, shakings, all so vain, into which the baffled consciousness helplessly resolved itself. The cage was the deluded condition, and Maggie having known delusion — rather! — understood the nature of cages. She walked around Charlotte's cautiously and in a very wide circle . . . She saw her companion's face, as that of a prisoner looking through bars. So it was that through bars richly gilt but firmly though discreetly planted, Charlotte finally struck her as making a grim attempt; from which at first the Princess drew back as instinctively as if the door of the cage had suddenly been opened from within.

Just as Maggie's final possession of the "truth" has filled her with a kind of orgiastic excitement which compensates for all her other wounded feelings — and even has obliterated the *nature* of the truth she has discovered — so in turn, conversely, the greatest Jamesian torture has become that of the "baffled consciousness," the "deluded condition," the terrible anxiety of *not* "knowing." And wasn't this a notable psychic cage which this cerebral artist had constructed for his suffering villainess? The later Jamesian imagery of the caged human psyche is a recurrent theme in his fiction; but this is a cage to beat all cages. The bars of which have to be both "richly gilt" and "discreetly" if firmly planted; and a cage which has to be "spacious," though suspended in the worst torments of the deluded mind! Even this last and best psychological prison in the world of the inheritors has to have a certain elegance, a touch of conspicuous luxury, a note of noble propriety.

In the famous bridge game of *The Golden Bowl* (and how the idle rich do amuse themselves) Charlotte, like the other Jamesian beast in the jungle, does spring at Maggie's throat — only again we have these two women thinking intensely in the dark, and uttering fatuous commonplaces to each other. For Charlotte doesn't quite ask, and Maggie obviously won't tell, anything which really bears on the central situation. The scene concludes with the false embrace of the two equally noncommittal Jamesian ladies, while Maggie relentlessly pursues her iron policy of evasion. "It was only a question of not by a hair's breadth deflecting into the truth" — which might be taken as the motto for all of Henry James's later work.

But does this Jamesian policy of "never deflecting into the truth" apply also to Adam Verver, when this infantile emblem of self-made American royalty braces himself for his foredoomed exile, and when the novel's descriptions of him become even more extravagant, laudatory, and lyrical?

From all the surrounding evidence in *The Golden Bowl*, James wrote the purple passages on Adam Verver in complete seriousness. Adam is the "innocent hero" of this phase of the novel who is being condemned by his own self-sacrificing will in order to ensure his daughter's happiness. The hyperbolic tone of these passages is both a tribute to Adam's sacrificial morality and perhaps another uneasy confession on James's part that the artist was making up in rhetorical extravagance for what he had so inadequately rendered in fact. From being a "supreme success," Adam Verver becomes, in this exacerbated Jamesian fantasy of great wealth and power, a sort of master magician. He "knows" and has known "all" about Charlotte, Maggie and the Prince. In his quiet, intense, powerful "originality" he has even devised, all unbeknownst to his doting daughter, his own forthcoming exile and expiation, and the subtle punishment for his wayward wife. He is described as singing to himself sotto voce, and weaving silently his mysterious spells. "The little man in the straw hat kept coming into view with his indescribable air of weaving his spell, weaving it off there by himself."

Like the evil magician of James's earliest fantasy, the Madame Merle-Merlin in *The Portrait of a Lady* — or rather unlike her — Adam is now a "good magician" who brings injustice (sexually, at least) to book. There are the descriptions of Charlotte's final subjugation by this powerful if childlike financier-collector — although her punishment is also a species of magic because it is never explained logically in the novel. In the daily round at Fawns, Charlotte now hung behind her husband with emphasized attention; she stopped when her husband stopped, but at the distance of a pace or two . . .

and the likeness of their connexion wouldn't have been wrongly figured if he had been thought of as holding in one of his pocketed hands the end of a long silken halter looped round her beautiful neck. He didn't twitch it, yet it was there; he didn't drag her, but she came; and those betrayals that I have described the Princess as finding irresistible in him were two or three mute facial intimations which his wife's presence didn't prevent his addressing his daughter — nor prevent his daughter, as she passed, it was doubtless to be added, from flushing a little at the receipt of.

Now Matthiessen was quite correct in saying that this passage, if James was conscious of his intention, was cruel. But if James *wasn't* conscious of it, as he was apparently not conscious of so much latent emotional content in his work, does it make the passage any the less cruel? Wasn't this in fact an overt example of the sadism which lingers just below the surface of all James's frustrations and inhibitions? Which is usually more subtle, however, or transformed into the intellectual "irony" of his central situations; and which lies behind, too, and has its share in the development of the whole strip-tease Jamesian narrative technique. Just as James was getting a little more careless in the prose effects of his later novels, perhaps he was relaxing the rigid censorship of the "intellect" over the emotional complexes in his own temperament — that is to say, when he did not distort or even glorify these perverse psychological strains in a remarkably obtuse fashion.

So here, the "betrayals" in Adam Verver which the Princess found so irresistible, those two or three mute facial intimations which he can't resist passing on to Maggie about Charlotte's plight (as not only a caged animal now but one on a psychological chain) and at which the Princess actually flushed a little — could anything have a more sexual overtone, as between father and daughter, or suggest a kind of little sexual intercourse, almost *over* the helpless body of the father's real wife? Very interesting; and yet apparently James simply meant to signify the triumph of wronged virtue in the Ververs — and he even went on to toy with, to amplify the same image. The mute facial intimations of Adam — and again the highest development of the "civilized" and sophisticated Jamesian drama of consciousness now lay, as it were, in these silent, almost imperceptible physiognomic movements; these facial intimations, James went on to say —

amounted perhaps only to a wordless, wordless smile, but the smile was the soft shake of the twisted silken rope, and Maggie's translation of it, held in her breast till she got well away, came out only, as if it might have been overheard, when some door was closed behind her. "Yes, you see — I lead her now by the neck, I lead her to her doom, and she doesn't so much as know what it is, though she has a fear in her heart which, if you had the chances to apply your ear there that I, as a husband, have, you would hear thump and thump and thump. She thinks it may be, her doom, the awful place over there — awful for her; but she's afraid to ask, don't you see? just as she's afraid of not asking; just as she's afraid of so many other thing that she sees multiplied all about her now as perils and portents. She'll know, however — when she does know.

Well now really; how sadistic can you get, albeit all unconsciously — or how infatuated with your own verbal conceits so that any other meaning — even the true meaning — of the imagery escapes your attention? Whether these words were the utterance of the husband who could apply his ear so intimately to his wife's thumping heart; or of the daughter who imagined these fatherly remarks, hardly matters. In their moment of revenge, their moment of intellectual triumph, the Ververs have become monsters of manipulation; just as James himself, in the display of the "mind" over the suppressed emotions, over the body and sexuality in particular, has become almost a similarly unconscious monster of "treatment" as to both people and human relations in relation to the plot line of all these latter narratives. Overcome by the fairytale magic of the American financier-collector in *The Golden Bowl*, and by the making of a true American princess, the artist has become indifferent to, even unaware of, the human cost which this triumph of moral virtue is exacting upon the victims of its process, or upon the victors.

Or do they really, the Prince and Charlotte, deserve — in the Jamesian mind — such a monstrous psychological punishment, although once again Charlotte's final anguish is not *knowing* what her doom is going to be? The all-dominant, all-controlling, all-inclusive "mind" in Henry James's fiction has its singular retributions. Part of Maggie's newborn nobility of spirit is her capacity to share in Charlotte's torment — yes, to share in it, but not possibly to mitigate, to lessen, or avert it! What was curious, too, in all the later Jamesian imagery, devised to describe Charlotte Stant's suffering, was the prevalence of bestiary symbols in an artist who had so rigorously excluded from his intellectual orbit all consideration of the "animal feelings." We've already noticed those later Jamesian prowling beasts always about to leap forth from their jungle lairs ("The Beast in the Jungle"), but it was curious that Henry James could at once present the Ververs in such a "pure" and noble context and yet use such direct animal symbolism in his descriptions of human "anxiety." (Or perhaps it was not curious at all, but quite a logical result of the deep Jamesian repressions.) Meanwhile what was the "awful doom" which the cunning little magician (Adam) had prepared for his faithless spouse Charlotte — faithless to Adam's daughter, it almost appears, more than to the noble and betrayed father himself, who had so little concern for the carnal aspects of his famous marriage of convenience? Well, the Ververs are now forced to leave "Europe" — Maggie, the Prince, their grandson the Principino, or in short, everything — for a permanent exile in "American City." That was still the worst fate that Henry James could imagine in the way of suffering, atonement, and cosmic torment: this was indeed "Hades, U.S.A.," as the later Scott Fitzgerald would call it.

"Lost to each other — father and I," Maggie wails to Fanny Ashingham. And lost, lost, lost; separated eternally by that terrible "American City" (a precursor of Sinclair Lewis's Zenith, too?) is the Jamesian refrain towards the close of *The Golden Bowl*. Almost mechanically again, Henry James invoked the romantic imagery of the French Revolution, of the suffering nobility in their last days of glory, to commemorate the tragic renunciation of this novel. (Jamesian critics all, make what you will of this.) But there were a few more twists of the melodrama yet, towards the close of this epic. To show her new power, her new security, her new womanhood, Maggie *makes* her Prince take Charlotte off somewhere together by themselves; even while she covers this maneuver with another striking declaration of daughterly love for her about-to-be-abandoned heroic father Adam.

But the Prince wisely refuses this gambit. "If Charlotte doesn't understand me," Maggie then declares, "it's because I've prevented her. I've chosen to deceive her and to lie to her." (Which, in the grand Jamesian psychomorality, apparently "covers" and excuses all her dubious behavior.) "But I've chosen to do the same," answers Amerigo; and their new marital "understanding" is based on this frank acknowledgment of their joint, their collective guile and duplicity. Yet Maggie is still forced to utter a long wail of protest. "I see it's *always* terrible for women," she says; and there is the much quoted rejoinder of the Prince: "Everything's terrible, cara — in the heart of man." So it is in truth; and there's no denying this Jamesian axiom. Only what is really terrible in the heart of man included so many things that Henry James never dreamed of; while in turn this rococo artist went so far out of his way to contrive a notable series of "terrible things" which the heart of man, or his mind, had never before imagined — and very likely never would again.

And now the making of a princess, à la Henry James, is almost complete. Well, that is, Amerigo still wants to let Charlotte "know" the real situation; which Charlotte should indeed by now quite obviously know. Isn't it his right, the Prince demands, really to "correct" Charlotte's view of Maggie herself; to which point, after letting the question "ring" long enough in the Prince's own ears, Maggie addresses herself:

"Correct her?" — and it was her own [voice] now that really rang. "Aren't you rather forgetting who she is?" After which, while he quite stared for it, as it was the very first clear majesty he had known her to use, she flung down her book and raised a warning hand. "The carriage. Come!" The "Come!" had matched for lucid firmness the rest of her speech, and when they were below in the hall there was a "Go!" for him, through the open doors and between the ranged servants, that matched even that. He received Royalty, bareheaded, therefore, in the persons of Mr. and Mrs. Verver, as it alighted on the pavement, and Maggie was at the threshold to welcome it to her house.

So Henry James wrote at the zenith of his famous "scenario method," or at the apex of his dramaturgical affliction; still possessed — or even more deeply obsessed — by his ruling and demented infatuation for the theatrical "scene": a scene, replete with such ringing "Come's" and "Go's," which you can envision, which you probably have witnessed at the center stage of any typical romance melodrama of his period. The real point is, of course, that the Jamesian passion for the stage had actually corrupted the texture of the writing in his later fiction — the process of becoming "theatrical" was almost complete. It had worked inward from the fictional concept of the novel, from the controlled, stagy behavior of the characters in their key scenes, from the fabricated human emotions, even to the point of a theatrical prose.

Notice also how James now reversed his themes for the sake of a new "effect." Thus all of a sudden the ignorant, outcast, provincial Ververs have become *the* royalty which the Italian prince receives bareheaded, paying his tribute amidst the ranks of ranged servants. (What has become of the penalty of the "private life" which Mr. Spender orated so eloquently about, or that "atonement" of the superior intelligences which Mr. Dupee described?) Even Charlotte must be accorded her royal due simply because she belongs to Adam Verver. And "belongs" quite literally; since throughout this final farewell scene in *The Golden Bowl*, Adam still weaves his potent web and still plays out "his long fine cord" which is looped around her neck. There is no doubt that Charlotte is at once enthroned, as it were, and chained; while just as clearly Maggie's ringing, royal imperatives have also harnessed for good and all the errant pagan Prince.

The ascent to nobility on the part of both Adam and Maggie also marks the rise to a connubial authoritarianism. There remains only the moment of Maggie's final reconciliation with Amerigo. Triumphant, dominant, at last the true (and total) mistress of her own house and husband, the American princess of high finance still has the interval of terror and suspense, as James wrote, which always precedes "on the part of the creature to be paid, the certification of the amount." Here again, as in all the later novels of Henry James, the moment of sexual passion is accompanied by, or is actually described in terms of, the cash nexus. When Maggie is about to confess her true love for the Prince, and sees the "love" in his eyes, James added another of these peculiar financial statements. "So far as seeing that she was 'paid' went, he might have been holding out the money-bag for her to come and take it." A moneybag, to be sure, which in the later Freudian imagery was a curiously feminine symbol of love; but which Henry James himself equated purely with the riches of love, as well as seeing in it the only and indispensable means of love. Very likely here James was consciously, if somewhat awkwardly, stressing the language of finance at the close of a novel which dealt with a master financier's daughter. But there was no doubt either, just as Adam Verver emerged as the triumphant, or even royal hero of *The Golden Bowl*, and Maggie as the true princess, that James himself certainly approved of this conclusion and this triumph of the big money *and* culture. Maggie's European education has made her fit for her fortune. If poverty is the Edenite sin in the Jamesian hierarchy of moral values, then wealth is the highest human good, and the more wealth, obviously, the greater the good. On another level still, love *meant* money to Henry James; and in accordance with those oral-anal, pre-oedipal and pre-sexual temperamental patterns which emerged so clearly in *The Sacred Fount*, money meant love.

But in any case the entirely baronial setting, psychology and conclusion of *The Golden Bowl* were never intended in an ironical, or even critical sense. James's own earliest and abiding convictions about life flowed naturally into this peculiar vessel of sensibility. The only trouble with the golden bowl was that it was not real gold — it was flawed. The whole point of the novel was that through the heroine's "suffering" and by her triumph of will (cunning, calculation, power) the Jamesian princess made, as it were, a *new* and better and perfect golden bowl out of her restored marriage, her own restored self-image, her reclaimed and regenerated (if harnessed and tamed) husband. Once again Henry James was the perfect Veblenian writer of his period, and of the national letters. He illustrated in all solemnity, with perfect belief, and absolute confidence, the whole ironic mythology of great wealth which the American sociologist had set forth, at about the same time historically, with so much insight and wit. James was the first great American leisure-class writer, as we've said, who perhaps necessarily outdid any other leisure-class writer up to his period and ours. He was the true believer in the cultural — or rather, artistic — usefulness of the great fortunes and the implicit merit of the *founders* of such fortunes, even though, as in the case of Adam Verver or of Chad Newsome, they would have to be taught the European social graces. But since he was so innocent himself as regards the real nature of the whole new epoch of finance capitalism at the end of the last century; since he viewed this scene in the naïve and sentimental terms of his own youth (which were not even true for the 1850's and '60's), the true drama of the American financiers, titans and barons would have to await the tougher, more realistic and sardonic mind of a Theodore Dreiser. For Henry James *exemplified* an epoch which he never remotely understood.

At bottom, also, this was an unholy quartet in *The Golden Bowl*; but precisely in the sense which Henry James did not see, intend, or render. So that the elements of true art which are in the novel, which are buried there by the writer's own unconscious; just those elements are in the end subverted and betrayed by the artist's incapacity to deal with them correctly — or even at all. Now very likely that is another facet of the fascination of the Jamesian fiction, quite apart from the struggle, or the puzzle, of learning how to decipher his peculiar literary idiom, his even more peculiar vision of life and art.

I mean the fascination, and the tragedy, of an artist who is so *close* to something real in his work, as this one was very often, and then is forced to convert his true material into something quite different, quite opposite, and altogether artificial. Henry James was akin to the "devil's party," as our Jacobite commentator said; and the real point is that he never allowed himself to know it. Maybe he stressed the "game of literature" so strongly because he suspected that literature was not a game.

11. The Ghost in the Jolly Corner

THAT WAS close to the heart of the matter. Everything came out clearly in the three famous novels of Henry James's so-called major phase. *The Wings of the Dove, The Ambassadors, The Golden Bowl* represented the climax of this astoundingly idiosyncratic temperament.

The rest of James's career through the 1900's was in the nature of a postscript, an epilogue. But an epilogue which, in the case of a writer now so utterly consumed in projecting a baroque personality under the universal guise of art, drew itself out for another decade; and a decade which then extended itself posthumously almost for another ten years (with new books by Henry James still continuing to appear) until the very brink of the 1920's. Moreover this semi-final, final, and post-final period of James's work, during which even his life appeared to be constrained into the elaborate form of his later literary method, still contained some memorable or notable literary material. Here indeed the final "secrets" of this singular artist emerged more clearly and positively; the true values, motives, prejudices of Henry James became transfixed by age, as it were, and remained there, all pure and translucently displayed in his last periods of work, for us to marvel at and ponder over in sheer incredulity.

Or, with a deferential bow to the Jacobites, who appear notoriously to have so little humor about the case of their master, we may even smile at the increasing eccentricity of the later James, and perhaps his increasing absurdity. Thus, in the postscript-Preface to *The Golden Bowl* itself, James went on talking enthusiastically about James. Quite typically for this master of literary intrigue, of the all-controlling plot line, of the victimized fictional characters, he declaimed against "the mere muffled majesty of irresponsible authorship." In his view, irresponsible authorship meant the author who presented directly his view of his own fiction, as opposed to the "modern" author like James himself, who gloried in a "still marked inveteracy of a certain indirect and oblique view of my presented action." In this Preface, too, we notice again how James dwelt on "the entertainment of the great game" which his fiction had become, or on the "actors in the offered play," or on "the inordinate intellectual 'sport' of it" — and the "it," of course, was what James now considered to be the art of fiction.

There was his final stress on the novelist's method rather than his content. You might say that content as such now mattered very little to James. He had rationalized away, through the emphasis on technique, his own lack of experience, of life and living and of human content, in favor of his game, his sport, his play-acting. But the euphoric tone persisted; as in his summary of the peculiar relation — the lack of relation — between the Prince and Maggie:

So it is that the admirably endowed pair, between them, as I retrace their fortune and my own method, point again for me the moral of the endless interest, endless worth for "delight," of the compositional contributions. Their chronicle strikes me as quite of the stuff to keep us from forgetting that absolutely no refinement of ingenuity or of precaution need be dreaded of as wasted in that most exquisite of all good causes, the appeal to variety, the appeal to incalculability, the appeal to a high refinement and a handsome wholeness of effect . . .

And so it was, under this Jamesian spell of compositional contributions, and of these refinements of ingenuity, and of this handsome wholeness of effect — that Maggie Verver became a mediocre little operator, all apparently unknowingly to the artist who was so consumed by his passion for "method"; while the handsome, pagan Prince was tamed and, so to speak, gelded: an admirably endowed pair whose chronicle was in fact highly dubious.

As for the tormented world of private sensibility, which Messrs. Spender and Dupee made so much of in the light of the moral corruption of modern society, James had a different view of that, too. Apologizing for the small number of characters in *The Golden Bowl*, the limited and mainly domestic scene remote from all out-side forces and influences — which was also, as we've seen, the logical climax of the leisure-class novel — James even took a special pleasure in this literary challenge. "That was my problem, so to speak, and my *gageure* — to play the small handful of values really for all they were worth — and to work my system, my particular propriety of appeal, particular degree of pressure on the spring of interest, for all that this specific ingenuity could produce." In-genuity — I had almost forgotten that typical Jamesian word in this now altogether private game of art. And the Preface was filled with other Jamesian tags of fictional "criticism," if that is what you wish to call it. There is the "bristling consciousness" of the author who is rereading his curious epic. There is his "consenting re-perusal" of his own material — or of this "blest good stuff, sit-ting up in its myriad forms, so touchingly responsive to new care of any sort whatever" — and now the note was that of the intel-lectual nursing mother, caressing its little verbal charge with an almost sexual gesture.

There was, among all the sonorous Latin phrases which James threw off so abundantly, so eloquently, so passionately in his dis-cussions of his beloved method, the relatively simple generalization about "the working secret of the revisionist." There was the in-terest of the "watched renewal" of a literary work (his own, natu-rally) as compared with the tediousness of "the accepted repeti-tion." And there was the typical Jamesian lament and appeal; the familiar cry of the wounded literary vanity, of the frustrated literary ego, urging on his audience to greater pains and effort. "What has the affair been at the worst, I am most moved to ask, but an earnest invitation to the reader to dream again in my company and in the interest of his own larger absorption of my sense?" But just as earlier, the note of "ingenuity" had been coupled with the Jamesian "system," and with the degree of pressure on the *spring* of human interest, in the Jamesian mixture of cleverness and power; so now the invitation "to dream again" — as though *that* was the meaning of art — was joined directly with "my company" and the larger absorption of "my sense," as indeed the only sense that James could finally make of the baffling and varied universe of man.

Yet the critic R. P. Blackmur called these Prefaces "the most sustained and I think the most eloquent and original pieces of literary criticism in existence." This critic, almost as romantic, metaphysical and rhetorical as James himself, collected the Prefaces into a volume called *The Art of the Novel* which formed the basis not only of the Jamesian esthetic in the mid-twentieth century, but almost of the so-called "modern esthetics" in our academic centers of fiction-writing at least. And this Jamesian esthetic, composed, as we've seen, of such a singular vision of life and art alike, compounded of such a series of higher and higher rationalizations of precisely the weakest elements in James's own fiction itself, has been used to mislead at least two generations of college and university students — not to mention the aspiring young professors of literature who turn out yearly their stint of "Jamesian" novels to the co-ordinated applause of their colleagues and the utter indifference of the outer world.

Well, meanwhile Henry James's next important book, or the book which the Jacobite revisionists of our historical epoch *made* important in a most revealing way, was *The American Scene*, in 1907. James had returned to the United States in 1904 for the first time since 1883. He spent the autumn with the William Jameses in New Hampshire, then in Cambridge. He revisited New York and went west to California, giving his standard two lectures on Balzac and on Speech,* before returning to Lamb House in Rye,

England. He had contracted with *Harper's Magazine* to publish his "impressions" of this American tour; and out of this "frenzied homecoming," adds Mr. Dupee (though why "frenzied"?) came *The American Scene*, "one of his inestimable books and one of the great American documents." And this baffling statement, one of the strangest in American literary criticism, represented the received opinion of the entire enchanted Jamesian circle. Just as Lionel Trilling had staked out *The Princess Casimassima* as the great American "counter-revolutionary" document in the vein of Dostoyevsky, so Dupee went on to celebrate *The American Scene* as an invaluable social documentary. Indeed he had already set the ground for this claim in his "analysis" of *The Golden Bowl*. "How strange, then, to charge James, as has so often been done, with here ignoring the world, when his doing so makes just the point of the novel, is just his sacrificial tribute to the tragic actualities of his characters. How short-sighted to maintain that his long exile attenuated his energy and confused his point of view, when it was precisely his vantage point abroad that permitted him to combine the American moral energy with the hard wisdom of the good European, to keep bravely abreast of world developments however damaging they might be to his own theories and desires, and so to remain profoundly creative into his sixties."

A touching eloquence, almost as fairy-talish in its view of James, however, as James was about the world he lived in. We have already seen on what curious grounds *The Princess* was completely misinterpreted and overestimated; the case of *The American Scene* is perhaps even more peculiar. And Dupee's own reasons for his lofty estimate of the book are also somewhat uneven or evasive. "Intensely wrought" in detail of sentence and paragraph, so we are told, this Jamesian travelogue yet has a structure which is

---

* Both of these lectures were reprinted in *The Question of Our Speech* (1905). *English Hours*, in the same year, was a collection of travel essays, most of which had already appeared in magazine or in book form. James never missed a chance, also, to exploit his own work, or to use it in every possible medium. He was indeed, during his own lifetime, already conducting his own literary revival.

"casual" — quite an understatement. What is the book's theme? "Here 'the very *donnée* of the piece' gets formulated," said Dupee about James's travels along the New Jersey shore: "The book will investigate the consequences of 'the great adventure of a society reaching out into the apparent void for the amenities, the con- summations, after having earnestly gathered in so many of the preparations and necessities.' "

He was quoting James — but was *that* the meaning of American society in the early 1900's; just when a popular, a national ground swell of radical protest and indignation was gathering all its force to attack, not indeed the search for "amenities and consum- mations," but the very base and nature of the new American finance-politics? I will skip the further pages of eulogy about *The American Scene* in Dupee's *Henry James*, including the fact that in a relatively short book, this critic includes almost complete James's purple passage on New York Harbor which uses such imagery as "an enormous system of steam-shuttles or electric bob- bins"; or a "monster . . . flinging abroad its loose limbs even as some unmannered young giant at his 'larks' "; or "some colossal set of clockworks, some steel-souled machine-room of brandished arms and hammering fists and opening and closing jaws." Imagery, that is, of the eighteenth century industrial revolution, but com- pletely inadequate to describe early twentieth century American corporate capitalism; and quite as romantic and rhetorical as James's stereotyped descriptions of the French Revolution. *The American Scene*, so Dupee added, was "remarkably forward-looking, a kind of source book of later American writing, full of the unborn spirits of poems by Hart Crane and plays by Eugene O'Neill." But O'Neill at least, who was never deeply concerned about the "amen- ities and consummations" of his society, would stir in his grave at such a claim.

The English poet, W. H. Auden, was somewhat more uneasy about *his* praise of *The American Scene* in the Scribner revival (1946) of this epic. At least Auden's Introduction was a hodgepodge of "insights," good, bad and indifferent, which gave the impression that the poet had not quite read the book, or did not care to discuss it. "Few writers have had less journalistic talent than James," said Auden, thereby demolishing the Dupee thesis in one phrase. And: "*The American Scene* is only the latest, most ambitious, and best of a series of topographical writings, beginning in 1870 with sketches of Saratoga and Newport" — equivocal praise at best for the editor of such a volume. Then Auden went on to mention "the overwhelming alliterative barrage, the annihilating adverbial scorn" of James, as compared with Dupee's "intensely wrought" paragraphs: and that the "facts" in the book "are, even for James, amazingly and, one would have thought, fatally few." One would have thought — or does one perhaps *still* think so? Yet Auden went on dutifully to praise the Jamesian "intuition," which replaced all the missing facts, and to say that *The American Scene*, if not an inestimable social documentary, and one of the great American documents, was in fact "a prose poem of the first order," in which "outside of fairy tales, I know of no book in which things so often and so naturally become persons" — as when the American buildings, places, and pullman cars *speak* to James, and he to them.

Auden did not mention the "insides" of fairy tales, which were the true insides of Henry James's work; but he was warm, and the rest of his Introduction dealt with the conflict between the European "*romanitas*" and its American rejection. But what then was *The American Scene* really about; and why, and how, could it have been elevated to an absolutely unfounded critical grandeur? This is the recurrent question about all of James's "great" books; and the answer in the present case is both illuminating and baroque. For the query which James put to himself about the American scene of the 1900's was hardly a new one. It was his earliest, deepest, most abiding conviction about the *lack* of amenities in his native land, as far back as the 1870's. His answers remained the same, in essence; and perhaps never was such a closed mind joined to so much proclaimed "curiosity" on the part of the "restless analyst" who is the central figure of this investigation. And James used other such tags to describe the shifting phases of his own rigidly embedded temperament.

There is "the repatriated immigrant," for example, or the "story-seeker curious of manners," or the "waiting observer," the "returning absentee," the "remembering mind," the "rootless returner," the "free observer," the "twice-alienated orphan refugee," the "shuddering pilgrim," the "repatriated absentee" (a twist on the returning absentee); or the "brooding visitor," the "earnest observer" (another variation on the "free" one); the "prepared sensibility," the "mooning observer" (still another twist); the "musing moralist," and so on. But unfortunately all these different phases and states of James always agreed on the same conclusions about the American scene: the same conclusions which the tormented, frustrated, ill and neurotic artist, the young James, had already decided upon in his apprentice years.

The style of *The American Scene*, intensely wrought as it is, is difficult even for the seasoned Jamesian reader. Perhaps never have so many words been used for so little content; probably this is really James's worst-written, and mainly most vacant, empty, and chatterbox book; as though the writer's own consciousness as regards his lack of real knowledge about his ostensible subject had impelled him into almost hysterical bursts of verbal virtuosity. (Here we might add a new term to the modern canon of Jamesian esthetics: that of "intensely skippable prose.") The subject of the book ranged from James's first impressions of the New England landscape which he still claimed to love — though it was clearly a landscape marked "by the absence of forms," and that is: without a Church, to begin with. Was there *no* American religion worth mentioning beyond "the shrill effect of the New England meeting-house"? Was Hawthorne, for example, purely deluded about the iron grip of puritanical Calvinism? Well, you must realize that just as James had viewed English religion, and par-

ticularly, in his later phase, English Catholicism for its purely
esthetic effect; so now he esteemed religion "socially" (in *his* social
scale) for its "seated solidity" and its cultural "order." But the
absence of true religion in New England, or New Hampshire at
least, was marked and matched by the perhaps worse absence of
"the pervasive Patron" who reigned throughout Europe from the
days of feudalism. No church, then, no pervasive patron, no
feudalism: so Henry James added to his earlier or original list of
"American lacks" and American nothings.

Was this really the first notable example in *The American Scene*
of James's memorable social commentary? One wonders what
William James, or Mark Twain, or Walt Whitman, all of whom
had celebrated precisely the democracy's *repudiation* of such an
outworn feudal heritage, might have rejoined to such an "indictment"; or would they have considered this aging Henry as merely
slightly "touched"? Meanwhile James himself also asked what
form *could* there be "in the almost sophisticated dinginess of the
present destitution" — except, that is, the underlying existence of
the *wage standard*. He was enraged at the violation of every grace
in life by the "cynically squalid rustics" of New Hampshire, who
insisted on being received at the front door of his brother's
house. Such was the prelude to Henry James's *The American
Scene*, the opening chord in this odd native ode of the returning
expatriate; and perhaps you may already suspect the further direction, the movement, the true tone of this "great American document." Though you still have to ask yourself, after all, just how
could the formalist American critics of the forties and fifties,
granting their attachment to a new and sterile literary conservatism;
or even the extremes of their disenchantment with the radical
movements of the 1930's; or yielding as they no doubt did to the
temper of the times, not to mention the coercive forces of official
or semi-official "purges" and brainwashing, native style — yet still,
and nevertheless, how *could* these formalists and Jacobites, when
all is said and done, pin their restored faith and their critical

reputation on such a novel as *The Princess Casamassima* or such a
social "documentary" as *The American Scene?*

Shades of the thirties indeed, age as it was of often brilliant
and vital social documents; of which *The American Scene* is a
travesty, an esoteric, unconscious farce! It is a puzzlement, the
key use of this Jamesian chronicle for our own period of conformity and barely repressed social anxiety; if it is not simply to
laugh. And was it quite true, as Henry insisted and proclaimed
in the overture to this volume, that his verdict on the missing
Church, State and Patron in the rural American scene, on the
rude manners of the overpaid American rustics, contained no trace
of bitterness or despair? — even though the singular sociological
insight about "the absence of forms" in American life also served
the purpose at times "positively to save the restless analyst from
madness . . . He could make the absence of forms responsible,
and he could thus react without bitterness — react absolutely with
pity; he could judge without cruelty and condemn without despair." This was a singular cluster of emotions in these pages of
The American Scene; for just what bitterness, just what cruelty
and what despair, what act of judging and condemning, and what
reaction of calm, aloof, intellectual and rational "pity" was Henry
James talking about? What one does feel in these early passages
of so-called social commentary is not only the residual and fixed
imprint of James's earlier prejudices about the American scene,
but the lingering embedded accents of the same quite morbid or
even deeply neurotic and pathological complex of anxiety, fear
and aversion which marked the very earliest Jamesian passages,
a quarter of a century before, about his native country.

The more Henry James "changed," the more he remained the
same. *Voilà.* And, if this was only the prelude to *The American
Scene,* the later commentary became altogether extraordinary. The
"thrilled, roundabouted pilgrim" (a fine variation on the "ancient
contemplative person" — though what was really "contemplative"
in this rehearsal of an emotional bias which had been contemplated

so many times before?) was delighted by "mellow, medieval Albany" — founding seat of the highly medieval James family — but then, approaching the *Boston* docks by primitive steamboat, he felt once again the true import of democracy:

The great presence that bristles for him on the sounding dock, and that shakes the planks, the loose boards of its theatric stage to an inordinate unprecedented rumble, is the monstrous form of Democracy, which is thereafter to project its shifting angular shadow, at one time and another, across every inch of the field of his vision. It is the huge democratic broom that has made the clearance and that one seems to see brandished in the empty sky.

Monstrous, yes, theatric (which was in other contexts so dear to Henry James), shifting, angular, huge, and brandished in the swept-clean sky of his native vista; and James only forgot, this once, to include his other favorite, recurrent American adjectives like "grey," "empty" and "barren." Moreover, in the study of "the working of democratic institutions," James reiterated his own special angle of approach. "The political, the civic, the economic view of them is a study that may be followed, more or less, at a distance; but the way in which they determine and qualify manners, feelings, communications, modes of contact and conceptions of life — this is a revelation that has its full force and its lively interest only on the spot where, when once caught, it becomes the only clue worth mentioning in the labyrinth." Yet, if ever a book showed up the dangers and deep deceptions involved in studying the political, the civic, the economic view of democratic institutions "at a distance," and then stressing manners, feelings, communications, modes of contact without reference to their socioeconomic-politico framework; if ever a book showed the highest reaches of folly which *can* be achieved by such an approach, it was surely Henry James's *The American Scene.*

Perhaps also this was James's most vicious book at its core, as the "rootless returner" — shall we say? — the orphan-exile from early childhood, the journalist-newspaperman-artist, now kicked out, in his own fantasies, from the European castle of culture, still clung to all its familiar furnishings while everywhere in the American scene revisited he found only the evidence to confirm his half-discredited but still rigidly embedded dream of foreign culture, his early and nightmarish revulsion from his own society.

His lingering nostalgia for Cambridge — the shadows and shades of his youth; since there are in effect no *living* persons in *The American Scene* except the restless analyst himself, and even those figures then alive, such as Howells, were treated with the ceremonial praise of the dead — was only another prelude to James's horror at the "alien races" who had conquered New York. At Ellis Island, the seat of the Commissioner of Immigration, in the bay of New York:

I was to catch later on a couple of hours of the ceaseless process of the recruiting of our race, of the plenishing of our huge national pot au feu, of the introduction of fresh — of perpetually fresh so far as it isn't perpetually stale — foreign matter into our heterogeneous system. But even without that a haunting wonder as to what might be becoming of us all, "typically," ethnically, and thereby physiognomically, linguistically, personally, was always in order . . .

Shortly before this, watching the young men flocking up for their degrees at the "new Harvard," Henry James had already asked himself: "Swarming ingenuous youths, *whom did they look like the sons of?*" Certainly not like the sons of Harrow, Oxford and Sandhurst, about whom the Jamesian observer in "The Lesson of the Master" had expressed such delight at having the fruit "of one's loins" arrive at that educational eminence.

What was interesting, in the New York passages, was the curious sense of the Jamesian proprietary interest in the now alien-dominated native scene — which he himself had rebelled against and deserted. Wasn't this a case of a Henry James in the manger? And he expressed his distaste clearly for those "inconceivable aliens" who had replaced, who had obliterated even his fondest ghost memories of the past. The "visionary tourist" — and with what visions now! — the "repatriated absentee" indeed — walked the streets of "the terrible town," as he had walked them so much more hopefully, romantically, and visionally in London while he was preparing his "material" for the anarchistic scene of *The Princess Casamassima.* But here in the melting pot of the democracy, even beyond and above "that perpetual passionate pecuniary purpose" which now dominated the American metropolis, he found "the obsession of the alien." "To inquire of these things on the spot, to betray, that is, one's sense of the 'chill' of which I have spoken, is of course to hear it admitted, promptly enough, that there is no claim to brotherhood with aliens in the first grossness of their alienism."

To whom was James talking, then, with this sense of chill, and with these prompt admissions of the great hidden truth of the democracy? (We are never told.) But Henry James at least questioned *himself* on this underlying issue:

If it be asked why, the alien still striking you so as an alien, the singleness of impression, throughout the place, should still be so marked, the answer, close at hand, would seem to be that the alien himself fairly makes the singleness of impression. Is not the universal sauce essentially his sauce, and do we not feel ourselves feeding, half the time, from the ladle, as greasy as he chooses to leave it for us, that he holds out?

This was of course the familiar refrain of the Old Republic about the new democracy; this was the fear and prejudice of Boston and New York about the rising tide of immigration in the nineties and the 1900's. But did James have to reflect it quite so purely, so thoughtlessly, so crudely, *au fond*, for a most sophisticated and civilized, as he prided himself, talent? Now Howells also had come from Boston to New York with much the same sense of indignation about the greasy sauce, the greasy ladle of the new immigrant

types — and shortly thereafter had selected a German socialist, or
even anarchist, for the hero of *A Hazard of New Fortunes*, in 1890,
over fifteen years earlier. The "inconceivable alien," the "ubiqui-
tous alien," as opposed to James's own Fifth Avenue heritage of
the now-shuddering pilgrim, the uneasy and chilled pilgrim: how
these pages of *The American Scene* echo and re-echo with such
phrases and such nightmarish fantasies of prejudice and doom!
Do Messrs. Trilling, Dupee, and Auden (of all people) really want
to be identified with this unhappy aspect of the American literary
mind? Have they read and understood what their master was
saying in this great American document?

For this became a recurrent and almost obsessive theme, in
The American Scene, on the part of this self-alienated orphan
artist, now finding himself twice alienated, as it were, and in his
older age newly orphaned. (But didn't this also, in a sense, *justify*
his own alienation and orphanhood?) On this dubious theme
James invented ever new phrases and tags, such as "the *launched*
foreign personality," while in the "electric cars" of New York he
found nothing else to think of.

*The carful, again and again, is a foreign carful; a row of faces, up and
down, testifying, without exception, to alienism unmistakable, alienism
undisguised and unashamed. You do here, in a manner perhaps, discriminate; the launched condition, as I have called it, is more developed
in some types than in others; but I remember observing how, in the
Broadway and the Bowery conveyances in especial, they tended, almost
alike, to make the observer gasp with the sense of isolation. It was not
for this that the observer on whose behalf I more particularly write had
sought to take up again the sweet sense of the natal air.*

Now, quite typically, James had apparently forgotten his own
earlier descriptions of almost a physical nausea, a sense of suf-
focating isolation as a youth, amidst all that "sweet sense of natal
air" which was then almost purely Nordic and Anglo-Saxon. On
a deeper level he completely ignored his own identification with

the wave of Irish immigrants who had been the earlier scapegoats and villains of the fearful and prejudiced New England mind. Quite logically (for this frightened, insecure, snobbish, and authoritarian temperament, that is) he now substituted the later immigrants as the new scapegoat, demon and villain on his own "native scene." And quite logically he had fled to the *English* nobility (the historical and hereditary masters and oppressors of the Irish) as a sanctuary and refuge (and cover mechanism) for his own "tainted" and inferior social status; to the England which was "superior" even to that Boston Brahmin culture which he then consistently ridiculed and snubbed.

Thus do the weak and haunted spirits of life find their peculiar modes of survival. Thus the vicious cycle of man's "superiority" to man is perpetuated in the highest realms of art and culture. (By contrast, Theodore Dreiser, as the spokesman for the new immigrant strains in American culture, would recognize, accept, identify with and celebrate his own "lowly" and "alien" and outcast social origins.) Meanwhile, in New York's East Side, Henry James's worst fears were confirmed, since these new Americans were not only gross and greasy, but apparently they were almost all Jewish. "There is no swarming like that of Israel when once Israel has got a start, and the scene here bristled, at every step, with the signs and sounds immitigable, unmistakable, of a Jewry that had burst all bounds." He went on to describe this "New Jerusalem" in terms which were even more lurid. He remembered the "dark, foul, stifling Ghettos" of European cities, while the New York whirlpool testified only to a "Jerusalem disinfected," filled everywhere with "insistent, defiant, unhumorous, exotic faces." Unhumorous: and here this portly, well-groomed, constrained, fastidious, supersensitive "Anglo-American" tourist deprived the immigrants of perhaps their greatest single spiritual resource: the Jewish humor itself. Who was being unhumorous now? But face after face in the swarming, alien sectors of the great metropolis were only, to Henry James, unmistakably "low." In one of those extended passages of imagery, so much praised by a later generation of formalist poet-critics, he compared "the Hebrew conquest of New York" — the alien children, the alien parents, the alien old people swarming everywhere in these streets, all for the purposes of "race rather than reason" — to some species of snakes or worms who, "when cut into pieces, wriggle away contentedly and live in the snippet as completely as in the whole."

Admirable and poetic imagery indeed from the leisure-class bard of civilizational nuances. And the Jamesian analogy extended from the subhuman reptiles to the posthuman skeletons and "grinning spectres" of the new racial conquest, this "all-unconscious impudence of the agency of future ravage." And then, reaching backward, as for refuge, into the Victorian myths of his youth, James suddenly called upon the resources of Anglo-Saxon romance to combat this ominous and threatening menace to *his* American scene. "For that honour that sits astride of the consecrated English tradition . . . quite as old knighthood astride of its caparisoned charger, the dragon most rousing, over the land, the proper spirit of St. George, is just this immensity of the alien presence climbing higher and higher, climbing itself into the very light of publicity."

But no modern St. George emerged in answer to Henry James's fervent appeal, unless it was the Germanic Hitler who used a more barbarous mythology, combined with all the skills of scientific-industrial technology, to quell the same alien presence. Yet in these pages of *The American Scene* James was just as ignorant and ridiculous about the new native upper classes as he was prejudiced about and terrified of the immigrants and aliens. What an unbearable and odious social snob he clearly revealed himself as being in these areas of "social analysis"; and maybe his single redeeming trait was, after all, a kind of amiable idiocy — or an idiosyncrasy of vision so remote from the actual facts of the material which it was presumably describing that you can't take it seriously. For it was in a Baltimore *country club*, of all places, that James suddenly found a new democratic vista, a new horizon of hope for the threatened, the menaced, the tarnished and already alien-dominated, the vulgar, gross and ill-fated American republic of his returning visit.

The Country Club was, for the restless analyst, "one of the great garden-lamps in which the flame of Democracy burns whitest and steadiest and most floods the subject; taking its place thus on the positive side of a line which has its other side overscored with negatives." The Country Club, indeed, was "blest," with its "inimitable, invaluable accent of American authority," with its "critical group at the windows," with its "supreme specimen, supreme for a documentary worth, even at Charleston." And it is blest (after some more vague Jamesian rhetoric about the "general theory of its nature and strength," its "unconscious heroism," and "sublime serenity") because, as we may gather, it beautifully resists the strain of "universal eligibility." It is blest because, in a word, everything is staked "on the conception of the young Family as a clear social unit," and this conception of Family "is, goodness knows, 'European' enough." Now the point is that Henry James was absolutely, solemnly, even devoutly serious in such passages, which might otherwise be construed as satire — or farce. And you can make what you will out of it, while you listen to the leading Jacobites all concur on the brilliance of this major American social document straight in the line of Tocqueville. But in the line of Tocqueville — to where? And wasn't this admiring observer of the American Country Club, incidentally, *the* Henry James, I mean, who described its kitchens, courts, baths, gardens, its "wonderful inside and outside palaestra" in such Dreiserian terms of awe — wasn't *he* the most vulgar of materialists when it suited his garden-struck and exclusive fancy?

Still proceeding south, however, in the later sections of *The American Scene*, James then delivered, quite majestically from his own orotund and pontifical presence, his final commentary on the race problem. For he had never before met the "African types" that he now began to encounter, such as the group of "tatter-

demalion darkies" who lounged and sunned themselves at one of
the railroad stations quite within his range. And: "To take in
with any attention two or three of these figures had surely been to
feel one's self introduced at a bound to the formidable question,
which rose suddenly like some beast that had sprung from the
jungle." (And now James repeated his best phrases, such as the
"sacred rage" also, almost indiscriminately in his prose.) For these
African types —

*These were its far outposts; they represented the Southern black as we
knew him not, and had not within the memory of man known him, at
the North; and to see him there, ragged and rudimentary, yet all portentous and "in possession of his rights as a man," was to be not a little
discomposed, was to be in fact very much admonished. One understood
at a glance how he must loom, how he must count, in a community in
which, in spite of the high ground it might cover, there were compara-
tively so few other things. The admonition accordingly remained, and
no further appeal was required, I felt, to disabuse a tactful mind of the
urgency of preaching, southward, a sweet reasonableness about him.*

Thus the "musing moralist" (shades of John Brown) has become the tactful mind, which feels no "urgency" — seeing at a
glance the true nature of the Southern Negro, realizing then the
error of the unfortunately deluded Northern mind; joining perhaps
in its own musing way the beastlike Negro to the low aliens, the
swarming Jews who had taken over *his* country: no indeed,
James felt no urgency to preach southward even a sweet reasonableness about the Negro question. (I translate these Jamesian
passages exactly, perhaps repetitiously, because the high gloss and
delicate sensitivity of his later prose may sometimes obscure the
real meaning — the vulgar and trite prejudices — of his modulated
sentences.) Shades of the whole Abolitionist movement! Perhaps
this was Henry James's most profound betrayal of his democratic
American heritage — since it had been also the deepest social
experience, presumably, of his own youth.

Was it the fact that these "darkies" dared to sun themselves at the railroad terminal "quite within his range," when they should have obviously been rushing around to attend to the travel necessities of the Southern preacher? Or that, ragged, rudimentary, portentous as they were, these looming African types somehow reminded James they were now in possession of their "rights" as men? (Obviously they needed a long period of training at the English court as slaves, playthings, jesters maybe.) In Florida, meditating over the crude service offered him by his waiter, Henry James "could have shed tears" — not for the Negro, but for the old Southern plantation aristocracy, because their servants had been so badly trained. Was it for this, he asked himself, that "they had fought and fallen"? The Negro waiter was surely not worth the Civil War.

Thus all the great moral issues of the mid-nineteenth century American scene were brought down to a purely "domestic" solution. And who fared worse in this incredible Jamesian sociology: the gray, sterile, barren native New Englanders, the swarming and conquering aliens, the apelike post-Civil War African types, or the newly oppressed (and so badly served) Southern whites? It is a question; but meanwhile, too, there was a curious Jamesian postscript to *The American Scene*, in which the young American girl herself of purest Jamesian fantasy was viewed more sharply now "as encountered in the great glare of her publicity, her uncorrected, unrelated state." She too, along with the American buildings, the cities, the pullmans, uttered a private appeal to the omnipotent — or omni-verbal — Jamesian ear:

For since I am, with my preposterous "position," falsely beguiled, pitilessly forsaken, thrust forth in my ignorance and folly, what do I know, helpless chit as I can but be, about manners or tone, about proportion or perspective, about modesty or mystery, about a condition of things that involves, for the interest and grace of life, other forms of existence than this poor little mine — pathetically broken reed as it is, just to find itself waving all alone in the wind? . . . Was there ever such a con-

spiracy, on the part of a whole social order, toward the exposure of incompetence? Were ever crude youth and crude presumption left so unadmonished as to their danger of giving themselves away? . . . Haven't I, however, as it is, been too long abandoned and too much betrayed? Isn't it too late, and am I not, don't you think, practically lost?

A touching, a desperate last little appeal this was on the part of the betrayed young American maiden, which also marked the end of the international theme, and James's own farewell to the heroine around whom he had centered such a large part of his literary cosmos. But was the "exposed maiden" of James's modern American scene really so different from James's earlier version of her? Or had he again simply and belatedly come closer to the *reality* of this young American girl whom his own adolescent and romantic fancy had persisted in keeping so "pure," so innocent, so ethereal. And wasn't this a "reality," as in the similar case of James's imaginary British nobility, which always became for him a species of nightmare when compared with his own innocent and glamorous and purified visions of what such a young girl *should* be?

When you really consider the whole line of those Jamesian heroines, from Daisy Miller to Milly Theale, what have you got? And what other so-called major writer of world fiction had ever developed such a restricted and inhibited line of heroines, and *had kept them like that*, through the exclusion of all sense of feminine experience and reality? Perhaps in turn the Innocent American Maiden had ruined Henry James himself; but meanwhile his "Julia Bride," in 1909 (though published previously in the New York Edition) was just the tale of a new and "modern" maiden; or of her reality as James now perceived it.*

* A year earlier, in 1908, James published *Views and Reviews* with an introduction by Le Roy Phillips, the first compiler of a Jamesian bibliography, who also collected and edited these essays on such Victorian figures as George Eliot, Browning, William Morris and Kipling. *Italian Hours* (1909) was another volume of travel sketches and essays.

Haven't we noticed, moreover, that whenever James described a "mature woman" in his fiction (from Madame Merle to Kate Croy or Charlotte Stant); a woman who knew what she wanted from life, or who had actually lived; a woman who was *not* the innocent young American maiden, but a woman who was a woman — that she was usually a criminal? Julia Bride herself was the portrait of the young maiden who has lived, who is no longer so pure and innocent. This was her dilemma in the story, because, rather like Edith Wharton's Lily Bart in *The House of Mirth,* four years earlier, Julia has had enough "experience" to make her slightly stale.

And that is to say, stale in terms of the "good marriage" which Julia must make; since, revising all his values elsewhere, Henry James still held to this implacable destiny for even his now slightly soiled, socially betrayed and utterly desperate modern heroine. Once again the story described the new epoch of cheap money and cheap sex as the background for the later line of Jamesian parents who are always participating in a sort of marital ring-around-a-rosy. But "The Jolly Corner," in the same year of 1909, was a far better story, even while it was a more highly personal and auto-biographical document. In effect this was another of the Jamesian ghost tales in which one side of Henry James pursued — or was pursued by — another side of Henry James. Could anything be more complete — as a Jamesian id fancy — cozier, or more revealing? And in fact "The Jolly Corner" was a fascinating study of the Imperial Henry James tracking down his own ghost, his alter ego, or himself, in the upper floors of the deserted house which had once contained the "happy memories" of his childhood.

That was the central situation of the ghostly tale, which reverted in part to the psychological terror of "The Turn of the Screw," and of a late tale which has been the subject of much critical speculation and interpretation. The hero is a man of fifty-six who, like the elderly exile of *The Ambassadors,* is too old to "live" any more, and has come back to New York, in this line of later Jamesian heroes, to rehearse his childhood experiences in a series of gossipy talks with a sympathetic confidante. (In this sense, now that the sexual barrier in James's work has been completely leveled by "old age," now when "good talk" is permissible as the *only* sexual link, these elderly, effeminate, gossipy Jamesian protagonists have just begun to live.) Spencer Brydon confides all this to Alice Staverton: that is, his speculations as to the financial titan he might have been if he had remained in America; and while, like the heroine of "The Beast in the Jungle," she reassures him about any possible "selfishness," or even morbidity on his part, he pursues his new obsession. For he still thinks that all things come back "to the question of what he personally might have been, how he might have led his life and 'turned out,' if he had not so, at the outset, given it up —

Not to have followed my perverse young course — and almost in the teeth of my father's curse, as I may say; not to have kept it up so, "over there," from that day to this, without a doubt or a pang; not above all, to have liked it, to have loved it, so much, loved it, no doubt, with such an abysmal conceit of my own preference: some variation from that, I say, must have produced some different effect for my life and for my "form."

There is no doubt as to the personal, autobiographical reference to James's own career in this statement; the lingering consciousness of his own early conflict, choice, and exile. But this spokesman of "The Jolly Corner" is again careful to discriminate the purpose of his late obsession. "If I had waited . . . then I might have been, by staying here, something nearer to one of those types who have been hammered so hard and made so keen by their conditions." This was his reference, one assumes, to the new financial titans and monopolists; but —

It isn't that I admire them so much — the question of any charm in them, or of any charm beyond that of the rank money-passion, exerted by their conditions for them, has nothing to do with the matter: it's

*only a question of what fantastic, yet perfectly possible, development
of my own nature I mayn't have missed. It comes over me that I had
then a strange* alter ego *deep down somewhere within me, as the full-
blown flower is in the small tight bud, and that I just took the course,
I just transferred him to the climate, that blighted him for once and
for ever.*

Thus, it was not a question of James (or his present hero)
preferring America and New York life to the European existence
which he had loved so much, without a doubt or pang. It was
not a question, really, of choosing to have been one of the new
robber barons whom he described so naïvely and in terms of floral
growths. It was simply that he now felt capable of leading *both*
lives; and this greedy ego could not forego any development of his
own nature. In the story the sympathetic Miss Staverton agrees
that this other flowering of the Jamesian temperament was possible,
too. "I feel it would have been quite splendid, quite huge and
monstrous." "Monstrous above all!" the hero echoes complacently,
"and I imagine, by the same stroke, quite hideous and offensive."
Would you like me to have been a billionaire? he asks her; to get
her comforting reassurance, "How should I not have liked you?"
And Spencer Brydon sets out to track down this Jamesian alter ego.

But note how often James himself now used the word "monstrous" himself, and how this insatiable fantasist is increasingly
identified with the beastlike animals who figure in his own imagery
of respectable, confined leisure-class life. Yet the ghostly atmosphere of "The Jolly Corner" is very well done; and high up in the
house of childhood, in a series of connected rooms with the final
room having no other outlet, the Jamesian ghost, tracked down,
at bay, and bristling, makes its stand. "Brydon at this instant
tasted probably of a sensation more complex than had ever before
found itself consistent with sanity." He feels both pride and terror;
pride that this other mask of himself is worthy of *him*; and terror
indeed while, "softly panting, he felt his eyes almost leave their
sockets." Those eyes — which have figured so largely throughout

the voyeuristic pattern of James's work; and those high connecting "upper rooms" of the James family's house, which could very logically be the bedrooms about which a whole series of Jamesian "observers" have made their nocturnal tours.

Now what was *in* the locked room of the Jamesian unconscious? The conventional sociological interpretation, first expounded by Matthiessen, is simply that James was writing a parable of what might have happened to his own character if he had stayed in the United States. For, desperately fleeing back down the long stairway, this once omnipotent ghost-tracker is not spared a final glimpse of a monstrous, alien countenance, not his own; but a hideous ghost whose ethereal hand is marked by mutilated fingers. The alter ego of the Jamesian billionaire has been corrupted and disfigured; he is a stranger.

The conventional Freudian interpretation of the story, however, as perhaps best expounded by Clifton Fadiman, explicitly following, as this critic acknowledged, "Dr. Saul Rosenzweig's remarkable monograph, 'The Ghost of Henry James: A Study in Thematic Apperception,'" is on a much more personal level. It is based on Henry's mysterious wound or "obscure hurt" at the time of the Civil War, which prevented him "from joining in the masculine activity of making war," in Mr. Fadiman's words, and which also (probably) prevented him "from experiencing normal sex relations." Thus the early injury of James's is represented in the symbolically castrated fingers of the ghostly alter ego, and it symbolized a certain death in James, according to Mr. Fadiman, "the death of passion," while "The withdrawal to Europe, the most important outward event of his long life was another symbol of the retreat from the American experience that, in a sense, had been too much for him."

And, continuing with this theory of thematic apperception, these early wounds and repressions of Henry James's rose up to consciousness in later life (this is perhaps a Jungian touch) and his last visit to the United States was a compulsive act to relive this ancient trauma. (The orthodox Freudian repetition-compulsion.) "As Dr. Rosenzweig so persuasively puts it," added Mr. Fadiman glowingly, the visit " 'was largely actuated by an impulse to repair, if possible, the injury and to complete the unfinished experience of his youth.' " James wrote the story all unconsciously, we are told finally, and quite correctly; but it is obvious "that James's ghosts anticipate and dramatize many of the findings of psychoanalysis."

Here again, James is being hailed as the (unconscious) father of the Freudian thought which all of our findings tend utterly to disprove. He was indeed the sublime example of classical face-saving rationalization which completely avoided the least vestige of the Freudian truths. During the course of these speculations (in Mr. Fadiman's *Short Stories of Henry James*), we are also told that "The Jolly Corner" is one of the most difficult of James's last stories:

Composed in his famous final manner, it serves as a fair example of the complexity of his mind, a complexity that forced him (as with Joyce and other innovators) virtually to invent a style.

Well, we have noticed that later Jamesian style whose "complexity" was often invented to cover a virtual absence of content. And this large statement represents an entire range of false, fatuous and grandiose claims which are recurrently made about James's work. His mind, as should be clear at this point of our study, was not so much "complex" as very often incredibly naïve. Once you have established the Jamesian hierarchy of values (strange as they are in any realistic appraisal of life), this famous mind becomes indeed almost conventional or trite — certainly clever or ingenious rather than profound. In one sense we can state categorically that Henry James *never had an idea*.

Mr. Fadiman has again joined the bewitched, bemused and Circe-ish circle of Jacobite commentators, at the loss, momentarily, one hopes, of his own normal intelligence. For there was no "death of passion" in James's life or career, simply because he had never reached the point of passion. His whole view of sex and love was on the oral, infantile, pre-oedipal and pre-sexual level. His own attitude is consistently that of the pubescent (at best) voyeur, "spying out" the hidden, mysterious, and ultimately sinful, area of "adult intimacy."

There was no "second death" in Henry James's withdrawal to Europe, simply because it was America which was always "death" to James. It was Europe which was, from his earliest literary fantasies of fame and the "good life," right down to the repeated affirmation of this theme by the divided hero in "The Jolly Corner" itself — it was Europe which was life, life, life to James. He could not possibly have returned to America to work out, to resolve these earlier traumas, because it is obvious throughout his career and his work that these traumas were buried deeply under layer upon layer of sublime rationalization. In his own life he possibly never even understood that there was a trauma — and in his work, as we have now seen, every issue of depth psychology was always resolved by a sentimental, romantic kind of "psycho-morality" — that is, when James was consciously aware of these issues at all. No, James returned to America simply to *confirm*, to expand, to applaud and to celebrate the whole purpose of his own European pilgrimage — as *The American Scene* shows without question; as the end of "The Jolly Corner" also proclaims. The only trouble with the Rosenzweig-Fadiman thesis is that, while fitting James into the conventional Freudian categories, it shows no knowledge of James's real motivation or temperament.

What was behind the locked door in the empty room of the Jamesian temperament — the room to which the omnipotent searcher of "The Jolly Corner" had pursued his psychological prey — was *the Jamesian unconscious.* (One should remember the early, recurrent dream of the young James during which he is chased down the long, empty corridors of an art museum by the hideous specter of his anxiety — only to turn upon, and to *defeat* this ogre by the sheer force of his will to power and to fame.) What lurked at bay in this empty, locked room was simply perhaps the real author of *The Sacred Fount*; or the artist who set down the curious oedipal-incestuous central situation in *The Golden Bowl* — and then refused to see it; or the writer-creator of a whole long series of neurotic, morbid, even hysterical "narrator-observers" in the Jamesian fiction who still persisted in denying the true nature of his own primary literary spokesmen. "Do you believe then — too dreadfully! — that I *am* as good as I might ever have been?" asks Spencer Brydon of "The Jolly Corner" in all the false modesty which covers his persistent, dominant concern with himself alone. But this monster egotist is still too clever, too self-protective, ever to stir — to *really* question — those hidden psychological depths lying deep down — not far up — within him.

The manner of this hero's "escape" from the repressed part of his own temperament is also interesting. For he surrenders abjectly. He is devoured by the necessity to "see" this hidden "monster" — to discover that in which "all the hunger of his prime need might have been met, his high curiosity crowned, his unrest assuaged." But he grasps at the idea of a saving, an inexorable and vital "discretion":

Discretion — he jumped at that; and yet not, verily at such a pitch, because it saved his nerves or his skin, but because, much more valuably, it saved the situation. When I say he "jumped" at it I feel the consonance of this term with the fact that — at the end indeed of I know not how long — he did move again, he crossed straight to the door. He wouldn't touch it — it seemed now that he might if he would: he would only just wait there a little, to show, to prove, that he wouldn't. He had thus another station, close to the thin partition by which revelation was denied to him; but with his eyes bent and his hands held off in a mere intensity of stillness. He listened as if there had been something to hear, but this attitude while it lasted, was his own communication. "If you won't then — good: I spare you and I give up. You affect

*me as by the appeal positively to pity: you convince me that for reasons
rigid and sublime — what do I know? — we both of us should have
suffered. I respect them then, and, though moved and privileged as,
I believe, it has never been given to man, I retire, I renounce — never,
on my honour, to try again. So rest for ever — and let me!"*

But wasn't this saving "discretion" the complete key to the
Jamesian fiction throughout his long career: the discretion of a
gentleman, say, though not of a major artist? What a fascinating
passage this was indeed: since it was also the perfect self-projection
of the Jamesian temperament and achievement alike. Wasn't the
"saving of the situation" a key theme in James's work — the saving
of "face," too, as in *The Golden Bowl*, by pretending in all one's
respectable middle class American virtue that the situation, which
was there, did not exist? (Not to mention the *other*, deeper
situation, also so consistently there in the novel, and just as consistently denied by James, and described as filial or parental love.)
Hovering by the closed door of the Jamesian unconscious, this
hero — like so many other Jamesian figures back to the sensitive
young Anglo-American observer in *The Portrait of a Lady* —
"wouldn't touch it," though he might if he would! This hero, in
the typically Jamesian vein, simply "waits," he listens, he "watches,"
though now with his eyes bent, and his hands held off, for the
"revelation" which is there, and which is denied to him. He re-
tires; he "renounces" — in the best Jamesian resolution of all
the great problems and issues of life; I mean of living. And still
he reasserts his own authority, his own ego, his own terrified but
deeply covered, protected, and impenetrable self-image, by feeling
that "appeal positively to pity." He is both moved and privileged,
by what he has *not* seen, as no man before him. "I spare you and
I give up." What a happy, face-saving and ego-saving solution;
which still leaves the weight of the decision not upon the menacing
Jamesian unconscious, but upon *him!* What then of "those reasons" — rigid indeed, if not possibly or entirely "sublime" — by

which both halves of the divided Jamesian temperament might have suffered if they had become clear? "So rest for ever — and let *me!*"

Again the final accent was on the Jamesian "I," the "Omnipotent Me," who has come to the edge of his own darkness, and then has retreated frantically, even hysterically — but still with "dignity," and with immutable "self-possession." The hero of "The Jolly Corner" does think fleetingly of suicide, by escaping from his demon through the upper-floor window *without* a ladder. He yearns for "some comforting common fact, some vulgar human note, the passage of a scavenger or a thief, some night-bird however base." And why are these symbolic associations of dirt, crime and baseness linked so directly here with the "vulgar human note"? Did the Jamesian snobbery penetrate so deeply even into these unconscious areas of his temperament? Or was this the *true* imagery of his buried self? Retreating down the long stairway of his childhood, of his family's empty and haunted house, this hero also is forced to catch at least a fleeting glimpse (which is exactly what one does catch in James's best work) of "the monster with the mutilated fingers" — or of, shall we say, the inhibited Jamesian "id." He faints and falls upon the floor. "They were cold, these marble squares of his youth" — and where indeed is the "Jolly Corner" of James's younger American experience?

Yet even this brilliant self-portrait, perhaps the best and most accurate description of James's whole body of literary work — as compared with the apologetic, the evasive, the self-glorifying "Prefaces" — was muffled again by the "false" (that is to say, the *conscious*) ending of the story. The hidden self of the Jamesian hero is indeed "monstrous." It is "evil, odious, blatant, vulgar" — James's worst terms of abuse. But it is surely, this hero thinks, the "face of a stranger" — as indeed it was in James's work. And though the gentle, good, tactful Alice Staverton accepts the possible explanation that it *might have been* this hero's personality, if he had remained in America; and she accepts the maimed specter also because it is his, Spencer Brydon's — she comforts him with "the cool charity and virtue of her lips." That "charity and virtue," in truth, which is also a synonym, in James's work, for "discretion" or "pity" or "waiting" or "watching" or "retiring" or "renouncing" — for all these barely concealed modes of nonrecognition, evasion, and flight as the "resolution" for the fleeting depth insights which appear indeed so hideous and so horrid to this neurotic and repressed late-Victorian artist who then rationalized and even glorified the obvious process of his literary sublimation.

Yet "Julia Bride" and "The Jolly Corner" were interesting stories in what they suggested and what they revealed. Although the resolution of the first tale was snobbish and vulgar, and that of the second was fearful and sentimental, they formed the prelude to James's last collection of short stories, *The Finer Grain*, in 1910, which contained also a few more chronicles of personal import or literary value.

"A Round of Visits," according to Morton Dauwen Zabel in *The Viking Portable Henry James*, reverts to the international theme; and it derived, like its two companion stories, "The Jolly Corner" and "Crapy Cornelia," "from James's momentous return to America in 1904, after an absence of twenty-one years." There we go again: for what was "momentous" about James's return to America, except that it led to the exotic, the bizarre, the ludicrous *American Scene* ("one of the great American documents") and to this last group of very mixed stories indeed. But such words as "momentous," not to mention James's own "portentous," are typical of the Jacobite addicts who, as it were, stimulate each other — even the usually judicious, although sometimes, yes, portentous M. D. Zabel — to higher and higher flights of lyrical (rather than critical) passages.

"A Round of Visits" was in fact another Jamesian romance melodrama on the "sensibility" of high finance. It was based squarely upon an innocent, a sentimental, a fairy-tale vision of the new age of finance capitalism; just as it was still concerned with the old-fashioned and "aristocratic" theme of one's *investments* — and just as it ended upon a dubious theatrical climax of a guilty embezzler shooting himself heroically just when the police are entering his apartment. A much lighter tale in *The Finer Grain*, "Crapy Cornelia," was a better story; although here again was the late-late Jamesian concept — notion? — of "old money" (inherited from *personal* real estate, perhaps) versus gross, vulgar, evil and ignorant "new money." Again, it was the sensibility, manners and cultivation of Old New York money which Henry James stressed; it was the blatant "bad taste" of the new American fortunes that he condemned — rather than the amoral ethics of their acquisition or the unjust and corrupt social consequences of these fortunes upon the whole texture of democratic society: the profound social change indeed of the older democracy into a modern oligarchy and empire around the turn of the century. But didn't Henry James admit this via the hero of "Crapy Cornelia" himself, to whom "the angular facts of current finance were as harsh and metallic and bewildering as some stacked 'exhibit' of ugly patented inventions, things his mediaeval mind forbade his taking in"?

Medieval mind, forsooth; while the two ancient personages of this story settle down happily with their mutual concern for each other's "beautiful old things" (antiques, I mean) and refuse to have any more "adventures." The story was another comedy, of course; James was not completely serious here. But there was no doubt as to the bliss of the narrative's White-Mason when he was confronted only by the endless sessions of Old New York gossip with Cornelia Rasch herself — without the constraints of a possible marriage, love, or of any other disturbing physical emotion. "Old age," beginning around forty-eight, was a relief and a blessing for the later Jamesian spokesmen, since now they can consider themselves as "high game" — as too old for all those other dangerous adventures or experiences in life from which White-Mason himself has escaped so successfully and so personally "right."

Old age, like old money and old real estate, was the later Jamesian solace and salvation — a sanctuary from life, now not only permissible but praiseworthy. For now his heroes can pursue, with no further qualms or conflicts, such Jamesian comforts, pleasures and delights as their collections of fine old pieces (still English, of course), and the gossipy conversation which was always a central feature and perhaps the highest achievement of leisure-class fiction. But if one notes this refrain in the other tales in *The Finer Grain*, what can be said about the central story called "The Bench of Desolation"?

Much *has* been said about this story, of course. It was among the last of the "blest nouvelles" — "that small reflector," as R. P. Blackmur said in one of his less rhetorical statements, "capable of illuminating or mirroring a great deal of material" — which James himself had developed as an almost necessary discipline for his natural capacity to "enlarge." (And Mr. Blackmur quickly atoned for his factuality: "To the artist who practised in it the difficulties of its economy were a constant seduction and an exalted delight.") "The Bench of Desolation" was included in M. D. Zabel's *Portable Henry James,* this editor told us, "not only because I consider it another masterpiece" — surely reason enough — but because "I agree with Edmund Wilson that it is 'one of the most beautifully written and wonderfully developed short pieces in the whole range of James's work.' " And here even the broader and usually more accurate critic, Edmund Wilson himself, succumbed to the Jacobite mania for finding more and more "masterpieces" among the lesser works of James.

"It deals, moreover, not with the life of social privilege and civilized existences usually thought to be his special province," added Editor Zabel, "but with the seamy world of poverty and hardship in which he is commonly considered inexpert but which — witness also *The Princess Casamassima* and 'In the Cage' — he was sometimes able to treat with extraordinary insight and compassion." Well, we have considered "In the Cage," whose young telegraphic heroine was so charmed to be able to assist in one of those noble love affairs so far outside her own narrow range — to get this vicarious glimpse of "real life." And Mr. Zabel forgot to mention "Brooksmith," in which that ineffable butler just pined away — went to pot — because he could no longer be present in the charmed circle of the higher conversation at tea or dinner. From *The Princess Casamassima* to *The Wings of the Dove*, we have also "witnessed," in Mr. Zabel's phrase, the Jamesian formula of the "little gent" of obscure social origins whose life is ennobled and whose whole character is elevated by even a fleeting contact with true nobility or the upper classes — so that the first of these heroes committed suicide rather than associate with his anarchist friends, and the second refused both a gratuitous fortune and the woman he craved, for the sake of an enchanted memory. (Not to mention Fleda Vetch of *The Spoils of Poynton*.)

"The Bench of Desolation" simply repeated this formula in a lighter vein, more ironically, and also more artificially. Where is all that extraordinary Jamesian insight and compassion about the seamy world of poverty and hardship? Herbert Dodd has been blackmailed by Kate Cookham on the threat of a "breach of promise" suit which he never has the courage to fight in the law courts, and which his "gentlemanly code" of behavior, his consuming fear of publicity and "vulgarity," prevent him from opposing. Thus his later marriage, his home and children, his rare-book shop, his whole life, in short, is eaten up by the need for this perpetual blackmail money which he is forced to disgorge to the relentless, terrible Kate Cookham. The accent of suffering is real in "The Bench of Desolation." This was the last Jamesian tale of the "wasted life" — and it is wasted precisely because the hero is too noble, in his own mind, to endure the vulgarity of life itself, or even to test it. Kate Cookham (and she did!) has no real case against the little Herbert Dodd; but his scruples have prevented him from finding this out, even while his lifelong misery is haunted by the suspicion that he should have found out.

The plot of the story is thus highly unlikely to begin with: that of mute, silent suffering under a dubious legal claim which is never contested. And throughout most of "The Bench of Desolation," the portrait of Herbert Dodd is highly ironical. He is the typical British "gentleman's gentleman" — he is or should be a valet rather than a book dealer. He is Brooksmith's inferior, never even glimpsing the nobility of the dinner table, and condemned to an even more ignominious existence of penury and misery through a benighted code of "chivalry" which simply masks his own weakness. And he almost knows this. Was this curious story another parable of James's own sense of personal failure; of the lurking suspicion that *his* outsider's view of the British royalty (as in *The Sacred Fount*) had also condemned him to a false code of manners and view of the world? — a spurious life of art in fact, simply because it was based on the false premise of being a "gentleman."

That is what "The Bench of Desolation" suggests, on the unconscious level and even almost overtly. And *if* this were true both Wilson and Zabel would be correct in hailing this story as a forgotten masterpiece. But the whole point of the story's ending is that Herbert Dodd is finally "rewarded" for his poor, pathetic mockery of a gentleman's behavior. Kate Cookham has become a true lady on her ill-gotten gains; she returns his pathetic fortune fivefold; and on top of this she offers him both herself and her glamorous new "social position." After punishing her with something of the same outraged gentlemanly dignity which Merton Densher used on the evil Kate Croy — and after pocketing the money which Kate returns to him — Herbert Dodd finally accepts this mysterious if fortunate conclusion to his blighted existence. His mysterious fate indeed! Since here again, as in all of James's work, if the artist had almost succeeded in breaking through (or seeing through) his own binding and strangling code of values, he had quickly — Henry James himself, I mean — imposed an altogether inadequate "happy ending," a fairy-tale conclusion, on what might have been an ironic and penetrating parable of lower middle class "respectability." This was the real Jamesian formula of fiction: to allow us a glimpse at the face of truth, and to cover it over hastily with artifice.

Thus, while "The Bench of Desolation" is highly improbable as a whole, the story's resolution is altogether impossible. Is that what Edmund Wilson means by one of the most "beautifully written and wonderfully developed short pieces in the whole range of James's work"? The Jamesian hero here is even more of an impossible prig in his new wealth and social "position" than he was in not standing up to Kate Cookham's contrived blackmail at the story's opening. Is the writing, or the structure, of fiction to be so completely divorced from all content or credibility? And perhaps, after all, it was simply the "lower class" scene of this tale which allowed James to view his own gentlemanly code so ironically — since Herbert Dodd naturally could never *be* a gentleman; and maybe it was this same noble little aspirant to breeding and "culture" who had to be rewarded in this fairy-tale way even for *trying* to ape his superiors. Whatever unconscious bearing "The Bench of Desolation" had on a certain part of the Jamesian temperament, had to be muffled and bound around tightly by the gentlemanly code itself — had to be repressed back into the silent and now almost forbidden depths of the artist's psyche.

That was a disfigured countenance indeed which the Jamesian ego had so briefly glimpsed in "The Jolly Corner," the real face of the Jamesian unconscious which the writer had covered with his mutilated (or inhibited) fingers. James's final work in this period, *The Outcry* (1911), was a sensationally bad novel, another lurid romance based on the "social problem" of England's great paintings being sold off secretly to the collections of the culture-hungry American financiers. But this time it was a popular melodrama so badly written, so ludicrously conceived, so poorly developed, that it is almost impossible to take it at all seriously.

Was it a play first, which James developed into the novel; or a novel again written with the barely hidden aim of a play to be pro-

duced from it? It hardly matters. Except that if you want to see
the true model of the Jamesian fiction clear — the hidden workings
which are also. buried in such major novels as *The Wings of the
Dove* or *The Golden Bowl* — the real motor which propelled all
that elaboráte and rarefied, esoteric, exotic and super-subtle "art
of fiction" — then *The Outcry* does have a certain scholarly interest. For the Jamesian tone of "high society" was even more highly
accentuated here. The "modern world," even in England herself,
was based on gambling, blackmail and promiscuous, shifting sexuality. The language of the British gentry became still more for-
malized and stilted.

In point of fact *The Outcry* was a potboiler of the lowest quality.
(And here was James plain, working out his "dramatic method" at
the popular level, and hence really exposing what we have seen to
be the hidden core of his best fiction.) Yet in the *Notebooks*,
Henry James still praised this work for "the manner of my late so
absorbing and endearing plunge into the whole process of *The Outcry*" — for its revelation of the new use of "action" in his fiction
which now took precedence over *everything* else. He could add that
"the process of *The Outcry* has been of enormous benefit and interest to me in all this connection — it has cast so large and rich and
vivid a light upon my path: the august light, I mean, of the whole
matter of method." And these were august words too, in the Jamesian cult of art, which were being applied to perhaps the single worst
book of Henry James's whole career.

Do I exaggerate? I mean as to the real quality of *The Outcry?*
Well, as the English professors of an earlier, less esthetic, less scientific, less methodological day used to say: Let us take any three
pages at random of the popular play-novel (which ran into four
editions, and hence perhaps somewhat confused James's own judgment of the work). Let's take one page from each of the "Three
Books" — the barely concealed three acts — of James's "absorbing
and endearing plunge" into the action, process and method of *The
Outcry*. Such as, from Book First:

THE OUTCRY

"I doubt if you can any more stay Mr. Bender's hand than you can empty his purse."

"Ah, the Despoilers!" said Crimble with strong expression. "But it's *we*," he added, "who are base."

" 'Base'?" — and Lord John's surprise was apparently genuine.

"To want only to 'do business,' I mean, with our treasures, with our glories."

Hugh's words exhaled such a sense of peril as to draw at once Lady Grace. "Ah, but if we're above that *here*, as you know —— !"

He stood smilingly corrected and contrite. "Of course I know — but you must forgive me if I have it on the brain. And show me first of all, won't you? the Moretto of Brescia."

"You know then about the Moretto of Brescia?"

"Why, didn't you tell me yourself?" It went on between them for the moment quite as if there had been no Lord John.

"Probably, yes," she recalled; "so how I must have swaggered!" After which she turned to the other visitor with a kindness strained clear of urgency. "Will you also come?"

He confessed to a difficulty — which his whole face begged her also to take account of. "I hoped you'd be at leisure — for something I've so at heart!"

This had its effect; she took a rapid decision and

51

Or, from Book Second:

THE OUTCRY

"The precious picture Lord Theign exposes?" —
she took his presumed sense faster than he had taken
hers. But she hung fire a moment with her reply to
it. "Well, will you keep the secret of everything I've
said or say?"

"To the death, to the stake, Lady Sandgate!"

"Then," she momentously returned, "I only want,
too, to make Bender impossible. If you ask me," she
pursued, "how I arrange that with my deep loyalty
to Lord Theign ——"

"I don't ask you anything of the sort," he interrupted — "I wouldn't ask you for the world; and my
own bright plan for achieving the *coup* you mention ——"

"You'll have time, at the most," she said, consulting
afresh her bracelet watch, "to explain to Lady Grace."
She reached an electric bell, which she touched — facing then her visitor again with an abrupt and slightly
embarrassed change of tone. "You do think *my* great
portrait splendid?"

He had strayed far from it and all too languidly
came back. "Your Lawrence there? As I said,
magnificent."

But the butler had come in, interrupting, straight
from the lobby; of whom she made her request. "Let
her ladyship know — Mr. Crimble."

Gotch looked hard at Hugh and the crumpled hat

124

Or, from Book Third:

THE OUTCRY

"Ah, we *can* at least go on talking!" she perversely sighed. "I can say anything I like so long as I don't say it to *him!*" she almost wailed. But she added with more firmness: "I can still hope — and I can still pray."

He set free again with a joyous gesture all his confidence. "Well, what more *could* you do, anyhow? So isn't that enough?"

It took her a moment to say, and even then she didn't. "Is it enough for *you,* Mr. Crimble?"

"What *is* enough for me" — he could for his part readily name it — "is the harm done you at our last meeting by my irruption; so that if you got his consent to see me —— !"

"I didn't get his consent!" — she had turned away from the searching eyes, but she faced them again to rectify: "I see you against his express command."

"Ah then thank God I came!" — it was like a bland breath on a *feu de joie:* he flamed so much higher.

"Thank God you've come, yes — for my deplorable exposure." And to justify her name for it before he could protest, "I *offered* him here not to see you," she rigorously explained.

" 'Offered' him?" — Hugh did drop for it. "Not to see me — ever again?"

She didn't falter. "Never again."

200

And so on, for 261 pages of this "rapid and precipitated Action" of *The Outcry* (in James's words), or the lurid "difficulties and dangers" of the Great English Painting Collectors, until we reach the "happy issue" of the novel, as to wit:

THE OUTCRY

They had fallen apart on the irruption, the pair discovered, but she flashed straight at her lover: "Then we can swagger now!"

Lord Theign had reached the open door. "I meet him below."

Demurring, debating, however, she stayed him a moment. "But oughtn't *I* — in my own house?"

His lordship caught her meaning. "You mean he may think — ?" But he as easily pronounced. "He shall think the Truth!" And with a kiss of his hand to her he was gone.

Lord John, who had gazed in some wonder at these demonstrations, was quickly about to follow, but she checked him with an authority she had never before used and which was clearly the next moment to prove irresistible. "Lord John, be so good as to stop." Looking about at the condition of a room on the point of receiving so august a character, she observed on the floor the fragments of the torn cheque, to which she sharply pointed. "And please pick up that litter!"

THE END.

And yet I suppose this Jamesian work, too, will be praised in those American colleges or universities where *The Complete Plays of Henry James,* edited by Mr. Leon Edel, is currently enjoying *its* revival, for reasons which have, I confess, altogether escaped the cognizance of the present historian of the Jacobite movement in the national letters.

The Prewar Years

12. Self-Revelation of James by James

"THE OUTCRY" was the last of the "popular" plays and play-novels whose dramatic method and "Action" so enthralled Henry James that he paid little attention to the literary content, or considered that content "good enough" to please the popular audience of his own day. But James was also on the edge of his last important work, the *Memoirs*, and of two more late novels.

A *Small Boy and Others*, in 1911, was the first volume of Memoirs, and it had an equivocal and interesting background. "I sit heavily stricken and in darkness," James wrote to a friend in the summer of 1910, when he was sixty-seven. (I am quoting from F. W. Dupee's introduction to the Criterion Books edition of the three autobiographical volumes.)

William James was dead; and William James, as he told his correspondent, had been his "ideal Elder Brother." In the course of a recent visit to Europe with his wife, William James had been taken suddenly ill. Accompanied by Henry James, long resident in England, the couple had hastened back to their summer house in the New Hampshire mountains, and there the brilliant philosopher and notable man had died. "His extinction changes the face of life for me," Henry added in the same letter. It also started him on the writing of his autobiography.

But just as James had resolved the early loss of his beloved cousin, Minny Temple, by the final consolation that perhaps *her* death had helped to liberate his own literary powers, so now it was not impossible that his brother William's was partly responsible for one more last burst of Henry's almost demonic creativity, on the edge of his seventies.

At least these Memoirs, which Dupee called *autobiography*, began "as a small work on a limited subject and then expanded into a lengthy one on a rather different and much more intricate subject." The Jamesian expansion was familiar; but what was the difference between the "limited subject" and the much more intricate one? "At Mrs. William James's suggestion," Dupee tells us, "he first determined to publish a selection from his brother's early letters together with a brief memoir of him. What he finally produced was an extended account of his own early development . . ." Well, naturally. Wasn't this the perfect ending to the sibling rivalry which had so obviously existed, if all apparently unconsciously, between these two talented brothers? Wasn't it the final triumph of the Jamesian ego (Henry's, I mean) in which the "limited subject" (William) becomes the more intricate subject (Henry); in which indeed William disappears completely from the first volume of the Memoirs, and then appears engagingly (if limitedly) in the second — since *after* Henry had established his own superiority, and was again in control of the whole literary cosmos of these semi-autobiographical volumes, he could well afford to be generous about the more limited subject of William?

Yet Mr. Dupee goes on solemnly to justify Henry's elimination of William, now extinct indeed. *"Justifying Henry"* — that was the grand purpose of the Jacobite movement in our letters, as well as the great game of our literary criticism during the last two decades — but a game which led otherwise sober practitioners of the literary craft to unforeseen extremes. Dupee quotes Theodora Bosanquet, James's secretary at the time, in her *Henry James at Work:* "By way of documentation, Miss Bosanquet remembered, James had only a bundle of family letters. 'No preliminary work was needed. A straight dive into the past brought to the surface treasure after treasure.' " And now even the *process* of writing it-self, usually so painful, laborious and conflicted, has succumbed to the romantic fairy-tale element in the Jamesian fiction, and the fairy-tale imagery. "Strolling around the room and dictating rapidly," so added Critic Dupee about these Memoirs, "while Miss Bosanquet took down his sentences on the typewriter, he appealed very largely to memory. In this way the book assumed an auto-biographical form and by degrees it prolonged itself."

It is good to know the Jamesian method of constructing "an autobiographical form," which in turn described "the growth of a mind from a state of relative moral servitude to the state of relative moral freedom" — the subject of these three volumes, according to Dupee, and of "much of his fiction." This was again the high moral approach to James's work, as typified by the ecstatic Mr. Blackmur also — but since when have we applied such terms as "servitude" to the development of the mind itself? Well, since Henry James, naturally; the artist who perhaps even described the human psyche in such terms of upper class and lower class intel-lects, or of intellectual masters and servants. And who or what imposed this proclaimed "moral servitude" upon the young hero of the Dupeean *autobiography*? *A Small Boy and Others* described the Albany and New York cousinship — "the blest group of us . . . and withal so fused and united and interlocked." But fused, united and interlocked, that is to say, *without* the family of the eccentric, rebellious, or even outcast Henry James Senior, and wist-fully gaped at by the small Henry James Junior. There is very little about Henry's own parents in *A Small Boy*. Along with William, they had to wait their turn while the biographer described the more worldly, glamorous (and even richer?) Jamesian cousins, uncles and aunts. The note of exile and orphanhood was struck early here, both in family and in personal terms — an orphanhood which held in itself something curiously exotic and *comforting* to the soli-tary child-hero whose existence was mainly that of "wondering and dawdling and gaping." Henry was about eight years old when the volume opened, yet the late-late James was positive about his early hero's state of mind. "Wonderful altogether in fact, I find, as I write, the quantity, the intensity of picture recoverable from even the blankest and tenderest state of the little canvas."

"We were for considerable periods, during our earliest time, nothing less than hotel-children" — and upon these American exiles and outcasts (or upon the young Henry in particular), there was pressed home " 'that sense of Europe' to which I feel that my very earliest consciousness waked." This early "perversity," or what James elsewhere called the "poison" of a legendary enchantment, was to become a central theme in the *autobiography*; but while the terms were accurate, what did James mean by them?

Well, for one thing, among all the charmed cousinships of the child Henry, there was a corresponding lack of any other interests — except, as James said, to go bad or to go to Paris. "The bright and empty air was void of 'careers' for a choice as of cathedral towers for a sketcher, and I passed my younger time, till within a year or two of the Civil War, with an absolute vagueness of impression as to how the political life of the country was carried on. The field was strictly covered, to my young eyes, I make out, by three classes, the busy, the tipsy, and Daniel Webster." Was this typical of the ruling merchant class of old New York, as Edith Wharton described it also, which had no interests beyond that of its own financial horizon? Was it even more typical of the descendants of this class who knew just enough to repudiate their own mercantile origins while finding no alternatives in life beyond those of wealth, travel and pleasure? Yet certainly this Jamesian observation could not have been true of his father (who appears later on as a follower and admirer of John Brown), just as it was not to be true of his brother William.

It is obvious, in short, that this view of empty careers in the American vista (also lacking its cathedral towers); that this description of American political life as being divided between the busy and the tipsy represented even more clearly Henry's values than it did those of his Albany-New York cousinships — among whom, too, he was drawn much more directly to the women rather than the men. But "history" was a different matter to the young hero of the Memoirs; that is to say, European and particularly French history. After the absolute void on the brink of the Civil War as to the parties, the movements, the issues, the gathering clouds of impending conflict (in one of the most intense, dramatic and colorful periods of the nation), there is suddenly "the admired appearance of my uncles 'Gus' and John James to announce to my father

that the Revolution had triumphed in Paris and Louis Philippe had fled to England. These last words, the flight of the king, linger on my ear at this hour even as they fell there; we had somehow waked early to a perception of Paris, and a vibration of my very most infantine sensibility under its sky had by the same stroke got itself preserved for subsequent wondering reference . . .

But who again was that "we" — except, naturally the royal Jamesian We, imperial and absolute — who had so early become immersed in these tragic and noble legends of foreign kings, while at the same time being so indifferent to the native and democratic (middle class, mercenary, vulgar) struggle over the slavery question? "I at any rate revert to the sound of the rich words on my uncles' lips," so James added here, "as to my positive initiation into History." An initiation which fairly impelled, and was consistent with, the later Jamesian notion of History as being solely a matter of rich, romantic legend; and in the course of which French history in particular was to be almost purely that of glossy "pictures." What a marvelous childlike fantasy there is, in these pages of *A Small Boy*, as to the whole great world of art and literature and the stage, so European and foreign in essence, and so directly opposed, so infinitely superior to the ordinary world of business, politics, or "real history" in the drab chronicle of the earliest American scene à la Henry James. The world of books figures here largely too; just as it was naturally the world of *English* books which took precedence over the narrow orbit of the American ones. But then: "All our books in that age were English, at least all our down-town ones —

I personally recall scarce any that were not; and I take the perception of that quality in them to have associated itself with more fond dreams and glimmering pictures than any other principle of growth. It was all a result of the deeply infected state: I had been prematurely poisoned — as I shall presently explain.

Now perhaps *I* should explain here (as compared with the Jamesian *I*) that at this point the Memoirs have already centered around the development of Henry's consciousness as their central theme. Even the Broadway Bookstore was "overwhelmingly and irresistibly English," was "tonically English." But what an odd "principle of growth" this was. "That I should have been so inquiring while still so destitute of primary data was doubtless rather an anomaly," James added — though wasn't *this* the primary principle of the Jamesian consciousness throughout his whole career? "And it was for that matter quite as if my infant divination proceeded by the light of nature: I divined that it would matter to me in the future that 'English life' should be of this or that fashion." And what an odd "light of nature."

James was aware that this early dream of Europe, of England, was in part the "daydream of infant ignorance"; but the texture and tone of *A Small Boy* take on all their eloquence and fervor here; while there were yet more remarkable passages to come on the infantine yearning for Europe and England:

This represented, no doubt, a failure to read into matters close at hand all the interest they were capable of yielding; but I had taken the twist, had sipped the poison, as I say, and was to feel it to that end the most salutary cup. I saw my parents homesick, as I conceived, for the ancient order and distressed and inconvenienced by many of the more immediate features of the modern, as the modern pressed upon us, and since their theory of our better living was from an early time that we should renew the quest of the ancient on the very first possibility I simply grew greater in the faith that somehow to manage that would constitute success in life. I never found myself deterred from this fond view, which was implied in every question I asked, every answer I got, and every plan I formed.

Remarkable, yes. And the older James, looking back at this possessed infant, could only add that "if success in life may perhaps be best defined as the performance in age of some intention arrested in youth I may frankly put in a claim to it." And here James himself, setting the key for his later critics, biographers and editors, was misrepresenting his immediate family as "homesick" for "the ancient order," as so distressed by the merely modern, so intent on renewing the quest for "better living." "As I conceive," added the late James; but this was certainly far from what Henry James Senior or William James had ever conceived about their own European experiences. Wasn't this statement a subtle distortion of the whole James family in order to justify Henry's own bias? Nobody could have been more "American" in the best sense, including the international and even the cosmic sense, than Henry James the father or William James the son and brother. It was only Henry, the Dark Prince already infatuated with his infantile legend, who so perverted this American "rediscovery of Europe," while the real James family of this period was really intent upon "discovering" and celebrating an *American* coming of age.

Yet a score of later Jacobite commentators followed this Jamesian lead in discussing the James family as a whole. (Notwithstanding the revealing phrase which Henry used to describe his European dream of success in life as "some intention *arrested* in youth.") Thus to accept one's fate, even to grasp at one's orphanhood, and to make it a nobler orphanhood, and then to return to one's ancient and superior home of Europe: that was the true, the underlying, the blessed and consecrated theme of the first volume of the Memoirs. And similarly, Henry's early passion for the stage was simply the yearning for another world of make-believe where the young orphan prince might feel at home.

The sections on the stage, even the elegant romances and lurid melodramas which prevailed in the American scene of the 1850's, form another blaze of "real life" in the Memoirs. The factual memory of Henry James about the details of stage production, costumes, actors was prodigious in *A Small Boy*; and this early addiction, too, was another kind of poison or obsession throughout James's later career. (We have already noticed how the echoes of the popular American stage romances of James's youth can still be felt in *The Golden Bowl* and in *The Outcry* equally.) And directly after these theatric sections there was again the recurrent refrain of the "romance of orphanhood," and the conjoined note of little Henry's personal sense of failure and alienation.

But this was a sense of alienation, almost a yearning for orphanhood, so James added, that was absolutely devoid of jealousy, of envy, competitiveness, ferocity of spirit, or even the sense of alternatives. What was apparent to him then was only his own "falling short," and the "yearning for otherness." "Envy, as I knew it at least, was simply of what they *were* . . . They were so *other* — that was what I felt; and to *be* other, other almost anyhow, seemed as good as the probable taste of the bright compound wistfully watched in the confectioner's window; unattainable, impossible, of course, but as to which just this impossibility and just that privation kept those active proceedings in which jealousy seeks relief quite out of the question."

Quite remarkable indeed the Jamesian ingenuity which imparted such a pure and wistful tone to the defeated little hero of *A Small Boy*. "A helpless little love of horizons, I certainly cherished, and could sometimes even care for my own . . . It wasn't that I wished to change with everyone, with anyone at a venture, but that I saw 'gifts' everywhere but as mine and that I scarce know whether to call the effect of this miserable or monstrous. It was the effect at least of self-abandonment — I mean to visions." Miserable and monstrous alike, perhaps, but these childhood "visions" were Henry James's true life — and there was no doubt as to their materialization both in his career and his art. Was the little Henry a complete failure in the erratic, fitful education which he received? And was William even more brilliantly successful by contrast? Henry took pleasure, it seemed, in describing his older brother's superiority — and here, too, the real nature of the brotherly relationship was concealed beyond recognition in layer upon layer of filial piety, affection and devotion: in these tones of sweet, tender, humble retrospect.

The little lost Henry was too lost, too alone, too defeated, too awkward, gaping and pensive; particularly perhaps because he had altogether eliminated any ordinary, running day-to-day relationship with mother, father, brothers or sister in *A Small Boy and Others*. The small boy is here all right; but where are the "others" — who should have been close to him, and who appear in this volume only, as it were, to display their "otherness"? There was the added factor that just as Henry James Senior had little use for the formal or conventional education of his time, so he had in fact less use — radical, free-thinking Swedenborgian that he was — for conventional religion. "What church do you go to?" was often asked of the James children; to which the answer was *none*, or in Henry Senior's words, "all." "To which I must add as well," his literary son added here, "that our 'fending' in this fashion for ourselves didn't so prepare us for invidious remark — remark, I mean, upon our pewless state, which involved, to my imagination, much the same discredit that a houseless or a cookless would . . ." And this "pewless state" in this early Jamesian world of childhood invoked "cold scrutiny," so Henry added, and "derisive comment," while their father's reply that then "we could plead nothing less than the whole privilege of Christendom" was even colder, for adequate response, "than any criticism I recall."

Behind the orphanage and exile of this bewildered and lost little ego, indeed, lay a lack of all authority, all rules, and of those social "forms" which the later James stressed to the point of inventing or fabricating them. Emerging from the identical background, how could William shine so clearly as the painter, scholar, scientist and philosopher while Henry, like a whole line of his later heroes, was the little plaintive outcast? But again there was his flight into fantasy, in *A Small Boy and Others*; his refuge in the world of the theater, and books — and that visionary world of "art" which was so closely linked with, which *was* "Europe." The orphan prince had already created a new, a better, a truly royal heritage for himself, which fell into the ancient pattern also of the myth or the birth of the hero. Did James in fact really know very little (except through a child's eyes, or a child's memories) of the Old New York society which he described so glamorously here? That Old New York *Dutch* society, mainly, which Edith Wharton did know so well, and had experienced in reality, and rebelled against so sharply, while in his old age James still clung to it so fervently as yet another shining illusion? Here as in his first adolescent impressions of Europe and England, he had created anew his own personal sense of "the rich burden of a Past," or a History that was all legend, mystery and romance.

At the close of the first voume of the Memoirs, the pattern was set, the hero's fate was sealed, the trap had closed. The little Henry was overcome by European paintings. "Art, art, art, don't you see? Learn, little gaping pilgrims, what *that* is!" Or by the European buildings, such as those in the Rue de Tournon, which also spoke their message so clearly. "Yes, small staring jeune homme, we are dignity and memory and measure, we are conscience and proportion and taste, not to mention strong sense too: for all of which good things take us — you won't find one of them when you find (as you're going soon to begin to at such a rate) vulgarity." In the great museum of contemporary French painting, Henry was enthralled by Delacroix and Paul Delaroche above all. "Yet Les Enfants d'Edouard thrilled me to a different tune, and

I couldn't doubt that the long-drawn odd face of the elder prince, sad and sore and sick, with his wide crimped sidelocks of fair hair and his violet legs marked by the Garter and dangling from the bed, was a reconstitution of far-off history of the subtlest and most 'last word' modern or psychologic kind."

Yes, *that* was art, was history, was psychology, was home. Speaking of another Delaroche painting, James affirmed it again:

There *was reconstituted history if one would, in the straw-littered scaffold, the distracted ladies with three-cornered coifs and those immense hanging sleeves that made them look as if they had bath-towels over their arms: in the block, the headsman, the bandaged eyes and groping hands of Lady Jane Grey — not less than in the noble indifference of Charles the First, compromised king but perfect gentleman, at his inscrutable ease in his chair and as if on his throne, while the Puritan soldiers insult and badger him . . .*

And little wonder that nothing in the dull democratic vista, the mediocre Puritan vulgarity of the New World, could compare with such exalted visions and scenes. These paintings *were* Europe, and they spoke to James in "a vast deafening chorus." The wondrous Galerie d'Apollon was style, was *glory*. "The glory meant ever so many things at once, not only beauty and art and supreme design, but history and fame and power." Power, yes! to this little bedraggled, gaping, wondering ego, ashamed, homeless and obsessed by the sense of its own exile and impotence. This young Henry had his sudden revelation of "the world in fine raised to the richest and noblest expression" — the world of the Second Empire which was on the spot "so amply radiant and elegant that it took to itself, took under its protection with a splendour of insolence, the state and ancientry of the whole scene . . . But who shall count the sources at which an intense young fancy (when a young fancy *is* intense) capriciously, absurdly drinks — so that the effect is, in twenty connections, that of a love-philtre or fear-philtre which fixes for the senses their supreme symbol of the fair or the strange."

Well, this was quite a vision of the world, of society, humanity, art, culture and history itself, upon which the child-hero, the child-prodigy, of A *Small Boy* had fixed his enchanted eyes. (And a vision which he would never change, in effect, and never relinquish; which in his old age he still described with the same intensity and magical exaltation that he had first felt in his boyhood.) But now, where was the lack of will, the lack of spirit, the distaste for competition, or the absence of jealousy and other such envious or wanting emotions, which James had repeatedly proclaimed as the dominant mood of his American childhood? Wasn't it simply that his own home, parents, siblings and friends — the American scene in general which could hardly compare to these kings and princes, ladies, of French romantic painting — had had nothing to *stir* the Jamesian emotions? It was at the Louvre too that the young Henry had "the appalling yet admirable nightmare of my life." That is, the nightmare which took place in the same Galerie d'Apollon, when suddenly emerging out of a room which "I had a moment before been desperately, and all the more abjectly, defending by the push of my shoulder against hard pressure on lock and bar from the other side," he, James, turned upon, pursued and vanquished "a just dimly descried figure" which had been pursuing *him*:

The lucidity, not to say the sublimity of the crisis had consisted of the great thought that I, in my appalled state, was probably still more appalling than the awful agent, creature or presence, whatever he was, whom I had guessed, in the suddenest wild start from sleep, the sleep within my sleep, to be making for my place of rest. The triumph of my impulse, perceived in a flash as I acted on it by myself at a bound, forcing the door outward, was the grand thing, but the great point of the whole was the wonder of my final recognition. Routed, dismayed, the tables turned upon him by my so surpassing him for straight aggression and dire intention, my visitant was already but a diminished spot on the long perspective, the tremendous, glorious hall, as I say, over the far-gleaming floor of which, cleared for the occasion of its great line of priceless vitrines down the middle, he sped for his life . . .

The central imagery of this dream is familiar, of course, through-out a whole line of ghostly tales from "The Turn of the Screw" to "The Jolly Corner"; or through a whole line of Jamesian novels whose central "action" so often takes place in French or English art museums. For this was the moment of James's own "immense hallucination," his awakening to all the glory of life in Europe, his repudiation of his own home, early life, and America. But what was in that haunted and locked room of the dream — his imprison-ment, his past — Henry James would never really understand. And that visionary, bold dream-hero, the Jamesian will or the Jamesian ego itself — both appalled and appalling indeed; surpass-ing the "awful agent" of this nightmare in "straight aggression and dire intention," putting to final rout the specter of its own neurotic anxiety: wasn't it already repressing the true sources of its own talent, the Jamesian unconscious itself? Yes, the all-triumphant Jamesian "will-ego," embodying its own defeated enemy-monster within itself, led directly to the artist who saw all life, all experience, all human relations in just such terms of ag-gression and "dire intentions," of "mental" attack and flight, flight and attack, of either the appalling or the appalled state — or in the equivalent terms of power, manipulation and control as the only condition, the only answer, for all the central human situa-tions in the Jamesian fiction.

The Jamesian hero of this nightmare dream was, in short, the author whom we have been studying: often so interesting and sym-pathetic in his inclinations of fear and flight, and often quite mon-strous indeed in his moments of "triumph." For who was it, even in the pre-Freudian age of Henry James's adolescence, who ever quite so gloriously vanquished all the ghosts of his unconscious — and what writer but Henry James would ever have wanted to? That memorable and bold rush and dash for freedom and libera-tion — inspired at base by "irresistible but shameful dread" — marked in fact the first step of the peculiarly Jamesian mode of esthetic imprisonment. The headlong charge for the "freedom" of Europe and Art led only to the esoteric career we have recorded in these pages; and that dreamlike "liberation" of the Jamesian temperament became the lifelong trap of Henry James's true talent.

The entire description of this early and profound, recurrent and obsessive dream nightmare set the tone for the prevailing mood of the Jamesian fiction. As early as this, Henry James himself became the omnipotent narrator-interrogator-inquisitor whose later development we have traced. The "lucidity, the sublimity" of the great thought "that *I*, in my appalled state was probably still more appalling . . ." "The triumph of *my* impulse, and "the wonder of *my* final recognition," and then: the "tables turned upon him by *my* so surpassing him . . ." And finally, that "visitant," who is the true specter of James's unconscious and morbid fear of life, and who becomes a mere spot speeding for *his* life down the immense, empty, gleaming halls of art with their "priceless vitrines": wasn't this the most intimate, revealing vision of the typical, recurrent, and yet ever astounding Henry James himself?

Meanwhile, however, the second volume of the Memoirs, *Notes of a Son and Brother*, a year later, in 1914, carried forward the Jamesian chronicle of the Self. There is another reference to the failure of his education on the part of this child-adolescent whose great need, as it appeared, was to be wounded. There is the glowing reference to the Théâtre Français's Racine with the actress Rachel. Young Henry was seventeen now, and the makings of the esthetic absolute were almost all present — the religious devotion to "art" at the expense of every other interest, and for the single purpose of overcoming his own sense of personal and social failure.

His early conflicts had been resolved at the stage of preadolescence. His solution was clear; all that was needed was the "method" to achieve it. All the themes had been sounded for the final break, which had actually taken place already in the child's psyche. Adolescence was therefore only a period of "waiting," of waiting and thinking and being "prepared" — just as this was also the dominant mood of the Jamesian fiction. In Newport, in 1860, on another of those American "returns" after the European years, James had noted his own curious "detachment" from the life around him. "Newport imposed itself at that period to so remarkable a degree as the one right residence, in all our great country, for those tainted, under whatever attenuations, with the quality and the effect of detachment. The effect of detachment was the fact of the experience of Europe."

There are interesting sections here, incidentally, on both Henry James Senior and on William James. It was William who continually made the playful and affectionate references to Mrs. James herself, the mother-wife of the Memoirs about whom Henry was almost entirely reticent. And quite similarly, in Henry's profile of the James family as a whole, there is no real description of their underlying or true relationships. This was still the development of *Henry's* consciousness, almost as immaculate as the esthetic absolute itself.

The tone of these family reminiscences, all pure affection, admiration, sweetness and filial devotion, was close to the particularly Jamesian hyperbole or euphoria. Only "If to be orphaned and free of range had affected my young fancy as the happy, that is the romantic lot . . ." was still the refrain in *Notes of a Son and Brother:* the unswerving desire, yearning and goal of the orphan prince. In this sense, too, as James commented, people in books were characters, "and other people roundabout us, were somehow not." And the "abstraction" of the father's philosophic ideas was somehow a snub to the young Henry's already developed pictorial sense. The father's insistence on the "freedom from pressure," as well as on the absence of all *forms*, social, moral, religious, to emphasize the freedom, the individuality of the human spirit, was again "positively embarrassing to us" (i.e., to Henry), even while the young exile brooded over the oddity of his filial case in "my small uneasy mind."

Henry never could really understand his father's philosophy. "It

was all a play I hadn't 'been to,' consciously at least — that was
the trouble; the curtain had fallen while I was still tucked in my
crib." (A crib, one is tempted to add, which was in itself the first
scene of this strange orphanhood. The infant exile indeed!) And
here, in the eloquent, but quite formal and "set" tribute to the
death of the all-sacrificing Mrs. James, was the original source of
that sexual and psychological "cannibalism" which was at the
center of *The Sacred Fount* and of James's own temperament.
"The only thing I might well have questioned on these occasions
was the possibility on the part of a selflessness so consistently and
unabatedly active of its having anything ever left *acutely* to
offer . . ." Now there was no question as to the mutual devotion
of the elder Jameses, or even about their direct physical bond; for
to Henry Senior, who advocated a kind of sensuous metaphysics
too, this was another essential part of the spiritual life. The intimacy of the parents was almost a household jest of the James
family; and the father died a year later than his wife, as we are told,
simply because he could not live without her.

Yet, by sacrificing everything so utterly to her husband and her
children, had Mrs. James (whose first name is rarely mentioned)
really been despoiled of her own personality — or was this another
of those elaborate cover mechanisms so familiar in the Jamesian orbit of life and literature? Wasn't it curious, too, that the esthetic
son would identify emotionally with *her*, in his own fear that
women, that love, and in particular sexual love, would consume or
"dry up" his own sources of creativity — since after all *she* had
maintained the father's literary career and life alike? By her giving
all, was there nothing really *left* of the mother? Or had she gained
more things, spiritual and physical, than Henry ever dreamed of —
or rather, just those things, later on, which he seemed to dream of
so consistently and so queerly in his fiction? Here too, very likely,
was the source of the charmed circle of "adult intimacy" which
the Jamesian literary children, and many of the childlike Jamesian
adults, were so constantly circling around — from the bedroom's

precious treasure in "The Aspern Papers" to the haunted upper floors of childhood's house in "The Jolly Corner."

This was in fact the original, mysterious abode of sexuality which the Jamesian children and adults alike — always ending up by "knowing all" — never did quite penetrate, or were always thrown out of. Meanwhile one notices that in Boston, to which the James family migrated in 1865, Mrs. James was not always well received, while Henry Senior (who wrote all her social letters, apparently, in Henry's account) talked even more affectionately of his "indisposed" wife. The two younger James sons had gone off to the Civil War, and Wilky was wounded during his service with Colonel Robert Shaw's Fifty-Fourth Massachusetts (the first body of colored soldiers raised in the North). Parenthetically, while the editorial Mr. Dupee praises "a work which is so subjective, so purposeful, and so well-organized as this one is," the Memoirs in fact wander quite verbosely from place to place and time to time, according to James's associative, or dictational, moods. And then follows the celebrated description of the Jamesian "wound," or "obscure hurt," on the eve of the Civil War itself:

Scarce at all to be stated, to begin with, the queer fusion or confusion established in my consciousness during the soft spring of '61 by the firing on Fort Sumter, Mr. Lincoln's instant first call for volunteers and a physical mishap, already referred to as having overtaken me at the same dark hour, and the effects of which were to draw themselves out incalculably and intolerably . . .

But this description was as obscure, ambiguous, shifting, perverse and puzzling as it was copious, verbose and abundant. Was this accident a "private catastrophe," as James said at times, or a "difficulty, bristling with embarrassments," or again merely a minor "physical mishap," and a "small affair"? What was clear, however, from the start of this inimitable passage, was that James had linked his own accident with the larger "accident" and wound of the Civil War itself. This had in his own mind "an association of the closest" which could not be expressed, as he added, but was both implicit and momentous. Didn't indeed his own personal "catastrophe" (wound, accident, mishap) finally conclude by becoming even *more* important than the Civil War — which after all ended in four years, while the effects of the Jamesian hurt continued to draw themselves out "incalculably and intolerably"?

"One had the sense I mean," so Henry James continued both mystically and mistily, "of a huge comprehensive ache, and there were hours at which one could scarce have told where it came most from one's poor organism, still so young and so meant for better things, but which had suffered a particular wrong, or from the enclosing social body, a body rent with a thousand wounds, and that thus treated one to the honour of a sort of tragic fellowship . . ." And thus James had in effect absorbed within his own poor suffering organism the national suffering of a thousand wounds — but quite *without* the proclaimed honor of a "tragic fellowship," since it was precisely this wound, this accident, this mishap which had prevented him — or was designed to prevent him — from entering the Civil War. What a rationalizing process was here, on the part of an artist whose whole career was based so largely on the single, divine, ego-saving and face-saving principle of the higher and higher rationalization! But more —

"Jammed into the acute angle between two high fences, where the rhythmic play of my arms, in tune with that of several other pairs, but at a dire disadvantage of position, induced a rural, a quasi-extemporized old engine to work, and a saving stream to flow, I had done myself, in face of a shabby conflagration, a horrid even if an obscure hurt . . ." *That* was the accident. Beneath this florid and romantic prose, pumping an old fire engine (whose "saving stream" was directed at the "shabby conflagration"), James had done himself some physical harm. But, in this curiously inflated and pictorially obscure scene, what about the "acute angle" between the two high fences of what childhood imprisonment, despite all the play of this hero's "rhythmic" arms? Wasn't this whole scene entirely dreamlike in essence; or almost imaginary in fact? "And what was interesting from the first was my not doubting in the least its duration," James added, in this section of *Notes of a Son and Brother*, " — though what seemed equally clear was that I needn't as a matter of course adopt and appropriate it, so to speak, or place it for increase of interest on exhibition."

But hadn't he done just this in the long years of his "suffering," and didn't he do it once again in the final recounting of this "obscure hurt," which was almost, indeed, a decisive factor in his decision to leave America and become an artist? How did he realize "from the first" the duration of this "wound," if he hadn't, also from the first, perhaps even planned and wanted such an injury — this remarkable and curious artist who did indeed "adopt and appropriate" everything around him — and particularly himself — for its increase of interest in a lifelong literary exhibition? And here again he proclaimed the very fact of the "interest" and the "exhibition" of his own accident, almost, obviously, *despite* his own proclaimed modesty.

Thus the Jamesian "wound" became the complete symbol, if not the alter ego, of the Civil War itself, and the life and death of our national existence — on the part of precisely that artist who had previously denied all value to the national existence. What had helped to support James during those trying years (at once of his own fate and of his country's), he then went on to declare, was the series of "sympathies, supports and reassurances" which, even at the cost of publicizing his illness, he had received from his friends, if not quite from the famous Boston medical specialist who had declared that Henry's celebrated ailment did not even exist. "The truth being that this interview settled my sad business," James wrote here, "settled it just in the saddest sense, for ever so long —

That action had come from the complete failure of our approached oracle either to warn, to comfort or to command — to do anything but

*make quite unassistingly light of the bewilderment exposed to him.
In default of other attention or suggestion he might by a mere warning
as to gravities only too possible, and already well advanced, have made
such a difference; but I have little forgotten how I felt myself, the
warning absent, treated but to a comparative pooh-pooh — an impression
I long looked back to as a sharp parting of the way, with an adoption
of the wrong one distinctly determined . . .*

"It was not simply small comfort, it was only a mystification the
more," so James concluded this mysterious account, "that the inconvenience of my state had to reckon with the strange fact of
there being nothing so to speak of the matter with me." That is,
there was no ailment, objectively, which only made the matter
worse, since the continuation of the ailment, in fact, simply proved
that the famous Boston specialist was wrong! For the great specialist, as events proved, was unquestionably wrong. Hadn't *he* turned
James on the wrong course by his ignorance; and wasn't the Jamesian conviction about his illness, his life, his destiny proved by
events to be *right*? That is the moral of this episode in the Memoirs;
and the Jamesian candor (along with the Jamesian obfuscation)
revealed all the effrontery of the infatuated and the betrayed ego.

But then, what *was* young Henry's obscure wound? According
to the orthodox Freudian interpretation, it was a form of castration,
whether physical or psychological. (There is a curious identification with Henry James Senior, who *had* lost his leg as a youth in
just such another typical firefighting episode.) But we have already reviewed this theory, in respect to "The Jolly Corner," and
there we noticed that the Jamesian "wound" marked not the
"death of passion," in actuality, but rather the *prevention* of passion. It was the physical confirmation of his lack of passion in any
adult or mature sense; it was the true mark of his psychic wound
or bloc. It served the purpose of bringing him all the attention
(the "publicity" he claimed to loathe), the sympathy and comfort
which, in his own mind at least, had been lacking in his im-

prisoned, orphaned youth; while it obviously prohibited any thought either of war or of women.

But was there any "castration" at all? Wasn't the wound, from all the evidence James himself submits, simply a back injury? — if there was any injury to speak of in this completely dream-like and mystic episode, which the great Boston medical specialist, and with some reason perhaps, simply had pooh-poohed. Here again the *causes* of the Jamesian neurosis, like the "causes" of his personality, or of his art, are veiled in true mystery, since this writer never tried to face them or understand them; and always saw them — for all his famous "seeing" and "understanding" — through the tinted, the infatuated, the visionary glass of his own ego. But what is fascinating, just the same, is the *manner* of this Jamesian "seeing," or the process of his whole reaction and ego-response to the threat of this veiled reality. The *origins* of the Jamesian temperament and art may fit into the Freudian categories; the results break these categories wide open. They can hardly contain the unique literary monster called Henry James.

There was no doubt a strong element of shame in the Jamesian recall of the Civil War episode; just as there is buried and concealed shame throughout the chronicle of his eccentric, anti- or nonsocial family. But then consider how the Jamesian "wound" is absolutely identified with the national wound of the war itself; how indeed it finally takes precedence over the war and the nation, as though Henry had embodied this wound, the war and the nation, and had finally come to suffer more — and longer — than anybody else. Just as he had returned to America not to relive the trauma of his exile — oh, no — but to confirm the essential rightness of his exile (by the fact that the American scene had disintegrated even *more* than he had suspected), so in his old age he relived the trauma of the war, not indeed to find the "truth" but in order to reach the higher justification for his buried, haunting experience. And didn't he, though! But perhaps, as we now realize, even the Freudian "truths," arrived at so painfully and laboriously, merely provide another set of living illusions for the tormented organism. And Henry James was the supreme example of this process of life-giving *illusion*, at the cost of any sense of reality.

He took over the Civil War not only psychologically by his greater suffering in *Notes of a Son and Brother*, but quite literally through his editorial "interpretations" of his brother Wilky's direct war experiences. Wilky's war letters are notable in this volume for their simplicity and clarity. The Jamesian commentary is again highly romantic, outstandingly "patriotic," sonorous, rhetorical, verbally orotund, and rather presumptuous when it is not faintly patronizing. It is "we" who suffered all the real horrors, humiliations and ordeals of the war, not to mention the actual wound that Wilky received — just as James even identified himself now with the role of "dear old Walt." I mean the Whitman who identified himself with the Civil War, rather than the war with him, and whom James had earlier dismissed as the poet of common, vulgar American life. And notice again, in the inflated and contrived Jamesian "recall" of the war, the complete lack of any knowledge or interest in the issues of the conflict: the moral values, the social or political or economic implications, the real meaning, in any sense, of the military struggle. The Jamesian "History" of the Civil War is couched in the same idiom precisely as his "histories" of the French Empire or the French Revolution — almost in the same romantic and lurid colors as those French paintings of mythological or royal scenes which had so impressed him as a boy.

In the Jamesian recording, the Civil War becomes another dimly remembered, glamorous and tragic fairy tale of "Boston genealogies," and "laughing, welcoming sunburnt young men" only less handsome than "their tawny-bearded Colonel" amidst all the "common grace of clear blue toggery." Luminous and beautiful indeed, if also "vaguely sinister and sad" was this "missed experience" of Henry's — as though that, too, was the tragedy of the war; that *he* had missed it! Remarkable, noteworthy, the spectacle of the late-late Jamesian ego finally coming to grips with the great trauma of its youth, and eating it up . . .* Then there are the concluding letters, in *Notes of a Son and Brother,* of the single great romantic heroine of James's youth, the dying Mary Temple herself, upon whose image and memory he had based a series of fictional portraits extending from the Isabel Archer of *The Portrait of a Lady* to the Milly Theale of *The Wings of the Dove.* Touching and entertaining letters these are too, though it is no surprise to discover they were written to another man, a "friend" with whom she was half in love — but not even addressed to William James, and certainly not to Henry who had gone off to Europe during her last tragic illness. This "central experience" of Henry James's life, as he claimed, was again of the second or third order of remoteness; but over which — again — the aging Henry had the last word.

Notes of a Son and Brother was the last complete volume of the Memoirs. The third book in the series was only a fragment, published posthumously in 1917, and edited by Percy Lubbock, another pioneer worker in the Jacobite ascension. Yet like most of the later Jamesian "fragments," *The Middle Years,* although brief and unfinished, is a document of considerable interest.

In this "meandering record," as James called it, more accurately than the critics who praise its structure or organization, there is the first moment of true "freedom" upon Henry's arrival, as an adult, in England. This was in 1869, according to his account; and the "somewhat disabled young man" who also viewed himself as "that intensely reacting small organism" felt he was truly at the gates of paradise. The opening note of *The Middle Years* was lyrical at the prospect of England and art, though the later style is even more abundant and redundant, pontifical, sonorous, polysyllabic. Dictating the memoirs from memory alone, embarking

---

* Yet even Edmund Wilson, in *Patriotic Gore* (1962), a book that is by turns brilliant, perverse and historically inadequate, quotes these Jamesian passages on the Civil War with much admiration and very little sense of their latent content. Thus a major critic, who finds evidence to question a historical figure of the stature of Abraham Lincoln, has also swallowed whole the Jamesian confectionary.

on his elaborate qualifying and parenthetical clause upon clause,
James sometimes lost track of his grammar altogether. For at last
he was in that "home of fancy" indeed, of romance, manners and
nobility in which he had really resided throughout his childhood,
and which had permanently affected his vision of life.

Yes, and Smollett and Hogarth, for the seamier, juicier side of
reality. "To return at all across the years to the gates of the paradise of the first larger initiation is to be ever so tempted to pass
them, to push in again and breathe the air of this, that and the
other plot of rising ground particularly associated for memory and
gratitude, with the quickening process . . ." Etcetera. And: "Let
me not here withal appear to pretend to say how far I then forsaw
myself likely to proceed, as it were, with the inimitable France
and the incomparable Italy; my real point . . ." But what was
his real point? He had already made up his mind, all definitely, all
rigidly, on *England* — the true scene of his childhood romances
and visions of glory — and the fog of the later prose is perhaps
meant only to conceal this steadfast choice, this iron if infantine
determination. It is often difficult, in these lyrical, rhapsodic pages,
to discover the actual subject of James's reflections, several sentences, several passages, or several pages back — it was difficult
for *him*, and sometimes he no longer bothered, and gave you, simply, your choice.

But the London social scene! These pages of the Memoirs vi-
brate with so much "excitation" that it is difficult to find any real
matter. For after all, in Henry's true yearning, "society" was perhaps even more important then the Art he proclaimed, which was
here again, at least, merely another cover mechanism. In this great
illusionary passion of the adult (or adolescent?) James for *London*,
facts were unimportant, and in these pages of *The Middle Years*
— which are really the earliest years of Henry's true life — the
facts are few. The central image is that of the solitary, young
"observer" roaming the streets of the enchanted town, gaping and
dawdling indeed, pressing that inquisitive little nose at the great

glass windowpane of "real life" which he long ago determined to break through, or to sidle and slide around. For he was home at last in the world that Dickens and Thackeray had built.

There is the account of his first meeting with George Eliot, and "the particular quality of my vibration" in seeing the kind of "great person" who simply did not exist in America. (There is the anecdote of how James silently left behind him the little volume of his early short stories, which the obtuse Mr. Lewes insisted on returning to him.) There is the first meeting of the young James with Mrs. Greville, a true English society aristocrat, even better than Mary Ann Evans maybe, or one who at least figures in *The Middle Years* far more prominently. Perhaps this was *really* home, for —

The red candles in the red shades have remained with me, inexplicably, as a vivid note of this pitch, shedding their rosy light, with the autumn gale, the averted reality, all shut out, upon such felicities of feminine helplessness as I couldn't have prefigured in advance and as exemplified, for further gathering in, the possibilities of the old tone. Nowhere had the evening curtains seemed so drawn, nowhere the copious service so soft, nowhere the second volume of the new novel, "half-uncut," so close to one's hand, nowhere the exquisite head and incomparable brush of the domesticated collie such an attestation of that standard at least, nowhere the harmonies of accident — of intention was more than one could say — so incapable of a wrong deflection . . .

Wasn't this another leisure-class vision of paradise indeed — complete with the incomparable brush of the "domesticated collie"? (And where then were the undomesticated collies?) The rosy light, the old tone, the soft but copious "service," the drawn curtains averting the autumn gale, the second volume, half uncut to be sure, of the latest novel: doesn't this remind you of "The Great Good Place," attributed as a rebuke to modern materialism by Mr. Fadiman, described as a religious utopia by Mr. Auden or Mr. Spender? No, this was a simple middle class vision of aristocratic luxury — with taste, with manners, with class. This was truly "another pearl," as James said, "for one's lengthening string." And: "I pass over what was doubtless the happiest stroke in the composition, the fact of its involving, as all-distinguished husband of the other daughter, an illustrious soldier and servant of his sovereigns that were successively to be, than against whose patient handsome bearded presence the whole complexus of femininities and futilities couldn't have been left . . ."

Well, this was also the tone of James's Civil War descriptions, which somehow became a "royal war," just as he had described the American Revolution as His Majesty's Rebellion, and sided of course with the Loyalists.

The quality of James's "pacifism," as illustrated in some of his ghostly tales, was dubious when it ran into these handsome, bearded, distinguished and illustrious servant-soldiers of their sovereigns. In *The Middle Years* was also the memoir of "my admirable old friend Fanny Kemble," and the chronicle fairly begins to glow with the "great names" and "great places" of English culture. (There is more content here, too, though the style is still the inflated, orotund, almost obese prose of the late-late James.) There was the distinct shock, for contrast, when the young Henry discovered, with something like horror, that "Tennyson was not Tennysonian," and he did not know who James Russell Lowell was when he met him — he did not even know it was Lowell. The gossip of these celebrities is the "great life" that James now celebrated; even while he frequented the company of "truly beautiful persons [who] might be old without being elderly." That is to say, those fading beauties of a still earlier time whose conversation provided him with so many invaluable "anecdotes" of high society.

Mrs. Greville was related to a relative of the Marquis de Sade.

There was the drive to Aldworth with this distinguished British lady, and the drive to Witley, although just as Henry was disappointed with Tennyson, he was not altogether satisfied with G. H. Lewes — if I read these complex sections of *The Middle Years* correctly. Louisa Lady Waterford, another aging Victorian or pre-

Victorian belle, was another matter. She was "illustrational, historically," said James, as the combination of "rare beauty with rare talent." "One made up one's mind thus that the only sure specimens were, and had to be, those acquainted with time, and with whom time, on its side, was acquainted; those in fine who had borne the test and still looked at it face to face . . ." Definitely Lady Waterford was the embodiment of that "tone of time" which lay behind the whole Jamesian quest, coming as this gaping pilgrim did from the blank, unhistorical expanses of the New World:

I mean that she reanimated for the fond analyst the age in which persons of her type could so greatly flourish — it being ever so pertinently of her type, or at least of that of the age, that she was regarded as having cast the spell of genius as well as of beauty. She painted, and on the largest scale . . . There it was that, like Mrs. Greville herself, yet in a still higher degree, she bore witness to the fine old felicity of the fortunate and the "great" under the "old" order which would have made it so good then to live could one but have been in their shoes . . .

Thus it was the still *older* feudal or medieval English life that James really craved: along with his visions of the *"ancien régime"* before the horrifying (but still pictorial, from the aristocratic side) French Revolution. Lady Waterford confirmed all his notions of the "happy effect" of such social apparitions. "We all now illustrated together, in higgledy-piggledy fashion, or as a vast monotonous mob, our own wonderful period and order, and nothing else; whereby the historic imagination, under its acuter need of facing backward, gropes before it with a vain gesture, missing, or all but missing the concrete *other* . . ." And thus England, too, was not really home; but only the gateway to the still older, still more historic, or legendary *true* home of Henry James. But what kind of "historic imagination" was this really? For curiously enough Lady Waterford, in the evocation of the early James by the late Henry James, appeared as much French as British, joined there together in the Jamesian fantasy, as it were, of prehistory. "The old as we call it, I recognize, doesn't disappear all at once; the *ancien régime* of our commonest reference survived the Revolution of our most horrific in patches and scraps . . . None the less it used to be one of the finest of pleasures to acclaim and cherish, in case of meeting them, one and another of the *complete* examples of the conditions irrecoverable . . . and for the enjoyment of that critical emotion to draw one's wanton line between the past and the present."

A wanton line indeed, which was only drawn between what James, as child, had envisioned life — and history — to be, and what James as an adult, even as an aging artist, did not consider to be life or history. Or this was "history" perhaps as it was envisioned in Shakespeare's romantic and chauvinistic pageants of the medieval English and French wars, conquests, villainies and dynasties. The "happy effect" of such personages and apparitions as Lady Waterford upon the gaping, romantic, predetermined young American pilgrim was that they made one draw that imaginary, legendary, pageantlike historical line "just where they might most profit from it." Or, that is, just where *he*, James, might most profit from it, in these pictorial yearnings which can hardly be classified as history. As to Lady Waterford's "class" as a whole, "they profited in that they recruited my group [*my* group indeed!] of the fatuously fortunate, the class, as I seemed to see it, that had had the longest and happiest innings in history — happier and longer, on the whole, even than their congeners of the old French time — and for whom the future wasn't going to be, by most signs, anything like as bland and benedictory as the past . . ."

Was there ever anything else like this Jamesian vision, early and late, of the past, of history, of the true material of life and art? The fading British aristocracy (or great ladies) of the 1870's and '80's served only as a link to the greater age of a century before, and there was little concern with the *present* anywhere in James, even in England. And no wonder that the "modern" British society, which no doubt had existed under his nose for the whole span of his career, was such a disenchantment when he came so belatedly, and for his own personal reasons of esthetic and dramatic rejection, upon it. If Tennyson was quite un-Tennysonian (in his rude manners, his domestic roars, his unawareness of his own guests, his poor style of reading his own lyrical, enchanted, pictorial, medieval verse) Lady Waterford was positively Lady Waterford. The Memoirs end, in effect, with the description of Lady Waterford's exhibition of her own paintings in Carlton House Terrace —

during which the reflection that "they" had indeed had their innings, and were still splendidly using for the purpose the very fag-end of the waning time, mixed itself for me with all the "wonderful colour" framed and arrayed, that blazed from the walls of the kindly great room lent for the advantage of a charity, and lost itself in the general chorus of immense comparison and tender consecration . . .

Familiar words and tone of time indeed in James. But what kind of "time" was this also? — a time that had stood forever still, as it were, in the enchanted visions of his alienated childhood. If *The Middle Years* was never completed, it ended on the correct note. The real chronicle of the Jamesian Memoirs, or *autobiography*, was continued in the rapt, ecstatic self-communications of *The Notebooks*, and in the Jamesian fiction itself. For now he led no other life than the meeting with such personages as preferably the Lady Waterfords, the collecting of those social "anecdotes" as the germ of his fiction, the notes to himself on his art; and the writing.

What a fantastical literary personage is revealed in these Memoirs, despite their difficulties and their defects. Where else is the central portrait of this dark prince, exiled and orphaned almost

from birth, restructuring his life, even his origins, from the fantasies of infancy — except in the classic myth of all the orphaned
and exiled heroes of antiquity, floating down their own immemorial stream of time from the epoch of Moses and before? Such was
the real hero of the Memoirs whom Dupee described as "exceed-
ingly modest," and such was the chronicle that Matthiessen
described as James's "self-effacing autobiographical volumes."
But what is in the slightest degree either "modest" or "self-effacing" in this full-blown, multivolumed chronicle of *Henry James*'s
spiritual development? How these critics are taken in — willingly,
consciously, devoutly — by the opaque varnish of the Jamesian
personality, the Jamesian craft! And to what an odd destination
had the (modern) Mosaic figure of little Henry propelled himself
at last in the Memoirs; and what an odd "destiny" he then set up
for his benighted, pagan tribe of fellow Americans. What factors
of temperament or environment could really lead to *this* esthetic
phenomenon; what causes, human, domestic or social could ever
really account for a Henry James?

    Was his earliest sense of orphanhood, in the midst of his gre-
garious, friendly, cultivated, eccentric family group, due to the obvious sibling rivalry with — the sense of mute despair before —
such a talented, socially charming brilliant older brother as William? Naturally; but not quite adequately, either. Was it due to
some deep, and equally mute, identification with the mother of the
family who, deeply in love with the father as she doubtless was,
had "orphaned" one of her sons, and yet not the other? A mother,
moreover, whom William accepted with the same easy familiarity
and affection as Henry Senior himself — with all *her* social defects
— and whom Henry Junior, with all his social sensitivity, could
well have been ashamed of.*

    * The final volume of Van Wyck Brooks's Memoirs, *From the Shadow of the
Mountain,* carries a curious letter from the mother of Thomas Sergeant Perry, an
early friend of the James brothers. It was not Cambridge that Henry found "deadly,"
according to Mrs. Perry, so much as the "poky banality" of his own home ruled over
by Mrs. James and her sister Miss Walsh: "large florid stupid seeming ladies . . ."

Wasn't he also, in his deepest heart, ashamed of Henry Senior, this itinerant, eccentric, free-thinking, mystic and grandly "philosophical" figure? — not altogether unlike the scoundrelly philosopher of "The Coxon Fund." Ashamed of this unconventional and lame father, and competing with him too, as he competed with William while ever denying it in those expressions of deepest filial devotion and loyalty. At least there is the series of heroic young children in James's work, talented prodigies like the Pupil, always viewed against their eccentric and exploiting families. There is the series of *diminutive* father-figures too, ending with Adam Verver, who are finally controlled and managed by the "daughter-son" with whom James was always identified. As far back as the ugly-duckling yet heroic daughter of "Washington Square," James's fiction records the triumph of all these outcast child-princelings over a callous and cruel adult world — or else, as in "The Turn of the Screw," their contamination and death.

Hence also the series of *shifting* fathers, mothers, brothers he devised. And just as James "invented" his own orphanhood and alienation, in a sense, so he contrived his salvation through "Europe" and through "art." What was notable in Henry James was not perhaps the neurosis as such, but the method of "adjustment," including the process of the infinite rationalization that we have traced, and the final end-product of this in his fiction. For weren't his esoteric "method" and his baroque "art" alike simply another means of justifying his own temperament, his own unlikely vision of life? Isn't it clear too that the twentieth century Jacobites, in their famous parlor game of "justifying Henry," were simply following, all devoutly, piously, un-critically, the Master's initial program? And Henry did it better.

Very likely the deeper wound of Henry James was on the pre-

Brooks's earlier study, *The Pilgrimage of Henry James,* and his account of Henry in the *Makers and Finders* series, contain brilliant analyses of James's moral and social values, though the center of the "Jamesian psychology" is never quite reached, and no wonder.

oedipal *social* level, which then forced him into the strange quest of a feudal or medieval European culture — quite similar to the emergent robber barons of his own period also trying to buy up the same false antiquity and gothic prestige. Furthermore, just as James had no conscious concern with social values, economics, politics — or with any of the real elements of the "history" which he worshiped as a kind of picture and legend — so the Memoirs showed how little he cared also for philosophy, or for ideas in themselves. (That was his father's province, or his brother's!) In point of fact, had any writer except James, had any writer pretending to major status ever been so purely concerned with the realm of "manners" — and manners which were completely divorced from all the social and historical context which formed them? Or take religion — wasn't James's only real concern with the increasing "Catholicism" in his work simply for its greater "pictorial" and dramatic value? (Well, perhaps there was also an implicit rebuke to the uncultivated Americans of his youth, who had in their turn patronized the Irish Catholic immigrants.) What is interesting, however, is how far he managed to carry forward such a narrow intellectual orbit of pure manners. And no wonder that he needed all the supporting props of melodrama and "method" to fill out his limited esthetic scene; as well as all the fertility of an endlessly subtle or tricky "metaphysical" imagination to devise twist upon twist for his slender themes.

This was the equivalent of the Jamesian stress on the "conscious mind" (in those lengthy passages of "critical analysis") with no regard for the depths — the *real* twists and quirks and hidden abysses — of the unconscious. And wasn't there, instead, a very sensitive and fearful Jamesian instinct to press *down* the unconscious wherever it began to form and show in his fiction — and thus to betray and distort all the real implications of his best stories? Pure manners and pure consciousness, only those remain. And perhaps never in the history of humane letters had a novelist done so much with so little content as Henry James himself: the

Dark Prince of the American leisure class, the self-made orphan of international culture, the romantic historian of the *ancien régime*, the European inheritor, the absolute esthete, the prime autocrat of contemporary (and contrived) art.

Now forgive the capitalizing above which is simply an attempt to cope with the enormity of Henry James's literary personality. That he was also the prime fictionalist of power, position and prestige; of almost completely fabricated "social forms"; of lurid schemes, intrigues, plots and plans; of an altogether abstract control and manipulation of his literary characters; that he was the typical, though altogether unconscious novelist of a late nineteenth century American finance capitalism, spurious and transient as this vision of life turned out to be — Well, that was just another irony of the cultural history which Henry James from the start had ignored and despised at the cost of his own development as an artist.

13. The End of Henry James —
and the Ascension

HE HAD BEEN ill since the time of *The Outcry*, however; he was bed-ridden and invalided for long periods. He was in his seventies; there were organic troubles and he had been suffering, as he told Desmond MacCarthy, from "the spiral of depression which . . . compelled him step after step, night after night, day after day, to descend." He would never have recovered, he thought, "had it not been for a life-line thrown to him by his brother William."

This is based on Mr. Dupee's account of the last years; and we have noticed the real meaning of the brotherly "life-line" — of William James's death — in sustaining Henry through those Memoirs which had started out as William's story. Even so, the First World War had cut through *The Middle Years* with its appalling impact. "He was not of course among the observers who had foreseen a world war," said Mr. Dupee with some measure of understatement; and this critic-biographer immediately and typically proceeded to explain away his own statement. "He assimilated the news, however with the assurance of one long familiar with the latent violence of modern life; and on August 5th he addressed to Howard Sturgis what has become a classic account of the war's moral impact:

The plunge of civilization into this abyss of blood and darkness by the wanton feat of those two infamous autocrats is a thing that so gives away the whole long age during which we have supposed the world to be, with whatever abatement, gradually bettering, that to have to take it all now for what the treacherous years were all the while really making for and meaning is too tragic for any words.

There is no doubt as to the late-late James's "assurance" about such matters; that was by now his public tone. But what "latent violence of modern life" was James ever really familiar with: what aspect of modern life did this romantic medievalist really comprehend, even in his studies of the "sensibility" of high finance? Perhaps Mr. Dupee means the "alien menace" of *The American Scene?* Or the "moral evil" of the modern world from which the superior protagonists of *The Golden Bowl* had retreated, according to the imaginative Mr. Spender? Or the melodramatic violence of "modern Anarchism" which the little revolutionary bookbinder (named Hyacinth) defied, according to Mr. Lionel Trilling, in *The Princess Casamassima?*

Come now. We have just noticed that the real world of the Jamesian yearning was the semifeudal and pictorial amalgam of French and English nobility in the *ancien régime* of Henry James's fictional fantasies. Our whole study of this extraordinary temperament has revealed not only a built-in cultural time lag in this writer who confused "history" with royal legend — and time itself with the enchanted visionary realm of childhood romance — but even a kind of biopsychic time lag. James had absolutely no comprehension that the First World War was about to break upon his head, as Mr. Dupee correctly stated at first. Since he had no real sense of history at all, he had no knowledge of the real issues of this war, too, except that of an elevated "moralism" and a fervent "patriotism" (towards England, naturally) of the blindest sort. In his "classic account of the war's moral impact" just notice the "abyss of blood and darkness," the "wanton feat of those two infamous autocrats," those "treacherous years" (during which other writers were already protesting the drift of historical events!) and the final "too tragic for any words." Is *that* the language of a historian?

It was close to the same visionary and romantic rhetoric with which James always described the great events of *his* personal history. I mean the French Revolution again, where the nobility behaved so gallantly to their last moments on the scaffold before the jeering commoners; the "King's War" against the rebellious (or treasonable) American Colony; the Civil War that we have described. Yet even a cultural historian like F. O. Matthiessen, still under the dark Jamesian spell, could add to this nonsense that "James broke off *The Ivory Tower* because the modern age had sounded its first alarm in July, 1914:

His sensitive antennae recorded at once an interpretation of what was happening. He had only a moment of shocked blankness that anything so "infamous" could happen "in an age that we have been living in and taking for our own as if it were of a high refinement of civilization . . ."

And I isolate, I stress this statement because it represents the high pitch of Matthiessen's own absurdity in the historical area when it concerned itself with Henry James: just as we have noticed previously the tangle of Matthiessen's esthetic judgments when they describe James. And both Dupee and Matthiessen are perhaps the *best* of the Jacobite critics, if we omit the inflamed and cloudy rhetoric of Mr. Blackmur; the pontifical "judgments" of Mr. Zabel; the "committed sensibility" of Mr. Edel; or the fervent metaphysical misinterpretations of Mr. Stallman; not to mention the sheer poetic license of the two expatriated English poets, Auden and Spender.

What a roster of illustrious modern names. (I leave out many others, to stress these typical Jamesian specialists; I omit the popular but "outside critic" Mr. Fadiman among others.) And what a farrago of nonsense they have all contributed to the remarkable case of Henry James.* Under the spell of this Circean wand they

* Amidst the heavy burden of this unanimous critical praise of Henry James's work on both sides of the ocean, perhaps only two voices were raised in dissent. In America Van Wyck Brooks continued calmly to show up the essential snobbery and

have become, if not quite an order of lower critical animals, very like unto the little children who were the heroes of a writer whose own mind was fixed and permanently embedded in childhood fantasy. *What* is so catching and contagious and befuddling in this transparent world of Jamesian "art"?

You have only to read a sampling of James's war letters (in *The Letters of Henry James,* edited by the early Jacobite, Percy Lubbock) to realize how ignorant and naïve, how "patriotic" and chauvinistic, how violent and melodramatic — how romantic and how vulgar in short — James really was about the First World War, where he beheld England as the citadel of civilization, and Germany *merely* as the barbaric, ruthless Hun. Yet this war, like his recapitulation of the Civil War, also served its purpose in the career of Henry James. After the United States took no "immediate action" upon the sinking of the *Lusitania,* he became, formally, an English citizen. He was ashamed of his own country (openly, that is, at last), and he took this opportunity — at last — of demonstrating his deep bond with England.

But this had always been the logical culmination of his deepest yearning; for which he had "waited" so patiently (and perhaps cunningly) throughout his adult life, just as he had dawdled and gaped (with his hidden, iron determination) through the period of adolescence until his inevitable break with America. And maybe this final act of James's marked the closing and healing of the earlier Civil War wound which had, in its own way, "determined" his youthful exile; but an exile, in fact, which had already been determined by the time of his tenth year of life.

"He survived some two and a half years of the war," said Dupee, "and was strenuously and variously active in Britain's cause." (So too was Edith Wharton, in much the same way, and with the same disastrous effect on her writing, which perhaps never quite recov-

---

antidemocratic bias of James; and in England J. B. Priestley (in his *Literature and Western Man*), while perhaps according to James more credit than he deserved, brilliantly described his limitations.

ered from her period of aristocratic and martial propaganda.) And
when Ford Madox Ford — who had changed *his* too Teutonic
name — was about to depart for the front, it was James who said:
"*Tu vas te battre pour le pays de Madame de Staël.*" Well, that
was what the war was really about, for Henry James; and he was
paying his belated price — a price no writer can afford to pay —
for his ignorance of history, society, politics and economics; not to
mention religion, social morality, ethics or philosophy. And not
to mention literature itself, from which he drew only his own peculiar inspiration.

Yet his application for English citizenship was sponsored by the
Prime Minister among others, as Dupee is careful to note. "Civis
Britannicus sum," he wrote to Edmund Gosse; and now perhaps
he was prepared to die. He suffered from a bad heart — "made
worse, perhaps, by his wartime exertions," so we are told. On December 2nd, 1915, he had a stroke; and there was his famous comment, heard by Henry as "another voice": "So here it is at last,
the distinguished thing!" (For even nature's afflictions had to be
notable in his case.) And on February 28th, 1916, he died.

He left the unfinished volume of the Memoirs, and two "fragments" of novels, *The Ivory Tower* and *The Sense of the Past*,
which are dismissed, perhaps too casually, by Mr. Dupee, and
which are "analyzed," perhaps too earnestly, by Mr. Matthiessen.
Both of these unfinished novels, published in 1917, and edited
by Mr. Lubbock, were drawn from James's outline summary (in
the *Notebooks*) of what was to be his last "American novel,"
and was tentatively called first "my K.B. case," and then "Mrs.
Max." Here again in his notes, or in what Matthiessen called
James's "fertile colloquy" with himself, James lavishly stressed the
Dramatic Method and the Action of his final works; which he
also discussed in terms of "Acts" — of stage sets and of stage entrances and exits, and hence, no doubt, of stage or theatrical *people*. There is, for example, in the original scenario of "Mrs. Max,"
the friend of the Heroine's, whom the Action must gather in.

"Yet, ah, *so* functional too must this figure be — in the sense, I mean, of what will depend on it; which is the *only* sense of the functional."

Is it, really? But of course the late-late James no longer even considered the mere functioning of a human character — not to mention the low, vulgar functioning of the human organism — simply in itself, as a display of character, of temperament, of life, or the way people are. "Functional" meant indeed "what will depend on it" in the future course of the action, or of the plot melodrama. The Jamesian esthetics, or more correctly the Jamesian dramatics, had drained off all the natural life of these literary characters for the sake of the original "idea," and then the "dramatic development," full of "effects," of this idea; and then the stage "moral," or final climax of this now so highly contrived literary concoction. Yes, the whole effect of the Jamesian play-novel, so devoutly studied in our academic Creative Writing courses, was simply to deprive the novel of its most characteristic and fruitful artistic freedom as a chronicle of human experiences, even while it was intended to produce those Jamesian "plays" which were so unsuitable for the stage itself.

Yet James continued to discuss, fervently and feverishly, the new discoveries, of a "method," which the Jamesian critics of the mid twentieth century have actually established as the "Art of Fiction." He referred back again to the "august light" which *The Outcry* had provided for his fiction. He used such terms as "action" again and always; or degrees and proportions and *kinds* of plasticity, and "theatrically (using the term scientifically and, ah, so non-vulgarly!) workable." "Oh, blest *Other House*," he cried here, referring to another dismally poor play, "which gives me thus at every step a precedent, a support, a divine little light to walk by. *Causons, causons, mon bon* — oh celestial, soothing, sanctifying process, with all the high sane forces of the sacred time fighting through it on my side! . . ."

Who was idiotic now? Though it was still very controlled and

dedicated: this insane esthetic rage of James's which has also entranced our best contemporary scholars and critics. "Let me fumble it gently and patiently out — with fever and fidget laid to rest
— as in all the enchanted months!" (And that is to say, of the enchanted love affair of James with his Art, the passion of James
for James.) "It only looms, it only shines and shimmers, *too* beautiful and too interesting; it only hangs there too rich and too full
and with too much to give and to pay; it only presents itself too
admirably and too vividly, too straight and square and vivid, as a
little organic and effective Action." *Action;* and the plot of "Mrs.
Max" which James outlined in the *Notebooks* was that of another
conventional Jamesian romance-melodrama which contained a rich
but sick husband to whom the heroine had devoted the best years of
her life. With his death, she is "free," in the Jamesian sense — free
to go to Europe, that is, and experience life; but her conflict is
simply whether she will go alone or *with* her husband's mother.
Her husband's mother, needless to say, controls the family fortunes;
and the real "problem" of the play-novel is whether the heroine will
knuckle under to the dominating mother-in-law for the sake of
the fortune, or will she be able to proclaim her own freedom as a
human being and live, though more simply, on the seven or eight
thousand dollars a year which she has from her own inheritance.

The outlines of the leisure-class novel and the world of the rentiers — of which the international theme was a branch — never
changed in the enchanted and embedded Jamesian vision of life.
(This "vision" which, as we have already seen, is so personal and
strange in the history of literature as the reflection of man's true
nature, aspirations and destiny in the world.) The *Notebooks* continued with the Jamesian stress on "the function of this Exposition," and the *"dénouement d'acte,"* and the process "I follow to
arrive logically and thrillingly at that determination of the elements." But just what determination of which elements did Henry
James arrive at in the actual portion of *The Ivory Tower* which
exists today?

The scene was the post-Civil War Newport, the earlier Jamesian "link" with America, but a scene which now also had succumbed to not so much the social, but the esthetic corruption of great wealth. This was the new-rich paradise of the rich-rich million-aires in the Jamesian version of the social change which had swept over the Democracy in the latter half of the nineteenth century. And the plot line of *The Ivory Tower* encompassed *two* of these millionaires, a good one, "Mr. Betterman," and a bad one, Mr. Gaw. They are both dying, together, as the novel opens; the ac-tion of the story takes place, indeed, around their entwined death-beds. The bad millionaire, Gaw, is of course the *richer* million-aire; and his daughter, Rosanna, patient, suffering, heavy, massive heiress (rather like the heroine of "Washington Square"), has atoned for an "ancient wrong" done to Betterman's nephew, Gra-ham Fielder, by calling him back from Europe in time to receive *his* fortune from the good millionaire.

This was still the world of the inheritors, as well as the rentiers; and never was the time lag in James's work (this prescient, sensi-tive "interpreter" of both the American scene and World War I) more apparent. Just as the language of these new millionaires, and their heirs, is that same midwestern dialect which James had used as early as *The American,* so the central concept of these new for-tunes is still that of the fortunate speculator rather than of finance capitalism. It is close to that of Howells' old-fashioned *Silas Lapham,* in 1885; while Dreiser's *The Financier,* in 1912, and *The Titan,* in 1914, had already described a completely different world of corporate finance; and a new breed of American man, abstract, calculating, nonhuman. The Jamesian chronicle, by contrast, still dealt with the "personal millionaires" of the mid-nineteenth cen-tury, rather than the new titans and barons of oil, coal, railroads, land, mining and the utility trusts. What was curious, too, in *The Ivory Tower* was that both of the dying rich men were again rather pathetic and childlike figures. Rosanna treats her own minus-cule millionaire in much the same way that Adam Verver's daugh-ter nursed and "managed" him.

The Jamesian father-figure is again infantile; the big, heavy, solid, plain daughter is the mature heroine — who, however, exists in a veritable nest of the evil, vicious, corrupt hangers-on of great wealth. Davy and Gussy Bradham are the "new-money" types of James's notorious American return, though the tone which he used to describe them was similar to that describing the decadent British aristocracy in *The Awkward Age* or *What Maisie Knew*. The Bradham crowd is fast, loose, unprincipled; ambitious (for even more wealth), hard and self-serving. Their stress on carnel pleasure (a "modern" invention, à la James) hardly conceals their self-interest, cunning, selfishness and malice. James is very good at describing these clever and voracious little social egos, all clamoring for recognition, for advancement, for personal gain.

For in *The Ivory Tower* the familiar Jamesian ambiguity: the mixed motives, the shields and covers and echoes and reflectors and traps and red herrings which are usually established to cover the real behavior of his characters, the continual series of false leads of which this artful writer was so prolific, the elaborate and countless mirrors of illusion in a prose which, as we've said, was designed to distort rather than to display the truth — Well, this ambiguity of Jamesian art, which far outdid the basic complexity of life, has divided off here into the black-and-white worlds of almost pure "good" and pure "evil" which were always at the base of Henry James's real vision of human experience.

All of the characters in this novel, with the exception of the heroic, disinterested, noble and wealthy Rosanna Gaw, are trying to get hold of the fortune which Fielder has again inherited, for no good reason to speak of, from Rosanna's father. The story is filled with the scheming, plotting and planning of its new-rich crowd (who are apparently not rich *enough*) devoted to this single purpose, and massed together in pursuit of their "easy money." Because Fielder again, as the noble European Jamesian hero, doesn't really care about this irrelevant fortune, which is also "contaminated" by such a corrupt social scene. Against this vulgar mass of humanity stand only the two noble (but comfortably off) protagonists, Rosanna and Fielder, who are also "old friends" rather than lovers. But what happened in *The Ivory Tower* was that it simply fell apart, so far as the Jamesian vision, method and craft were concerned, and the two halves of his literary world (which always lay beneath his elaborate attempts at mystification and dissimula‚ tion) were completely visible.

This novel was in fact a kind of skillful light parlor comedy, English in essence, of cunning, sadism, malice, "teasing" and what we may call minor evil. Now James was still very good at this — but that is not what he is supposed to be good at. What happens now to the long line of contemporary critics who have stressed the "higher morality" of Henry James, or the "development of the moral consciousness" as his major contribution to fiction, or the "civilizing impact" of his work? In the Notes to the unfinished *Ivory Tower*, too, James himself was apparently quite unconscious, again, of what his novel had turned out to be. But for the most part the scenario he had sketched out is dull reading except, again, for the clear "moral" which he wanted to establish in this late-late fiction. "I want Gray absolutely to inherit the money, to have it, to have had it, and to let it go . . ." This was still the sensibility of high finance, the dramatic peril of contaminated cash, as in "A Round of Visits," or even as in the "noble" development of Merton Densher's moral consciousness where he too repudiates the fortune which has been given to him for his deception of Milly Theale. Thus the world of the inheritors now included those who were given fortunes for their charm and innocence (Isabel Archer); those who *refuse* their tainted fortunes (from Densher to Graham Fielder, and perhaps we should include the equally noble Fleda Vetch of *The Spoils of Poynton*); and those others, from Kate Croy to the present group of Newport scoundrels and schemers, who are simply out to get a fortune — by any means, that is, except by working for one. The unfinished Notes for the unfinished *Ivory Tower* again stressed Gray Fielder's "moral consciousness" in this utterly exotic context of falsely inherited wealth which is then repudiated. And what a fertility of imaginative twists, what cornucopias of esthetic nomenclature Henry James still displayed in the development of what was obviously the weakest, emptiest, most contrived and theatrical of plots.

He no longer *cared*, involved only with his famous "method," about what kind of content the method was to produce; and in this way his basic values showed up clearly. There was still the "bad," the "black," the "evil" world of malice in *The Ivory Tower*, the "money power" and the "money prestige" which this good hero would repudiate. "Don't I really see the Bradhams then as *predatory*? Predatory on the very rich, that is," James asked himself here. Not a bad idea, incidentally, if it worked; and the Jamesian world of rentiers now included the rich, the very rich, and the rich who wanted to be richer, to be very, very rich. But wasn't this an interesting statement from the leisure-class novelist who had, in his own career, elevated the predatory emotions into the realm of art — into the central areas of the psyche? Now James was simply repudiating the *obvious* predatory area of the cash nexus around which his whole literary world, his whole sense of human beings, of human relations and human experience, was actually centered. The "big haul" in the outlined plot for *The Ivory Tower* was necessary in order to have "the big sacrifice" of the noble, good, sensitive old-world young man; but again *who* had contrived so carefully both the "big haul" and the "big sacrifice," and whose novel was to revolve around this axis of real greed and spurious nobility?

Oh yes, Henry James was "deep, deep, deep!" as he said so often through the false voices of his literary characters . . . And the second of the unfinished novels, *The Sense of the Past*, published in the same year (1917) as *The Ivory Tower*, had a similar quality of ultimate and pure, if altogether unconscious, self-revelation. The novel had a curious history, as was true with so many Jamesian works — so that in a sense their origins and their postscripts are as interesting as the work itself.

He had started *The Sense of the Past* in 1899, as another commercial "ghost story," in the vein of "The Turn of the Screw," for
Doubleday who then withdrew their offer; a "betrayal" James did
not forget. In July-August of 1900, Howells suggested the idea of
an "international ghost" which appealed to James as a continuation of his story, but — "I fumble, I yearn, *je tâtonne*, a good deal
for an alternative to *that* idea, which proves in execution so damn-
ably difficult and complex . . . The ideal is something as simple
as *The Turn of the Screw,* only different and less grossly and
merely apparitional." *

There were things, "admirably beautiful and possible things,"
in James's preliminary idea for *The Sense of the Past,* as he confessed to himself; and "it's only the idea which can give me the
situation" — which was another interesting illumination on the
part of this "metaphysical," say, but non-ideological novelist, who
became increasingly concerned with the twists of his plot to develop
his "moral." But he could not work out the story in 1900, "and I
fear I must simply confess to my funk at the danger, the risk, the
possibility of the waste of *present,* precious hours —

*Let me lay the many pages I've worried out of it piously away — where
some better occasion may find them again. I must proceed now with
a more rigorous economy, and I turn about, I finger other things over,
asking, praying, to feel something that will do instead. I take up, in other
words, this little blessed, this sacred small, "ciphering" pen that has
stood me in such stead often already, and I call down on it the bene-*

---

* This statement, incidentally, made not for publication, but in James's private
communings with himself, should lay once and forever the "Freudian Ghost" of a
theory that there are no ghosts in "The Turn of the Screw" — that the whole drama
exists in the mind of the governess. A nice theory; but untenable to anybody who
has studied the story closely, and who knows the whole body of James's pre-, non-,
and "anti-Freudian" work, as we have seen. It was precisely those "grossly and
merely apparitional" ghosts who *made* the governess nearly mad, and over whom she
triumphed. Nor did James "believe" in ghosts, as the neo-mystic and neo-religious
critics state. They were the props of a commercial tale which was also a *jeu d'esprit,*
in the vogue of ghost stories which prevailed in the 1890's.

diction of the old days, I invoke the aid of the old patience and passion
and piety. They are always there — by which I mean here — if I give
myself the chance to appeal to them. There are tails of things that one
must, with one's quick expert hand, catch firm hold of the tip of. They
seem to whisk about me — to ask only for a little taking of the time,
a little of the old patient mystic pressure and "push." Adumbrations
of "little subjects" flash before me, in short, and the thing is to . . .

Now this was the familiar, innermost, mystic note of the Jamesian religion of art: along with the Jamesian doubts, and the reassuring Jamesian self-assurances as to "one's quick expert hand"
grasping those slippery, flashing tips of his literary "tails" (tales).
But what was the true meaning of the invocation to the "old days,"
to the "old patience and passion and piety," which is a constant
refrain in the *Notebooks* from the 1890's to the writing of *The*
Sense of the Past itself — to the very end?

Was it — this "benediction" of the past which James so tragi-
cally kept invoking — referring to the days of his early success
with the gently satiric *The American*, the romantic and touching
Portrait of a Lady, the controversial "Daisy Miller"? The days
of his popular fame, that is, before the failure of *The Bostonians,*
The Princess Casamassima, The Tragic Muse. And before the
horrid, the undignified, the most deeply wounding dramaturgical
crisis — which Henry James then "reconstructed" for almost two
decades into the "dramatic method" of his fiction, and the relentless series of play-novels or novelistic plays which he continued to
"produce, produce, produce." While Sigmund Freud indeed, during
these same years, was penetrating down through all the melancholy and complex depths of human self-delusion, Henry James
was providing one of the clearest, best examples of the way the
human organism really works, survives and even flourishes through
the repression of all unpleasant or damaging facts, including, let
us say, any kind of objective truth itself. James was thus a perfect
illustration of the Freudian hypothesis about human nature in its
natural, illusionary state. He was a whole psychology course in

himself — although not in the sense attributed to him by the rational-moral critics who accept all his transparent fictions at face value, and then proclaim Henry James as the Master of Freudian insights.

In *The Sense of the Past*, too, notice the familiar lure of the legendary British estate which the story's hero has *inherited* — almost the same donnée (speaking as the Jacobites always do of the Jamesian données which are never to be questioned) which James first used in the "Passionate Pilgrim" of the 1870's. Thus this master fictionalist completed the full cycle of his fiction and fantasy life alike: a cycle, however, which also remained fixed and immutable from the point of its origins — a perpetual, but unchanging cycle.

The last novel's hero, Ralph Pendrel, is another weak and clinging young "historian" who is involved with "the sense of the past" in precisely the Jamesian mode: the past of legend, nobility, romance, glamour, and pictorial color in early nineteenth century England. (But this visionary sense of the past is bolstered up, perhaps, by the solid immutable base of "old property.") Ralph is indeed consumed by the "backward vision," the "recovery of the lost." He yearns for "the very tick of the old stopped clocks." Now this was what Henry James had always meant by "history," and those ancient clocks had really stopped ticking before James's birth. Quite like Henry, Ralph leaves New York (and the rather attractive heroine called Aurora) to gain possession of his enchanted London house and his special, private, solitary "romance" with the past. Now the leisure-class novel à la James has descended (or ascended) to *one* character alone with his legendary property, and his private visions of a nobler past; and one wonders what evil of "the modern world" Mr. Dupee, Mr. Spender, or even Mr. Matthiessen could read into this literary situation.

But the unfinished novel was also a kind of reverse-twist on "The Jolly Corner," since the hero is to meet his "true" alter ego: no demon, no apparition, this time, but an enchanted, glorious cavalier of a "happy" (British) status. And once back in the 1810 English scene (after this elaborate introduction), the Jamesian prose takes on all the trappings of the popular novel, or of his historical romances such as *Guy Domville*.

Ralph Pendrel's family have been Loyalists, of course, in the King's War against the rebellious American settlers — in the rigor of which they had emigrated, restoring themselves to England for a ten years' stay. And somehow (James is rather vague) they have also amassed a fortune during their subsequent return to the lost, I mean the newly emancipated, American Colony. Returning once more to the Motherland, meeting his Midmore cousins at their great English estate of Drydown, Ralph, putting on the mask of his ghostly alter ego, is a noble young man of arms, action, and intrigue. Only this is another false world of romance that James has set up at the opening of *The Sense of the Past*; an enforced mode of gaiety in which Molly Midmore, continually tossing up her head, also calls her glowering, suspicious brother "merry Perry." It is the *wrong* sister whom Ralph has been taken in by (there is again the familiar Jamesian "cousinship of passion"); and this hero gives himself away bit by bit. For all his wit, sparkle, and sophistication, he is actually in a box or a trap which is slowly closing upon him. The fairy-tale romance turns shortly into another Jamesian psychological nightmare very close not to "The Turn of the Screw," as James believed, but to *The Sacred Fount*.

Ralph is really walking on a tightrope of the past (of which he is half aware, and half ignorant), and one false move will disclose his true — or his false — personality to this whole group of older British nobility. Even the "cleverness" which he prides himself on to get out of each new predicament leads him only into another one. That is the basic situation in *The Sense of the Past*, beneath all the romantic chatter that James now dispensed with such ease and fluidity; and it is a familiar, recurrent theme in James's work. Molly, the wrong sister, has Ralph's letters to her, as she claims, but where are *her* letters to him? And he hasn't even heard of

Nan — the right sister for him. Well, he gets over this hurdle through his "intellect" and quick wit; and he rejoices at "the pleasure of being certain, when he could be certain." On top of this slippery heap again, he "laughed out his desire." But Perry Midmore is increasingly suspicious of Ralph's behavior, and there appears "Sir Cantopher," an early nineteenth century English clown (modeled perhaps on James's reading of Smollett, Fielding, etc.), who is the agent in the drama who has set out to "catch" Ralph for good, or almost to catch him. He is "the terrible man" who "knows," or appears to know Ralph's "secret" of being an impostor — and all the Jamesian tags, and all the Jamesian psychological states, come together here.

The omnipotent "inquisitor" of the Jamesian chronicles, in this case Ralph Pendrel himself, is now being quizzed. His growing sense of panic goes along with the English group's growing suspicion of him; and if the Jamesian hero is not about to fall off the tightrope of his false identity, he is always on the edge of a chasm. The psychological states are genuine in *The Sense of the Past*, though the expression is often either flowery or tedious; and what is effective in the novel is just the alternation of mood between Ralph's false omnipotence and his true panic at the fear of "exposure" — or the "exhibition" of his true personality. (Of his being both naked and a scoundrel, so to speak.) These sections of the novel are like a sleepwalker's terror, where one false step leads to a catastrophe. Yet this Jamesian hero, too, is "indomitable" — his fear of "disclosure" is matched by his impudicity. "Ralph felt himself in the box, but also that never was a witness to have seen his embarrassment so enrich his interest." (Or was it, at base, that he *wanted* to be disclosed, revealed, exhibited as a naked scoundrel?) At least he treads this tightrope, he walks the edge of this chasm; he escapes from this box, momentarily, with aplomb as well as with alarm.

"I keep my balance here, for all your so watching me, as if I were on the tight-rope; and, so far as she or I at least are concerned, will

rule the scene there from the — wherever the place is: wait a minute, wait!" says the quite incredible hero in this dream-nightmare
chronicle. And again he is, in his own mind, the observer-
manipulator, still "ruling the scene" from his tightrope, his chasm,
his trap, and his box. But the elations of his "knowledge" (power)
are matched by the constant awareness of his danger and his "ignorance" — by his impotence. Or else he discovers that he "knows
too much," which is quite as dangerous for his situation as not
knowing enough. "I'm not mad, Cousin Perry," he says in almost
the same tone as the inquisitive, snooping, and beseeching observer of *The Sacred Fount*. (He has also "terrified" Perry Midmore with his mystic knowledge of events he shouldn't know.)
Here too are that late-late mood and words of *James plain* — the
mood of the Jamesian characters who so delight in "tormenting"
each other with their secrets and their hidden stratagems. "The
least I could do would be to torment you in return," says Molly
to Ralph quite "playfully." And there is the panicky awareness on
the part of this late-late Jamesian hero that his own body, his facial
expressions, as well as his speech, may be giving him away.

"If he only hadn't, once more, all the same, to wince the while
with awareness of that overdone grimace of his own!" And that is
to say, he winces more because he has already winced, or grimaced.
He gives himself away, again, because he has already given himself
away. As in the sphere of minor malice, where the aging James
was still effective in *The Ivory Tower*, so here the sections on both
a fancied omnipotence and a real self-disclosure are notable in *The
Sense of the Past*. As in *The Sacred Fount*, too, there is a gradually
enveloping atmosphere of nocturnal terror and fear (far more real
than that of the "mere vulgar apparitions" in "The Turn of the
Screw").

There is a growing fear and terror on the part of the English nobility as to this "alien" in their midst. And no wonder that James
was so sensitive to the "alien menace" in *The American Scene*;
since wasn't *he*, in the deepest core of his fantasy, always identi-

fied with the alien hero in England — an alien himself, at base, in *both* countries? But "identified with" the aliens only in the sense of also accepting as "superior" the British nobility which, in *The Sacred Fount*, had finally discovered and had kicked out the snooping hero simply because he had lacked, not indeed their mind, but their tone!

Henry James himself had tried desperately to conform to this tone, this life and these manners which he had read about and yearned for since early childhood. Hadn't he even "outdone" the British nobility in what William James called the "crustacean" mode of his formality? Wasn't he just as "physiognomic" (so the hero of *The Sacred Fount* had cried) as these most handsome, physiognomically, British? And yet no woman had loved the earlier Jamesian hero; and no man had treated him with quite the respect he deserved — and they had all united finally in treating him as "mad," as an outcast. Just so, in *The Sense of the Past*, Ralph hears himself laughing the most nervous of his laughs — after the false romantic paranoid glow of his early entrance and power over this little English group — his "glamour," his "authority." "Why is it, please, that you provide so for our hating you?" inquires Mrs. Midmore "in all gentleness and elegance." It sounds so dreadfully, she adds, "as if you knew something — !" And a page or so later comes the hero's equivocal answer. "I ask myself, when you tell me that I strike you as 'knowing' something, 'what it is I can know that wouldn't be a good deal more to your advantage than to mine if you were to find it out! I don't know anything that I *conceal*,' he smiled and smiled . . ."

So even the final, vaunted Jamesian stress on "knowing" is a form of disadvantage to the hero, a liability as he says, that can be turned against him. But smiling and smiling, what this last Jamesian figurehead *does* know is that the British nobility already suspect him, and will shortly and inevitably hate him, because he actually is an alien, an obvious outsider — a brilliant and deceitful fake. And wasn't this obviously the innermost panic and

fear of Henry James himself, however concealed in the fabric of his
fiction or his life alike? That is the real import, the underlying
message of *The Sense of the Past*. Although the little hero of the
Memoirs yearned, when he came "home" to the England of the
1870's, for a still earlier, still more "romantic" English scene of the
early nineteenth century, he was only to prove, in Henry James's
last novel, that he was still again, and perhaps even more, the
perfidious impostor. Yes, the real Henry James too, throughout his
own English life and career — so anxious to conform, and finally so
rejected both as fictionalist and dramatist — was walking the same
kind of tightrope, circling the same chasm, enclosed in the same
fatal box of all those mysterious "social forms" and inherited modes
of style, tone and grace as this last hero in *The Sense of the Past* for
whom one false step (in his own mind) would be the end.

What a curious and revealing chronicle this was in the obviously
unconscious Jamesian "moral" of the cultural superman, tran-
scending two ages, two cultures — and of the alien, even criminal,
intruder-impostor. Here was another characteristic set of alter egos
in the fantasy life of Henry James in which lay the final significance
of his whole life and literary career. In his deepest desire wasn't *he*
a similar superman of high art, straddling two nations, two societies as he did; and also then in the hidden core of his own
deepest anxiety — as in the prevalent "malaise" of his last unfinished novel — always and forever the alien outsider, the social impostor? A dominant mood of his most personal fiction, this was
the key to his whole public play-acting role of the Gentleman-
Artist. Just so, it was the reason for all that feverish, almost hysterical clinging to and stressing of the "social forms," or that which
"saved face," as in *The Golden Bowl*, at the expense of all truth
and depth, all reality, in his fiction. A crustacean Henry was indeed, as William had said, at the cost of all living and moving
human life and experience in himself, in his work. *Henry James*
was the real "American Pretender" from the earliest time of the
falsely inherited English estate in "A Passionate Pilgrim." And

what we have called the "biological orphanhood" of this enigmatic artist — or the self-made noble outcast — was certainly reinforced, was made almost intolerable, by the underlying anxiety of
James's having to conform, every moment of the day and night,
even, it appears, in his dreams, to his earliest vision of what the
British nobility *should be like*. That is the psychological burden of
both *The Sense of the Past* and *The Sacred Fount*, among the
many other works and passages of Henry James which support and
corroborate this point.

It has other aspects of course. Just as this central nightmarish
anxiety of "discovery" and "revelation" may be also biological and
sexual in the sense of Jame's predominant voyeurism and exhibitionism — in his *wanting* to be revealed — it was even more clearly
social and repressive and deeply inhibited in Henry James's equal
need *not* to be revealed for what in his heart, and in his most pertinent fiction, he believed himself to be. And these last insights as
regards the Jamesian temperament, the Jamesian predicament,
which are offered to us by *The Sense of the Past* explain something
else about the celebrated Jamesian "method" and "craft," which
employed such elaborate devices to expound or conceal the mysteries, the ambiguities, the enigmas, the subterfuges of his art. How
can an artist be direct or honest when his whole life and character
are based upon evasion, repression and dishonesty? Thus the famous Jamesian "development of consciousness" is stressed by the
Jacobite cult as a major contribution to the novel form. But what
a curious form this took in *The Sense of the Past*, where one half of
the hero's personality was "watching" the other half living a false
existence, wearing a false personality, so "triumphantly" and yet
so uneasily. This was also an accurate description (since the artist
had given up his vaunted "ambiguity" in the last novels where his
pure fantasy life displayed itself, unchecked by his earlier restraints
and inhibitions, mirrors and reflectors, in the transparent spheres
of good and bad, black and white — the world of James plain) of
how Henry James himself had "assimilated" his role of the English

Gentleman-Artist. And yet with the "wavering margin" which he also described, this constant threat of underlying distress and danger.

So then, with all the "beauties" and "miracles" of James's last fictional subject, as he said in his Notes, all the "magnificence" of his hero's being the "other man," and yet not being him, of adopting a false personality which was at once masterful and panic-ridden; of all this anxious, critical "living in his 'own' self" which was not his own self! — Well, dear God, no wonder his unfinished novel, just like the Jamesian psyche itself, from which this whole unique art form derived, was filled with a recurrent sense of "malaise"; with this uneasy watching, watching, watching on the part of his hero, or himself. Ralph Pendrel is also haunted by the hovering presence of the "real aristocrat" of 1820 whose place he has taken; a menacing figure which has not the appearance or effect "of reassuring or relieving him, but only of really quite mocking and not pitying him," of showing him to himself as " 'sold,' horribly sold." And how often the same refrain of being mocked at and menaced, of being "sold, sold, sold" appeared in the work of the later Henry James. Wasn't he at least half aware, and then having constantly to repress the thought, that he himself and his whole literary career had also been so horribly sold by his infantile-adolescent yearning and need for an aristocratic and old-world, a "European" or an "English" status? In *The Sense of the Past* the hero's depression — "his unspeakable homesickness for his own time and place" — was to increase and deepen. And this was James plain again, brooding, at the end, upon his own "unspeakable homesickness" for the *American* scene which he had abandoned, even in a sense betrayed, for the sake of his cut-off, rootless, forever false and formal, and desperately repressed and fearful British existence. How could he not realize somewhere in his tormented depths (though never, again, quite consciously) that the exile of his childhood years had simply been confirmed and reinforced by the alienism and exile, the stifling crustacean formality, both false and foreign, of his mature life.

In the Notes for the unfinished *Sense of the Past*, James sought to balance off the prevailing malaise of his hero, or of the novel itself, by another romantic love affair, or what he called "the romantic hocuspocus of my sought total effect." (Odd and revealing term — "hocuspocus" — since James was "throwing in" the love affair for the sake of his popular audience as much as for the technical balance of mood — which didn't really exist.) Yet again there was the late-late Jamesian refrain, complaint, lament, as to Ralph Pendrel's being "so 'cut off,' so now conclusively and hopelessly cut off, from the life of the whole magnificent world from which he is truant." This was the final despair of the now aging, the now aged, Henry James about his own "wasted life," and about that whole magnificent world indeed from which he himself had been so truant. And not merely in his English sojourn, but even in the quality of that British existence which was so hopelessly blank in experiential terms, in terms of *real*, rather than purely "artistic" or "mental" experience, as in those rare moments — such as in "The Beast in the Jungle" — he himself had felt, acknowledged and expressed.

And yet — and yet —. Henry James still had to add the familiar, reassuring and rationalizing climax to all this curiously open and revealing spiritual torment in both *The Sense of the Past* and the Notes for its conclusion. Again, the latent content of his fiction had to have its *conscious* negation, denial; and affirmative "moral triumph." (That which the Jacobite critics always seize upon to avoid the real psychological import of the Jamesian fiction.) For Ralph Pendrel was to be changed by this ghostly excursion into the legendary past; he was to have profited by it! "But I grant at once" — said in conclusion the old, familiar once-again-omniscient Henry James to the anguished Henry James of the Notes — "that Ralph has emerged from all trouble and now is, for the whole situation, supreme master and controller." *That* was to be the last point of James's last novel, as we have seen it to be the real point of all his later fiction. And who, may I ask for almost the last time, was the true "supreme master and controller" of James's literary puppet in *The Sense of the Past* — this curious fictional master and controller (unlikely as Ralph Pendrel was for this role) whose final power and authority were still, for the late-late-late Henry James, the whole meaning of human experience and character? Or at least the only possible answer he could devise for the human torment and anguish which was expressed in the body of the novel itself.

The Jamesian hero was to come out of his ordeal "all right," as had, so virtuously and blandly and complacently (on the conscious level), the hero of "Crapy Cornelia" from the near-fatality of actually marrying the series of women he had loved. Emerging safely, victoriously, all-masterfully from the harrowing ordeal of his double life in the past, Ralph Pendrel "*re-connects, on the spot, with all the lucidity and authority we can desire of him*" — and he reconnects, of course, with his distinguished friend in *The Sense of the Past*, the American ambassador himself. Thus the final, familiar, "conscious, moral, rational" triumph of the last Jamesian hero, who was also the anxiety-ridden superman of two cultures.

Yes, but haven't we said enough — though more could be said about Henry James; there is always more to be said about James — in respect to the strange history of this strange artist? Maybe he is so interesting just because, with all the appearance of a major talent, he produced only a minor body of work: with its narrow and fabricated frame of values, its inhibited and artificial range of emotions, its lack of any reference to the general human situation of his time or our time, or any time . . . No, Henry James could never possibly be called a great writer; he was only the great magician that he so revealingly called himself, and one who contrived an endless series of puzzles to fill up the empty box of his art, and his life. So he wasn't the "greatest American writer" that he has been described as so repetitiously during the middle decades of the twentieth century American literary scene. Compared with Melville, Whitman, Mark Twain, Dreiser — or even with Hawthorne

the "romancier" whom James took such pains to dismiss from the
native scene before him — Henry becomes a prodigy, yes, or some
kind of exotic literary monster in truth: but a child prodigy, as
we've seen, and even a childlike or childish sort of monster.

Based as his life and career were on his earliest, deepest infantile
dreams of "Europe, Art and Culture" — that embedded yearning
of the orphan prince which all experience confirmed, and no experience affected — Henry James is the most fascinating case of
arrested development in the history of belles lettres. At base his
whole literary world was the "pure" fantasy world of an adolescent,
or preadolescent vision of how things "should be," and never were,
and never could be. In the history of this career, too, we've noticed
the gradual emergence, under cover of these romantic visions, under this aura of perfect nobility, beauty and goodness, of another
Jamesian orbit of power, manipulation and control. I mean the
true Jamesian sphere of the buying and selling of human souls, the
managing and "fixing" of human destinies, so completely suited, so
well embodied in his famous "method" of the plotted and *controlled* novel. That was also the Jamesian "evil" which emerged in
the teasing and "playing" which was the product of the tormented
psyche and the blocked pleasure impulses.

Maybe this was the underlying appeal of the Jamesian fiction to
those critics who stressed his noble morality, his moral-rational
judgments, or the growth of the "moral consciousness" in his work,
which really shows quite the opposite: the growth of a thwarted,
unappeased and unfulfilled, a frustrated, devouring and sealed-off
egotism. At least what James himself finally called the romantic
"hocuspocus" of his narratives, and his highfalutin "morals," also
invalidated, to a large degree, the real psychological content (as in
The Wings of the Dove, as in *The Golden Bowl*) of the fiction
itself. We have noticed the buried incestuous background of so
many of these tales, long and short — the sphere of "domestic evil,"
so to speak, or of the earliest, most primitive and childlike human
desire — which James persisted in both portraying and betraying —

or in setting forth in his celebrated données, and ignoring in his
literary conclusions. Nor should we forget the very curious element
of the shifting parental relations in the enchanted visions of this
Dark Princeling — or sometimes the absolute sewer, as it appeared,
of promiscuous adult "sexuality" around the edges of which the
Jamesian infants sniff and pry. Those typical protagonists of our
self-made noble outcast, I mean, including the triumphant child-
heroine of *What Maisie Knew*; or the other-worldly child prodigy
of "The Pupil" who was exploited by his "bohemian" parents; or
the martyred child victims of "The Turn of the Screw," also
tainted by the crimes of others in the coarse, vulgar, sinful world
of adult sexuality.

We should remember the very earliest child-victim of Henry
James, the beautiful, unearthly infant in "The Author of Beltraffio,"
who at base was sacrificed for the "sexual-esthetics" of his pagan
father. Or the scholar-publisher of "The Aspern Papers," snooping in darkest night around the hidden treasure in the bedroom
of the ancient, witchlike mistress of the dead lover. These scenes
of an infantile and prurient sexuality occur too often, too persistently in the work of Henry James — they are revealed too
clearly in his later work — for us to take the conventional, the lofty
moral and rational interpretation of them. And this infantile-
pubescent, this thwarted sexuality of Henry James's, resulted directly in that equally dubious, shifting literary world of power and
conquest in which we have seen the final Jamesian reliance on the
one solid element of the cash nexus. If to be poor was the greatest
Jamesian sin, in women particularly, as with Kate Croy or Charlotte Stant or even the charming and betrayed Mme. Vionnet —
since poverty, with handsome women (and that is of course *relative* poverty), can only lead to sexuality and to crime; just so, a
well-inherited fortune was the greatest virtue in this elevated realm
of the inheritors and the rentiers, in the leisure-class orbit of power
without passion, or "passion" without love.

Thus Henry James became the perfect Veblenian novelist. He

was, as we've noticed, the novelist of the great American fortunes whose real mission in life, as he himself implied, was to teach the rich how to *use* their wealth. Henry James's basic values were in reality very close to those of the titans and financiers of his own period, if he hadn't the slightest comprehension of *how* these new fortunes were made, or of what profound and pervasive moral damage they did to both the old American republic and the modern American democracy. We have seen also that the closest Jamesian approach to this area was the unconsciously entertaining later phase of the "Sensibility of High Finance." Just as Henry James was the first (and perhaps last) American leisure-class novelist, his most bitter disappointment was that all this New Money made during his own lifetime did not recognize the superior taste, habits and manners of (just a little older) Old Money.

Thus he kept on writing of the sweet, innocent, childlike "good millionaires" of his fancy (Christopher Newman, Adam Verver, Mr. Betterman), as well as the other bad millionaires of the empty, bleak, sterile, "formless" American scene of his youth. But in any case money was essential to the Jamesian literary universe; the more of it the better — since it was only the *making* of money that led to vulgarity; or the taint of money not inherited "correctly," to evil. His "good heroines" were those who received their fortunes for their charm (starting with Isabel Archer); or later, his typical "good heroes" were those who *refused* an undeserved or contaminated fortune (Merton Densher, Gray Fielder); while his bad heroines or heroes alike showed mainly a lack of taste in their greed. Yes, the real crime in the whole range of Jamesian fiction was simply to have no cash (I mean, again, not *enough* cash); and even the suffering and Job-like "little gent" in "The Bench of Desolation" received his little lower class fortune in the end.

Did the blocked faculties of pleasure lead to this hidden craving for power in the Jamesian temperament; or was the power-need so strong (the mask for impotence) as to block off all the comforts, pleasures and luxuries of life, or of the body, which are so necessary to sustain the human psyche in its moments of need? No matter which way the cycle went in Henry James, the result was the same in this curious temperament which always "saw itself" (without ever seeing the truth about itself) as the little powerless and outcast child-orphan, as in the Memoirs, gaping and dawdling through its inferior, isolated existence with no thought of envy, jealousy, malice, competition or other such ordinary impulses. What a notable study of pure egotism, in the pre-, non-, or anti-Freudian sense, Henry James also was! Of the unconscious but all-devouring, absolute, implacable and finally altogether dictatorial, authoritarian and tyrannical ego, which sublimated and rationalized all of life to its own yearnings and needs, its own self-enclosed and idiosyncratic vision of "life."

But why continue to rehearse and summarize these Jamesian traits and "conclusions" so baldly here without their proper sources and contexts which we have already described. These abstract generalizations are hardly so interesting, too, as the whole process of their revelation in an author who disguised more than he displayed in both his temperament and his craft; whose prose style was designed to mislead the reader as often as to lead him; whose own alter ego — or the true ego of the present study — was either almost unknown to, or as in *The Sacred Fount,* "The Jolly Corner," and *The Sense of the Past,* was so definitely rejected and renounced by the artist himself.

We have, though, traced in some detail and with sufficient space the temperament, the character, and the work, of this utterly singular and quite fantastical writer, whose actual literary production might otherwise hardly warrant such consideration. Maybe Henry James is the most fascinating of all the minor writers in the world simply because he behaved like a major writer (and was often so close to this line, and always failed to achieve it); and because the real intensity, the real dedication of his talent was completely imprisoned, was fatally trapped, by the peculiarities of his personality. Perhaps it was just because he dedicated himself utterly and completely to "Art" itself (as was suggested by "The Middle Years"); because art was his *only* life, that in the end his art was so removed from, or devoid of, what we commonly recognize as life. And if he was only, in the end, a master magician of the verbal order — if his true literary orbit was entertainment of a very special kind, rather than the edification which the great novelists always bring to us — well, what a puzzle, an enigma, a drama he managed to make of his own shortcomings. And what a drama his modern critics have made of him!

If Henry James was the age, as our New Critic pronounced at the outset of the present study, he was certainly not *his* age, either in the America he scorned or the England he saw through the glass of his own legendary and antiquarian visions. In this sense Henry James's work was "ageless," just as it was "timeless" and "place-less" — in the sense that it floated in the high, pure, weightless outer space of pure esthetics and pure fairy tale. But in an odd way Henry James did become the age of the mid-twentieth century United States literary environment and atmosphere; and the symbol of a curious kind of literary or critical imagination in the 1940's and '50's.

For this was the epoch of a peculiar "prosperity" and a false "normalcy": an age of conformity and of sterility, as I said at the time (in my *American Moderns*, in 1958); of the "peace" which went under the name of the Cold War, and of new, unparalleled world tensions in the period from McCarthy to Sputnik. In terms of the national spirit, the Zeitgeist, it was also a period of alto-gether Jamesian euphoria which had simply blocked out, denied, or "reconstructed" all the hard, unpleasant, dangerous or threatening facets and facts of the "real world," the larger world around us, including our own defeats and our failures to deal with this outer and surrounding world, ominous and threatening.

In literature this period marked the decline of the classic modern American writers (Hemingway, Faulkner, Steinbeck, Dos Passos among others) while they were at the peak of their popular and worldly reputations. In criticism there was the movement towards higher and higher levels of esthetic, or scholastic absolutes. The mid-twentieth century American literary scene was the apogee of the so-called new criticism, which cared little for anything new or creative in the national letters, but concentrated all the weight and density of its own "scientific" methodology upon a thin list of "approved" writers, Eliot, Pound, and James foremost among them. In the authoritarian epoch of the "teacher-critics" or the "teacher-poets" or the "teacher-novelists" (when the arts themselves had retreated to the academic sanctuaries), there was a formidable body of "received opinion" about good writers and bad writers. And they were "fools," as one of these official spokesman said, who dared to ignore or defy this prevailing School; this arbitrary, dogmatic and agreed-upon literary coda as regards the whole wide panorama, varied, multiformed and complex, of both native and world literature.

Well then, thank God, I say, for the Fools; who in ancient culture were viewed as the emissaries of the Lord.

Described by our imaginative Jamesian critic-poet, W. H. Auden, as the Age of Anxiety, this was also an Age of Mediocrity when few good writers emerged, or were noticed when they did appear, while a host of minor talents, all skillful, all uttering the same commonplaces, were "accepted" and often celebrated. And in this academic, theoretical, genteel pseudoclassical and "pure" literary environment which was dominated by the absolutist coda of the New Criticism — who cared? One might have welcomed another H. L. Mencken to pursue the battle against this resuscitated and reinforced and even more powerful revival of "the Academy" upon the American scene — an academy which was more threatening precisely because it included some of the best-known modern names, and an Academic Humanism (Mr. Trilling's "Liberal Imagination," devoid of any taint of vulgar progressivism) which made the official humanism of the 1920's almost look humanist. But no Mencken, no Sinclair Lewis appeared to deflate such high-minded, officious and quite tyrannical critical opinion. It was not a fresh period indeed, those 1940's and 1950's, as I said at the time; but then how could it be? The social atmosphere was so heavy, oppressive and ominous; the esthetic air was so thin, pure, abstract and sterile — or perhaps disinfected was a better word.

Thus it was an age of literary revivals, rather than literary creativity; and wasn't our own Henry James the perfect symptomatic and symbolic figure, on all these accounts, of such a period? At least Henry represented all that Herman Wouk's Marjorie Morningstar craved in her fictional apotheosis of wealth, status, respectability and "culture" — if this was only, alas, in a suburban and middle class Westchester hamlet. James was superior to this, truly; James was the real thing. He was the perfect English gentleman, superficially at least, for those critics who refused to notice his underlying fear and anxiety — as well as the price which he paid in his art for his formal and spurious respectability. Didn't these Jacobite critics themselves yearn for just what Henry James had yearned for; and receive it through the cult of James at the same cost?

Henry James was, above all, the pure artist. Just the thing for the new criticism with its own stress on method which also negated, or obliterated, the historical and the human elements alike in the "pure" work of art. Just the thing too, this aristocratic Anglo-American artist — with his elaborate rationalizations of his own work and temperament; with his non-political (well, royalist), non-social, non-economic and non-historical sense of "history" which was all romantic legend and noble pageantry as we've seen — for the ex-radical critics in the 1940's and '50's who were making haste to block-out and "reconstruct," quite in the Jamesian mode, their own now "subversive" ties or connections, or perhaps even their radical utterances (I don't mean beliefs) in the 1930's. How perfect Henry James was in all these respects; how beautifully he fitted the new period in every respect, joint, hinge or *clou* as he might

have said. For James was certainly superior to the contemporary
writers who illustrated the same cultural drift in the mid-century
American literary scene. He was certainly better than Herman
Wouk or J. D. Salinger who were popular for much the same reasons. He was far superior even to his own Jacobite critics who rehearsed and rehearsed the same old stereotyped "virtues" in his
fiction; and refused to notice all the fascinating faults and limitations of Henry James, the curious if momentary lapses in his literary role beneath the encrusted self-armor, the momentary episodes
of self-satire and (if only partly conscious) self-illumination.

Henry James was at least a supreme example of the artist
manqué, and he shows us *why*. While the twentieth century Jacobite circle was comprised, on the whole, of demi-critics who showed
us in the end nothing — nothing more, that is to say, than what
was on the surface of James and his work, or what he consciously
wished to show . . . But wasn't the cult of James a revealing symbol and symptom of an age and a society which wanted to dwell
like him in some imaginary world of false art and false culture?
Just like James, the United States of the 1950's was rooted in a
fabricated fantasy life of its own "leisure class" existence; while
also, just as in the Jamesian temperament and achievement, this
narrow and rigid "vision" of itself had obvious undertones of anxiety, fear or hysteria. For this *was* in effect a leisure-class nation
among all the troubled, impoverished, chaotic or revolutionary nations of the world with whom the U.S.A. could barely communi-
cate, and often appeared to have no understanding of. Those other
dark and "alien," poverty-stricken, coarse, vulgar or "lower class"
nations of the universe, I mean, whose destinies had not yet elevated them above, beyond, the age-old level of impoverished, wanting, restless, and trouble-ridden human existence.

But then, wasn't the cult of Henry James a sign of danger, too,
for a nation which found itself for the first time in its history — or
for the first time in the history of mankind perhaps — quite in
this Jamesian social and moral position; and using the same kind of

elevated "moral-rational" stance, the same purified "stream of consciousness," if not always of thought, insight or intelligence, in order to rationalize or justify its own visionary and romantic view of
itself?

I think so. And thus Henry James really *was* the Age in a sense
which our New Critic hardly meant or envisaged. James and his
cult represented the imaginary and fictional age of the American
democracy in the mid-twentieth century, which was in effect another kind of enchanted fairyland, and "legendary" (borrowed,
nouveau-riche, spurious) nobility amid all the latent, repressed,
anxiety-provoking symptoms of the real world in which it existed;
but which it refused to acknowledge — to "see" or to "know."
Thus, in the 1940's and '50's, the Jamesian esthetics was the perfect
register, reverberator, mirror, reflector for changing and distorting,
or for eliminating, the realities of world history which a large sector
of the American intellectuals no longer wished to understand and
deal with. Henry James was a symbol of national make-believe
on the highest level of intellectual or cultural status and respectability. And to the point that the Honorable John F. Kennedy,
President of the United States, was fashionable enough to link the
work of William Faulkner, upon that novelist's death, with the
"great body" of Henry James's writing. Now what could be better
— for the Jacobite cult at least?

Only — now for the voice of an Emerson or a Thoreau, very
different indeed; or of a Melville, a Whitman, a Howells, a Mark
Twain, a Dreiser! But the great age had gone, so it appeared, and
the age of the Literary Pretenders had arrived. Thus if you scan
the columns of any of the fashionable literary periodicals, you are
likely to find still another laudatory, devout, euphoric appraisal
of "The Enduring Fame of Henry James," which simply repeats
all the clichés and truisms, not to mention the self-styled "hocuspocus," of two decades of Jamesian criticism. Even as this book
goes to press, we are witnessing the publication of the second and
third volumes of the "definitive biography" of Henry James and the

new New York Edition of James's Collected Works with, let us
hope, those two errant chapters in *The Ambassadors* finally put to
rest.

And so be it; and none are so blind; and in this case, as we know,
a little child (though a most prodigious and fantastical little child
prodigy) was leading them; and the Jacobite Emperor was naked
amid the universal acclaim.

Index

Index

Aesthetics: analysis substituted for action, 227-229; dramatic method, 125-127, 140, 156, 167, 174, 243, 293, 416-417; form of the novel, 106-108; manipulation vs. experience, 230, 233; manners the true subject, 410; novel vs. drama, 169; realism vs. magic, 245; statement of, 247-255; thinness of experience glorified, 187-188; victory of method over content, 336-337; writing as a game, 143-144, 159-160, 247, 290, 295, 307-308, 314, 334

Album, The (1894), 120

Alexander, George, 124

Alienation, theme of: justified (*American Scene*), 347-349; final statement of (*Sense of the Past*), 427-431

"Altar of the Dead, The," 131-132; related to "The Great Good Place," 195

Ambassadors, The (1903), 219, 264-290; analysis of, 271-290; artificial method of, 284; cultist view of, 11, 268-271; family patterns in, 281; Preface, 291-297; reversal of

Ambassadors, The (1903) (*Cont.*) chapters in, 265-266, 444; scenario of, 266-268; theme of money in, 305

Ambient, Mark ("Author of Beltraffio"), 57-59

Ambiguity, use of, 44

American, The (1877), 22-26; associated with days of early success, 424; dramatized, 119, 120-121; pattern of, 98

American Moderns (Geismar), 439

American Revolution: the King's War, 426

American Scene, The (1907), 338-354; American girl in, 353-354; Auden on, 340-341; conception of democracy in, 351; Dupee on, 339-340; race problem, 352-353; resentment of aliens, 347-349, of Jews, 349-350; restatement of earlier prejudices, 344, 348; Zabel on, 364

American scene reflected by James, 7-8, 14; "American disease" stated, 32; exile from happiness, 330, 360; the "good millionaire," 22-26; ignorance of, 90-91; indictment of,

Experience: artistic vs. human, 134-
135; avoidance of ("Beast in the
Jungle"), 261; defined as of the
mind, 100-101, 105; final despair
at lack of, 433; glimpsed and then
covered by artifice ("Bench of
Desolation"), 368-369; lack of,
turned into mystique, 187; vs.
manipulation (*Wings*), 230, 244
Expression, verbal: later elaborations
of, 174

Fadiman, Clifton, 132, 414; on "The
Birthplace," 256; on *Bundle of
Letters*, 36n; on Faulkner, 272;
on "The Great Good Place," 193-
194; on "The Jolly Corner," 358-
360
Family pattern: Jameses', reflected
in "The Pupil," 116-117; of new
America, first stated in *Daisy Miller*, 28-29; snobbish conception of
(*American Scene*), 351
Family relationships: of Henry with
parents, 95-96, 408; of Henry
with William, 96, 380, 387, 408;
of Henry's parents, 203, 394; infantile fantasies of (*Golden Bowl*),
316-317, 321-322, (*Memoirs*), 385
Farange, Maisie (*What Maisie
Knew*), 147-155, 436; compared
with Mamie Pocock, 296
Faulkner, William, 272, 439
Feminism: in James's novels, 48-49;
movement satirized, 61-63
"Fiction, The Art of" (1888), 99-
102
Fielder, Graham (*Ivory Tower*),
419-422; a "good hero," 437

"Figure in the Carpet, The," 137-
139, 180
Finer Grain, The (1910), 364-369
Fitzgerald, Scott: "Babylon Revisited" quoted, 133n; copies James's
ideas of wealth, 56; on the American family, 29; on "Hades U.S.A.,"
330; a reader of James, 3
"Flickerbridge," 255n
Follett, Wilson, 198-199
Ford, Ford Madox, 416
"Four Meetings," 31, 32-33
France: attitude toward, in *The
American*, 23-26, in "The Rever-
berator," 78-80; real culture of vs.
bohemianism, 273; shift to, after
disillusion with England, 268, 274,
285-286
French Poets and Novelists (1878),
27n
Freudian interpretation: of James as
an example of repression and ra-
tionalization, 424-425; of "Jolly
Corner," 358-359
"Friends of the Friends, The," 140n,
165
From the Shadow of the Mountain
(Van Wyck Brooks), 408n

Galerie d'Apollon, 389; scene of
James's nightmare, 390
Gaw, Rosanna (*Ivory Tower*), 419-
421
Gedge, Morris ("The Birthplace"),
256
"Georgina's Reasons," 60
Gereth, Mrs. (*Spoils of Poynton*),
142-143, 145, 192
Gerhardt, Jennie, 37